W9-BUE-936

ARNULFO L. OLIVEIRA MEMORIAL LIBRARY
1825 MAY STREET
BROWNSVILLE, TEXAS 78520

Studies in the Eighteenth Century

David Nichol Smith, 1876-1962
(From a photograph taken in the Rare Book Room of the Alexander Turnbull Library, Wellington, New Zealand, in 1951. By courtesy of the National Library of Australia.)

Studies in the Eighteenth Century

Papers presented at the
David Nichol Smith Memorial Seminar
Canberra 1966

Edited by
R.F.Brissenden

ARNULFO L. OLIVEIRA MEMORIAL LIBRARY
1825 MAY STREET
BROWNSVILLE, TEXAS 78520

1968

Australian National University Press
Canberra

First Published 1968

This book is copyright; reproduction in whole or part,
without written permission of the publishers, is forbidden

Printed and manufactured in Australia

Registered in Australia for transmission by post as a book

Library of Congress Catalog Card no. 68-18428

National Library of Australia reg. no. AUS 67-895

SBN # 7081 # 0069 # 4

In Memoriam
H.J.D.

Contents

Illustrations

Preface

IN THE PREFACE to his *Oxford Book of Eighteenth Century Verse,*
David Nichol Smith observed that 'our attitude to the century is
still in process of readjustment'. The one thing reasonably certain
was that 'a new verdict, favourable or unfavourable', would be given
by the present age. That was in 1926. Forty years later we can say
with confidence that the new verdict, if not finally delivered, is at
least beginning to take shape. It is a verdict which embraces, of
course, not merely the poetry but the general cultural achievement
of the eighteenth century. That it should be so largely favourable
owes an incalculable amount to the work of men such as David
Nichol Smith.

As a scholar he obviously felt that it was his primary responsibility
to present the literature of the past to his contemporaries in such a
way that it could be seen clearly for what it was. 'I sometimes think
we should get a truer view of the poetry of [the eighteenth] century',
he remarked in his Alexander Lectures at Toronto, 'if we could
rediscover it for ourselves and forget all the critics have said about
it.' To the task of making such a rediscovery possible he devoted his
talent and energy.

The working tool of the scholar is the library. D.N.S. had at his
command the wealth of the Bodleian, the British Museum, and
other great collections in Europe and America. In the course of his
life he also built up a judiciously chosen personal library of some
8,000 volumes, about half of which consist of books printed before
1800. No scholar working in Australia can ever hope, to have such
extensive resources at his disposal. The acquisition by the National
Library of Australia of Nichol Smith's books is thus an event of
singular importance. Together with certain other holdings in the
National Library they now form the nucleus of a growing collection
in which scholars concerned with the seventeenth and eighteenth
centuries can do useful and positive work. That David Nichol Smith
should have actively desired his library to come to this country is
something for which he will always be remembered with gratitude
and affection.

It seemed fitting that the arrival of his books in Canberra should
be publicly celebrated. The National Library, the Australian
National University, and the Australian Humanities Research
Council therefore decided to sponsor a David Nichol Smith
Memorial Seminar in Eighteenth-Century Studies. This, it was

hoped, would both honour the memory of the man and stimulate the further growth of scholarly activity in the field to which he had made such a notable contribution.

The seminar was held at the Australian National University during the week 15-19 August 1966. The papers delivered at the seminar, with two exceptions, are brought together in this volume. The exceptions are 'The Birth of Tristram Shandy: Sterne and Dr Burton' by Arthur H. Cash, and 'Analytical Bibliography: Some Problems of Method', by D. F. McKenzie. Professor Cash's paper had been included in the seminar program, but he was unexpectedly prevented at the last minute from delivering it. We consider ourselves fortunate in being able to present it now. Dr McKenzie's paper was delivered at the seminar but since it had already been accepted for publication elsewhere we are unable to print it in this volume.

As a contribution to the seminar the National Library of Australia undertook the preparation of a *Short Title Catalogue of books printed in the British Isles, the British Colonies and the United States of America and of English books printed elsewhere, 1701-1800, held in the libraries of the Australian Capital Territory.* The catalogue was edited by Professor William J. Cameron of McMaster University and Mrs Diana J. Carroll of the National Library. It was published during the seminar. The National Library also mounted an exhibition of books, manuscripts, and prints, designed 'to illustrate David Nichol Smith, the man and the scholar'.

During the seminar a concert of eighteenth-century chamber music was presented. The concert was organised by Mr David Woolley, principal oboist with the Sydney Symphony Orchestra; and it was made possible through the generous sponsorship of Colonel Aubrey Gibson. To both these people we extend our thanks.

The seminar itself could not have taken place, of course, without considerable assistance from a number of sources. We are extremely grateful in particular to the Australian-American Educational Foundation, the Commonwealth Office of Education, the Humanities Research Council of Canada, the University of Oxford, the University of Saskatchewan, and the Victoria University of Wellington. Through their help we were able to bring together for the seminar scholars from the United States and Canada, from the United Kingdom, and from New Zealand. Many Australian universities also contributed to the cost of sending speakers and seminar members to Canberra for the occasion.

It is pleasant and not unjustified to think that David Nichol Smith would have thoroughly approved the notion of holding a conference on the eighteenth century in the Antipodes—despite Johnson's firm advice to Boswell that nothing could be learnt from a visit to the regions of 'Otaheité and New-Zealand'. D.N.S. was amongst the first to recognise and welcome the extent to which the study of English civilisation in the eighteenth century had ceased to be a purely English pursuit. Many of the students who worked with him at Oxford came from distant parts of the world; and he visited and taught in universities in the United States, Canada, Australia, New Zealand, and other countries.

When *Essays on the Eighteenth Century,* the *Festschrift* presented to him on his seventieth birthday, was compiled, its editors regretted that because of the bad times in which it had been prepared they were unable to include 'any contributors from the Dominions and from France'. In one respect at least this volume may redress the balance. We hope also that it may be found not unworthy to stand on the same shelf beside that earlier volume; and that it too will play a useful part in ensuring that the verdict of our own age on the eighteenth century is just, well informed, and honest.

R.F.B.

Australian National University
Canberra

Notes on Contributors

AUSTIN, M. N., M.A., B.D., Professor of Classics and Ancient History, University of Western Australia. Professor Austin is the author of *An Ignorant Man Thinking* (essays and addresses on classical and university education), and *Samuel Johnson on Education.*

BRISSENDEN, R. F., M.A., PH.D., Senior Research Fellow in the History of Ideas, Australian National University. Dr Brissenden has published monographs and articles on eighteenth-century and contemporary literature. At the moment he is working on a study of sentimentalism, and on editions of *Pamela* and *Joseph Andrews.*

BURKE, Joseph, M.A., O.B.E., Herald Professor of Fine Arts, University of Melbourne. Professor Burke has published a critical edition of William Hogarth's *Analysis of Beauty* and autobiographical notes, as well as numerous articles on eighteenth-century English art. He is at present engaged on Volume IX of the *Oxford History of English Art.*

CAMERON, W. J., M.A., PH.D., Professor of English, McMaster University. Professor Cameron's main work has been in bibliography. He is an advisory editor of *Biography,* and is editor of Volume V of the Yale edition of *Poems on Affairs of State. The Short Title Catalogue, 1701-1800,* of books held in the libraries of the Australian Capital Territory, published by the National Library as a contribution to the David Nichol Smith Memorial Seminar, was prepared under his supervision.

CASH, Arthur H., A.B., M.S., PH.D., Professor of English, State University College, New Paltz, New York. Professor Cash, author of *Sterne's Comedy of Moral Sentiments* and numerous articles on Sterne, is currently writing a full-scale biography of the novelist. He will be program chairman for the Bicentenary Conference on Laurence Sterne to be held at York University in 1968. His paper unfortunately was not delivered at the seminar as Professor Cash found himself at the last minute unable to be present.

COHEN, Ralph., M.A., PH.D., Member of the Center for Advanced Studies and Professor of English, University of Virginia. Professor Cohen is on the editorial board of *Eighteenth Century Studies,* and is an advisory editor to the *Augustan Reprint Society.* He is the author of *The Art of Discrimination,* and editor of *The Essential Works of David Hume.*

DAVIS, Herbert J., F.B.A., LL.D., LITT.D., Professor Emeritus, University of Oxford. Professor Davis was a most distinguished scholar, and also a friend and colleague of David Nichol Smith. His monumental edition of Swift's *Prose,* and his numerous critical discussions of that author's work, rank among the major contributions of our day to eighteenth century studies. His memorial address on D.N.S. was the highlight of the seminar, and it is an occasion for very great regret that he is not alive to see its appearance in print in this volume.

FORD, Franklin L., PH.D., Professor of History and Dean of the Faculty of Arts and Sciences, Harvard University. Professor Ford touched on various aspects of the Enlightenment in two books, *Robe and Sword: The Regrouping of the French Aristocracy after Louis XIV,* and *Strasbourg in Transition, 1648-1789.* He has also written sections dealing with the period for Columbia University's *Chapters in Contemporary Civilization,* and for the newly published *Traditions of The Western World.*

GRAVE, S. A., M.A., PH.D., Professor of Philosophy, University of Western Australia. Professor Grave, who took his doctorate at Aberdeen, is the author of *The Scottish Philosophy of Common Sense.*

HARDY, John, M.A., D.PHIL., Professor of English, University of New England; formerly a Junior Research Fellow of Magdalen College, Oxford, and Assistant Professor at the University of Toronto. Professor Hardy was an editor of, and contributor to, *Johnson, Boswell and their Circle.* His edition of Johnson's major political writings is in press. He is presently working on editions of *Rasselas* and the *Life of Milton,* and on a study of Johnson's criticism of Shakespeare.

HOPE, A. D., B.A., Professor of English, Australian National University. Professor Hope is the author of several volumes of poetry, and of a collection of critical essays, *The Cave and the Spring.* In 1966 he shared the Britannica Australia Award for literature.

HORNE, Colin J., M.A., B.LITT., Jury Professor of English Language and Literature, University of Adelaide. Professor Horne is the editor of *Swift on His Age,* and a contributor to the eighteenth-century volume of *The Pelican Guide to English Literature.* He has published articles on several authors of the period, and is preparing a book on Swift's poetry.

SPATE, O. H. K., M.A., PH.D., Professor of Geography, Dean of the Research School of Pacific Studies, Australian National University. Professor Spate took the English Tripos Part I at Cambridge before going on to geography. His publications, which cover a wide range of themes in history and geography, generally have a literary bias. This is perhaps best illustrated in his volume of essays, entitled *Let Me Enjoy.*

TISCH, Johann Hermann, D.PHIL., Professor of German, joint Head of the Department of Modern Languages, University of Tasmania. Professor Tisch is particularly interested in seventeenth- and eighteenth-century German and comparative literature, and has produced articles on the concept of baroque, on Gryphius, Milton, Gottsched, the Early Enlightenment, and Schiller. He is presently working on a book on the reception of Milton in Germany and on a study of seventeenth- and eighteenth-century drama.

WATT, Ian Pierre, M.A., Professor of English, Stanford University. Educated at St John's College, Cambridge, The Sorbonne, University of California, and Harvard, Professor Watt is the author of *The Rise of the Novel: Studies in Defoe, Richardson and Fielding,* 1957, and of numerous articles on eighteenth-century and modern literature.

xiv

WILES, Roy McKeen, B.A., A.M., PH.D., F.R.S.C., Professor of English, McMaster University, member of the Humanities Research Council of Canada. Professor Wiles has published books and articles on literature and society in eighteenth-century England, notably *Serial Publication in England Before 1750,* and *Freshest Advices: Early Provincial Newspapers in England.* He is at present completing a study of eighteenth-century English provincial life.

WOLPER, Roy S., PH.D., Assistant Professor in English, University of Saskatchewan. Professor Wolper has delivered papers on the eighteenth century in Canada and Scotland, as well as in Australia, and has also published several articles on the same period. He is at present working on a study of *Gulliver's Travels* as a satire on modes of perception.

D.N.S.

A Biographical Note

DAVID NICHOL SMITH was eighty-six years of age when he died in 1962. He was educated at the University of Edinburgh and the Sorbonne, and he began his academic career at Armstrong College, Newcastle upon Tyne, then part of the University of Durham, and the predecessor of the present University of Newcastle upon Tyne. He was Professor of English Language and Literature at Armstrong College from 1904 to 1908. In 1908 he became Goldsmiths' Reader at Oxford, the university in which he was to pass most of his academic life. In 1921 he became a Fellow of Merton College; and from 1929 to 1946 he was Merton Professor of English Literature.

In the early part of his career he became best known for his editions of works from the seventeenth and eighteenth centuries, the most notable being the *Oxford Book of Eighteenth Century Verse,* and his edition of the *Poems of Samuel Johnson.* He also published several collections of lectures and essays on eighteenth-century literature, among them *Shakespeare in the Eighteenth Century, Some Observations on Eighteenth Century Poetry,* and *John Dryden.* The full list of his publications is extremely extensive.

In his later years at Oxford he became increasingly interested in graduate studies. 'Pupils came (and still come) to Oxford from many parts of the world to join those who have read the Oxford English School', observed the author of the obituary in *The Times.* 'He took a personal interest in them all, and often helped them to a career. In this and other ways his influence on English studies was wide and deep.'

After retiring from the Chair at Merton in 1946 he held a number of visiting lectureships and professorships. He visited, amongst other institutions, the Universities of Chicago, Cambridge, Cairo, Edinburgh, Adelaide, and New Zealand. He held the Chair of English at Adelaide in 1950-1, and it was no doubt partly as a result of the time he spent in Adelaide that he eventually welcomed the suggestion that his library should come to this country after his death.

He was elected to the British Academy in 1932, and to an Honorary Fellowship of Merton College in 1947. In the course of his life he received honorary degrees from Australian, English, French, Scottish, and United States universities; and his death was noticed in countries other than his own.

A comment in the *Johnsonian News Letter* may suffice to indicate the very great esteem in which this scholar was held by the academic community at large:

> For many of us the passing of D.N.S. will seem like the ending of an era. He was one of the older scholars whom we all revered —one who stood for something solid and real. Certainly he was one of the major forces which influenced the slow rise of the reputation of 18th-century studies.

Studies in the Eighteenth Century

David Nichol Smith

Herbert Davis

I first saw David Nichol Smith in the summer of 1912, when I attended his lectures which he gave three times a week. He was then thirty-seven, and had been since 1908 Goldsmiths' Reader in the University.

The impression that he gave was of a serious learned scholar, a literary historian who packed an immense amount of information into his lectures, who was concerned to extend the limits of our knowledge of the writers of the period; who was not afraid to mix biography and history and criticism, to give names and dates and details of the composition and publication of books, on the accuracy of which it was always safe to rely.

He would certainly not have thought of himself, nor did we think of him, as concerned only with eighteenth-century studies. Let me remind you of what he had published before he came to Oxford, what particular plans Raleigh had in mind when he invited him, and his main associations after he got there, in order to emphasise the broad base of his scholarly interests and activities, and to place him in the great Scottish tradition established at the University of Edinburgh by Masson and Saintsbury.

He began by editing Boileau and Dryden; essays by Hazlitt and Macaulay; and more important than this, two plays for the Warwick edition of Shakespeare—*Henry VIII* and *King Lear*. If this was mainly work for the booksellers, before his first academic appointment, it provided him with five years of scholarly activity prompted by what he had seen of the work of men like Saintsbury and Brunetière; work not supervised for a doctoral thesis, but prepared for the publishers with great care and skill. All this made it possible for him to publish in 1903, when he was only twenty-eight, such a distinguished volume as *Eighteenth Century Essays on Shakespeare*, carefully annotated and introduced by an essay on Shakespearian scholarship during the century, remarkable for its originality, its learning, and its critical acumen.

1

Its purpose was to give a correct account of Shakespeare's reputation during the eighteenth century, 'and to suggest that there are
grounds for reconsidering the common opinion that the century did
not give him his due'.[1] It may thus be regarded as the beginning
of a campaign in which he was to play so large a part, a campaign
to change our attitude and to reassess the whole historical and
critical account of eighteenth-century English literature.

But this volume should also remind us that he was then equally
concerned with problems of editing the text of Shakespeare. Professor Sutherland has touched upon this very delightfully in his
British Academy notice,[2] where he quotes a letter from D.N.S.,
after his eightieth birthday, to Professor Dover Wilson:

> The Warwick edition came out 58 years ago . . . It belongs
> to my Edinburgh days when I was waiting for something to
> turn up—which came at the end of 1902 when I joined Raleigh
> in Glasgow. I don't like looking at it now, but I remember that
> my chief guides were Johnson and Aldis Wright, not a poor
> couple. When Raleigh had moved to Oxford and I was in
> Newcastle he got me chosen by the Clarendon Press for their
> edition of Shakespeare, which was to conform as far as reason-
> able to the first Folio. It was to be a simple job—so Raleigh in
> his enthusiasm seemed to think—I had only to remove obvious
> errors and be in effect a competent printer's reader. Then
> Raleigh contrived to bring me to Oxford and the way was
> understood to be clear for speedy publication. How it was I
> forget, but I spent most time on *King Lear*—it was the chief
> occupation of my spare time for several years. What happened
> was that I taught myself the problems of Shakespearian editing
> (I got little or no help) and gradually learned that I had
> better abandon them and own myself beaten. I suspect that
> Raleigh thought me pedantic. He sometimes showed an un-
> canny gift of solving a difficulty at sight, but some of the
> problems that bothered me I could not get him to understand.
> This is almost all forgotten now, but you seem to me to have
> put on record that I once was a wrestler with these textual
> problems, and in doing so you have pleased me greatly.

And, again, in his acknowledgment of the volume of *Essays on the
Eighteenth Century* in honour of his seventieth birthday he wrote
to Professor Sutherland:

> I see myself henceforward even more cursedly confined to one
> century. The reviewers already deny me any desire to cast eyes
> promiscuously on the others. I must get busy with the Malone

[1] D. Nichol Smith (ed.), *Eighteenth Century Essays on Shakespeare*, 2nd ed.,
New York, 1962, p. v.
[2] *Proceedings of the British Academy*, Vol. XLVIII, London, 1962, p. 455.

Society and now that *Arden of Feversham* is finished pass on to
Mother Bombie. It may all be of no use in extricating me from
the bonds which you have taken an almost malicious pleasure
in winding round me. . . .[3]

I like to remember that his last months were largely occupied in
revising *Eighteenth Century Essays on Shakespeare* for a second
corrected edition, which was published after his death sixty years
after the first Glasgow printing. Little was left for Professor Wilson
and myself to do except see it through the press. I have since been
reminded that we all failed to correct one error which had
appeared in a note accusing Dr Johnson of forgetfulness, when he
defined tragedy and comedy as

> compositions intended to promote different ends by contrary
> means, and considered as so little allied, that I do not recollect
> among the Greeks or Romans a single writer who attempted
> both.[4]

The note rightly refers to a similar statement of Dryden in the
Essay on Dramatic Poesy but adds tersely: 'Johnson forgets the
Cyclops of Euripides'.[5] In a letter to me from Dr Powell, written
after his eightieth birthday, Johnson is triumphantly vindicated:

> The Cyclops of Euripides is not a comedy; see Gilbert Murray
> on the subject. It is a satyr play, a genre unknown to us. D.N.S.
> could not have read it. Perhaps in his notes he described it as
> 'satyric' drama following Shelley and then thought this equiva-
> lent to or meant for 'satiric' drama, which might well indicate
> a comedy of sorts.
>
> I am astonished that this note has gone uncorrected for sixty
> years. Last winter I went through the ancient dramatists and
> the only one who had attempted both tragedy and comedy was
> perhaps Ennius and his efforts only survive in fragments.

I think the error, if such it be, may well be traced to the Department
of Classics at Glasgow, where Jebb had been Professor before he
went to Cambridge. In his account of the *Cyclops* as 'satyric'
drama, he goes so far as to use such terms as 'farce' and 'broad
comedy', though indicating that Euripides was not too successful
in this travesty of the heroic.

He delivered his inaugural lecture as Goldsmiths' Reader in
February 1909, on *The Functions of Criticism,* a subject he had
chosen because of the new interest that had been shown in the aims
and methods of criticism in the academic world in England as

3 Ibid.
4 Samuel Johnson, 'Preface to Edition of Shakespeare (1765)', in *Eighteenth
Century Essays on Shakespeare,* pp. 118-19.
5 *Eighteenth Century Essays on Shakespeare,* p. 322, n. 118.

particularly indicated by Saintsbury's *History of Criticism and Literary Taste in Europe,* 1900-4, and the collections of critical essays which were being published by the Clarendon Press—his elder brother, Gregory Smith's volume of *Elizabethan Critical Essays,* 1904, and Spingarn's edition of *Seventeenth Century Essays,* 1908, which he was then actually engaged in reviewing.

It is not a performance of which I think he would be very proud, and I cannot remember his ever once mentioning it. It is marked by a curious impersonality and reticence, perhaps assumed as a protection against the rather formidable audience before which it was to be read. Yet it in a way is very characteristic; it was not a time for adventuring into new fields, but an occasion when it was best to draw upon all those resources which would enable him to speak with authority out of the depth of this knowledge and experience. He does in fact draw upon everything that he had published in the last ten years—his translation of Brunetière, his edition of Boileau, his familiarity with French literary historians and critics, his studies of Dryden and Johnson, and Hazlitt and Jeffrey, his reviewing of the volumes of Courthope's *History of Poetry* as they appeared, even his encyclopaedia article on 'Literary Criticism'. It thus serves admirably to show his interests and to mark what he had already done up to this point, which was the beginning of his long career in the University of Oxford.

For the next ten years he was to continue ably to support Professor Raleigh, an original critic with a delightful pen, and a fascinating lecturer, but one who tried to preserve the tradition of the brilliant amateur, which made a splendid combination with the quiet, sound, and, I think one should say, professional scholarship of D.N.S. He admired Raleigh and recognised his brilliance, and his charm—and his weaknesses. It was said, he told me one day, that Raleigh could put together a most impressive lecture, as he strolled into the city across the meadows from his house at Hinksey. 'But I am afraid', he said with a grin, 'he was sometimes out for a duck.' And then he added quietly but with some conviction, 'I don't think I was ever out for a duck'. Professor Renwick, writing in the *Scotsman* in January 1962, quotes Raleigh's remark: 'I'm a gas man myself, but I don't allow any other gas men on the premises', and makes the comparison between them:

> In lectures, Raleigh delighted his audience by his wit, gusto, and sometimes inspiration; Nichol Smith did his duty by them in presenting a steady stream of valuable knowledge, often hard-earned and always admirably arranged. He was at his best as a tutor, and happiest of all as a supervisor of postgraduate students in the eighteenth-century, studies of which he had a

profound and comprehensive knowledge and understanding, not only in literature but in biography and social history, gathered from newspapers and fugitive pamphlets as well as from books.

In those days when I was listening to his lectures, 1912-14, he was busy first at his chapter for the *Cambridge History of English Literature,* Vol. X, on Johnson and Boswell, and on his edition for the Roxburghe Club of *The Letters of Thomas Burnet to George Duckett,* 1712-22. This was the kind of task he particularly delighted in, bringing to light unpublished material with fresh information about happenings in the world of letters. It delighted him when he had occasion to take out of its case this handsomely printed and sumptuously bound volume. This happened once, as George Sherburn told me, when he went as a young man to visit him for the first time in Oxford. But I will quote from the letter written to me in 1962:

> I saw him first, I think, in 1922. I had come across the letters of Tom Burnett and George Duckett in the B.M. manuscript room. I was most elated, and when I met Nichol Smith in his study I was full of it. 'Where did you find these things?' he asked, and I told him. When I said 'In the B.M.' he replied 'but they're all here', and pulled out of a low shelf his edition of them for the Roxburghe Club. The B.M. people had not told me of the edition, and didn't have a copy of the printed book. But thereafter D.N.S. more or less 'accepted' me.

His next job was to take him a little further in the direction of specialising in Johnsonian studies—his revision of Courtney's *Bibliography of Johnson* which appeared in 1915. But in all this time he was reviewing books about Shakespeare and Elizabethan drama, as well as earlier volumes of the *Cambridge History* dealing with the sixteenth century, and he edited a selection of Shakespeare criticism and contributed a chapter to *Shakespeare's England.*

In 1918 he published one of his most valuable little books, *Characters from the Histories and Memoirs of the Seventeenth Century,* with an admirable introductory essay. In 1920 he revised and completed for the Clarendon Press the edition of Swift's *Tale of a Tub,* which had been prepared by A. C. Guthkelch, who had been killed in the war.

These works showed the depth and extent of his knowledge of the history and literature of the seventeenth century—the England of the lifetime of John Dryden, the England in which Swift grew up and the period whose writers Johnson was mainly concerned with.

I would also suggest—as D.N.S. would have liked it to be known —that we should detect here some marks of the influence and benefit of his warm friendship with that great historian, Sir Charles Firth, who did so much to support the work of Raleigh and Nichol Smith, both outsiders in Oxford—though they came to be fully accepted there at last—in founding the English School at Oxford, which I can remember was still regarded in some quarters with extreme suspicion even when I was an undergraduate. I may say that my moral tutor at St John's did his best in 1912 to dissuade me from wasting my time in such frivolous studies.

In that other world before 1914, the English School remained small, with only two or three college tutors like George Gordon and Brett-Smith to support the Professor and the Goldsmiths' Reader. But the standards were high, and were raised by the number of senior students with degrees from other universities in Scotland and Wales and in the Commonwealth who took English Schools. Not more than one or two—like Tucker Brooke from Yale and F. P. Wilson from Birmingham—had taken the advanced degree of B.Litt.

I think it is worth while emphasising that then the more serious professional academic study of English language and literature was still being done in France and Germany, where most of our philologists had had their training, and in the United States. Even in Scotland the study of English had been mainly part of the general education of the undergraduates. Most of the scholarly work that was being published in Great Britain was done by men who had been brought up in the older disciplines, or who had been educated abroad. It was, I suppose, as a part of the concern on all sides in the twenties for a further development of the work of the universities that plans were made in the English School under George Gordon, who came back as Merton Professor in 1922, and Nichol Smith for encouraging advanced studies in the subject beyond the undergraduate level. I do not think it matters that Gordon was himself concerned in a negative way to prevent what he feared might be an inrush of candidates for the doctoral degree; and perhaps also to keep himself clear of having to take over too much responsibility for administering what could be called a school of graduate studies. Certainly Nichol Smith saw it as a positive thing to provide for the first time proper supervision and even some further instruction at an advanced level.

They were both aware of the sources of help to be found outside the teaching Faculty—they were in touch with the great undertakings at the Press, like the Dictionary and the series of editions of English writers; and they decided very wisely to draw in such men as Percy Simpson, brought back to edit Ben Jonson, and others at the Bodleian and the Press, like Strickland Gibson and R. W.

Chapman, to help in teaching bibliography and textual criticism. This was the kind of world to which Nichol Smith properly belonged; and he inevitably became the centre of it. After he became Merton Professor in 1929 he still managed to devote most of his energies to this part of his work, for which he was so admirably fitted. Already in 1937 when he came out to Toronto to give the Alexander Lectures, he was able to arrange thereafter a sort of triumphal progress through the United States, visiting his pupils who were strategically placed across the whole continent. He followed their careers with the greatest interest, and always welcomed them back to his study in 20 Merton Street, where one was sometimes surprised to learn the latest news of what was happening in universities in California or Australia. Nothing is more remarkable in him than the ease with which he could stretch his interests and enlarge his sympathies in response to those of his pupils who in one way or another had gained his respect.

It was, I like to think, a source of encouragement and strength; he enjoyed this recognition which he received abroad, and was proud of the position which he was rightly given in the international world of English scholarship. Though he was inclined sometimes to be rather scornful of the latest fashions in poetry and in criticism, he had an extraordinary ability to detect real quality of character and intelligence, even sometimes where one might not have expected it. It was on his first visit to the United States that he was invited to stay over by two of his former students at the University of Louisiana; and I very well remember his satisfaction and confidence as he told me of the impressions he had brought away from that southern university. 'There are two young men there whom you would do well to watch; I think they will both go far.' They both did; though perhaps not always quite in the direction that he had expected. One of them was Penn Warren, and the other Cleanth Brooks.

Much later it always gave him pleasure to surprise a visitor who had come to pay homage to the doyen of eighteenth-century studies, by boasting that one of the last candidates whose work he supervised for the doctorate was Professor Norman Jeffares—and the subject of his thesis was the poetry of Yeats.

But it is time that I should remember the particular occasion and the fact that, as shown by the character of his library, which now forms the Nichol Smith collection there in the National Library, and also evidenced by his most important work, he was quite properly regarded as one of those scholars who in his generation had exercised a very powerful influence on the course of eighteenth-century studies in English literature. We should all

7

agree with the comment from the *Johnsonian News Letter* quoted by Dr Brissenden—certainly he was one of the major forces which influenced the slow rise of the reputation of eighteenth-century studies[6]—but I should like to make a further special claim, because I have noticed that in some of the accounts that have been written about him, notably in the obituary in *The Times,* nothing was said about his remarkable work in the earlier part of the eighteenth century, and particularly the part that he played in guiding and directing as well as contributing to the work done on Pope and Swift.

He did not publish much on Pope, but he lectured for many years about him and most of the editors of the Twickenham edition were his pupils. In the first of his Alexander Lectures at Toronto in 1937, he had some wise remarks to make on Pope's 'poetic diction'. He had been concerned with Pope as an editor and critic of Shakespeare, and he delights to point out Pope's perceptions, and to quote his neat explanation of Shakespeare's weaknesses:

> Most of his [Shakespeare's] faults are less to be ascribed to his wrong judgment as a Poet, than to his right judgment as a Player.[7]

He likes to surprise us by quoting remarks of Pope, which sound very different from the conventions he is often supposed to have accepted. Pope is not afraid, for instance, to talk of 'inspiration' or to speak with admiration of Gothic splendours:

> The Poetry of Shakespear was Inspiration indeed: he is not so much an Imitator, as an Instrument, of Nature; and 'tis not so just to say that he speaks from her, as that she speaks thro' him.[8]

Or,

> One may look upon his works, . . . as upon an ancient majestick piece of *Gothick* Architecture, compar'd with a neat Modern building: The latter is more elegant and glaring, but the former is more strong and more solemn.[9]

He loved to pick out, as he was able to do in his anthology of eighteenth-century poetry, lines from Pope's later work, where in the dialogue, in all the familiarity of a conversational tone, he is

---

[6] *Johnsonian News Letter,* Vol. XXII, No. 1, March 1962, p. 3. Quoted in the brochure which initially announced the David Nichol Smith Memorial Seminar.

[7] Alexander Pope, 'Preface to Edition of Shakespeare (1725)', in *Eighteenth Century Essays on Shakespeare,* p. 51. Quoted by D. Nichol Smith in a lecture at Birkbeck College, London, 1928.

[8] Pope, 'Preface to Edition of Shakespeare (1725)', p. 48.

[9] Ibid., p. 62.

able to produce poetry so powerful and so passionate, burning with a clear bright flame:

> When Truth or Virtue an Affront endures,
> Th' Affront is mine, my Friend, and should be yours.
> Mine, as a Foe profess'd to false Pretence,
> Who think a Coxcomb's Honour like his Sense;
> Mine, as a Friend to ev'ry worthy mind;
> And mine as Man, who feel for all Mankind.
> *Friend:* You're strangely proud.
> *Poet:*   So proud, I am no Slave:
> So impudent, I own myself no Knave:
> So odd, my Country's Ruin makes me grave.
> Yes, I am proud: I must be proud to see
> Men not afraid of God, afraid of me: . . .[10]

Though he was not quite by temperament so near to Pope and Swift as he was to Johnson, he always liked to be dealing with literature that was concerned with contemporary society, that demanded an acquaintance with history and politics and journalism and the world of learning; and I do not know that he ever enjoyed any of his tasks more than he did his editing of Swift, though he left it unfinished.

I should like to say something about his work on Swift, since its importance may easily be overlooked, as he began by taking over the Guthkelch edition of *A Tale of a Tub,* and accepted the text he had prepared, but gave much care to revising and supplementing the Introduction and adding new matter to the notes. Some parts of the Introduction, the account of the authorship of the fifth edition with the Apology and Notes, and the section on Swift's reading bear, I think, clear traces of his handiwork, and the explanatory notes throughout have been carefully trimmed and cut in his most characteristic fashion.

He was fully aware of the danger of trying to annotate such a book, of not falling into the traps laid for the unwary commentator by a humorist at the height of his youthful powers. But he provides all the information we need, and adequate comment for the understanding of a difficult book. It may be admitted that the textual apparatus was not complete and some of the misprints which had entered in the course of reprinting were not removed. This was, however, done in the revised edition; but he refused to use the opportunity to adopt the method of Greg and Bowers and take the first edition as copy-text, and incorporate into it the corrections of the fifth edition. He had taken pains to show that Swift himself

---

10 From 'Epilogue to the Satires', in D. Nichol Smith (ed.), *The Oxford Book of Eighteenth Century Verse,* Oxford, 1926, p. 138.

9

was responsible for the substantive changes made for the edition of 1710; and he remained unconvinced of the importance of restoring the accidentals of the first edition, even though it may be assumed that the first printed text would be the nearest to Swift's original manuscript.

Fifteen years later, in 1935, he published his edition of *The Letters of Jonathan Swift to Charles Ford,* a volume containing much entirely new information about Swift, especially during the twenty years from 1713 to 1733, when the bulk of these letters were written. Only one of the fifty-one letters from Swift had appeared before. They are all printed here from Swift's autographs. They had remained hidden among the papers of Sir John Hynde Cotton, Ford's executor, at Madingley Hall, Cambridge. They are now in the great Rothschild collection, which has been presented to Trinity College, Cambridge. The volume also contains the text of a number of poems printed from manuscripts in the hand of Swift and of Ford, which were among these papers—birthday poems to Stella and to Ford and poems written about their visits to Ford's country house in Ireland, Woodpark; also letters to Ford from Gay, Pope, Bolingbroke, etc. I should say that this is the most important contribution to our knowledge of Swift that has appeared since the days of Forster. But I cannot do better than let the editor speak:

> . . . the importance of these letters lies in the new light which they throw upon Swift. Of all his many friends there was none to whom he habitually wrote at once so easily, even so care-lessly, and on terms so equal . . .
>
> When he writes to Ford he is under no constraint . . . All has the freedom of conversation in which nothing that is said will be misunderstood . . . their distinction is that, better than any series of letters to any other friend, they give us Swift in undress. We know him the better for seeing him in undress. From beginning to end there is not one word which even the most squeamish editor would wish to omit.[11]

It is particularly valuable for the light it throws on the composition and publication of *Gulliver's Travels,* and on Swift's attempt to restore it to its original state when it was reprinted by George Faulkner in the third volume of Swift's *Collected Works,* published in Dublin in 1735. From 15 April 1721 to 16 August 1725 there are seven reports on the progress of the *Travels,* and it was to Ford that he announced on finishing his *Travels* that 'they are admirable things and will wonderfully mend the world'.

---

11 *The Letters of Jonathan Swift to Charles Ford,* ed., D. Nichol Smith, Oxford, 1935, pp. xxvii-xxviii.

Nichol Smith remarks that we have no evidence that anyone ever saw the manuscript except Ford, and when the book was published in October 1726, it was Ford who had the original manuscript and compared it with the printed text. He made a list containing every single alteration from the original copy. But later, when Swift was preparing the copy for Faulkner, it is evident that the manuscript had been lost or destroyed. And he applies to Ford for help:

> I think you had a Gulliver interleaved and set right in those mangled and murdered pages.[12]

Finally the editor makes this emphatic and authoritative statement:

> It is *Gulliver's Travels* as issued by Faulkner in 1735 that is the first authentic edition, finally approved by its author . . . and Swift's two letters to Ford confirm its authority.[13]

In this matter of the text of *Gulliver's Travels,* he was himself particularly concerned, for he had undertaken to edit *Gulliver's Travels* for the Clarendon Press.

It is a project which I think goes back as far as the twenties when Sir Charles Firth read a paper before the British Academy on 'The political significance of *Gulliver's Travels*' and later sent a further note to the *Review of English Studies* in 1926. When he died, he left his notes to D.N.S. to be used in annotating the book. It was a task which was postponed until his retirement. But then he became involved in travels of his own to the United States, to Egypt, and to this country, where, as you know, he spent a year at the University of Adelaide. When at last he settled at home in Merton Street, his energies were flagging. When I inquired from time to time about his progress, I was told that he was busy working at the notes, and he would occasionally report that a note was finished—the problem of the 'Bristol barrel' solved. I was indeed under the impression that he had completed the notes for the first two books—but I understand from Professor Sutherland to whom he had bequeathed the task that he found among the papers only the notes for Lilliput.

He did not waste his time; he indulged in few frivolities. He did not even take much delight in the pleasure of reading, though he never refused to look through a manuscript for a friend—or to give his opinion on it to the Press.

He continued to the last to interest himself in all the work of his friends and his pupils—and they all went to 20 Merton Street to report. There was little that was going on in the whole field of eighteenth-century studies that he was not aware of. His advice was sought and readily available in all kinds of projects, large and

12 Ibid., p. xliv.
13 Ibid.

small. But advice did not satisfy him; he enjoyed supervision. At least, in my experience, he always gave the impression that he liked to be asked to look through a manuscript; and when it came back, it always bore the marks of a careful reading. If there were no serious matters to be challenged, there were always little improvements to be made in the style. I think he rather enjoyed this job of tidying up.

Perhaps I may be pardoned for speaking at length about his work on Swift; for I was in a position to know how far he had been concerned in the planning and shaping, and sometimes revising, of the work of his fellow editors like Sir Harold Williams and myself. For example, I was once persuaded by Dr Francis Bourke of Dublin to reproduce as an early portrait of Swift a picture in the possession of Mr Briscoe of Bellinter in Ireland. It formed the frontispiece to Volume II of my edition of Swift, published early in 1940. On 12 February he wrote to me, first referring to the other portraits in the volume:

> I greet Partridge with a knowing wink, but how the artist must have flattered him. Isaac Bickerstaff is new to me—I did not know that any copy of the *Tatler* contained that rare frontispiece—and I salute him with a respectful bow. I don't know what to say about the new portrait of Swift. I assume that its history is well authenticated, and there's a look in the eye which I do not find suggested in any other portrait. Early portraits, before the features and the character are set, provide surprises. To judge from the costume this portrait was painted before Swift took orders—when he was writing his poems and being fancied by William III—but I should like to have my doubts removed.

Then, he evidently went back and had another look at it, for after he had finished the letter, he added a postscript, in which he set out all his doubts:

> I am really very doubtful about that portrait. What about the eyebrows? And the point of the nose? And the mouth? The mouth may well have firmed with age and experience, but the contour of the nose doesn't change much. If it is Swift, he must have been very young. Where was it painted? At Temple's? We should not expect a portrait of him in his T.C.D. days.
>
> I write with a bluntness which will assure you that I do not yet regard you as an American.
>
> And if I am wrong, smite me as hard as you like. I am still a Scot, and will take all I deserve.

I recall that when he went to hospital three days before his death he took with him the galley proof of the Preface to Williams's edition of *The Correspondence of Jonathan Swift*; and the final printed version was not quite the same as the author's original manuscript. Even Middleton Murry, in the Preface to his biography of Swift in 1954, acknowledged that the edition of Swift's *Letters to Ford* was 'the most notable addition to the work of Swift in our time'. But alas he made the terrible mistake of referring to 'the late Mr D. Nichol Smith' when he was still enjoying his seventies. When Murry came to Oxford a few years later I urged him to call and make his apologies and see for himself how very much alive D.N.S. still was. He promised he would; but he did not have the courage to face him, knowing, I fear, that much of his work had been judged and found wanting.

Though D.N.S. never indulged in Johnsonian violence, he could express stern and cold disapproval and was intolerant of much in the modern world. He remained unalterable in many of his Tory prejudices, his careful frugal ways, and his rather puritanical principles. In his early chapter on Johnson published in the *Cambridge History of English Literature* in 1913, he writes about him in words which might be applied to himself:

> There are no distinct periods in Johnson's literary develop-ment, no sudden access of power, no change in his outlook, no novelties in his methods. He continued as he had begun. He grew in confidence and facility; he perfected his command of expression; but there was not any change in the spirit of his expression or in what he wished to express.[14]

It is very right and proper that we should remember him finally as a Johnsonian. He began and continued to the end a critic of Johnson's sort; he understood the poetry of the eighteenth century and its criticism as he studied it with Johnson as his guide. Indeed, some of those who have felt strongly that he was unfair in his judgment of Theobald and Warburton and neglected to modify his views in his revised edition of *Eighteenth Century Essays on Shakes-peare* will notice that he is content to fortify his opinion by quoting that very injudicious outburst of Johnson's that 'Warbur-ton as a critic would make "two and fifty Theobalds, cut into slices".' But it should be remembered that in his lectures on the same subject published in 1928 he had called Theobald 'the first of our Shakespeare scholars, and for these reasons: he respected the readings of the old editions and did not give full rein to his taste'.

It was in 1913 that he undertook to edit Johnson's *Poems* for the Clarendon Press. The volume finally appeared with the help of Professor E. L. McAdam in 1940. What happened is described very characteristically in the Preface:

14 *Cambridge History of English Literature*, Vol. X, Cambridge, 1913, p. 160.

When its progress was checked by the events of the next five years, some parts had been completed more or less as they are now printed. But work interrupted is not always easily resumed, and this editor, while continuing to collect material for a volume which he never doubted to see published, found many obstacles to making a good end.[15]

Meanwhile McAdam had prepared an edition for his Doctor's degree at Yale, and it was soon decided to bring out a joint edition. Fortunately many of Johnson's manuscripts had come to light in the meantime, and in 1936-7 Nichol Smith was himself able to use Mrs Thrale's manuscripts in the Huntington Library. This must be regarded as his main contribution to the work of fixing the canon of Johnson's writings, and providing for the first time a satisfactory text of the *Poems*. But he contributed a good deal more to the study of Johnson than is evident from his published works. In addition to the lecture on Johnson which was published in the Alexander Lectures which he gave at University College, Toronto, in 1936, there is a manuscript volume among the many papers left to the Bodleian, containing lectures on Johnson given at the Sorbonne in 1933, and at Tucson and Pasadena in 1936; *Recent Studies of Johnson,* dealing particularly with Powell's revision of Birkbeck Hill's edition of Boswell's *Life*; and a very clear account of the whole dramatic story of the finding of the Boswell Papers in Fettercairn and at Malahide Castle, down to the unexpected discovery of the last batch which did not reach Colonel Isham in New York until after the war, in 1946. In the following year he came to stay with us for some time at Smith College, where we celebrated the occasion by arranging an eighteenth-century seminar in honour of Chauncey Tinker and Nichol Smith. There he met Colonel Isham, and was invited to call at his apartment and see those Johnson manuscripts.

Colonel Isham was himself too Boswellian a character to be properly appreciated by some of the more sober and serious academic scholars who were concerned with Boswell's and Johnson's papers. Sometimes, indeed, he treated them with little respect. I was curious to see how he would treat Nichol Smith, and what would come of their meeting. I cannot do better than give you Nichol Smith's own account, which I found among his papers, first drafted in his own hand with a corrected fair copy in typescript. For it shows him in the ripeness of his years, warmed by the recognition that he had received especially among scholars in the United States, rewarded by this rare privilege of being present as the very last of

[15] *The Poems of Samuel Johnson,* ed. D. Nichol Smith and E. L. McAdam, Oxford, 1941, p. v.

the treasures were taken out of the old trunk under the table, and rather enjoying his ability to recognise immediately and talk about the scraps of manuscripts as Isham placed them in his hands. It was an occasion that I like to remember.

In January 1947 Isham asked me to dine with him in his flat in New York. Bundles of the papers were lying on tables still unassorted, though one or two treasures had been singled out. He showed me a character sketch of Goldsmith all in the handwriting of Sir Joshua Reynolds, which proved that the great painter who always conveyed on his canvases the characters of the men and women whom he painted, had skill with his pen as well as with his brush. When Isham read it out to me, I thought it the best character sketch of Goldsmith that I could hope to know. He showed me part of the manuscript of Johnson's *London,* the only part that is known to survive. He showed me the only manuscript of *The Vanity of Human Wishes,* and it is of particular interest in view of a remark that Johnson made to Boswell about his method of composing verses. 'I have generally had them in my mind', he said, 'perhaps fifty at a time, walking up and down in my room, and then I have written them down, and often from laziness have written only half lines'. Here was corroboration of this remark: the second half of many of the lines was in a darker ink than the first half. You will believe that the hours passed quickly in this unforgettable evening and early morning, for I did not get away to my hotel till long after midnight. No less memorable was my last visit to him a day or two before returning to England. He had no sooner greeted me than he said 'I have something to show you'. It was a slip of paper on which Boswell had written two lines of *The Vanity of Human Wishes,* and one word of it was corrected in Johnson's handwriting. The lines are in the passage which mentions the Bodleian Library,—'O'er Bodley's dome his future labours spread'. Boswell pointed out to Johnson that the word 'spread' occurred in two adjacent lines, and Johnson at once substituted another word in one of them. This he did in talk, but it was an authentic emendation that had to be put on record. 'For perfect authenticity' Boswell says, 'I now had it done with his own hand', and he adds in a footnote that he deposited the slip of paper in the Bodleian. As we had sought for it there in vain we had concluded that it was lost; but it had never been there; Boswell had forgotten to carry out his intention. The slip of paper had come to light in New York. When I pointed this out to Isham he sat quiet for a moment, and then he said, firmly, 'Take it back with you.' A collector such as Isham cannot escape criticism. I have called him a determined collector, but I would add that in my relations with him he has been an eminently just collector. I took the slip back with me by plane, and I have often wondered what the observations of Johnson and Boswell would have been had they known of its flight over the Atlantic. My first duty when I got back to Oxford was to do what Boswell had intended. I deposited the slip in the Bodleian.[16]

[16] Bodleian MS. Eng. Misc. e. 551. [This passage has in fact been published before, and in Australia. It appeared in *Meanjin*, Vol. XI, No. 3 (1952), pp. 292-3, under the title, 'A Boswell Fragment', and with the following note: 'A previously unpublished extract from an address, "Samuel Johnson and the New Boswell Papers", delivered last year at the University of Melbourne by Professor D. Nichol Smith. . . .'—R.F.B.]

The Enlightenment: Towards a Useful Redefinition

Franklin L. Ford

When I consider the titles of the other papers to be delivered during this seminar, each one expressive of deep and sharply focused erudition, my own topic seems ambitious to the point of *hubris*. However, an effort to redefine the place of the early modern Enlightenment in our cultural history, drawing on old sources and new scholarship, has for some time tempted me, if only as an exercise in self-education. Rather more generously, I might add that a preliminary reconnaissance of eighteenth-century Europe's intellectual terrain is perhaps a defensible opening for the David Nichol Smith Memorial Seminar and for the philosophical, literary, and historical discussions it will comprise. In any case, as Captain Cook must have said more than once, it is too late to turn back now.

The title of this paper, as announced, points to national and social variants;[1] and I shall, in fact, want to say something about both those aspects of the Enlightenment. Nevertheless, my ultimate purpose is to try to get beyond the mere notation of variety to a useful redefinition of the movement as a whole, a redefinition broad enough to accommodate internal diversity, yet explicit enough to cut away elements which ought not to be, though they often are, included.

An essay at redefinition must, of course, pay heed to definitions past. The Enlightenment surely demands at least a brief review of this kind; for the connotations of the term have shifted a great deal in the course of the past one hundred years, without ever becoming altogether precise. Its German original, *Aufklärung*, was used admiringly, even proudly, by Immanuel Kant in his celebrated essay of 1784, 'What Is Enlightenment?' But in the 1860s, 1870s, and 1880s, when the English equivalent of *Aufklärung* came into general use as a capitalised label for a movement, it usually carried

---

[1] This paper was delivered at the seminar under the title, 'The Enlightenment: Some National and Social Variants'.

17

overtones of contempt for the preceding century's allegedly shallow rationalism and irreverence. Thus, the *Oxford English Dictionary* reminds us, James H. Stirling, discussing Hegel just about one hundred years ago, castigated 'Deism, Atheism, Pantheism, *and all manner of isms* due to the Enlightenment'.[2] Our own century has witnessed a certain revival of esteem for the Enlightenment, resulting partly, no doubt, from Herr Hitler's having startled the world into considering possible alternatives to his own appeal to Germans to 'think with their blood'. More important to this re-evaluation, however, has been increased attention to the relevant texts themselves. Beginning with Lanson in France and continuing with Cassirer in Germany, Cobban in England, Brinton, Manuel, Gay in America, and other scholars in a number of different countries, there has been displayed a mounting determination at least to do the *philosophes* the courtesy of studying what they actually said.[3]

Yet much writing on the subject, whether scholarly or popular, continues to rely on stereotypes and over-simplifications. The fact that some of these are complimentary while others are sneering does not render any of them less deplorable. Even the witty and literate Carl Becker, in his *Heavenly City of the Eighteenth Century Philosophers,* New Haven, 1932, lapsed repeatedly into the role of a detractor who was not fair to the clearly expressed views of his victims. As for admirers of the *philosophes,* they too can be guilty of putting clichés in place of critical appreciation. Many a self-styled 'Enlightenment man', I fear, has no more real right to the title he has assumed, in terms of understanding what it means, than does his more athletic rival, the 'Renaissance man'.

What I have just said is not intended to be unsympathetic. The difficulties of definition and comprehension are real. They are rooted in the fact that a cultural movement, being a cluster of ideas and of people who espouse some or all of them, in differing combinations, inevitably lacks simple, unarguable boundaries. The ideas seem to mesh one moment and to clash the next. Some, which in one context appear central to the movement, in another may appear peripheral. The people, too, refuse to hold still. They

[2] J. H. Stirling, *The Secret of Hegel,* London, 1865, p. xxvii.

[3] See especially G. Lanson, *Histoire de la littérature française,* 8th ed., Paris, 1903; E. Cassirer, *Die Philosophie der Aufklärung,* Tübingen, 1932, trans. F. C. A. Koelln and J. P. Pettegrove, Princeton, 1951; also his *Rousseau, Kant, Goethe* (English ed., Princeton, 1945); A. Cobban, *In Search of Humanity,* London, 1960; Crane Brinton's introduction to *The Portable Age of Reason Reader,* New York, 1956; F. E. Manuel, *The Eighteenth Century Confronts the Gods,* Cambridge, Mass., 1959, and *The Prophets of Paris,* Cambridge, Mass., 1962; P. Gay, *Voltaire's Politics,* Princeton, 1959, and *The Party of Humanity,* New York, 1964. An earlier summary of the author's own views appeared as an essay, 'The World of the Enlightenment', in Columbia University's *Chapters in Western Civilization,* 3rd ed., Vol. I, New York, 1961, pp. 530-80.

quarrel among themselves, wander off on tangents, sometimes become totally disillusioned and recant.

Faced with such difficulties, a student of the Enlightenment may easily be drawn in one or the other of two very dangerous directions. In his desire to achieve clarity, he may settle for too narrow a range of phenomena, too few ideas, too sparse a cast of human characters. If carried far enough, the process of getting rid of every theme or individual not accounted for by a simple conception, early arrived at, could leave the student with only one theme, be it a view of nature or religion or freedom or morals, and perhaps at last just a single spokesman, the only one to have displayed the common decency to behave himself, saying on all occasions no more and no less than was expected of him. I am not aware of anyone who has fallen into quite so dire a predicament; but the game of intellectual give-away, of discarding significant, if puzzling, material in the rush to find a key, remains as tempting as it is apt to be impoverishing.

Yet the opposite danger, that of failing to draw any outlines at all, is at least equally threatening. It is not uncommon, for example, to encounter the Enlightenment being discussed as though it were synonymous with 'European thought in the eighteenth century'— this despite the fact that the Enlightenment did not exactly coincide with the eighteenth century even in terms of time. This also despite the fact that it is hard enough to bring Lessing and Voltaire, Kant and Benjamin Franklin, Diderot and Jeremy Bentham under the same intellectual umbrella, without having in addition to accommodate Giovanni Battista Vico in his isolated Neapolitan garret, John Wesley in his open-air pulpit, Justus Möser in his beloved, archaic Osnabrück, or Abbé Berger and the numerous other French *anti-philosophes* in their chapels and university chairs.[4] Just think how Dr Johnson would have felt about being confused in any way with the acknowledged *lumières,* Sam Johnson who said of one of them: 'Rousseau, Sir, is a very bad man. I would sooner sign a sentence for his transportation, than that of any felon who has gone from the Old Bailey these many years. Yes, I should like to have him work in the plantations.' (When pressed by Boswell to compare Rousseau and Voltaire, Johnson gave up: 'Why, Sir, it is difficult to settle the proportion of iniquity between them.')[5]

Surely we need not accept a formless nominalism which would refuse to recognise anything more coherent than a crowd of indi-

[4] For an interesting study of some leading *anti-philosophes,* notably Berger, see R. R. Palmer, *Catholics and Unbelievers in Eighteenth Century France,* Princeton, 1939.

[5] James Boswell, *The Life of Samuel Johnson,* Saturday, 15 Feb. 1766. (Gay's choice for the epigraph to *The Party of Humanity.*)

ARNULFO L. OLIVEIRA MEMORIAL LIBRARY
1825 MAY STREET
BROWNSVILLE, TEXAS 78520

viduals linked by the accident of time, arguing away the interval between the Wars of Religion and the French and Industrial Revolutions! It is my own belief that the rich variety of the Enlightenment can be appreciated without trying to credit or charge it with much that may be intrinsically interesting but remains, for present purposes, irrelevant. It is my further belief that a definition of the Enlightenment need not be so restrictive as to exclude one figure after another merely because his life's work ranged at times outside that definition or remained confined to only a part of the area within it. In short, I believe that the frame on which to rest our understanding of the Enlightenment need not be that of a Procrustean bed. If I am wrong, you will have an opportunity to conclude as much in the course of this paper. If I am right, there is no reason why we cannot go on disagreeing in our particular judgments about a major chapter in the history of ideas, while agreeing that at least it *was* a recognisable chapter.

Let me now say a bit more about the internal diversity of the Enlightenment. It is this very diversity which gives colour and life, paradox and humour to a movement which might otherwise deserve the accusations of monotony and self-righteous conformity levelled against it by its enemies. But let us admit that if diversity can defeat the would-be simplifier, it can also threaten to baffle the most responsible historian.

Take the matter of national variations. We know that there were men in Holland, Italy, Austria, Scandinavia, and the Iberian countries who were glad to be considered *lumières*. Their numbers, however, were sufficiently small to permit differences among them to be explained by personal, as opposed to national, idiosyncrasies. The same cannot be said of the French, the Germans, or the British; and I hope I may be permitted to divide the latter, for some purposes, by introducing the Atlantic Ocean and speaking of the Americans. The Enlightenment, for all its cosmopolitan aspirations, for all its exponents' avidity for fresh reading from abroad and their amazing feats as letter-writers, was not exactly the same in any two of these, its central countries.

Much depended, of course, on the questions which a given national situation made live and pressing. To the Americans, if I may anticipate a little in the use of 'national', to Franklin, Jefferson, Adams, Madison, and the temporarily adopted Tom Paine, whatever may have been their initial fascination with scientific, ethical, or educational issues, the political implications of Enlightenment became central. This was so because their own crisis, like that of their seventeenth-century English forefathers, was a crisis of governance, of the rights of rulers and of citizens. Yet

20

because they faced no entrenched feudal aristocracy and no mighty established church allied to privilege, the Americans never even approached the range or the intensity of French social and anti-clerical criticism.

It was, I suppose, the glory of the *philosophes* in France that no major aspect of the Enlightenment, however broadly one at last defines it, escaped their voracious curiosity and their fervent advocacy. Government, social relations, religion, economics, personal ethics, natural science, education, psychology all drew the attention, often generous, sometimes rancorous, of a bickering array of Frenchmen. In this respect, it is no more than fair that it should be their names which still spring first to our lips in any discussion of the Enlightenment. All the same, there is an element of distortion inherent in the Gallocentric view. The French range of interests was broad; but it was not uniform in the emphasis accorded different themes, nor was it without some characteristic premises grounded in the specifically French experience of the *ancien régime*. For example, much as I admire the work of my fellow-countryman, Peter Gay, his emphasis on the 'paganism' of the Enlightenment has often seemed to me exaggerated, until I have paused to reflect that he writes, most of the time, quite explicitly about the French Enlightenment.[6] Similarly, debates over the relationship between the Enlightenment and political or social revolution have had to concentrate on the French case, with only occasional side glances at the American.

If one does no more than take in the Germans, the canvas at once becomes broader, and more complicated. A scholar such as Ernst Cassirer, like Troeltsch and Dilthey before him,[7] depicts the *Aufklärung* as including some sceptical ideas about religion but also, and very importantly, as Christian in many of its concerns. From Leibniz through Thomasius and Wolff to Kant, the Christian *Aufklärer,* even when critical of existing Christian forms, have left us no choice. Conversely, the political and economic conditions of the Holy Roman Empire scarcely offered the challenges or kindled the hopes which call forth great treatises on public policy.

[6] Note the subtitle of Gay's *The Party of Humanity: Studies in the French Enlightenment.* In a more recent article, however, 'The Family of Freedom', *Columbia University Forum,* Winter 1966, Gay goes rather further. Having opened by asserting (p. 21) that 'there were many *philosophes* . . . but there was one Enlightenment', he goes on to examine (pp. 25-6) what he calls the 'turn from Christianity to paganism' in general, European terms. It is only that extension that troubles me.

[7] See, for example, E. Troeltsch, *Protestantism and Progress,* London, 1912; W. Dilthey, *Studien zur Geschichte des deutschen Geistes* (1901-11), recently collected and republished as Vol. III of Dilthey's *Gesammelte Schriften,* Stuttgart, 1962.

Well, but what are we to make of the British? It is undeniably true, though its significance may easily be overstated, that few Scots and fewer Englishmen, even those who looked to foreigners most like men of the Enlightenment, would have described themselves in just those words. Horace Walpole might have, and Alexander Pope—both were proud of their ties with the Continent—and Bentham, Godwin, Priestley would all, I suspect, at least have accepted the title of *philosophe* with complacency. But neither Hume nor Gibbon nor Adam Smith, though in touch with the *lumières* across the Channel, felt any need to style himself one of them. The question is not, it seems to me, whether Leslie Stephen could write his two volumes on *English Thought in the Eighteenth Century*, discarding Descartes at the outset and thereafter ignoring the Enlightenment. He not only could, but did.[8] The real question is whether we could adequately discuss the European Enlightenment, leaving out the English and Scottish thinkers. The answer, quite clearly, is that we could not. If many of them in the eighteenth century assumed that Great Britain needed no Enlightenment, since it had already had its Glorious Revolution and its scientific revolution, its Locke and Newton, we are bound to reply that that is not all the Enlightenment was about; and the characteristic swing in Britain towards ethics, economics, epistemology, and history suggests that the gentlemen in question knew this was so.

Another kind of variation appears in the social backgrounds of the *philosophes,* considered now without reference to nationality. Let me cite just a single illustration. One of the most curious myths concerning the Enlightenment has been that it was an expression of 'middle-class interests', presumably formulated by a phalanx of middle-class men. Whatever 'middle-class' meant in different countries during the seventeenth and eighteenth centuries (and nowhere was it equivalent to that much abused order, the *bourgeoisie!*), the notion remains as I say, a curious one in that it attempts to make a matter of opinion something about which there is not the slightest need for guesswork. Either the men of the Enlightenment were all or nearly all middle-class by background, or they were not. It may well be that many of the movement's assertions and programs suited an audience of educated commoners and laymen more than the aristocracy and the higher clergy. Sustained criticism of the existing state of affairs was likely to do so. But what would the Enlightenment have been without Baron de Montesquieu and Baron d'Holbach, the Marquis de Condorcet, the

8 The one possible exception, the discussion of 'The French Influence', to which Stephen devoted nine pages (3rd ed., Vol. II, London, 1902, pp. 186-95), is almost entirely negative concerning the reality of such influence.

Earl of Shaftesbury, the Marchese di Beccaria, and other titled
philosophes from Bolingbroke through Condillac to Turgot? Some
characteristically aristocratic views of freedom and resistance informed the entire movement, just as an aristocratic fascination with
personality, motives, virtue, justice endowed it with a sensitivity not
guaranteed by businesslike common sense alone.

Even after we have acknowledged the national and social variations which must be covered by a general definition of the
Enlightenment, there remain the men themselves, stubbornly
resistant, in their personal complexities, to any easy generalisation.
Was Hume a *philosophe* when he struck at that foundation stone
of orderly thought and scientific inquiry, the notion of cause and
effect? Yet Hume's essay of 1741, 'On Money', stands as a small
classic of closely argued economic analysis, to which Adam Smith
no less than the French physiocrats could look with gratitude. Did
not the Goethe of *Sturm und Drang*, of *Werther* and the first part
of *Faust* reject the erudition and intellectual clarity so prized by
the *philosophes*? Yet an older Goethe, the octogenarian cosmopolite
and classicist who identified the romantic with the sick, looked back
kindly on the Enlightenment he once had scorned. Do we try to fit
him in—or leave him out?

Rousseau is doubtless the most troublesome personality and
hence the best test case of all. He has been claimed by the
Romantics and called an *anti-philosophe,* a playwright who came
to denounce the theatre as distracting and corrupting, an encyclopaedist who broke violently with Diderot, a theorist of community
discipline who once called Sparta the ideal Greek city state precisely because it had no philosophers,[9] a critic of almost everything
that for Voltaire made civilisation civilised. Yet Rousseau, the
enemy of privilege and pretence, the moralist who saw natural man
not as a 'noble savage' but as an ideal type somewhere within us,
needing desperately to be reconciled with society, the reformer not
always a utopian, surely that Rousseau cannot be abandoned as a
'drop-out' from the Enlightenment.[10]

From even this brief reminder of personal complexities it is
possible, I think, to derive an important truth about the study of
an intellectual movement, any intellectual movement. That is that
if we are to identify its central tenets and values, we must avoid

[9] In *Réponse à M. Bordes,* cited by Judith N. Shklar in her excellent article,
'Rousseau's Two Models: Sparta and the Age of Gold', *Political Science
Quarterly*, March 1966, p. 31.
[10] I have benefited greatly from Peter Gay's discussion of biographical and
critical works on Rousseau, Chapter 8 of *The Party of Humanity*, and, like him,
from such recent French inquiries as Robert Derathé's *Le Rationalisme de Jean-
Jacques Rousseau*, Paris, 1948, and the same author's *Jean-Jacques Rousseau et
la science politique de son temps*, Paris, 1950.

what might be called the 'fallacy of personification'. It is at once necessary and helpful to take account of human variety; but it is neither necessary nor helpful to assume that a movement in the history of ideas is the sum total of everything everyone connected with it ever said or did. It is possible to get at the essentials of Marxism, for instance, including its evolution over five or six human generations, without having to make its central propositions explain all the political tactics of Lenin and all the decisions of the British Labour Party, let alone the specific behaviour of sometime 'Marxists' such as Benito Mussolini and Josef Goebbels or self-styled ones such as Lee Harvey Oswald. By the same token, it is possible to see in the Enlightenment a body of assumptions and concerns which since the later seventeenth century numerous thinkers have been able, as individuals, to adopt in some connexions and not in others, to espouse wholeheartedly and to reject impatiently at different times in their lives—and incidentally, in some cases to misunderstand and misrepresent, to the confusion of posterity. A few men, the mathematician and encyclopaedist d'Alembert for one, appear to have lived so happily within its boundaries that it is impossible to think of them ever wandering outside. Other men—Rousseau, Hume, Herder, Burke—cannot be understood wholly in terms of the Enlightenment, but neither can they be understood if they are thought of as wholly beyond its pale.

Our task, I suggested at the outset, is to try to derive from old texts and new scholarship a conception which can respect and encompass variety, while refusing to be torn apart by it. The twin dangers of excluding so much as to leave nothing worth defining and of including so much as to disappear in meaningless profusion have had to be remarked. So have some examples of national, social, and personal variation. In arguing that the Enlightenment was something other than a mass of biographers, I have not sought to dehumanise it; nor should I like to be thought of as underrating the lively interest to be found in the study of different nationalities and classes or status groups.[11] The search for a useful, general conception, however, cannot stop there.

My own endeavour to arrive at such a conception has led me to single out four attitudes, each based on identifiable assumptions which in turn seem to me at once characteristic of and essential to

11 There is, of course, still another kind of variation, the chronological, to which a longer treatment would have to devote considerable attention. In the present essay, I can only signal the differences separating the generation of Locke, Leibniz, Newton, and Bayle from that of Diderot, Hume, and Lessing, not to mention the differences between both these older groups, on the one hand, and the generation of Condorcet and Bentham, or even that of Kant, on the other.

the movement as a whole. This process of selection has involved the reclassification of some traditionally much stressed aspects as either atypical or misrepresented. Of these I shall speak briefly in closing. But first, what are the four themes I ask you to consider the features *sine qua non* of the Enlightenment?

The first is secular humanism. Humanism must here be taken in both its restricted and its several extended senses. That is, for the *philosophe,* man was truly the measure of all things—his mind, his body, his passions, his well-being, his relations with his fellow men. Humanism also still carried, as it had since the Renaissance, the implication of reverence for classical antiquity. Such reverence had long since ceased to be abject. The men of the Enlightenment could admire the heroes of Plutarch and the *Odes* of Horace without surrendering to the past, even the Graeco-Roman past. But the classics did inform the rhetoric and provide the favourite examples of the movement. Beyond that, humanism shaded into humanitarianism, as what might be called the applied aspect of a general value system. Sound thinking and good will had finally to show results under the banner of beneficence.

As for secularism, it was important despite the fact that Christian humanists, dominant in the sixteenth century, still numerous in the seventeenth, were by no means lacking in the eighteenth. More characteristic of the Enlightenment, however, was the demand for a morality independent of theology and a charity unrelated to hopes of the soul's salvation. I agree with the many commentators who have seen in Enlightenment thought important elements of both Christianity and Stoicism; but, once blended, they produced a genuinely new compound, an ideal of virtue and justice for living men, unsupported by transcendental sanctions or rewards.

The second element I wish to emphasise is the reliance, so far as intellectual method was concerned, on *analysis* as the orderly, rational, deductive treatment of data assembled from experience and observation. It is much better, I think, to insist on the importance of deductive-empirical analysis than it is to settle for the vaguer notion of an 'age of reason'. That phrase has always seemed unfair to earlier ages (thoughts of Socrates and St Thomas Aquinas inevitably cross the mind); but in addition, it is unfair to the seventeenth and especially to the eighteenth century. For one thing, it suggests that Reason was enthroned as a deity safe from all doubt, whereas in fact we know how much effort men such as Hume and Rousseau, Diderot and Kant put into analysing reason itself, its limits, its pitfalls, its needed controls.

For another thing, analysis according to Descartes's laws of breaking down a problem to its irreducible components, self-evident ideas, had by the eighteenth century been coupled with Locke's insistence on experience, including controlled experiment, as the source of such ideas. The result was a *particular way* of reasoning, as well as a particular view of what men can reason about. We may complain that the Enlightenment was too sure of the clarity of sensory perception, the reliability of verbal communication, and hence the solidity of conclusions agreed upon by right-thinking men; but we ought not to underestimate the hard work and in many cases the very considerable ingenuity which went into the search for such conclusions. It is useful to recall that Enlightenment, the product of learning and analysis, the shared property of reasonable men, stood for the exact opposite of its mystical Latinate cousin, 'Illumination'; and it still does.

Now a secular humanism armed with deductive-empirical analysis might or might not accept the existing order of things as essentially static, subject to improvements in detail perhaps, or characterised by the flux of aimless surface motion, but fundamentally static none the less. Hence, a third attitude of the Enlightenment must be lifted out and made explicit: the conviction that basic changes were occurring in man's condition, that more would occur in the future, and that an effort to control the nature and direction of such changes was not only intellectually respectable but indeed imperative. I am fully aware at this point of the need to step carefully. The Enlightenment's typical view of the physical universe *was* static, in its insistence on the regularity and predictability of natural phenomena, its rejection of occasional, miraculous changes in the rules. It must also be said that very few of the *philosophes* failed to experience, and to express, periodic doubts about the meaning and value of change. Nevertheless, within the dependable frame of the material world, human affairs, human behaviour were generally seen as changeable, and the changes themselves as at least potentially amenable to direction. This may seem a fairly modest assertion, but it had tremendous implications for both the tenor and the substance of Enlightenment thought.

The fourth theme or attitude I should like to single out is the widespread sense of liberation, of breaking shackles. The spokesmen of Enlightenment saw themselves as seeking truth and purveying knowledge in the service of something higher still: freedom—from senseless privilege, from superstition, from stultifying ignorance, from capricious authority. Some of them saw liberation as an achievement of the mind; thus Kant wrote in his essay on *Aufklärung*:

> Enlightenment is man's release from his self-incurred tutelage.
> Tutelage is man's inability to make use of his understanding

without direction from another . . . *Sapere aude!* 'Have courage to use your own reason!'—that is the motto of Enlightenment. Others attacked satisfyingly concrete targets, the Church, the *Parlements,* and various other established institutions in Voltaire's case, cruel and ineffectual legal procedures in Beccaria's. Some of them, depending on the political circumstances, were persuaded that a strong, wise monarch could be used to bring low the worst enemies of freedom. Others lumped kings and ministers with the rest of the oppressors. But all demanded that the change in man's lot, achievable through the exercise of beneficent reason, be in the direction of liberty.

Needless to say, in nominating as the Enlightenment's basic features secular humanism, a faith in rational analysis, a concern with the direction of unblinkable changes, and a sense of dedication to the cause of liberty, I may have chosen too many or too few to satisfy another observer. But these four were not determined *a priori,* at the expense of other possible themes. Instead, they recur endlessly, with many permutations, over a wide range of early modern thought. They do, in short, emerge from the sources. A theorist of the time who rejected any one of them would, I believe, seem to an objective reader to deviate, in that respect, from the main stream of the Enlightenment. A theorist who rejected all of them—Möser in Germany, for example, or de Maistre in Savoy— did not belong to that stream at all.

One set of corollaries to the formula presented here involves the explicit rejection of several time-worn, though not exactly time-proven, views about the Enlightenment.

1. It was not content with a bloodless, cock-sure rationalism. I have tried to recall the inquiries into reason itself which occupied a number of the *philosophes.* Furthermore, respect for sentiment, for the emotions, was far too widespread to support the claims of some Romantics that they had rescued man's feelings from the dry dust of the eighteenth century.

2. Nor was an unbridled naturalism a hallmark of the Enlightenment. Nature appeared comprehensible, but it was not without its excesses and its tragedies. How to curb or channel nature, including human nature, was part of the problem of liberating the thinking, moral individual. Whatever the Marquis de Sade may have been, besides a bore, in claiming that any action that is possible is *ipso facto* natural, and hence unobjectionable, he was assuredly not a man of the Enlightenment.

3. If the *lumières* were not smug rationalists, if they were not wild men, neither were they systematic sceptics. Indeed, their characteristic mistrust of philosophical systems, as such, more often

than not expressed itself in the search for (presumably attainable) particular truths. They were doubters about many traditions, institutions, delivered dogmas; but they were not sceptical in the broad sense of doubting the possibility of firm, communicable knowledge. David Hume did show such scepticism in some of his work, though he did not spend his life as though he believed it. Some of Rousseau's late, desperate writings have the nihilistic tone of true Pyrrhonism. Nevertheless, an often touching confidence in human knowledge and a faith in the possibility of finding unanswerable arguments were the more common hallmarks of Enlightenment thought. They were also, be it noted, invitations to bitter disappointment, something your genuine sceptic spares himself in advance.

4. Still another cliché consists in branding the Enlightenment an effusion of naïve faith in simple, unilinear progress. As I have already suggested, doubts and uncertainties on this score were legion. A few philosophers, notably Turgot, Godwin, and Condorcet, deserve to be called 'progressionists' in some of their writings; but like Hume at his most sceptical, they actually appear unrepresentative when speaking thus. One finds far less progressionist emphasis in the eighteenth century than one does in the nineteenth. Not surprisingly, it was the opponents of such figures as Hegel, Comte, Marx, and Huxley who sometimes dubbed them '*philosophes* after the letter' and comfortably blamed the eighteenth century for everything.

5. Finally, let me challenge the picture of the Enlightenment as primarily destructive, the expression of a negative liberalism obsessed with freedom *from* restraints and uninterested in freedom *to* achieve certain positive ends, including self-discipline. The point is that self-control was one of the highest aims of the *philosophes*, from Shaftesbury through Rousseau to Kant. But self-control is meaningless without freedom of choice; so the abolition of irrational external constraint could be viewed as the necessary pre-condition for moral behaviour, the true end of man. Few figures of speech were as popular among the *lumières* as that of 'clearing the ground', sweeping away the accumulated rubble of prejudice and the underbrush of injustice. No doubt for some, especially in France, this ground-clearing proved to be so exhilarating as to become an end in itself. Yet the ultimate justification for it remained a belief that if they could *écraser l'infâme*, they, or others after them, could build new and better laws and social relations for free men. Call this visionary and superficial if you like—it frequently was both. But it was not negative. If you had asked an exponent of Enlightenment whether he was striving to destroy old

wrongs or to create new happiness, he might have replied, using another favourite simile of his times, that this was like asking a surgeon whether he was amputating a gangrenous limb to keep the patient from dying, or to help him achieve good health.

In most of what I have said here, the tone and the argument have been friendly to the Enlightenment. It is unlikely, in fact, that one could aproach any intellectual movement in a state of prior distrust and hostility and still hope to learn from its spokesmen what they thought were its central themes. This is not to say that we have no task but that of understanding, that we have no obligation to evaluate, to judge the quality of the ideas themselves; but there is time enough to criticise, to expose inconsistencies, to cite omissions and blind spots, after the witnesses have had their day in court. As I have tried to show, a fair hearing destroys the basis for some criticisms and caricatures which simply do not deserve any longer to colour our judgments. On the other hand, it would be foolish to deny that the Enlightenment provided inadequate answers for many problems which still plague us. In some cases, it did not even perceive problems which to us appear immense. The same can be said of Greek antiquity, of the Middle Ages, of the Renaissance. The same will be said, in due course, of the best we ourselves may produce. For the richest heritage of thought is never adequate alone to cope with unforeseen developments in the human condition or to assimilate every new accretion of knowledge. That is why the interest of intellectual history lies not in admiring final triumphs, but in calculating margins of advance.

The Development of Eighteenth-Century Studies in the British Commonwealth

W. J. Cameron

The title of my paper may be misleading to some of you. I am addressing you in the Commonwealth of Australia, so the word 'British' is needed to define a larger area. But I come from a country, Canada, where that adjective is in some areas not very popular for defining the loose association of sovereign states to which most of us belong. And I was born and bred in another country, New Zealand, which is so British that it would be an insult not to use the adjective. Despite these dilemmas, the title of my paper is accurate. I am concerned with the development of eighteenth-century studies in English in those three Commonwealth countries where the British tradition is strongest—New Zealand, Australia, and Canada, especially English Canada. The economic jargon of today classes these countries as 'developed' rather than 'developing' or 'underdeveloped'. I believe, however, that despite the activities of a scatter of scholars and dedicated teachers, all three countries are underdeveloped in the intellectual field of scholarly studies (including the eighteenth century), and it is my purpose to suggest, using the eighteenth century as an example, how we might become as fully developed in intellectual as in economic terms. Indeed I intend to take for my theme a very British pronouncement by a very sturdy Englishman.

Nearly three hundred years ago, John Dryden affirmed of his own sphere of activity:

> [For] we live in an age so sceptical, that as it determines little, so it takes nothing on trust; and I profess to have no other ambition in this Essay than that poetry may not go backward, when all other arts and sciences are advancing.

31

Now eighteenth-century studies are flourishing (and, we hope, advancing) in the United States and the United Kingdom. The existence of such societies as the Johnsonian Society of the Great Lakes Region suggests that Canada benefits from contiguity with the United States, and the much higher output of scholarly publications from Canada suggests that scholarship is more active there than in Australia or New Zealand. Nevertheless, we seem to share in Canada the common experience of the Antipodes which observes that students on the whole are not interested in the eighteenth century, and, as some Australians have complained to me, *cannot* be interested in that century which was the cradle of our present cultures.

Those of us who believe that there is real value and pleasure in detailed knowledge of British culture in the eighteenth century ought to be not only teaching our subject but doing our best to encourage original research in the period. To achieve this aim, we ought to be firstly determining what resources we have in our own countries, and secondly using and developing these resources for the pleasure and instruction of our countrymen. I therefore propose first of all to give a preliminary survey of the major resources of original eighteenth-century imprints in the three countries. Secondly, I propose to offer a few suggestions as to how these resources may be best used and developed 'so that [eighteenth-century studies] may not go backward, when all other [fields of study] are advancing'. My aim is to provoke rather than advise, for I am sure that the exchange of ideas during this week's activities will be of much more lasting value than any tentative conclusions I might arrive at.

Now, let me draw your attention to the second of the three appendixes to this paper. It is a very brief summary of the holdings of the twenty-one libraries in the three countries that contain over a thousand volumes (*not* titles, please note) printed in the eighteenth century in the British Isles, the British colonies, and the United States of America, or in English elsewhere. The last column gives the estimated holdings of each library, and the figure is an extrapolation from a sample testing of the library's general catalogues to which has been added the figure in the second-to-last column. This additional figure may represent books in a printed catalogue (such as the 3,993 titles in the Redpath collection at McGill); in a separate library within a larger one (such as the 251 titles in the Dixson Library), or uncatalogued material (such as the 1,400 volumes in the Macdonald collection and the 2,100 volumes in other collections in the Fisher Library).

Two surprising facts emerge from the table. Only four libraries have 10,000 volumes or more, and all other libraries have 5,000 or less. New Zealand's largest collection belongs in the second category, and only one Australian library is in the first. Wellington and Canberra should obviously be the major centres for eighteenth-century research in the two countries. But what of Canada? Three major collections within the main area of population and none elsewhere make the resources of the United States seem more significant for most Canadians, especially as the three major collections are themselves not of outstanding quality. And further development of these major collections poses a problem of rationalisation which is quite different from the problem in the Antipodes. More detailed analysis of the three collections reveals certain weaknesses in each collection, weaknesses which are to a certain extent evident in the first six columns of the table. Comparable figures taken from the British Museum catalogue have been supplied to help keep matters in perspective. The first two columns reveal that McGill has a strong drama collection and the University of Toronto a relatively weak one. The second two columns show that the University of Toronto is strong in poetry, and McGill relatively weak. The last two columns of the six would suggest McMaster's superiority in prose to both McGill and Toronto, were it not for the fact that most of the Redpath collection (not included in the sample) consists of prose pamphlets. A further breakdown of the sample upon which these figures are based confirms the conclusion that McMaster has the most generally balanced, but smallest collection of the three, and that there are grave weaknesses in all three. The figures for the Australian National Library make that collection appear better than the Canadian ones, but this is largely because of special strengths in Alexander Pope and Jonathan Swift, which inflate the total number of items in the poetry and prose columns. The actual number of authors from the sample is a fairer indication of its relative strength. If one were to include McMaster's collection of Oliver Goldsmith in the sample, its figures would be similarly inflated. As it is, McMaster's figures are slightly inflated by its fairly strong Smollett collection. Both McMaster and the Australian National Library have a confirmable total of 10,000 volumes. The figures for McGill and Toronto are extrapolations that cannot be confirmed. I hesitate to attempt to extrapolate from the figures for the British Museum.

Now the four major collections have had very different historical origins, and this fact has left its mark on them. McGill has built slowly and somewhat erratically on a strong nineteenth-century benefaction. Toronto, like McGill, has benefited from being developed under the felt needs of graduate teaching and research.

Both collections show signs of sporadic buying in certain well defined areas of academic interest. Unfortunately, this often means that the books bought were those that were not already available in the private library of the professor who used them, either for his own research or for that of a student. When that professor left the university, he took with him the core of the collection, leaving an unevenly balanced and often unusable collection behind him.

McMaster, two years ago, had only 500 volumes in the field, and its collection of 10,000 volumes has been carefully put together by bulk purchasing (either from dealers or from duplicate collections in other libraries) and by buying individual items to round out the collection for research purposes. It is hoped that within a year this policy will produce the largest and most useful collection in Canada.

The Australian National Library owes its strength to outright purchase of three major collections put together by different methods. The first of these, the economics collection, was one of those fine subject-collections put together by a book-dealer called Kashnor. Other Kashnor collections are to be found in Milan and other centres for research in economic history. The very valuable one which came to Australia is strong in Irish and Scottish economic affairs, and thus serves as a complement to, rather than a rival of, the magnificent collection in the Kress Library of Business at Harvard. The second major collection was the lifetime acquisition of a working scholar—David Nichol Smith, in whose honour and memory this seminar is being held. It is strong in literature, especially Jonathan Swift. Some items from Nichol Smith's library went to their proper resting-place in the great libraries of Scotland and England. There they play an important role in completing the coverage of research material to which we must all resort when our local resources fail. But the bulk of his collection, with its innumerable notes and secondary material, makes it a mine of information for scholars here in Australia.

The third major collection is the library of the Clifford family of Ugbrooke. Over two-thirds of the pre-1800 material is of Continental origin, and its strengths still need to be carefully assessed. But the English material reflects the lives of a recusant or Catholic family with great fidelity. Practical manuals, devotional literature, and standard reference books are cheek-by-jowl with books on literature, politics, economics, and history. Not surprisingly, the Cliffords showed very little interest in English philosophy, theology, and intellectual history. Indeed, these three areas are probably the greatest weakness in the National Library collection as a whole.

You may judge for yourself, however, for the publication of the short-title catalogue of eighteenth-century books in the A.C.T. will show in detail what is at present available in the National Library. A short-title catalogue of the collection at McMaster is available on cards in the Mills Memorial Library in Hamilton, Ontario, and when bulk purchasing has ceased, it may possibly serve as a basis for a printed short-title catalogue of books in Canadian libraries, just as the one in Canberra (I hope) may be developed into a union short-title catalogue for Australia.

So much for the major collections. You may of course ask for details about the collections and of my sampling technique later. What of the medium-sized collections? Most of them have special strengths as well as obvious weaknesses. The Turnbull Library in New Zealand is stronger in poetry than any Canadian library and is superior to all except one Australian library in most other fields. Only one university library in Australia is comparable with the major public repositories; only one Canadian public library is comparable with the university libraries. In New Zealand the honours are divided. Semi-private collections (only the theological collection in St Mark's Rectory, Niagara-on-the-Lake, has sufficient books to be included in the table) usually have a special strength which makes them very valuable, out of all proportion to the total number of volumes. But a close study of the table will indicate roughly the size and strengths of collections between 1,000 and 5,000, and I shall be pleased to offer further details at question time.

Now let us turn to Appendix III. This is designed to give point to a question often asked. What proportion of a university library should reasonably be expected to be devoted to original research material? In absolute terms, I should guess that 100,000 volumes is a minimum for serious research in depth in our special field. But a student may have his appetite whetted by a much smaller collection if he knows that a larger one is available at not too great a distance. Those who are familiar with any of the libraries listed might therefore decide whether the resources are adequate or inadequate by comparing them with other libraries. McMaster's 5 per cent is a greatly exaggerated figure because we have embarked on a deliberate policy of specialising in the eighteenth century. The percentage will come down as secondary material is collected, and as other areas are developed according to plan. McGill and Toronto represent figures resulting from haphazard development during a highly respectable longevity. Mount Allison, with its special collection of ballad and folk-song material, has a distinction much to be admired in a university with no pretension to graduate studies. Otago reflects the care with which the original De Beer collection is being developed, and Western Ontario shows how another benefactor can give strength to a modest collection. But need I go on? Each university will have to decide whether or not it thinks it worth while to develop the collection it already has, and knowledge of what books are in other collections may help in making a decision. Nevertheless, I should like to offer some encouragement to those who believe that their collections *ought* to be developed.

When, in 1962, Walter Stone published my short-title catalogue of 'Wing' books in Australian libraries, I wrote an introduction to it on the development of rare book collections and research facilities in Australian and New Zealand libraries. Although English books of the period 1640-1700 were used to illustrate and explain the opinions expressed there, the general message is essentially the same for eighteenth-century studies. In 1962, I made a plea to librarians and scholars to complete the task of making known the true resources of Australia and New Zealand in seventeenth-century books, so that orderly development of seventeenth-century studies could be undertaken in this geographical area. The plea has not fallen on deaf ears, for Miss Jean Whyte has published supplements, and a dedicated band led by Wallace Kirsop is still carrying on the good work. Thus I have been greatly encouraged to do the same kind of work for the eighteenth century. The result has been a fruitful collaboration with Mrs Diana Carroll of the National Library in producing what I hope Australians will soon make the first of a series of short-title catalogues which will reveal the true resources of Australia.

Let me parody what I wrote in 1962: if every eighteenth-century book in Australian, New Zealand, and Canadian libraries were to be gathered together in one library, we might be proud of the collection that resulted. No one would question the assumption that it was our duty to develop such a collection until it became a great centre of research in the period. But in my opinion the geographical dispersal of these treasures is a great advantage for the future encouragement of research. It is much simpler to build a small specialised collection to encourage scholars *to begin* a research project locally than to expect a man to undertake the beginning, the middle, and the end of such a project in a large library at a great distance from his day-to-day work—teaching, or whatever it may be. If in the odd moments of a busy life a man is able to lay the groundwork of his project in a local library with very limited resources, he will be encouraged to travel to larger centres in our geographical area for, say, a week's concentrated work, the results of which may be developed locally. This pattern of work may then be repeated until it becomes absolutely necessary to take advantage of the immense resources of the larger libraries overseas to complete the work.

So, the essential needs of a scholar in the eighteenth-century humanities in our underdeveloped parts of the world are firstly, adequate (though limited) local resources to begin a project and to keep the work going; secondly, sufficient national resources to enable the major part of the work to be completed; and thirdly, opportunities to complete the work in a major English or American library. If the work done in Australia, New Zealand, or Canada has been well done, the time and money required to complete the work in the great libraries of the world should be reduced to an absolute minimum, and the advantages to a man of keeping intellectually alive by doing even limited research work in conjunction with his normal day-to-day activities is enormous.

I believe this to be true still. And I find plenty of evidence in Canada that such ideas fall on sympathetic ears. In New Zealand I tried to demonstrate by my own publications that it was a valid way of combating the problem of isolation, and one student of mine who is just about to complete his Ph.D. has rather triumphantly succeeded in showing that it can be done by others, even with the rather poor facilities of New Zealand libraries. But I find Australian academics very backward indeed. I believe they have better resources than they deserve, for the rather chaotic state of retrospective collections in Australia is largely due to the lack of academic demands put on the libraries. The prevalence of rather barren Leavisite criticism in Departments of English has no doubt contributed, and it seems that Modern Languages Departments are relatively much more active in scholarly activity.

I cannot generalise about other disciplines, but it does seem that graduate work in Australia is far too restricted in subject-matter. In the field of English literature, there are adequate resources in Australia to encourage students to do good work on Jonathan Swift, for instance. Because of this, it may be worth while suggesting that eighteenth-century men in Australia form a Swift Society on the pattern of the various Johnsonian Societies in North America, to keep people informed of work being done and work needing to be done on Swift and his contemporaries. Good Irish collections also prompt the suggestion. Close watch may be kept on the Swift collections in various libraries so that collectors may be encouraged to fill in the gaps. The relationship between the major collection in the National Library, the next best at Monash, the fairly substantial ones at the University of Adelaide and the State Library of Victoria could also be worked out. Bibliographical work done on valuable copies of Swift material scattered round Australia may keep the spotlight on the value of Australian resources in eighteenth-century material.

But even if individual directors of graduate work manage to draw the attention of students to the fascination of such research work, the general climate of opinion at the undergraduate level will not be changed until the relevance of eighteenth-century studies to present-day realities has been properly demonstrated by dedicated teaching. The major barrier to this broadening of the cultural interests of students is probably an almost compulsive preoccupation with Australiana, with the literature and history of Australia. This is, in itself, not to be deplored. What is to be deplored is the isolation of such studies from the study of the parent culture and even of the sibling cultures of the present day. The phenomenon seems to be more obvious in Australia than in New Zealand or Canada, but the general tendency to foreshorten history, to isolate geographically or culturally, is common in all three countries. Present-mindedness, nationalism, parochialism, and anti-intellectualism abound in each country, and it is useless to fulminate against such an inevitable trait of an intellectually underdeveloped country. What we must do, if we care about intellectual health, is to harness such forces to the humanist cause of 'sweetness and light'. One method is to encourage provenance study. Let me illustrate from a Canadian example, and provide a few hints for Australia and New Zealand.

Just before leaving Canada three months ago, my bibliographical assistant George McKnight and I finished short-title cataloguing the library at St Mark's Rectory, Niagara-on-the-Lake. This library has been looked at by half a dozen scholars in the past ten years, but as it was uncatalogued, nothing much could be done with it. Local historians are very interested in it, not because it is a superb collection of eighteenth-century philosophy and theological controversy, but because it was brought to Canada by the first missionary on the Niagara frontier. As about a quarter of the books have evidence of ownership in them, from book-plates to signed annotations, it seemed possible to redirect local and national pride by provenance study into serious consideration of the intellectual tradition which Robert Addison brought with him in 1791.

The story, in fact, is an absorbing one, and I hope to complete it by next year in time for the centenary of both the nation and the local parish. Robert Addison in 1781 became curate of Upwell, Norfolk, which is partly in the Isle of Ely. That same year, a Reverend Richard Atkinson died in Whittlesea, Isle of Ely, just south of Peterborough, and Addison seems to have acquired his library. Atkinson had himself built a modest library (dates in some of his books range from 1734 to 1766), but he had also, somehow, acquired the library of one William Beale after Beale died in 1772. William Beale put his name (and usually a date of purchase or of binding) in about 250 of his books. Because of this, we may follow his intellectual development and his tastes in theology and even secular literature with amazing fidelity. Beale had taken holy orders, probably did a little teaching, and was a chaplain in the navy before becoming vicar of Whittlesea in 1742. Probably at this time he took over the library of his predecessor, Thomas Topping, who had been vicar of Whittlesea since 1704. Once again, we find it possible to trace the intellectual interests of the man, for thirty-four of his books contain his name, and in most cases the date of acquisition. His close reading of a voluminous author like Joseph Bingham is attested by a series of dates with which he marked his progress.

Topping has been confused with another man of the same name in some standard reference books, so his annotations help to clear up ambiguities. His theological interests are remarkably like Beale's, whom he may have influenced. Thus, the major part of Robert Addison's library was kept (and used) in the vicarage of Whittlesea from 1704 to 1772, and was given a special emphasis by the personalities of the two major collectors. But additions after 1772 can also be analysed to fix the characteristics of Richard Atkinson and Robert Addison. This is not all. A study of nonce-owners reveals a surprising number of parsons within a day's ride of Whittlesea. The dates suggest that Thomas Topping often borrowed his friends' books and was not over-scrupulous about returning them! And the circle of friends who gave books to other owners can often be determined.

When the library reached Niagara-on-the-Lake in 1792, Addison had added books bought at a sale in Quebec. The town of Niagara-on-the-Lake was burned to the ground by the Americans during the 1812 war, but the library was housed in a farmhouse outside the town and was thus preserved. When the British troops at Fort Niagara moved out, they left many of their books with Robert Addison, and so the library preserves practically the only relics of that frontier society that was so rudely destroyed by the conflagration.

I give a rough outline of this example of provenance study in order to encourage similar analyses of early collections in Australia and New Zealand, especially collections intended for educational purposes in the early days of the colonies. Walter Stone, in his excellent little periodical, *Biblionews,* has printed Peter Orlovich's account of an early Sydney library, The Philosophical Society Library, 1821-2. This is just the kind of thing I mean. Christchurch College, Christchurch, New Zealand, still owns the original collection presented by the Bishop designate of Lyttleton and his personal friends in August 1850. In some books, alterations in the date have been made (over the signature A.P.P.); and in others, several owners' names are to be found. Cream of the eighteenth-century material is a collection of 514 sermons in twenty-three volumes once belonging to 'Edw. Rowney Æd Christi Alumnus'. The collection deserves study—and perhaps comparison with another collection in a Wakefield settlement, now in St Barnabas College, Belair, Adelaide. A collection of 140 sermons in seven volumes of the same period, which belonged to one J. Hinton, can be traced through various owners to its final repository. Most of the original clerical lending library of Adelaide is also to be found there.

The gift of 'the associates of the late Rev. Dr. Bray', this library was sent out in 1846, and the volumes were serially numbered on the spine. The moderate Anglicanism of the collection is probably symbolised by the first choice of the benefactors—Burnet on the thirty-nine articles. But the first 200 volumes should be analysed more thoroughly. Though some have disappeared, attempts to keep the collection intact were still being made in 1882, as a substitute No. 4 (Chillingworth's *Works*) shows. The whereabouts of some of the 'borrowed' volumes may be revealed by a union catalogue of eighteenth-century books. Dr Bray's associates started the intellectual life of many a diocese, and the distinctive book-plates are to be found in many a theological collection. At Moore Theological College in Sydney are seventy of the original 1809 gift to Samuel Marsden's lending library—and some others that were part of similar collections in New Zealand and Australia. But probably of greater interest at Moore College is a collection of about two hundred eighteenth-century books that formed part of a collection of a thousand books chosen by Coleridge and Pusey for William Grant Broughton, the first bishop, and sent out to Sydney in 1839. The Tractarian bias provoked someone to send out yet another collection, of which about fifty or sixty are still on the shelves. In a formidable black book-plate pasted into about fifty or sixty eighteenth-century books is to be found the inscription, 'To the Protestant Church of Australia from some bachelors and undergraduates of the University of Oxford'. Thus the religious controversies of England were transplanted in 1839 to the developing colony. Meanwhile, the less partisan associates of Dr Bray continued to enrich the lending libraries. Indeed, books were still being sent to Moore College as late as 1953.

Anglican collections are not the only ones that invite provenance study. The earliest library catalogue that I have seen here in Australia is the manuscript catalogue of St Mary's Roman Catholic

Cathedral, Sydney, 1859. It lists 5,698 volumes, about five hundred of which are eighteenth-century English imprints. Almost half the collection consisted of books printed before 1800. As might be expected, some are Australiana. More surprising is the amount of Protestant material and books of secular interest. Most of the collection has survived and is to be found at St Patrick's College, Manly. Evidence from a copy of Hume's *History of England,* 1762, suggests that the library in 1859 included a collection sent out from Cheltenham some time after 1835 by a Mrs Sarah Neve. In a letter to Bishop Polding, she proposed to mark the books in this collection with the initials 'N.S.W.' to indicate that they were to belong to the Bishop in perpetuity. An additional 'M' would indicate that the books so marked could be used for missionary purposes. No books with these marks have yet been discovered, but the annotation in Mrs Neve's Hume echoes the proposal in her letter. The 'N.S.W. M' books may turn up in other Australian libraries once a union list of eighteenth-century books is available.

The Benedictine influence on Australia's Catholic clergy can possibly be traced by analysis of other books that were brought out by the first Vicar-General, Ullathorne, and the first Bishop, Polding. Although the task of identifying their books in the 1859 collection may be rather difficult, the work is worth doing. I leave the task of finding other collections in Australia, New Zealand, and Canada to local enthusiasts, but I might add some comments first.

Mr Allan Horton, Librarian at the University of New South Wales, told me of his discovery among some archives of a manuscript list of books dated 1810 and labelled 'List of books belonging to Government from Governor Bligh's papers'. He intends to try to track down the sixty or seventy titles in the public collections in Sydney. Would not Australians like to know what early governments thought were useful books for their purposes? Would not Australians like to know what founding families thought was valuable among the books printed during the Enlightenment? Indeed, I hear on the grape-vine that the Macarthur family's library may soon be broken up for sale. Should not a little provenance study be done on it before it is dispersed? And should not due tribute be paid in Canada and Australia to the book-collectors who so frequently helped to mould the major collections? Mr Eric McCormick has begun the work in New Zealand with his pamphlet, *The Fascinating Folly.*

Most frequently, the collections that provide the greatest amount of information for provenance study are those in libraries isolated from the major public and university repositories. Preconceived notions about the nature of collections in theological or other specialised colleges must be broken down. Law and classics (especially Juvenal) in the eighteenth century are better represented in the Leeper Library, Trinity College, Melbourne, than in most secular libraries in Australia. And the central philosophical and historical interests of the eighteenth century may be better represented in what seems to be a theological collection (such as the Shoultz collection housed in the University of Otago library) than in a largely secular library. Indeed, the Shoultz collection at Otago and the Clifford collection in the National Library, Canberra, have many surprises in store for the curious eighteenth-century man.

At this point I should like to leave provenance study to make another relevant point. Students and their teachers may frequently have their horizons greatly broadened when they are brought into actual contact with even modest collections of original material that cut across linguistic and subject boundaries. Narrowing disciplines—English literature, history, or whatever—tend to restrict one's interests in the culture of a previous age. By confining my survey to eighteenth-century studies in English, I fear that I may be contributing unwittingly to this bad trend. Predominantly English collections such as De Beer's at Otago, Nichol Smith's in Canberra, Macdonald's in the Fisher Library, Sydney, or the Redpath collection at McGill fit our university disciplines very nicely, and will no doubt be exploited by researchers. But other collections can introduce the narrowly specialised student to architecture, painting, social history, philosophy, and other aspects of European thought in a way that secondary material cannot. Imaginative display of such collections could be undertaken by librarians if they are encouraged by academics.

The small collection thus has a function other than providing original material for research purposes. If a student's interest in the culture of the eighteenth century can be aroused by showing him the books, manuscripts, or art objects of that period, his teachers must be ready and able to help him find material to cultivate that interest. So we come back to our first point. The resources of our three countries *must* be adequately assessed and publicised. Hence the need for developing bibliographical studies even at the expense of critical studies. A student, properly directed, may produce very valuable contributions to international scholarship by being invited to produce bibliographical work as a by-product of his studies. In the intellectually underdeveloped state of our culture, it seems most unwise to popularise the notion that bibliography (either analytic or enumerative) is a discipline with an end in itself, or that, as a means to an end, it is beneath the dignity of a cultivated university man. And both notions are far too common in library and university circles.

If the short-title catalogue that is being issued to mark the occasion of this seminar is used seriously, Australians may be able to assess the value of their national and local resources—and produce supplements to show where the books may be found. The National Library will use it as an acquisition tool, so that their already respectable collection may be enriched for the use of all Australians. If academics help librarians to decide what 'feeder' collections could be developed locally, and give advice on what kinds of material are needed in the National Library to balance the already existing collections, the development of resources should benefit all. Indeed, there is far too little co-operation between academics and librarians, not only in Australia, but also in Canada and New Zealand. I find librarians on the whole eager for advice and direction from academics, but although the library is supposed to be the humanist's equivalent to the scientist's laboratory, the academic who plays an active role in developing library resources is a rarity. In the present stage of intellectual development, this is disastrous. Everyone should face up to the questions: in what way *could* our eighteenth-century resources be improved? in what way *should* they be developed? The answer to the latter question in any particular university must be modified or shaped by full knowledge of local, national, and international resources.

The pattern of graduate study in the past has not helped much to develop the resources of the underdeveloped British Commonwealth countries. Students have gone to England or the United States for postgraduate training, and on their return (if they returned) they found the vast gap between the great libraries and those of their own country to be too great for them to use their research experience properly. By sending Canadian students to Australia or New Zealand, or Australian students to Canada, and so on, the strengths of our lop-sided collections may be utilised for the benefit of all. After completing a rather superficial survey of Australian resources, I would now have no hesitation in advising a Canadian student to come to Australia to do graduate research on Jonathan Swift, for example. I should hope that an Australian would have no hesitation in sending a student to McGill to work on eighteenth-century drama, especially with three reasonably good collections at Western Ontario, Toronto, and McMaster within a cheap train-journey's distance to supplement McGill's resources. And I hope that within a year prose and drama, philosophy and history, will have become major fields to attract Australians or New Zealanders to McMaster. But for eighteenth-century poetry the combined resources of Australia and New Zealand will probably never be equalled in Canada. Experience in British Commonwealth universities with approximately the same growth problems, and in British Commonwealth countries with fairly similar cultural backgrounds, should provide lively graduate students with ideas that will help them develop the limited resources of their own country. To help them decide where they may get the best facilities, their teachers must keep them informed of the resources available in different geographical areas. I have given a state-by-state summary of Australian resources in the introduction to the short-title catalogue. Let me end this paper with a province-by-province and centre-by-centre summary for Canada and New Zealand.[1]

1 This summary appears as Appendix I.

APPENDIX I

Eighteenth-Century Collections in Australia, Canada, and New Zealand, by State, Province, or Centre

AUSTRALIA

New South Wales: The University of Sydney has 5,000 volumes, and the Public Library of New South Wales (including the Mitchell and Dixson Libraries) has about 2,000 volumes. Nearly 10,000 volumes in the state.

Victoria: The State Library of Victoria probably has about 2,600 volumes, and the University of Melbourne 1,600. About 5,500 volumes in the state.

South Australia: The University of Adelaide has 1,500 volumes, and the Public Library of South Australia 1,200. About 3,500 volumes in the state.

Queensland: Less than 1,000 volumes in the state.

Tasmania: About 500 volumes in the state.

Western Australia: No significant collection.

Australian Capital Territory: About 10,000 volumes, of which 95 per cent are in the Australian National Library.

CANADA

Ontario: Roughly comparable to the whole of Australia. The University of Toronto and McMaster University both have over 10,000 volumes.

Quebec: McGill has the largest collection in Canada (13,000?), but all other collections in the province are very small.

British Columbia: The University of British Columbia has the largest collection (about 2,000). Total resources of the province are probably comparable to South Australia.

New Brunswick: Fredericton can muster almost 1,000 volumes (704 in the Cathedral Library, nearly 300 in the University of New Brunswick).

Nova Scotia, Manitoba, and Saskatchewan: The largest collection in each province (Dalhousie University, University of Manitoba, University of Saskatchewan) has about 500 volumes.

Alberta: The University at Edmonton has 163 titles.

Newfoundland and Prince Edward Island: No significant collection.

NEW ZEALAND

(This is a corrected form of the pioneering survey made by Keith Maslen in the periodical *New Zealand Libraries,* May 1962.)

Wellington: About 6,000 volumes are held among four institutions.

Dunedin: About 3,000 volumes are to be found in Dunedin libraries.

Auckland: About 2,000 volumes, mainly in two institutions.

Christchurch: Comparable with Fredericton, New Brunswick, with 1,000 volumes in two institutions.

New Zealand as a whole is richer than any state in Australia and any province in Canada except Ontario and Quebec. Australian scholars overlook New Zealand resources at their peril.

APPENDIX II

Summary of Sample Findings

The sample: 55 dramatists whose names begin with C
24 poets whose names begin with P
42 prose writers whose names begin with S

<u>121</u> authors

LIBRARY	No. of dramatists	No. of titles	No. of poets	No. of titles	No. of prose writers	No. of titles	No. of authors	Total No. of titles	Vols. not covered by sample	Estimated No. of vols. in collection
British Museum	47	881	22	667	42	1,538	111	3,093	?	?
McGill Univ., Montreal	25	149	11	65	28	139	64	353	over 4,000	13,000
Univ. of Toronto	22	87	17	98	30	228	69	413	—	12,000
National Library of Australia	27	109	13	142	26	285	66	536	—	10,000
McMaster Univ., Hamilton, Ontario	22	113	13	82	34	233	69	428	—	10,000
Alexander Turnbull Library, Wellington	18	61	13	98	20	103	51	262	20-30	5,000
Fisher Library, Univ. of Sydney	7	20	10	23	17	64	34	107	3,500	5,000
State Library of Victoria	19	53	9	33	27	67	55	153	250	2,600
Univ. of Western Ontario	17	61	10	32	21	62	48	155	100	2,500
Univ. of British Columbia	14	28	8	20	23	44	45	92	300	2,000

A P P E N D I X II—continued

LIBRARY	No. of dramatists	No. of titles	No. of poets	No. of titles	No. of prose writers	No. of titles	No. of authors	Total No. of titles	Vols. not covered by sample	Estimated No. of vols. in collection
Public Library of N.S.W. (including Mitchell)	18	52	11	24	23	64	52	140	250 in Dixson Library	2,000
Otago Univ., Dunedin	16	31	16	61	19	47	51	139	100	2,000
St Mark's Rectory, Niagara-on-the-Lake	2	2	2	2	9	33	13	37	—	2,000
Univ. of Melbourne	5	6	7	10	14	21	26	37	750	1,600
Queen's Univ., Kingston, Ontario	9	31	5	19	18	58	32	108	100	1,600
Univ. of Adelaide	11	20	8	43	16	48	35	111	—	1,500
Public Library of South Australia	13	36	6	12	13	31	32	79	—	1,200
Univ. of Auckland	9	13	5	12	18	29	32	54	—	1,000
Auckland Public Library	3	14	4	7	12	28	19	49	400	1,000
Toronto Public Library	7	15	4	6	15	28	26	49	—	1,000?
Mount Allison Univ., Sackville, New Brunswick	6	7	5	11	10	22	21	40	—	1,000?

APPENDIX III

English Imprints of the Eighteenth Century

A comparison of approximate strengths of university libraries
containing collections of appreciable size
(Bookstock as estimated in mid-1965)

Library	Estimated No. of volumes to nearest 100	Total bookstock to nearest 10,000	% of total bookstock
McMaster, Hamilton, Ont.	10,000	200,000	5·00
McGill, Montreal, Quebec	13,000	970,000	1·34
Toronto	12,000	1,210,000	0·99
Mt Allison, Sackville, N.B.	1,000	130,000	0·77
Otago, Dunedin	2,000	280,000	0·71
Western Ontario	2,500	390,000	0·64
Sydney	5,000	930,000	0·54
Auckland	1,000	210,000	0·48
Melbourne	1,600	425,000	0·38
Adelaide	1,500	440,000	0·34
Queens, Kingston, Ont.	1,600	490,000	0·33
British Columbia, Vancouver	2,000	760,000	0·26
Dalhousie, Halifax, N.S.	500	240,000	0·21
New Brunswick, Fredericton	300	150,000	0·20
Monash, Clayton, Vic.	400	200,000	0·20
Saskatchewan, Saskatoon	500	300,000	0·17
Victoria Univ. of Wellington	300	180,000	0·17
Manitoba, Winnipeg	500	340,000	0·15
New South Wales, Sydney	500	370,000	0·14
Tasmania	200	170,000	0·12

All other university libraries in Canada, New Zealand, and Australia have less
than one-tenth of 1 per cent or the figures available are too unreliable to form
estimates.

Middle-Class Literacy in Eighteenth-Century England: Fresh Evidence

R. M. Wiles

Forty years ago A. S. Collins published in the *Review of English Studies* an informative article on 'The Growth of the Reading Public During the Eighteenth Century'.[1] Drawing upon material in John Nichols's *Literary Anecdotes* and citing the spread of education, the numerous editions of Garth's *Dispensary* and other books, the increase in the production of novels, the extensive circulation of the *Craftsman* and the *Gentleman's Magazine,* and the development of circulating libraries, Collins showed that in the period with which he was dealing—1726 to 1780—there had been a considerable expansion in the number of English people who could read and did read. In support of this claim Collins also quoted statements by James Lackington, a successful London bookseller, who in 1791 declared that his plan to sell books at low prices had enabled 'prodigious numbers in inferior or *reduced* situations of life' to obtain books. Lackington felt that he could take some credit for 'diffusing that general desire for READING' which he said was then 'prevalent among the inferior orders of society'.[2] Whether that eagerness to buy books resulted from what he called his customers' 'natural propensity for the acquisition of knowledge' or from Lackington's own shrewdness in making books available 'on easy terms', this man who had ventured into the bookselling business with only five pounds' worth of stock in 1775 was by 1791 selling 'more than one hundred thousand volumes annually'.[3] The

---

[1] *Review of English Studies*, Vol. II, 1926, pp. 284-94, 428-38. This essay forms Section 4 in the fourth chapter of A. S. Collins, *Authorship in the Days of Johnson: Being a Study of the Relation between Author, Patron, Publisher and Public, 1726-1780*, London, 1927.

[2] J. Lackington, *Memoirs of the First Forty-Five Years of the Life of James Lackington*, London, 1791, Letter XXX, pp. 227-8.

[3] Ibid., Letter XXXV. This letter is numbered XLII in the eighth edition (1794) and the tenth edition (1795) of Lackington's book.

case for increased literacy may seem to require no further demonstration.

Yet not all the evidence has been assembled, and not all of the evidence thus far brought forward has been accepted. In the past four decades the subject has been further investigated by scholars who have thrown light on particular aspects of bookselling and the reading public.[4] A succinct account of literacy in the age of Johnson is in the second chapter of Richard Altick's *The English Common Reader: A Social History of the Mass Reading Public.*[5] Professor Altick does not accept James Lackington's statement that 'a general desire for reading' was then 'prevalent among the inferior orders of society', insisting that although followers of Wesley were expected to read as much as they could find time for, other members of the working classes in town and country did not read, partly because they were illiterate and partly because books were not available. Professor Altick also questions Samuel Johnson's observation in his account of Milton that 'General literature now [i.e. in 1779] pervades the nation through all its ranks'.[6]

I should like to begin my examination of this matter by suggesting that Lackington did not say that he sold books exclusively or mainly to poor people; his statements in Letter XXX[7] make it clear that he believed people of all classes were buying books and reading them. Here are Lackington's words:

> . . . I cannot help observing, that the sale of books in general has increased prodigiously within the last twenty years. According to the best estimation I have been able to make, I suppose that more than four times the number of books are sold now than were sold twenty years hence . . . In short, all ranks and degrees now READ.

It is the purpose of my paper to adduce what I take to be fresh evidence supporting both Johnson and Lackington in their declarations that reading was not limited to a few aristocrats and academics.

Of course there were men of taste whose substantial incomes allowed them to buy books and build up their ancestral libraries. They read because they had had private tutors or had gone to Eton, Westminster, Harrow, or Winchester and had further developed

4 See, for example, F. A. Mumby, *Publishing and Bookselling: A History from the Earliest Times to the Present Day,* London, 1930; Marjorie Plant, *The English Book Trade: An Economic History of the Making and Sale of Books,* London, 1939; Q. D. Leavis, *Fiction and the Reading Public,* London, 1939; and R. M. Wiles, *Serial Publication in England before 1750,* Cambridge, 1957.

5 R. Altick, *The English Common Reader: A Social History of the Mass Reading Public,* Chicago, 1957.

6 Samuel Johnson, *Lives of the Poets,* World's Classics, Vol. I, pp. 103-4.

7 So numbered in the first edition of Lackington, *Memoirs* (1791); it is Letter XXXIX in the eighth and tenth editions. I have not seen the ninth.

their appetite for books at one or other of the universities. On the
other hand, if the satirists are to be trusted, there were people of
high rank who had no use for books except as decorative features of
household equipment. In the *Lay Monk* No. 8 (2 Dec. 1713) and in
the *Universal Spectator* No. 254 (18 Aug. 1733) there are amusing
accounts of country knights who ordered books by the running yard
to fill up their library shelves in order to keep up with fashion.[8]
Defoe and Pope also poked fun at men who owned books but did
not read them.[9]

Likewise illiterate, though with more excuse, were the many
people in city and country alike who could not read because education had been denied them; economic conditions required them
to struggle for pence in order to keep alive. But there were charity
schools, and there is evidence to support Shenstone's observation
that 'every village mark'd with little spire' had a school of sorts.
Certainly most provincial towns had schools, for the local newspapers frequently carried notices of school openings and announce-
ments of teaching positions vacant.[10] Such schools as the middle
and lower class children could attend probably brought the
youngsters beyond the hornbook stage to some degree of literacy.
But the full account of education in eighteenth-century England
has not yet been written.

One of the notions held by many in that century was that reading was not a good thing for people of humble origin. It was all
very well for the 'polite' part of society to dip into books, but what
justification could there be for teaching poor people to read? Let a
pauper learn to read and he will grow discontented with his state
of life. An illuminating comment on this idea is to be found in the
Grub-Street Journal No. 247 (19 Sept. 1734)—illuminating not
merely because it voices disapproval but because it testifies to the
plain fact that many poor people were so eager to buy books that
they neglected the normal necessities of life rather than go without
reading matter. The writer of the statement in the *Grub-Street
Journal* expressed dismay at what he called this 'national *Insania*'
and deplored the fact that so many 'persons in the lowest Stations
of Life' were 'more intent upon cultivating their Minds than upon
feeding and cloathing their Bodies'. One should not accept as
typical the declaration by Samuel Richardson's little country
servant girl, Pamela, that while she was suffering distractions in

[8] For further examples see Wiles, *Serial Publication*, pp. 11-13.
[9] See Pope's account of the library in Timon's villa in *An Epistle to the Right
Honourable Richard Earl of Burlington*, 1731, and Defoe's *The Compleat
English Gentleman*, ed., K. Bulbring, London, 1890, p. 135.
[10] For some illustrative details see R. M. Wiles, *Freshest Advices: Early Provincial Newspapers in England*, Columbus, Ohio, 1965, pp. 352-3.

Lincolnshire she went to the library for books to read,[11] for it is possible that Richardson was here drawing not upon life but upon Sidney's *Arcadia,* in which the earlier Pamela had sought comfort in books—and she was a princess, not a servant. Yet evidence that servant girls sometimes did read books is to be found in actual journals and letters. One such girl, Mary Leapor, a cook-maid in a Northamptonshire village, was able to acquire some books, including works of Dryden and Pope, and before the end of her short life she produced original verses of her own that were published by subscription in 1748.[12]

If knights and maidservants and people of all ranks in between wished to buy books, there were plenty to buy, as one can see by glancing at the lists in the *Gentleman's Magazine* or the *London Magazine* or at the advertisements in newspapers. People who did not wish to buy books could borrow them from circulating libraries, of which there were many, both in London and in the country. In addition to Samuel Fancourt's large and varied collection in Salisbury (1734-40) and later in Crane Court, London,[13] and the well stocked libraries of Wright, Rowland, Mynors, and others who supplied Polly Honeycomb with reading matter, there were stocks of books available on loan for small fees in many provincial towns and cities, among them Leeds, Bristol, Bath, Nottingham, Chichester, and Liverpool. One of the earliest shows up in an advertisement of 1718. In the *St Ives Post Boy* No. 20 (28 Oct. 1718) George Barton, a bookseller with shops in Huntingdon, Peterborough, St Neots, and St Ives, offered 'All sorts of bound Books New and Old, at reasonable Rates', and 'Plays, or any other Books to let out to Read by the Week'. Forty years later Joseph Wilson announced his plan to open a circulating library in Leeds. In the *Leedes Intelligencer* on 27 November 1758 he expressed the hope that ladies and gentlemen of the region would become subscribers, since (as he said) 'the Utility of a well-regulated Circulating Library, for reading the most valuable *new Books*' immediately after publication had been 'universally approv'd' elsewhere.

There were those who feared that if people could borrow books

11 Samuel Richardson, *Pamela,* Letter XXXII: '. . . I went directly, and pick'd out some books from the Library, with which I filled a Shelf in the Closet she [Mrs Jewkes] gave me Possession of; and from these I hope to receive Improvement, as well as Amusement.'

12 See 'D.N.B.', *Gentleman's Magazine,* Vol. LIV, 1784, pp. 806-7, and *Purefoy Letters 1735-1755,* ed. G. Eland, Vol. II, London, 1931, pp. 278-80.

13 Fancourt describes his struggles to establish his library in *The Narrative,* London, 1747. Eighteenth-century circulating and subscription libraries are discussed by Hilda M. Hamlyn in 'Eighteenth-century Circulating Libraries in England', *Library,* Ser. 5, Vol. I, No. 3 (Dec. 1946); No. 4 (March 1947), pp. 197-222. They are now under study by Professor D. P. Varma of Dalhousie University, Halifax, Nova Scotia, Canada.

—especially new ones—for a small fee they would not buy any. Such a fear had been expressed by the author of the *Champion* in 1742 —it was James Ralph—who in No. 426 (10 Aug.) argued strongly against the establishing of a circulating library, and he was equally vehement against what he called the 'scandalous and low Custom' then prevailing among the proprietors of coffee houses of buying one copy of a new book as soon as it was published and 'lending it by Turns to such Gentlemen as read as frequent *their* Coffeehouse'. Both practices, the writer said, ought to be discouraged. But his twofold complaint now serves to show that people were keen to read; what better evidence could one have than that an opportunity to read the latest book was used by the proprietors of coffee houses to attract customers, much as television is used today in places where men at leisure congregate?[14]

Such a man as Samuel Johnson, who 'knew more books than any man alive' (as Adam Smith said), had his own extensive library and did not need to depend on lending libraries for books; and the same can be said of Henry Fielding and others. But one does not demonstrate increased literacy in England by citing the collections owned by men of letters. Who else reads books?

The answer will never be complete, but one can begin by examining the lists of subscribers that are found in some works published in the century. Another source, scanty but unchallengeable, is the ledgers of retail booksellers, one of the very few surviving records of this kind being the 'Gentleman's Ledger B' kept by Robert Gosling, a prosperous London bookseller to whose shop against St Dunstan's Church in Fleet Street many customers came.[15] A third source is the manuscript journals and letters recording the day-by-day experiences of English men and women of the period, many of whom bought books and read them.

One such record is the diary of Thomas Turner (1729-89), a shopkeeper in East Hoathly, Sussex.[16] Turner was a regular reader of the *Sussex Weekly Advertiser, or Lewes Journal,* and he also spent much of his time in reading more substantial publications. His tastes ran from Pope's translation of Homer to *As You Like It,* Addison's *Spectator* papers on *Paradise Lost,* Boyle's *Lectures,* and the

[14] It is well known that coffee houses in London and all over England regularly took in the current newspapers. Isaac Bickerstaff said in his *Tatler* No. 163 (25 April 1710) that on the morning when Ned Softly confronted him with his silly verses he had gone early to Will's coffee house 'with a design to read over all the newspapers'.

[15] The document is Bodleian MS. Eng. Misc. c. 296.

[16] The record of Turner's doings between 1754 and 1765 has been edited by the shopkeeper's great-great-granddaughter, in *The Diary of Thomas Turner of East Hoathly, 1754-1765,* ed. Florence Maris Turner, London, 1925, the text being based on that brought out by the Sussex Archaeological Society in 1923.

sermons of Tillotson, Gibson, and Sherlock. He looked upon Richardson's *Clarissa* as 'a very well-wrote thing, tho' it must be allowed it is too prolix', and he said he liked the ending of that work 'better than if it had terminated in more happy consequences'. Turner often had an evening 'out' and far too often he came home 'a little matter enlivened by liquor' or in a much worse state; but there were many occasions when, after shopkeeping hours, he and his wife enjoyed good literature. On a Friday in August 1755 he read part of the fourth volume of the *Tatler*, obviously finding its instruction helpful: 'the oftener I read it', he said, 'the better I like it. I think I never found the vice of drinking so well exploded in my life, as in one of the numbers.' The effects of that explosion, however, soon wore off, and there are many entries like that of 28 March 1756, when he recorded that he and a friend had drunk a bowl of punch and 'two muggs of bumboo'. It filled his heart with horror that he should have done such a thing, 'and on a Sunday too'. As usual, he resolved 'never, no never to be guilty of the same again'; but the struggle was not over. Turner's 'too eager thirst after knowledge' likewise gave him some twinges of conscience, but only because trade was poor and he felt that he should not be spending so much time on books.

Turner's diary is, of course, not the only intimate document conveniently available in print to students of eighteenth-century cultural history. Another, equally illuminating for the present purpose, is a long run of letters, mainly written by Henry Purefoy and his widowed mother in the period 1735 to 1753.[17] Henry was an Oriel man, a member of one of the oldest county families, and, as his epitaph states, 'He conversed more with Books than Men . . .'; but he was rather an enjoyer of books than a dedicated student of literature. He lived a busy life in Shalstone Manor House, Buckinghamshire. His diaries, his account books, and his letters are filled with an astonishing variety of details.[18] In many of the letters there are references to the clocks, portable barometers, fruit trees, harness buckles, lottery tickets, and books which he ordered. As early as 1728 he made a catalogue of his 376 books, and there are indications in the letters and account books that in later years he bought many other volumes. He was a regular subscriber to the *Gentleman's Magazine,* and month after month for many years he took in the successive parts of Thomas Salmon's *Modern History; or, the Present State of All Nations.* Additions to his library included translations of Plautus, Terence, Quintus Curtius, and Thucydides, the letters of Balzac, and practical treatises on phar-

17 *Purefoy Letters,* 1931.
18 See ibid., Vol. I, pp. xix-xxxi.

macopoeia, gardening, and the gout. I cannot suppose that Henry
Purefoy was the only man in Buckinghamshire who loved books,
bought them, had them bound, and read them.

Certainly it was not difficult for people living in the provinces to
obtain books. Distance from London was no barrier, for there were
booksellers in all the provincial cities and towns. Lackington
thought the bookshops in York, Newcastle, Leeds, Manchester,
Preston, and other places in the north and west of England carried
very limited stocks. At York and Leeds, he said, 'there were a few
(and but very few) good books; but in all the other towns between
London and Edinburgh nothing but trash was to be found . . . .'[19]
Even if the actual stock was scanty, any book in print could be
obtained from London. Presumably John Clay's bookshop in
Daventry was typical. It is fortunate that Clay's ledgers and day
books have been preserved—they are at the Northamptonshire
Record Office, Delapré Abbey, Northampton—for they offer a
fascinating and detailed record of the books, pamphlets, periodicals,
and stationery supplies sold over his counter in the course of more
than forty years. The lists of special orders for single books and for
the successive numbers of books published in parts give clear
indication that Clay had many customers, at least twenty-five of
whom got their copies of the *Gentleman's Magazine* from him.

Many London publishers advertised their latest books and pamphlets in the country newspapers. People who lived at a distance
from the provincial bookshops or who did not find the books they
wanted at the bookstalls on market days could not only place orders
for the desired publications through the newspaper carriers but
have the books delivered by those newsmen on their regular weekly
rounds. It is not generally known that the printer of an eighteenth-
century country newspaper usually had on his shelves a miscellaneous assortment of commodities, including not only his own pamphlets and printed forms but also medicines, candles, shoe polish,
soap, and other articles not obtainable at newspaper offices in the
present century.[20] All of these things, and small parcels entrusted
to them by townspeople, were transported by the hundreds of
newsmen who in any one week covered a very fine network of roads
and paths criss-crossing the whole country and thus provided a
most economic and dependable means of distributing literature to
the remotest corners of the land. Such notices as the following, from
the *Western Flying Post; or, Sherborne and Yeovil Mercury* No. 89
(8 Oct. 1750) are common:

19 Lackington, *Memoirs*, Letter XXXVI.
20 For details see Wiles, *Freshest Advices*, pp. 131-5, 140-1.

⁎ Gentleman and Others, living in the Country, may be supplied by the Newsmen, with all Sorts of New Books, Pamphlets, Maps, and Prints, as cheap as in London, from the Printing Office in Sherborne.[21]

There is abundant evidence that the services of the newsmen were used extensively for the transporting of books ordered through the local printing offices.

One of the most widely distributed newspapers in England was the *Western Flying Post*. Its printer, Robert Goadby, asserted in the issues of 24 September 1750 and 18 March 1751 that it was taken to all the towns and parishes in Dorsetshire, Somersetshire, Devon, Cornwall, and part of Wiltshire.[22] Among those to whom it went regularly was the Reverend William Borlase, eminent naturalist and historian. His account books for the years 1734 and 1772 may still be seen at the Royal Institute of Cornwall, and they show that he made use of the 'Sherborne Riders'—as the distributors of the *Western Flying Post* were called—to obtain not only newspapers but books, pamphlets, and magazines, as well as coffee and supplies of all kinds. Borlase knew what books he wanted, ordered them, and got them.

One kind of publication which could easily be conveyed to people regularly served by the news carriers was the 'number' book, the book published in weekly or fortnightly or monthly parts. Hundreds of titles were issued in this way.[23] This trade in number books would not be worth considering if the list of books published in fascicules 'stitch'd in blue paper' had nothing to show but the kind of 'heavy, unread, folio lump' which, as Henry Fielding declared in *Tom Jones,* could find purchasers only when 'piecemealed into numbers'.[24] Possibly Fielding's unkind term fits some of the volumes of sermons, the histories of Rome, the commentaries on the Bible, and editions of Josephus which were published in weekly numbers; but there were other works that make

[21] Benjamin Collins used precisely the same wording in his *Salisbury Journal* and in the local edition of that paper, the *Portsmouth and Gosport Gazette,* on 24 February 1752.

[22] In the *Western Flying Post* No. 250 (10 Dec. 1753), Goadby placed under the title of his paper a long note beginning with this statement: 'This Paper is distributed every Week, in great Numbers, in all the Cities, Towns, Villages, Parishes, &c., of the four great Western Counties, so noted for their Populousness, Viz., *Dorset, Somerset, Devon,* and *Cornwall,* in which *no other Paper* is circulated; besides Part of Wiltshire . . . .' The only rivals to the *Western Flying Post* in the southwest at that time were *Andrew Brice's Old Exeter Journal* and the papers printed in Bristol.

[23] To the 383 items listed in Wiles, *Serial Publication,* I can now add 40 more titles; and for the second half of the eighteenth century the list becomes much more extensive.

[24] Henry Fielding, *Tom Jones,* introductory chapter to Bk XIII.

the list quite impressive, for among them were *Paradise Lost,* rival translations of Pierre Bayle's *Dictionnaire historique et critique,* Robert James's *Medicinal Dictionary,* Johnson's *Dictionary* (immediately after the first edition), the *Harleian Miscellany,* and scores of works that are now found on the shelves of the world's greatest libraries. The range of subject matter is as wide as one finds in books published in the regular way: biography, history, fiction, natural science, travel, music, penmanship, mathematics, the Latin classics, architecture, masonry, drama, reports of state trials, antiquities, medicine, painting. The quality of the printing and paper was often excellent. Many of the books published in numbers 'took' so well that the early numbers had to be reprinted. One example is *The Travels of the Late Charles Thompson, Esq.,* published in fifty numbers by John Newbery and Charles Micklewright, at the Bible and Crown in the Market Place, Reading, beginning on the last Monday in June 1743. Before the end of November Newbery and Micklewright advertised in various newspapers that nearly two thousand subscribers were taking the work and that the early numbers were being reprinted to meet the demand from those who had not bought the numbers from the beginning.

An enumeration of specific titles would only be bewildering. It is worth pointing out, nevertheless, that many of these works issued in fascicules were really substantial. Thomas Salmon's *Modern History* —the one taken regularly by Henry Purefoy—began in 1724 and filled thirty-one octavo volumes before the last of the numbers appeared in 1738. After a second edition in three quarto volumes appeared in 1739 it was again issued in numbers in 1744-6, this time in folio and with a royal licence granting Longman, Osborne, Shuckburgh, Hitch, and Austen sole rights for fourteen years. Another very popular work published in numbers over a long period was the Reverend Nicholas Tindal's translation of Paul de Rapin de Thoyras's *Histoire d'Angleterre.* This translation, with Tindal's notes, filled fifteen octavo volumes when James and John Knapton first brought it out in monthly numbers at 1s. each from 1725 to 1732; it was immediately reprinted in folio numbers making two volumes in 1732-3, at the same time as a rival translation by John Kelly was also being published; and it came out in a third edition in eighty-four folio numbers in 1743-4. Even before that third edition began to appear, it was reported in the *Grub-Street Journal* on 19 September 1734 that the Knaptons' profit on the Rapin-Tindal work was between £8,000 and £10,000. If it is true, as was reported in the *Norwich Mercury* and other newspapers, that 'about 15,000' of each number of the Tindal translation were printed in 1732, that work outsold Tobias Smollett's later *History of England* by 2,000.[25] If these figures seem unimpressive, it is important to remember that they should be judged in relation to the total population of the time. A sale of 15,000 copies in a population of some six or six and a half million persons represents a sale of 100,000 copies in England's present population. Not many books achieve such sales in our time. Another work of considerable dimensions issued in numbers was *A New General Collection of Voyages and Travels,* edited by John Green and published by Thomas Astley. The 164 weekly numbers of this work made four fat quarto volumes comprising 2,800 pages, with maps and plates. The royal licence under which this work appeared was dated 18 October 1743. This popular collection had two substantial contemporary rivals, both published in weekly sixpenny folio numbers —the third edition of Awnsham and John Churchill's *Collection of Voyages and Travels* (first published in 1704 and reprinted or reissued in 1732 with two additional volumes), and John Harris's *Navigantium atque Itinerantium Bibliotheca,* the latter issued in 143 numbers beginning in April 1744 (under royal licence dated 23 Feb. 1743/4), the former issued in 271 numbers, also beginning early in 1744. Each of these two works had aggressive proprietors who made great efforts to outsell Astley's quarto work, with the result that the newspapers contained heated and lengthy arguments by the respective publishers, each denouncing the others and claiming superiority for his own publication.[26]

Astley undoubtedly achieved wide sales in the provinces as well as in London, for his list of 1,048 subscribers printed in the first volume includes 77 individual subscribers in Bristol and also two booksellers in that city, Mrs Martha Lewis, who took 106 sets of the numbers as they came out, and Mr Peter Brown, who took 25 sets. In his second, third, and fourth volumes Astley added more names but apologised to subscribers not mentioned, explaining that notwithstanding repeated requests to the booksellers in the country,

25 Add. MS. 38730 in the British Museum gives full details of the financial aspects of the Smollett *History,* showing that the printer, Richard Baldwin, was paid over £7,500 for printing 421,625 numbers of that work between February 1758 and the end of the following year.

26 One such letter, dated at London on 20 March 1744 and printed in several provincial newspapers, appeared in the *Sherborne Mercury* on 3 April 1744 offering to 'all those Persons that had rather have Original Authors than dry and injudicious Abridgments' the privilege of turning in every number of the Astley collection already bought and receiving in exchange, without cost, the Churchill numbers as they were published by John Osborn and sold by John Cook, bookseller in Sherborne. Astley's rivals apparently succeeded in hampering the sale of the later numbers of his *New General Collection of Voyages and Travels,* for records now being prepared for publication by Dr D. F. McKenzie show that Astley's order to his printer, Charles Ackers, was ultimately cut in half.

scarcely half of the names had been sent in.[27] Taken together, these
and other lists of subscribers to substantial books published in
fascicules represent all classes of society—not just university men, the
clergy, and schoolmasters, but tradesmen and others in considerable
numbers. To these subscribers the weekly numbers were taken as
regularly as the weekly newspapers, and in fact were usually
delivered free of charge by the same men as carried the local
newspaper.[28]

In view of the large number of books offered to the public in
inexpensive fascicules, and in view of the ease with which they were
distributed all over England, these number books must be seen as a
cause and a symptom of a substantial increase in reading. Such was
the opinion expressed in a London newspaper—the *Grub-Street
Journal*—as early as 1732, when the mode of publishing in fascicules
was just becoming popular: 'This Method of Weekly Publication
allures Multitudes to peruse Books into which they would otherwise
never have looked.'[29]

If the publishing of inexpensive weekly fascicules of substantial
books helped to develop the reading habit all over England, there
is also much to be said in support of the view that the newspapers
and periodicals added momentum to the spread of literacy in
London and in a thousand lesser communities throughout the
kingdom. At first glance one might prefer to give greater credit to
the eminently successful monthly collections of news and articles,
the *Gentleman's Magazine*, its closest rival, the *London Magazine*,
and their numerous imitators.[30] There is no doubt that these sixpenny magazines enjoyed a circulation of several thousands and
that many issues were reprinted.[31] The newspapers of the eighteenth
century are now harder to find because of their ephemeral nature,

27 For the references to lists of subscribers to other works published in
numbers, see Wiles, *Serial Publication*, pp. 229-31.
28 Advertisements of Astley's *New General Collection of Voyages and Travels*,
for example, indicated that the numbers would be delivered punctually every
week, 'at any Distance, clean and free of any Expence' by the distributors of
the newspaper.
29 *Grub-Street Journal* No. 148 (26 Oct. 1732).
30 For these see W. Graham, *English Literary Periodicals*, New York, 1930;
G. F. Barwick, 'Some Magazines of the Eighteenth Century', *Transactions of
the Bibliographical Society*, Vol. X, 1908-9, pp. 109-40; R. M. Wiles, 'Early
Georgian Provincial Magazines', *Library*, Ser. 5, Vol. XIX, 1964 (publication
delayed).
31 See *Boswell's Life of Johnson*, ed., G. B. Hill, rev. and enlarged L. F.
Powell, Vol. I, Oxford, 1934-50, p. 112, n. 1, and p. 152, n. 1; W. B. Todd, 'A
Bibliographical Account of *The Gentleman's Magazine*, 1731-1754', *Studies in
Bibliography: Papers of the Bibliographical Society of the University of Virginia*,
Vol. XVIII, 1965, pp. 81-109. Dr D. F. McKenzie will in the near future publish
exact figures showing the size of editions of the *London Magazine* in the period
1732-47.

but in their day they may well have been even more influential, both directly and indirectly, in luring Englishmen to read. Both in London and in the provinces the eighteenth century saw an enormous growth in the number of both newspapers and periodicals and in the extent of their circulation. A careful look at the chronological index in R. S. Crane and F. B. Kaye, *A Census of British Newspapers and Periodicals, 1660-1800*[32] shows that whereas only 25 serials were appearing in Britain in the first year of the eighteenth century, there were 70 in the year when George II ascended the throne, over 100 at the end of that reign, and 250 by the end of the century—and those figures can now be shown to be far from complete. More important than the number of new papers that were established in successive decades of the century is the fact that many of the papers survived for a very long time—some of them are still appearing— and increased enormously in their circulation. Robert L. Haig has shown how strong was the impact of the *Gazetteer* (1735-97), which took up where the *Daily Courant* (1702-35) left off;[33] and more recently there have been important studies of other influential newspapers.[34] Much remains to be done in the investigation of the London newspaper press in the eighteenth century, for the material is so vast and so few of the original issues have survived that the comprehensive accounts published since H. R. Foxe Bourne's *English Newspapers* (1887) do not succeed in setting forth the whole history of eighteenth-century journalism in detail.[35] Two books— Dr G. A. Cranfield's *The Development of the Provincial Newspaper 1700-1760*[36] and my own *Freshest Advices: Early Provincial Newspapers in England*—have made a beginning at telling the exciting story of English journalism in the provinces.

Reference was made earlier to the wide distribution of one of those provincial newspapers, the *Western Flying Post*. Many other provincial papers also achieved wide distribution—nothing like the incredibly vast circulation of the great daily newspapers now printed in London, but large enough to dispel the notion that local news-

[32] R. S. Crane and F. B. Kaye, *A Census of British Newspapers and Periodicals, 1660-1800*, Chapel Hill, North Carolina, 1927, pp. 179-201.
[33] R. L. Haig, *The Gazetteer 1735-1797: A Study in the Eighteenth Century English Newspaper*, Carbondale, Illinois, 1960.
[34] R. R. Rea, *The English Press in Politics 1760-1774*, Lincoln, Nebraska, 1963; Lucyle Werkmeister, *The London Daily Press 1772-1792*, Lincoln, Nebraska, 1963.
[35] See H. Herd, *The March of Journalism: The Story of the British Press from 1662 to the Present Day*, London, 1952; F. Williams, *Dangerous Estate: The Anatomy of Newspapers*, London, 1957. The physical aspects of London newspapers are admirably set forth in S. Morison, *The English Newspaper: Some Account of the Physical Development of Journals Printed in London between 1622 and the Present Day*, Cambridge, 1932.
[36] G. A. Cranfield, *The Development of the Provincial Newspaper, 1700-1760*, Oxford, 1962.

papers became influential only in the nineteenth century. Some years ago Professor James Sutherland brought forward illuminating details on the circulation of English newspapers and periodicals in the period 1700-30,[37] and between us Dr Cranfield and I—though we worked quite independently—have found evidence to show that by the fourth decade of the century a distribution of 2,000 copies per week was not unknown.[38] While that figure is doubtless somewhat about the average, many a well established country newspaper must have sold at least a thousand copies each week; others may have sold only a few hundred copies, but in some years there were twenty-five or thirty *different* newspapers being published concurrently in the provinces, and their total circulation was anything but scanty.

Beyond question many of those local newspapers were distributed over a large area. Soon after the *Northampton Mercury* was established in 1720 its proprietors made emphatic and perhaps exaggerated claims of circulation in nineteen counties,[39] and five years later the same proprietors declared that their other newspaper, the *Gloucester Journal,* went into thirteen districts, each district having its own supervisor and corps of local newsmen.[40] During the next quarter-century such papers as the *Leeds Mercury,* the *Nottingham Weekly Courant,* the *York Gazetteer,* and its rival, the *York Journal,* regularly listed in the colophon the distributors in twenty-five or thirty towns. Later in the century the claims to wide distribution leave no doubt that, taken together, the weekly provincial newspapers reached tens of thousands of homes.

Evidence to support this statement could be cited from many newspapers; in 1755, for example, the *Doncaster Flying Post* had under its date-line a list of fifty-one towns in which it was distributed; in 1772 the *British Chronicle, or, Pugh's Hereford Journal* named many agents and printed the statement that it was 'universally read by the Inhabitants of the City of *Hereford*', and had also 'an extensive Circuit in *Herefordshire, Shropshire, Worcestershire, Gloucestershire, Monmouthshire, Glamorganshire, Breconshire, Radnorshire,* &c.'. The *Newcastle Journal,* which had achieved a circulation of 'nearly 2,000' in its first year (1739), thirty-five years later made the claim that it covered an area in which there were 250 towns and was 'conveyed One Hundred Miles South, West, and North, on the Day of Publication'.[41] More specific details are given

---

[37] *Library,* Ser. 4, Vol. XV, 1934, pp. 110-24.
[38] Cranfield, *The Development of the Provincial Newspaper,* pp. 168-84; Wiles, *Freshest Advices,* pp. 95-100.
[39] *Northampton Mercury* No. 5, 31 May 1720.
[40] *Gloucester Journal* No. 160, 24 April 1725.
[41] *Newcastle Journal* No. 1846, 8 Oct. 1774.

in the *Cumberland Pacquet,* which announced on 28 November 1776 that the number of copies required weekly had lately increased greatly, 'the manner of their circulation requiring several hundreds of them to be thirty miles out of town by one o'clock on Thursday morning'. The statement went on thus:

> We think it incumbent upon us to acquaint our Readers, that by some necessary alteration in the distribution, more than three hundred of these Papers are conveyed ninety-six miles by 5 o'clock on the Thursday evening, exclusive of 500 and upwards disposed of on the road, and the quantity distributed in this town, and the other sea ports of this county, seven principal towns in Lancashire, and a great number forwarded by Post to every capital town in the kingdom.

Thousands of persons must have seen the *Cumberland Pacquet* every week.

All of this—and scores of further details could be cited—shows that newspapers became more and more abundant as the century advanced and that their circulation expanded significantly. The question to be asked is this: what bearing has the increased distribution of newspapers on the development of the nation's literacy?

The answer to that question was provided by the eighteenth century itself and is to be found in the first issue of the *Liverpool Chronicle: and Marine Gazetteer* (6 May 1757). In a passage quoted from 'a dissertation on the Utility of News Papers' reference is made to 'the Essays that are from time to time communicated to the public therein'. The author (whom I have not identified) expressed the conviction that the articles of news

> seem to be a natural decoy to draw great numbers to the reading these short dissertations, who, perhaps, scarce read any thing else; and who indeed, were it not for our news writers, might happen to forget reading at all.

The great mass of material apart from news and advertisements which is to be found in English newspapers of the eighteenth century has by some been dismissed as mere column-stuffing, used by printers of newspapers who were less concerned to provide good reading matter than to fill a sheet and a half and thereby evade the stamp tax of 1712. Up to a point there is truth in that notion; but when a second Act put an end to this dodge in 1725 and newspapers were printed on a large half-sheet bearing a stamp, the belles-lettres continued, obviously because readers wished to have not only news and discussions of political matters but instalments of recent novels, geography, history, biography, translations of Italian *novelle,* essays on embalming, on tar water, on turning to the East during the saying of the Creed, and on a thousand other subjects.[42] There were times when news was scarce and other material had to be used to fill space, but one is not justified in assuming that entertaining prose and verse were used only when there was a 'Dearth of News'.

That there was a real demand for 'literary' matter is evident not only from the files of the newspapers themselves but from the fact that some proprietors of country newspapers reprinted in volumes the articles which had been featured in their papers, and from the further fact that several proprietors published supplementary 'magazines' or collections of articles for which they could not find room in their regular columns. For instance, in 1745 David Henry, printer of the *Reading Journal,* published two little collections under the title *Seasonable Miscellany.* In 1750 Elizabeth Adams published under the title *The Chester Miscellany* a much more substantial collection comprising 'Several Pieces, both in Prose and Verse, Which were in the *Chester Courant* from January 1745, to May 1750'. Still more extensive was the *Agreeable Miscellany; or Something to please every Man's Taste,* a fortnightly periodical issued in 1749-50, containing prose and verse for which Thomas Ashburner could not find room in his *Kendal Weekly Mercury.*

Equally ambitious efforts to give readers of newspapers something more than news came from the presses in Newcastle and Sherborne. From its earliest days the *Newcastle Journal* had in almost every issue what the Proposals (1739) described as 'a short Essay, Letter, or Discourse, on some useful Subject, Art or Science'; thirty years later the proprietors of the *Newcastle Journal* announced the publication of a *Literary Register: or, Weekly Miscellany,* which was to be 'a repository or digest of the best essayical pieces of the times' and was to be available to the subscribers to the *Newcastle Journal* at three halfpence. In 1772 the proprietors of the *Western Flying Post; or, Sherborne and Yeovil Mercury* announced a similar low-cost weekly supplement. In the first issue of that new collection of pieces (6 Jan. 1772) the proprietors explained their objective in terms that are relevant to the present study:

> As there are great Numbers (some of whom have testified it)
> that would be very glad of a *Weekly Entertainment* for the
> Mind, besides the News of the Week, and who wish to have as
> well what may afford real Improvement, as merely a temporary
> Entertainment, the Printer of the Sherborne *Mercury* thinks
> he shall give pleasure to his Customers, by beginning the *New*

---

[42] Comprehensive accounts of such matters are to be found in Cranfield, *The Development of the Provincial Newspaper,* pp. 99-116, and in Wiles, *Freshest Advices,* pp. 303-38.

Year with an Appendix to the Sherborne Mercury, Under the Title of
A Weekly Magazine;
Which will contain *four large Pages* printed on a *good Paper,* which he has determined to render to the Customers of his Paper, but to None Else, at the very inconsiderable Price of One Halfpenny.

The weekly fare thus provided 'for the Mind' has much variety, for there is a good deal of prose fiction, there are extracts from new books, there are instalments of 'A Survey of the Works of God', and there are articles on such convenient themes as 'A Method of preparing Dun Peas for Hogs' and 'Hints for the Cure of Squinting in young Persons'.

That article on preparing dun peas for hogs can hardly prove that by 1772 the reading habits of Englishmen had achieved a new standard in quality or in quantity; but in reckoning the extent of general literacy in the eighteenth century one must see the local newspaper office as responsible for distributing not only weekly bulletins of news but an enormous variety of other reading matter which many thousands of people all over England bought regularly and kept on demanding. And not all the complimentary matter dealt with squinting and hog fodder. In a paper which I read earlier this year at the Chicago meeting of the Johnson Society of the Great Lakes Region, I pointed out that the country newspapers in 1750, 1751, and 1752 were the medium for circulating far more copies of Samuel Johnson's *Rambler* essays than the London subscribers and casual purchasers were buying—in many instances ten times more than were printed by Payne and Bouquet in the original run.

There is no doubt that London and provincial newspapers were seen by steadily increasing numbers of readers throughout the century. Those newspapers might have collapsed under the successive stamp taxes that were imposed; they did not collapse but grew in number and strength. There is also no doubt that, from 1730 onwards, great numbers of books issued in weekly parts were bought by an eager public. That experiment of selling books in parts might have proved to be a disastrous failure; it did not fail. On the contrary, it became such a large-scale mode of publication that great 'congers' of London's most respectable publishers invested heavily in the number-book trade, paid large sums for shares in individual works, and reaped handsome profits.[43] Multitudes of people of all classes bought the numbers. And the sale was not limited to London; they were *all* available anywhere in England. The impact of this

[43] Figures are given in Wiles, *Serial Publication,* pp. 5, 6, 97, 149-54.

typically eighteenth-century mode of publication must have been very great in town and country.

My case for increased literacy, then, does not depend upon conjectures concerning changes in the proportion of illiterates in the population, and although something is to be learned from such records and observations as those left by James Lackington, John Clay, William Borlase, Robert Gosling, Thomas Turner, and Henry Purefoy, it is in two 'middle-class' forms of publication—the number books and the newspapers (especially the local papers)—that I see convincing evidence that far more people in England were reading printed pages by the end of the eighteenth century than were doing so when Queen Anne ascended the throne.

Two Historical Aspects of the Augustan Tradition

Ian Watt

There can be few terms in English literary history which are used with such widely different chronological reference as 'Augustan'. At one extreme it can mean only the literature of 1702 to 1714, of the reign of Queen Anne; at the other, it covers the whole period from the Restoration in 1660 to the end of the eighteenth century; and there are many other intermediate and conflicting ways in which the term is employed by scholars and critics. This situation seemed to call for investigation, and two possible historical approaches suggested themselves: firstly, a brief analysis of the parallel with the culture of Augustan Rome; and secondly, a tentative inquiry into what other social and historical causes could help to account for the common qualities widely attributed to much of the literature written in England between 1660 and 1800.

The Roman Parallel: Three Phases

It is a commonplace that much of the historical development of European culture since the Middle Ages can be defined in terms of its changing understanding and awareness of different elements in Greek and Roman civilisation. At no time, probably, was there so pervasive an admiration of the Roman cultural model as in the seventeenth and eighteenth centuries; and it was, of course, the Age of Augustus which had the deepest appeal, because it had combined the triumph of a centralised political autocracy with supreme achievements in the arts.

1655-1700. The most obvious signs of the consciousness of the parallel between Rome under Augustus and seventeenth-century England is the use of the appellation 'Augustus' for the ruler. The tradition was initiated in 1655, with reference to Oliver Cromwell, in Edmund Waller's *A Panegyric to My Lord Protector,* and it was memorably continued by Dryden, in *Astraea Redux,* where he welcomed the restoration of Charles II in 1660, and in *Threnodia Augustalis,* where he mourned his death.[1] The same parallel is implicit in the growing use of the term 'Augusta' for London,[2] as in Dryden's *MacFlecknoe,* 1682, Pope's *Windsor Forest,* 1713, Defoe's *Augusta Triumphans,* 1728, and Thomson's *The Seasons,* 1728.

The habit of comparing England with Augustan Rome was one thing; the belief that there existed any real substance in the analogy was quite another. The writers of the reign of Charles II certainly did not think so at the time. The specific analogy seems first to have been advanced by Francis Atterbury in 1690, when he wrote, in the Preface to *The Second Part of Mr. Waller's Poems:*

> He undoubtedly stands first in the list of Refiners, and, for ought I know, last too; for I question whether in Charles II's reign English did not come into its full perfection; and whether it has not had its Augustan Age as well as Latin.

Atterbury was speaking primarily of the climactic development of the English language rather than of literature; but a generation later John Oldmixon had literature especially in mind when he wrote, in *Reflections on Dr. Swift's Letter to the Earl of Oxford about the English Tongue,* 1712, that the reign of Charles II 'probably may be the *Augustan* Age of *English* Poetry'.[3] This view of the Restoration period never found very widespread support, but it was implicitly canonised later by Dr Johnson's famous statement in *The Lives of the Poets:* 'What was said of Rome, adorned by Augustus, may be applied by an easy metaphor to English poetry embellished by Dryden, "lateritiam invenit, marmoriam relinquit", he found it brick and left it marble'.

'Native brick, imported marble', comments Robert Graves,[4] damning the whole classical period of English literature as an unhealthy foreign interruption. Whether the marble was a Roman or a French import hardly affects the present argument, since many of the cultural achievements of France under Louis XIV were themselves guided or inspired by what had happened under Augustus Caesar. French, like Latin, has no literary term corresponding to 'Augustan' in English; but Louis XIV was often addressed as Augustus,[5] and the parallel with Rome became extremely pervasive

---

[1] Waller also called Charles II 'Augustus' in 'On St. James's Park' (l. 123).

[2] Under the reign of Augustus the name was given to many towns of the Roman Empire; later it was applied to London by Ammianus Marcellinus, in the fourth century A.D.

[3] P. 19.

[4] *The Crowning Privilege,* London, 1955, p. 26.

[5] As in Boileau's 'Pour chanter un Auguste, il faut être un Virgile', *Discours au Roi,* 1665.

in France as soon as he personally took up the reins of government in 1661. In any case there is certainly no doubt that for Dryden the parallel was an important and conscious influence. Dryden's essays, for instance, are largely concerned with relating English forms to Latin models; and his translations of Virgil, Horace, and Ovid were perhaps the most important of his works as regards influence on later poetry and poetic taste.

But the closer the Augustan analogy was pressed, the more the differences became apparent. Charles II actually had considerably less power than his predecessors on the throne, and in any case no previous English monarch had ever had quite the power, or the resources, that Augustus Caesar had acquired. Throughout the whole republican period the Latin word *augustus* had signified religious awe, and when the title 'Augustus' had been bestowed on the Emperor Octavius it was to mark his god-like status. In France, Louis XVI, *le roi soleil*, had claimed, and been granted, some such numinous authority. But in England it was much more difficult to attribute quasi-divine powers to the king, at least after Charles I had failed to rise again.

In cultural matters, admittedly, there was a slight parallel, since Charles II was something of a patron of the arts and sciences, and Dryden became his Poet Laureate and Historiographer Royal. Unlike Augustus, however, Charles was neither a poet, a scholar, nor a playwright; and the straitened privy purse was wider open to other pleasures. For instance, Lord Lansdowne related that Charles was 'extremely fond' of Wycherley, and often 'chose him for a Companion at his leisure Hours, as Augustus did Horace', but although Charles promised Wycherley a pension, it came so irregularly that he actually spent four years in prison during the later part of Charles's reign.[6] Nor, unfortunately, was there any Maecenas at Charles's court to make good the King's cultural and financial deficiencies; and, as Boileau put the trade-union view of the poets, '. . . sans un Mécénas à quoi sert un Auguste?'[7]

Dryden's efforts to follow the pattern set by Virgil, Horace, and Livy were therefore doomed to failure. He gave up his planned epic poem because he was, he said, 'discouraged in the beginning of an attempt' by the fact that his salary as Poet Laureate was 'ill paid', and that he had no prospect of future subsistence.[8] In any

[6] 'Character of Mr. Wycherley', quoted in James Sutherland, 'The Impact of Charles II on Restoration Literature', in Carroll Camden (ed.), *Restoration and Eighteenth-Century Literature: Essays in Honor of Alan Dugald McKillop*, Chicago, 1963, p. 255.

[7] *Satire I*, 1660, l. 86.

[8] Quoted in Sutherland, 'The Impact of Charles II on Restoration Literature', p. 256.

case, though Dryden was no doubt willing enough to celebrate his King's achievements, where were they? He was forced to fall back on the most conventional general formulae, and on his own invention. Consequently his poems of state sound hollow and false: as when, in the *Threnodia Augustalis,* Charles is described as 'Intrepid, pious, merciful and brave'. Under Charles there would be no question of the heroic celebrations of Augustus by Virgil or Horace; it was only by dint of endless contrivances, in which Dryden's great political satires had played a considerable part, that Charles was not completely overwhelmed by foreign and domestic enemies, and by the acute religious divisions which, in *Religio Laici* and *The Hind and the Panther,* provided Dryden with his greatest poetic themes. Then, after the Glorious Revolution in 1688 the monarchy itself became much weaker, and Dryden himself fell out of favour.

The Augustan analogy was equally problematic in its application to the wider literary and historical context. Roman history could reasonably be seen as a continuously broadening stream of political liberty, which had finally been exchanged under Augustus for peace, prosperity, and the country's greatest age of artistic and literary achievement. But in England the course of events had been quite different: civil war had brought back monarchy, it is true, but it had not brought back absolutism, nor a cultural renaissance. In literature, however much Dryden and his contemporaries might flatter themselves on the increasing correctness and refinement of English poetry, Chaucer, Spenser, Shakespeare, and Ben Jonson, the giant race before the flood, were still there to say nothing of Milton. Thus the writers of the English equivalents of Horace's *Art of Poetry* or Boileau's *Art Poétique* were faced with an impossible task: to pretend that there was a steady curve of cultural progress leading to a pre-ordained Augustan apogee meant making 'correctness' and 'refinement' the primary criteria of literary greatness. This was completely at variance with the obvious facts; they knew it; and when they forgot it they sounded unconvinced as well as unconvincing.

1700-44. The term 'The Augustans', without any qualifier, makes us think first of the writers who came to prominence after the death of Dryden in 1700—of Addison, Swift, Pope, and their friends. But this is a retrospective application of the term; they themselves did not think of themselves as the English Augustans—indeed no writers have. They were, it is true, much concerned with the parallel between their own times and those of Augustan Rome, but they actually viewed it in an increasingly pessimistic vein, especially after the accession of George I.

Still, what we call the English Augustans were identified as such fairly early. Thus Thomas Tickell wrote in the 1721 Preface to Addison's *Poems* that Addison 'first distinguished himself by his *Latin* compositions, published in the *Musae Anglicanae,* and was admired as one of the best authors since the Augustan Age . . . .' It was, however, Addison's Latin verse that Tickell had in mind, and it was not until a generation later that Joseph Warton[9] in 1756, and Oliver Goldsmith in 1759, described the age of Addison and Pope as England's Augustan period.

The most extended discussion of when, if at all, England had had an Augustan Age, in the sense of a national literary apogee, was that of Goldsmith in his essay, 'An Account of the Augustan Age of England', published in the *Bee* of 24 November 1759. Goldsmith thought that for other countries it was easy enough to decide 'that period . . . when language and learning arrived at its highest perfection'. 'The age of Leo X in Italy, is confessed to be the Augustan age with them'; and 'the French writers seem agreed to give the same appellation to that of Lewis XIV'. In England, however,

> The English are yet undetermined with respect to themselves. Some have looked upon the writers in the times of Queen Elizabeth as the true standard for future imitation; others have descended to the reign of James I, and others still lower to that of Charles II. Were I to be permitted to offer an opinion upon this subject, I should readily give my vote for the reign of Queen Anne, or some years before that period.[10]

Goldsmith's chief reason is an interesting reflection of his own preoccupations with the economic context of writing. It was, he thinks, under the ministries of Somers, and later of Harley, that is, between 1697 and 1714, that 'patronage was fashionable among our nobility',[11] and that there then

> seemed to be a just balance between patronage and the press. Before it, men were little esteemed whose only merit was genius; and since, men who can prudently be content to catch the public are certain of living without dependence. But the writers

9 *Essay on the Genius and Writings of Pope,* Vol. I, London, 1806, pp. 153-4. Warton remarks that the 'common opinion' that 'the dissolute reign of Charles II . . . was the Augustan age in England, is excessively false. A just taste was by no means yet formed'. He goes on to assert, 'If I was to name a time when the arts, and polite literature, were at their height in this nation, I should mention the latter end of King William, and the reign of Queen Anne'.
10 *Collected Works of Oliver Goldsmith* (hereafter cited as *Collected Works*), ed. A. Friedman, Vol. I, Oxford, 1966, p. 49. Goldsmith wrote to the same general effect in *An Inquiry into the Present State of Polite Learning,* Ch. VII, 1759 (*Collected Works,* Vol. I, p. 291).
11 *Collected Works,* Vol. I, p. 311.

of the period of which I am speaking, were sufficiently esteemed by the great, and not rewarded enough by booksellers, to set them above independance. Fame consequently then was the truest road to happiness.[12]

As in many other discussions of the Augustan analogy, Goldsmith writes in a spirit of envious retrospective nostalgia. But it is true that it was the writers of the age of King William and Queen Anne who experienced the great transition between the old system of patronage and the new; between a primary orientation of literature to the king, the court and its chief noblemen, and a primary orientation to the demands of the miscellaneous reading public as mediated by the booksellers or publishers. The days when Lord Chancellor Somers was a member of the Kit-Kat Club, and when Swift, Pope, Prior, and Gay were the intimates of another chief minister, Lord Treasurer Harley, were certainly the closest English parallel to the close friendship and munificent generosity with which Augustus Caesar and his minister Maecenas had favoured Virgil and Horace and Livy. But William and Anne themselves had actually had no particular interest in literature, so that in England it had been largely a question of noble, not of royal, patronage. In any case everything changed with the advent of the Hanoverians and Walpole, as Goldsmith recognised.[13]

Lavish and discriminating patronage was an essential component of the Augustan analogy, taking its cue from Martial's *'Sint Maecenates, non deerunt, Flacce, Marones'*.[14] But the lack of any real equivalents to Maecenas was obvious enough, and had become a common complaint by the time of Pope. The difference in patronage is implicit, for instance, in the first use of 'Augustan' given in the *Oxford Dictionary,* where Nicholas Rowe refers longingly, in the Dedication of *Ulysses* to Lord Godolphin, 1704, to the 'Favour and Protection which Poetry found in the famous Augustan Age'. Gay's satire on patronage, *The Fourth Epistle, To The Right Honorable Paul Methuen, Esq.,* 1720, made an even more specific and disadvantageous comparison:

> Why flourished verse in great *Augustus'* reign?
> He and Maecenas loved the Muse's strain.
> But now that wight in poverty must mourn
> Who was (O cruel stars!) a Poet born.

When George II came to the throne, his second name, Augustus, stimulated many derogatory comparisons. In 1727 Pope wrote to

12 Ibid., p. 499.
13 The 'link' was 'entirely broken . . . since the days of a certain prime minister of inglorious memory' (ibid., p. 311).
14 *Epigrams,* Bk VII, No. 56, l. 5.

Swift: 'Horace might keep his coach in Augustus's time, if he pleas'd, but I won't in the time of our Augustus'.[15] More important than the lack of judicious royal patronage, however, was the way that, as Pope and Swift saw it, the party system had destroyed not only all discriminating patronage, but all sense of moral, social, and political community, and thus made it impossible for literature to play the normative role in civilisation which the classical tradition assigned to it. If 'Men of Genius', Swift wrote to Pope, 'could be united [they] would drive the world before them; I think it was so among the Poets in the time of Augustus, but Envy and party and pride have hindered it among us'; and so whereas 'Virgil and Horace are equally read by Whigs and Tories',[16] there was no contemporary writer who could hope for this unanimity under the Hanoverians and the reign of faction.

Swift seems to have been more conscious of the historical aspects of the Augustan parallel than any other English writer: on the one hand he was bitter because there was no English equivalent to the privileged position of writers in the Augustan Age of Rome; on the other hand the purely historical parallel itself seemed to augur a gloomy future for England.

For two reasons. The first arose from the position of Augustus as the heir of Julius Caesar. When, in *The Inferno,* Dante had placed Brutus next to Judas Iscariot, he was following the medieval tradition which had converted Julius Caesar, and therefore his successor Augustus, into the divinely sanctioned founders of the Holy Roman Empire, and therefore of the universal secular order. This view of the Caesars was not challenged until, during the struggles of the Florentine republic against Milan early in the fifteenth century, the civic humanists such as Leonardo Bruni, Poggio, and Salutati completely reinterpreted Roman history and attacked Julius Caesar as a tyrant who had destroyed the former liberties of republican Rome.[17] This political alignment continued. Those who supported the autocratic rulers, whether of quattrocento Milan, or of the great nation-states of seventeenth-century Europe, were protagonists of Caesar and Augustus; whereas those who stood for republican ideas, or for political liberty in general, made Cato and Brutus their heroes. Swift, like Addison in *Cato,* took the traditional republican and libertarian position, as is implicit in Swift's admiration for

[15] 22 Oct. 1727 (*The Correspondence of Alexander Pope,* ed. G. Sherburn, Vol. I, Oxford, 1956, p. 455).
[16] 20 Sept. 1723 (*The Correspondence of Jonathan Swift,* ed. H. Williams, Vol. II, Oxford, 1963-5, p. 465).
[17] See Hans Baron, *The Crisis of the Early Italian Renaissance: Humanism and Republican Liberty in an Age of Classicism and Tyranny,* Princeton, 1966, pp. 49-78, 121-9, 352-3, 477-9.

Marcus Brutus,[18] and in his calling George I 'Caesar' in the *Drapier's Letters*.[19]

With the death of Queen Anne, the theme of Hanoverian tyranny as a repetition of that of Augustus became commonplace among the Tory opposition, including Gay, Arbuthnot, and Bolingbroke. Swift was particularly insistent. His early 'Discourse of the Contests and Dissentions Between the Nobles and Commons in Athens and Rome', 1701, had been concerned with the parallel growth of the power of the Commons in Rome and England: in Rome, Swift wrote, it had concluded with an 'entire Subversion of the Roman Liberty and Constitution' and, with Octavius, 'the vilest tyranny that Heaven, in its anger, ever inflicted'.[20] In the thirties Swift's historical gloom knew no bounds, and he feared that he himself 'might outlive liberty in England. It hath continued longer than in any other monarchy, and must end as all others have done'.[21]

Swift's second use of the historical parallel was to make the religious laxity of England prefigure, as in imperial Rome, an inevitable political, moral, and literary decline. Thus in his *Thoughts on Various Subjects,* Swift wrote:

> The *Epicureans* began to spread at Rome in the Empire of Augustus, as the *Socinians,* and even the *Epicureans* too, did in England towards the End of King *Charles* the Second's Reign; which is reckoned, though very absurdly, our *Augustan* Age. They both seem to be Corruptions occasioned by Luxury and Peace, and by Politeness beginning to decline.[22]

Swift did not, then, think that England had ever had an Augustan Age in any favourable literary sense; he saw a parallel to Rome only in the parallel process whereby moral decay led remorselessly to political collapse. 'The Ruin of a State', he wrote in 1709, 'is generally preceded by an universal Degeneracy of Manners, and Contempt of Religion; which is entirely our Case at present.'[23]

Swift's pessimism here was buttressed by a pessimistic theory of the cyclical rise and fall of civilisations. This view was widespread in England, and it pervaded many of the contemporary histories of

---

[18] 'Letter to a Whig Lord', 1712, in *Prose Works of Jonathan Swift* (hereafter cited as *Prose Works*), ed. Herbert Davis, Vol. VI, Oxford, 1939-59, p. 134.

[19] Jack C. Gilbert has suggested that the initials M. B. in the *Drapier's Letters* stand for Marcus Brutus (*Notes and Queries,* June 1963, p. 217). Fielding also made Brutus the hero of liberty ('Liberty: to George Lyttleton, Esq.' 1. 16).

[20] *Prose Works,* Vol. I, pp. 221-2.

[21] Swift to William Pulteney, 12 May 1735 (*Correspondence of Jonathan Swift,* Vol. IV, p. 336); see also Swift to John Barber, 3 Sept. 1735 (ibid., p. 381).

[22] J. W. Johnson, 'The Meaning of "Augustan"', *Journal of the History of Ideas,* Vol. XIX, 1958, p. 513. I am much indebted to this valuable pioneering study.

[23] *Prose Works,* Vol. II, p. 57.

Rome. Polybius had given the general idea currency; then Livy, Dionysius of Halicarnassus, and later Plutarch and Florus, had made the reign of Augustus the beginning of an irreversible process of political and cultural decline. This perspective was incorporated into the standard English histories of Rome, from Polydore Vergil to Laurence Eachard's *The Roman History, From the Building of the City, to the Perfect Settlement of the Empire by Augustus Caesar,* 1699; and during the reign of the first two Hanoverians the immediate implications of the analogy for England made it a matter of political polemic, with the Tories asserting the parallel, and the Whigs, Dennis, Concanen, and Oldmixon trying to refute it.[24]

The inherent complexities of the Augustan analogy, then, combined with rapid historical change, do much to explain the generally accepted division of the Age of Pope and Swift into two parts—those before and after the death of Queen Anne. Before then, the patronage of such men as Somers and Harley, together with the writers to the court and the government, made possible a somewhat closer analogy to the favoured position of writers under Augustus. Afterwards, with the accession of George I in 1714, the Tories saw everything through darker spectacles, and consequently Augustus became both a tyrant in himself and the precursor of Rome's decline and fall.

Not, of course, that the Tories were wholly consistent; they remained unwilling to forgo the other aspect of the parallel, by which the Hanoverians and Sir Robert Walpole could be damned by showing how in the matter of state patronage England had been put to shame by Augustus and his Maecenas. The poetic climax of this use of the Augustan analogy occurs in Pope's *Epistle to Augustus,* in 1737.

Horace had written his *Epistle* in answer to Augustus's friendly and repeated invitations, and he had used the occasion for measuring the arts of his time against those of the earlier Greek and Roman traditions. Horace was certain enough both about Augustus's virtues as a ruler, and about the greatness of the literature of his own time, to affirm the poet's lofty traditional role as *utilis urbi,* as the conscience of the state; and his tone showed that he could take for granted the friendly interest and full agreement of Augustus.

Pope's version is totally different, because the Horatian parallel hardly applied either on the literary or the political side. Pope cannot see the development of English poetry and drama as one of continuous improvement and refinement, although he does his best

[24] There are many references to this controversy in J. W. Johnson's article, 'The Meaning of "Augustan" ', pp. 513-16.

with the poetic reforms of Waller and Dryden, and the moral purity of Roscommon and Addison. Nor can Pope share Horace's easy solidarity with the social, political, and literary life of his own time; Pope's poem is primarily destructive, and it succeeds as poetry only when it is animated by the energy of contemptuous exasperation. Where Horace had affirmed the social value of poetry, and given as one example the songs of traditional rural piety, Pope's imitation mocks Hopkins and Sternhold's popular metrical versions of the Psalms:

> How could devotion touch the country pews,
> Unless the gods bestow'd a proper Muse?
> Verse cheers their leisure, verse assists their work,
> Verse prays for peace, or sings down Pope and Turk.
> The silenced preacher yields to potent strains,
> And feels that grace his prayer besought in vain;
> The blessing thrills through all the labouring throng,
> And Heaven is won by violence of song.

There is the same ironic reversal in political matters. Horace had jokingly opened with his fear of intruding on the Emperor's more important political concerns; Pope opens with savage irony on George's absence abroad in the arms of his mistress, Madame Walmoden, apparently quite oblivious of the Spanish privateers who roam the main cutting off Jenkins's ear:

> While you, great patron of mankind! sustain
> The balanced world, and open all the main;
> Your country, chief, in arms abroad defend,
> At home, with morals, arts and laws amend;
> How shall the Muse from such a monarch steal
> An hour, and not defraud the public weal?

The terms of Pope's preliminary advertisement to the poem reveal a wholly ironical set of attitudes towards the society of his time:

> The Reflections of Horace, and the Judgments past in his Epistle to Augustus, seem'd so seasonable to the present Times, that I could not help applying them to the use of my own country. The Author thought them considerable enough to address them to His Prince; whom he paints with the great and good qualities of a Monarch, upon whom the Romans depended for the Encrease of an Absolute Empire. But to make the poem entirely English, I was willing to add one or two of those which contribute to the Happiness of a Free People, and are more consistent with the Welfare of our Neighbours.

In this context Pope's dry irony about 'consistency with the welfare of our neighbours' really achieves its derogatory parallel with Rome only by implicitly reproving George II and Walpole for being

76

insufficiently belligerent; the reader is not reminded that although the *Pax Augusta* was no doubt nobler, it was also much bloodier. Similarly Pope's joke about the 'happiness of a free people' glosses over the awkward fact that Pope owed his independence as a writer to conditions which were equally inconceivable either in Augustan Rome or in the France of Louis XIV. As is made clear by the sequel, where, to reprove George II for the indiscriminate nature of his patronage, Pope goes well beyond the facts in claiming that Augustus 'not only prohibited all but the Best Writers to name him, but recommended that Care to the Civil Magistrate'. It was only because the Stuarts had eventually lost most of the royal prerogatives that George's magistrates could not send Pope to join Ovid in exile on the Black Sea for his calculated *lèse-majesté*. On this contrast between Augustan Rome and Hanoverian England one imagines that Pope and his readers were equally ambivalent: as long as they enjoyed the advantages of peace, prosperity, and *habeas corpus,* they were quite willing to enjoy the ironic denunciations which the parallel with a more absolutist political and social structure made possible.

Of course, on the essential issue, that of the monarch's traditional responsibility for civilisation as a whole, Pope's ironic contrast between the two Augustuses was wholly justified, as was made abundantly clear by George Augustus's own comment: 'Who is this Pope that I hear so much about? I cannot discover what is his merit. Why will not my subjects write in prose?'

Reuben Brower has written that Pope and his circle 'often saw their world through Horace's eyes and to a surprising degree tried to shape the actuality to fit the dream'.[25] During the reign of Queen Anne their letters, their social life, and to some extent their writings, recreated the wide-eyed urbanity of the Horatian manner. But with the death of Queen Anne their perspective changed completely. Once the Whigs returned to power, the Tories had to see the Hanoverians as venal tyrants triumphing over the traditional English liberties through their standing armies, bribed electors, and corrupt placemen. Consequently the Augustan analogy became entirely negative politically. In Book III of the *Dunciad* Settle is termed, ironically, 'Th' Augustus born to bring Saturnian Times'; and this is part of a general trend in Pope and Swift towards satire, and towards a satire more unrelieved, more pessimistic, more intense, at times more tragic, than anything one finds in Horace or even Juvenal.

In the last analysis, then, both the similarities and the differences between eighteenth-century England and Augustan Rome only

25 *Alexander Pope, The Poetry of Allusion,* Oxford, 1959, p. 164.

served to sharpen Pope's and Swift's awareness of how unheroic and disordered their own world was. History had moved beyond them, chaos really threatened, and the only possible posture was public denunciation and an unremitting rearguard action. Embattled and embittered, Pope and Swift became that very un-Horatian thing, an intransigent minority. One may doubt the social and historical judgments that underlie the absolute pessimism of the perspective; but one must admit that it gave them an advantage denied to the other Augustan writers, the ironic advantage that the very un-reality of the Augustan analogy freed them from its inhibiting moderation and balance. And more than freed them; impelled them to create negative fictions of the highest order of imaginative intensity and conviction.

1744-98. During the second half of the eighteenth century the Augustan analogy naturally played a smaller role. Whatever divinity may have hedged, the Hanoverians remained invisible to any open eye; and the monarchical framework became largely irrelevant, not only to the actual operations of government, but to the world of literature. Of course, the stipendiary dunces of the court continued to celebrate victories and birthdays; but nobody listened. Newspapers, periodicals, and the booksellers now provided the patronage and the audience for literature; and while people continued to admire Augustan Rome, there was no longer any question of emulating its literary institutions and attitudes.

What literary history has uneasily recognised, then, as three separate phases of Augustan literature in England, is only partly and unevenly illuminated by the analogy with Augustan Rome. In the first phase there were some genuine parallels, and even some conscious effort to achieve for England what classical literature had achieved for Rome. But political life under Charles II was too unstable and turbulent to make it possible even to approximate to the genuinely impressive political and cultural parallel brought about in France under Louis XIV. In the last days of William III, and even more under Queen Anne, there was a momentary recreation of the Roman pattern; but after 1714, in the period when Pope and Swift did most of their writing, the Augustan analogy became both a literary mockery and a dire historical warning. In the last half of the eighteenth century the analogy largely passed from view, and we must therefore look elsewhere for whatever justification there may be in applying the term 'Augustan' to Johnson, Goldsmith, Burke, Gibbon, and many other writers who flourished between the death of Pope and the publication of *The Lyrical Ballads*.

There are, of course, many elements of continuity: in literature, the couplet, the periodic sentence, the pervasiveness of neo-classical critical assumptions; and there is no marked break in the general cultural background. On the other hand there are many contrary tendencies—the revival of other verse forms, the increase in prose fiction, 'sentimentalism'—which make it difficult to attribute the elements of what cohesion the literature of the later eighteenth century is generally thought to exhibit, to any community of critical or philosophical doctrines. It is, no doubt, impossible to over-estimate the power of inertia in literary as in other human affairs; and the mere existence of the achievements of the preceding literary period as models for the taste of readers and writers would therefore account for much of the continuity exhibited in the literature of the later eighteenth century; but some allowance must also be made for the influence of the substantial political and social uniformity of the century as a whole.

Augustan Literature and the Landed Interest
If we trace the line of development of most of the main political forces—ecclesiastical or parliamentary power, for instance—in England between the Restoration and the end of the eighteenth century, we are likely to get a decline or at best a zig-zag; but the power and wealth of the landed interest goes in a straight line, and up, from 1640 until towards the end of the eighteenth century.

From 1660 onwards this interest comprised the 160 or so temporal peers, and the much larger class of gentry, baronets, knights, esquires, and gentlemen, comprising perhaps some 20,000 families.[26] Jointly, they commanded a virtual monopoly of political power throughout the kingdom. In London the peers, of course, controlled not only the House of Lords, but the most important ministerial and court offices; in the country they were the Lords Lieutenant. Below them, the gentry, through the property qualification for members of Parliament and through personal local influence, controlled the House of Commons; as justices of the peace they controlled the day-to-day life of the countryside.

The civil war had been largely caused by the struggles of the landowners against Stuart economic and judicial encroachment; and the Puritan party had had many supporters among the peers and gentry. Very soon, however, they found they had personal cause to fear the dangers of religious and political equality; and at the Restoration they largely shed their Puritan and revolutionary allegiances, and united, in the words of Clarendon in 1661, to avoid

[26] G. E. Mingay, *English Landed Society in the Eighteenth Century*, London and Toronto, 1963, pp. 4-12.

any recurrence of 'that accursed dose . . . a commonwealth' the first ingredient of which had been 'the confounding the Commons of England . . . with the common people of England'.[27] The land-owning classes saw to it that they were the main beneficiaries of the Restoration Settlement. Almost everything of the political and legal *status quo* of 1641 was restored in 1660, but not the conditions of land tenure; whereas the monarchy lost all its feudal preroga-tives as head of the landholding system, the landowners, freed of their obligations to the crown, retained their own feudal rights and manorial courts.[28]

Thus fortified, the landed interest held the balance of political power from 1660 till the end of the next century. Not that the landowners were in opposition to the rapidly growing power of trade and industry centred in London; they were allied with it for the defence of property both against the weakened powers of church and state, and against the mass of propertyless labourers in town and country; and it was only very late in the eighteenth century that this alliance was threatened by the growing power and independence of commerce and industry, manifested in the reform movements associated with such Londoners as Beckford and Wilkes.[29] Later, in 1783, when Pitt the younger came to power with the support of the City and the reforming interest, the shift in the balance of power became more evident; but it was only with the Reform Bill of 1832 and the subsequent abolition of the Corn Laws that trade and industry gained a controlling political voice. Before 1640 the crown and the church had been dominant; after 1832 it was trade and industry; but between these two periods, and therefore throughout all the periods that have been called Augustan, England was dominated, as never before or since, by the landed interest.

What of this for literature? More specifically, what political and social attitudes are characteristic of the landed interest of the period which are also characteristic of the Augustan writers?

As far as I know, F. W. Bateson is the only scholar to attempt an answer to this question. Bateson's 'A Word for Waller'[30] presents him as the Augustan Wyatt; and he relates this to Waller's prescient awareness of the basic strategy required to ensure the political and

27 C. Hill, *The Century of Revolution, 1603-1714*, London, 1961, p. 222.
28 T. B. Macaulay, *The History of England from the Accession of James the Second*, Vol. I, London, 1850, p. 153; D. Ogg, *England in the Reign of Charles II*, Vol. I, Oxford, 1934, pp. 159-61.
29 See, for instance, the discussion of the social composition of the supporters of Wilkes in G. Rudé, *Wilkes and Liberty: A Social Study of 1763 to 1774*, Oxford, 1962, esp. pp. 82, 136-7, 193.
30 In *English Poetry: A Critical Introduction*, London, 1950, pp. 165-74.

social position of his own class. Thus it was Waller who, in the Commons debates of 1641 about Episcopacy, declared that 'if, by multiplying hands and petitions [the people] prevail for an equality in things ecclesiastical, the next demand may perhaps be *Lex Agraria,* the like equality in things temporal'.[31] Bateson goes on to suggest that 'the ultimate explanation of the pretentiousness and emptiness of much Augustan poetry' is the central contradiction between the 'community of sense' which was ideally supposed to comprise the whole of literate society, and the 'rigid social stratification' which gave decisive power to a landed aristocracy on grounds that were wholly devoid either of any 'rational basis' or of any 'mystical or traditional basis of authority'.

We must surely agree with at least one of Bateson's points—our sense both of Augustan literature and of its society is very much dominated by an impression of a complex but pervasive and rigid class-structure throughout the country. This social stratification may itself be regarded as one aspect of the landed interest's general strategy: the defence of the *status quo.* Such a defensive strategy permeated many social institutions after 1660. The Church of England, for instance, became largely an instrument of social discipline, especially in the country, and a political servant of the government.

This general defensive strategy also required a special political attitude, and an appropriate intellectual temper. The political attitude is the one which Bateson describes as the Augustan ideal— the effort to encompass in a system of basic agreement the whole 'community of sense'; a community that should encompass what was actually the relatively small fraction of the total population which owned real property. The intellectual temper required to avoid any recurrences of the excesses of the civil war may be described an anti-theoretical, sceptical, and pragmatic;[32] it was a temper which came easily to an aristocracy and gentry that had learned a good deal about the need for piecemeal accommodation to other forces during the civil war.

The consistency with which the aristocracy avoided making themselves politically isolated or socially exclusive can be seen by comparing them with their French counterparts. In England there was none of that tessellated structure of different degrees of nobility, all with special legal, political, social, and economic prerogatives, which made the French aristocracy so hateful to outsiders, and yet so divided within itself. Apart from the right of the English nobility

31 Ibid., p. 171.
32 See G. N. Clark, *The Later Stuarts, 1660-1714,* Oxford, 1940, pp. 34-5; B. Williams, *The Whig Supremacy 1714-1760,* Oxford, 1949, p. 143.

to trial by their peers, the common law obtained universally; and the social and political dealings of the English aristocracy with other classes show a tolerance and lack of exclusiveness that is very striking compared with the traditions of the European aristocracies.[33]

The anti-theoretical, sceptical, and pragmatic intellectual temper of the landed interest in England also differentiates it from that of the Continent. When people had got too excited about political and religious theory, civil war had ensued; ideological principles, apparently, were dangerous in themselves. Political and religious divisions continued, certainly, to divide men under Charles II and James II, until Locke and the Glorious Revolution provided the solutions. But the silent skill with which the ruling class turned against the successive threats of Monmouth, James II, and the Stuart Pretenders shows a remarkable subordination of theoretical to practical consideration. This pragmatic temper of the nobility and gentry was also evident in the predominantly practical interests of the Royal Society, and later flourished in the leading part played by the peers and great landowners in the improvements of farming methods which brought about the agricultural revolution.

To go from the general characteristics of a dominant class to those of a literary tradition is an uncomfortably abstract and theoretical operation; but some very general connexions seem plausible.

The supreme value for any landed interest is obviously the land, and it is surely the land, as much as anything else, that we think of in connexion with Augustan literature. That great monument in the history of the heroic couplet, Sir John Denham's *Cooper's Hill*, 1642, also set the pattern for the innumerable topographical poems of the ensuing period. The life of the countryside is also the subject of two other popular poetic forms—the poem of retreat, and the agricultural Georgic. These are three of the period's most characteristic poetic forms, and they all presuppose an ideal of human civilisation in a rural setting.

This ideal is also the theme of many of the finest poems of the period, from Pope's *Epistle to Burlington* to Goldsmith's *The Deserted Village*. Behind both of these is the myth of the Golden Age, a myth which no doubt provided some of the inspiration for one of the supreme aesthetic successes of eighteenth-century culture —its transformation of the countryside through emparkment and landscape gardening. This transformation, together with the ideal-

33 See especially H. J. Habbakuk, 'England', and J. McManners, 'France', in A. Goodwin (ed.), *The European Nobility in the Eighteenth Century*, London, 1953, pp. 1-42.

isation of a 'Sweet Auburn' which never really existed, gave the rural ideology an ever wider extension. For even today the picturesque lanes, hedges, parkland, and villages, which were largely the achievement of the eighteenth-century landowners, have become the attractive, though for two centuries now the misleading, symbol of England itself.

So much for the direct parallel in subject matter. The landowners' concentration on the defence of their property rights, their basically defensive strategy, is paralleled by many of the other characteristics of Augustan literature. Much has been written on the period's literary and philosophical concern with an ordered hierarchy of classes, and with the threats to it arising from human pride, which makes the individual dissatisfied with the place to which it has pleased God to call him. Earlier periods had also, of course, assumed a hierarchical order: but in the Augustan world that hierarchy is characteristically limited and social in its emphasis. On the one hand we notice that at the top of the pyramid God and the King are much less important; on the other it is evident that sceptical inquiry stops short of any challenge to the justice and permanence of the inferior position of the lower orders. Even for the most destructive and subversive minds of the eighteenth century, as we see in Mandeville or Hume, in Swift's *Directions to Servants* or Sterne's treatment of Corporal Trim, there is no question but that the mob is the mob and that servants ought to be content with their lot.

A less self-evident connexion comes from the defensive posture itself, from the landed interest's concentration on maintaining the *status quo* rather than on trying to change it for the better. Augustan literature, too, is basically defensive, and in a number of ways. Its poetry, for instance, takes more notice of Virgilian farming methods than of the great agricultural and industrial revolutions that were changing the face of England. More significant, the Augustan writers often looked back as a way of measuring the deterioration of the present; they were obsessed with decline. One aspect of this is the assumption—constant from Pope and Swift to Goldsmith and Burke —that the very fabric of society is threatened as never before. This is closely connected with the value which the Augustans placed on history: the contemplation of the civilisation of the past could guide man in the present. If the Augustan parallel itself had called attention to the urgent lesson for England of Gibbon's great theme in *Decline and Fall of the Roman Empire*, so Burke's famous perorations on Windsor Castle and on the death of Marie Antoinette drew from the traditions which never forgot the larger warning implicit in the martyrdom of Charles I. More generally, the defensive postures of the landed interest and of Augustan literature can themselves be seen as having the same essential movement: to survey the broad acres of the human inheritance, to value them duly, and to unite for their preservation.

The supreme values of the landed interest and of Augustan literature were alike, then, in their rural nature, and in their emphasis on preservation and constructive improvement rather than on radical change. This normative tendency is also evident in the effort of Augustan literature to provide positive models in every sphere of life. In its most external aspect, this emphasis is seen in the concern for dress, furnishing, and behaviour; they are the mere outward symbol of uniformity, to be sure, but they can increase or decrease the circle of the acceptably civilised community. Here the aims of the *Spectator* are characteristic. Addison's preoccupation with manners and decorum is not social in a superficial or frivolous sense: civilisation itself, it was assumed, depended on a shared moral and social code; and it was the writer's primary task to propagate agreement about it. Today we may not all find such terms as 'manners', 'propriety', 'civility', 'decorum', 'sense', 'reason', 'nature', 'taste', 'elegance', 'improvement', either attractive in themselves, or self-evident in their meaning; yet we cannot but be impressed when we consider what a continuous, concerted, and controlled effort must have been needed to establish them as the effective key words of a society for so long. In this context, the Augustan period's persistent collective concern for codifying society's positive standards, and for defending them against formlessness and anarchy, Beau Nash's reforms at Bath and Dr Johnson's labours at the *Dictionary* are seen to have a common purpose with Butler's *Hudibras* and Gibbon's *Decline and Fall*.

In the last analysis, the pragmatic and normative orientation of the Augustans meant that man's mind was mainly regarded as an arbiter of socially agreed ideas and attitudes; and this was probably hostile to the basic presuppositions of what we now call creative literature: the collective and codified experience of instructed mankind became much more important than any one individual's interpretation or imaginative remodelling of it; life, in fact, and specifically social life, was more important than literature. Here, perhaps, we can find a clue to one of the paradoxes in contemporary attitudes to the Augustan tradition; today we can wholeheartedly admire it as a way of life without regarding its literature, and especially its poetry and drama, with the same enthusiasm. Our most unqualified admiration, indeed, tends to go to those Augustan writings which are closest to being direct records of the life and attitudes of the period—to its essays, dialogues, letters; we also have the same admiration for the Augustan achievement in what may be called the literature of knowledge—Adam Smith's *The Wealth of Nations*, say, or White's *The Natural History of Selborne*; and the books of the period which live the most immediately today, from *Robinson Crusoe* to Boswell's *Journals*, belong to that special miscellaneous category which may be called the literature of experience.

I should be foolish indeed to argue that the landed classes of the period, merely by virtue of being such, were the direct cause of the characteristic qualities in Augustan literature. For one thing the political and social attitudes of the landed interest were probably not very different in most ways from those of the urban propertied classes. For another, most of their ideas and attitudes were highly traditional, and none, probably, was intrinsically new. What makes their ideology seem relatively distinctive is probably mainly the result of the processes whereby many of the other traditional features of the social, political, and intellectual scene—monarchy, the central importance of the court, the transcendental sanctions that had been assumed to underwrite the whole religious and secular order—had lost their compelling power; and this process affected the landed classes, and literature, in parallel ways.

In any case, the landed nobility and gentry of England had obviously absorbed many of the current stock ideas of European civilisation in general, including the doctrines of neo-classicism. This doctrine was itself the literary expression of the Counter-Reformation ideology, in which, faced by religious and civil dissension, church and state had combined to set up more centralised and codified systems of order; and in the course of so doing they found a useful parallel in the political, social, and cultural life of Augustan Rome. That very few of the doctrines of neo-classicism were taken wholly seriously by the writers of Augustan England is probably true; the parallel in the general historical situation does at least as much as any critical theory to explain the pervasive appeal of the writers of Augustan Rome to English authors and readers alike after 1660. The fact that both Horace and Virgil lived on their farms and were conservative in their values merely gave a special kind of almost religious sanction to general social and literary attitudes which would no doubt have been powerful in eighteenth-century England without them.

It may at first seem paradoxical, if not mistaken, to connect a literature which—from Etherege and Dryden to Pope and Johnson—is often urban in setting as well as conspicuously urbane in manner, with the dominance of the landed gentry; especially when, throughout the period, London was probably the largest cit in Europe, and England as a whole was becoming increasingly urbanized. But the relationship suggested between Augustan literature and the landed gentry primarily depends only on the assumption that the predominant social and political power was in the hands of a relatively homogeneous and conservative *élite*; an *élite* whose great and conscious distance from the labouring population below them gave England its closest historical approximation to the leisured class of classical times, based on the system of slavery. That some of the dominant class lived wholly in London, that many others spent much time there, or even that the cities of provincial England undoubtedly showed an increasing cultural autonomy, is of secondary importance: the Augustan attitudes fairly obviously depend on a powerful social *élite*, in which the landed interest happened to hold supreme power.

In any case, just as even for those who derived their income from trade the acquisition of a country seat was the final test of social success, so in literature even the most urban works, such as Pope's *Rape of the Lock,* Gay's *Trivia,* or Johnson's *London,* assume the superiority of rural wholesomeness over urban corruption. In these poems and in many of the novels and plays of the period, the contrast or conflict between the town and the country is a characteristic theme; and we may regard the tension as deriving from the conflict between the conservative and backward-looking posture of Augustan literature, and what was actually happening to England. Ultimately, indeed, the preference given to the superior values of the country may be seen as the literary counterpart of the basic political strategy of the period: a no doubt unconscious but functional inattention to many of the realities of England's situation —the growing importance of commerce, colonial expansion, and the Industrial Revolution, for instance.

Blake's 'London' and 'Chimney Sweeper' are significant exceptions. Blake was a Londoner, and the only important writer of the century who was born and remained a small independent tradesman; as an engraver his economic and social independence gave him opportunities for a literary and intellectual independence which were unique in the century. But the Augustan social and literary tradition goes on throughout Blake's lifetime wherever the writers are not directly exposed to the growing forces of urban radicalism and industrialisation. This surely is why, in defiance of chronology, we think of Cowper, Crabbe, Jane Austen, and Peacock as Augustan. Jane Austen's novels remind us of how, from Restoration comedy onwards, Augustan writers draw even sharper lines of discrimination between true and false norms; and for this no detail of speech, dress, or manners is too small to be morally diagnostic. Similarly

Peacock sets his novels in country houses, where he wages the last rearguard action against the Dunces, the prophets of the Age of Brass, and of the forces which are undermining the old landed order.

Today the word 'Augustan', it may be surmised, is often used to denote not a chronological period of literature, but a general cultural attitude that is only loosely, and sometimes confusingly, connected with it. It often stands, that is, not for a particular historical and literary parallel, but rather for a whole way of life defined by a leisured, sober, elegant, and determined conservatism. Here a consideration of other general terms used for the period helps to make the point. No one seems yet to have talked about Hanoverian literature as a category of literary history; and when Thackeray wrote of the Four Georges, his quarternion surely implied an attitude of jocular contempt; but the word 'Georgian' has long been wholly approbative, perhaps because the word itself denotes, in the realm of the applied arts, the enduring remains of the attitude of which the Augustan tradition was the literary and intellectual counterpart. Both were primarily concerned with imposing style on all the arts of life. The practical arts, it may be noted, such as architecture, landscape, dress, and manners, even letter-writing and obituary inscriptions, are much more immediately amenable to collective effort than the more imaginative and intense forms of literary achievement; and they also have the advantage of being, or at least appearing to be, of their very nature untheoretical and unideological.

On the other hand the very different applications of 'Georgian' and of 'Augustan' in its narrower sense, help to clarify a duality in our modern attitudes towards the eighteenth century. On the one hand we think of the lost Georgian world as the pinnacle of human achievement in all the arts of life; our age, which has made the landscape a parking lot for houses, the house a parking lot for people, and the city—just a parking lot, cannot but envy an earlier age which discovered the secret of building human houses, and harmoniously setting them in gardens and arranging them in cities. On the other hand, and especially in the academy, Pope and Swift support the intellectual's image of himself as a passionate defender of the last citadels of human reason against the mounting tide of folly, vulgarity, and commercialism. The *Dunciad* has become a prophetic book, and the fate of Gulliver among the Houyhnhnms seems a prescient enactment of the very process of human alienation. So we can have it both ways. The great Augustan writers of Queen Anne prefigure the modern writer as the voice of radical dissent from an ignominious world, while Georgian culture in general embodies our nostalgia for reasonable and aesthetic and widely-shared solutions to the problems of social life.

And there is yet another revealing contradiction in modern attitudes to the Augustan achievement. It takes, alas, considerable experience of untidiness and anarchy to appreciate why people should be content to give their best efforts merely to preserve civilisation, and realise the supreme value for this purpose of a few clear distinctions. The civil war had made this evident in England to succeeding generations; but for most of us only the years can be our instructor. So we should be neither surprised nor disappointed that the values and attitudes of Augustan literature are not the most popular ones among our pupils. For a young Augustan is as anomalous a notion, perhaps, as an ancient Venus.

I am indebted to Professor Malvin Zirker, at whose invitation I read an earlier version of parts of this paper at the University of Indiana on 23 April 1965; also to Professor Bertrand H. Bronson, who illumined the darkness of the original draft.

'Sentiment': Some Uses of the Word in the Writings of David Hume

R. F. Brissenden

'Sentiment' has long been recognised as one of the most significant words in the language of the eighteenth century. Together with several associated terms, notably 'sense', 'sensibility', and 'sentimental', it occupied a key place in the philosophical, moral, and literary vocabularies of the age. It is not surprising, then, that 'sentiment', both in the singular and the plural form, should appear with great frequency in the writings of David Hume. It occurs in his earliest work and in his latest, and it emerges as a term of central importance in both his moral and his epistemological theory.

In the Introduction to his first book, *A Treatise of Human Nature*, published in 1739, Hume observes:

> the sole end of logic is to explain the principles and operations of our reasoning faculty, and the nature of our ideas: morals and criticism regard our tastes and sentiments: and politics consider men as united in society, and dependent on each other.[1]

In one of the last things he wrote, the Advertisement to the 1777 edition of his *Essays and Treatises*, he states: 'the Author desires that the following Pieces may alone be regarded as containing his philosophical sentiments and principles'.[2]

The meaning of 'sentiments' in the latter quotation seems quite simple. If a contemporary reader had been in any doubt, a glance at Johnson's *Dictionary* would have soon clarified the matter for him: 'sentiment' is there defined first as 'thought; notion; opinion'; and secondly as 'the sense considered distinctly from the language

---

[1] David Hume, *A Treatise of Human Nature* (hereafter cited as *Treatise*), ed. L. A. Selby-Bigge, Oxford, 1949, p. xix.
[2] Quoted in the Introduction to *The Essential Works of David Hume* (hereafter cited as *Essential Works*), ed. with Introduction by R. Cohen, Bantam Books, New York, Toronto, and London, 1965, p. 11.

89

or things; a striking sentence in a composition'.[3] Any other dictionary would have given much the same account of the word. Erik
Erämetsä, in his valuable *Study of the Word 'Sentimental'*, quotes
some twenty definitions taken from a number of dictionaries published (and republished) between 1689 and 1812; and in those which
appeared prior to 1777 the following synonyms are given for 'sentiment': 'opinion', 'verdict', 'judgment', 'thought', 'mind', 'notion',
and 'inclinations'.[4]

'Sentiment' (or, more usually, 'sentiments') was commonly used
throughout the period to signify a body of philosophic doctrine, a
theory, or a set of arguments. A good illustration of this usage can
be seen in the Table of Contents in Thomas Reid's *Essays on the
Intellectual Powers of Man*, which was published in 1785. The
following are titles to some of the chapters: 'Sentiments of Philosophers about the Perceptions of External Objects; and, first, of the
Theory of Father Malebranche'; 'Bishop Berkeley's Sentiments of
the Nature of Ideas'; 'Of the Sentiments of Mr. Locke'; 'Of the
Sentiments of Mr. Hume'.[5]

Hume himself regularly employed the word in this way. Many
examples could be cited: one, taken from Book I of the *Treatise*,
demonstrates the connotations the word had for him when he was
using it in this sense. He is discussing here the classical theory of
being:

> But these philosophers carry their fictions still farther in
> their sentiments concerning *occult qualities*, and both suppose
> a substance supporting, which they do not understand, and an
> accident supported, of which they have as imperfect an idea . . .
> In considering this subject we may observe a gradation of
> three opinions, that rise above each other, according as the
> persons, who form them, acquire new degrees of reason and
> knowledge. These opinions are that of the vulgar, that of a
> false philosophy, and that of the true; where we shall find upon
> enquiry, that the true philosophy approaches nearer to the
> sentiments of the vulgar, than to those of a mistaken know-
> ledge. 'Tis natural for men, in their common and careless way

[3] This is the definition given in the first edition (1755) and also the fourth
(1778).

[4] See E. Erämetsä, *A Study of the Word 'Sentimental'*, Helsinki, 1951, p. 24,
for his full list of the definitions of 'sentiment'. Erämetsä does not seem to have
consulted the *Dictionarium Britannicum or a more compleat universal etymo-
logical English Dictionary*, by N[athan] Bailey, and others, 2nd ed., 1736, which
defines 'sentiment' as 'thoughts, mind, opinion, inclination; also passion'. This
is the largest edition of Bailey, the numerous and varying editions of which had
a much wider distribution throughout the century than Johnson. 'Passion'
apparently is not given as a meaning in the many smaller editions. Bailey did
not attempt to distinguish, as did Johnson, between 'low' and 'correct' usage.

[5] Thomas Reid, *Essays on the Intellectual Powers of Man*, ed. and abridged
A. D. Woozley, London, 1941, pp. xli-xlii.

of thinking, to imagine they perceive a connexion betwixt such objects as they have constantly found united together; and because custom has rendered it difficult to separate the ideas, they are apt to fancy such a separation to be in itself impossible and absurd. But philosophers, who abstract from the effects of custom, and compare the ideas of objects, immediately perceive the falsehood of these vulgar sentiments, and discover that there is no known connexion among objects.[6]

I have quoted this passage at length because the context in which 'sentiments' is here operating seems to establish in a very obvious way its meaning. The sentiments Hume is discussing in this passage are opinions or theories which result from the acquisition of knowledge and the exercise of reason. They can be investigated by the usual methods of philosophical inquiry and demonstrated to be true or false, reasonable or (as he says elsewhere) 'unreasonable'.[7] In 1777, in what was perhaps the last work he wrote for publication, Hume is still using the word in this way. The brief Advertisement to the last revised edition of his works begins with the following sentence: 'Most of the principles, and reasonings, contained in this volume, were published in . . . *A Treatise of Human Nature*'.[8] It concludes with the statement, which I have already quoted,[9] in which he refers to his 'philosophical sentiments and principles'. 'Sentiments' and 'reasonings' seem, in this context, if not exactly synonymous, intimately related in meaning. Hume's 'philosophical sentiments and principles' are quite clearly nothing more nor less than his philosophical theories, theories which are the result of and incorporate what he describes in the concluding paragraph of *An Enquiry Concerning Human Understanding* as *'experimental reasoning concerning fact and existence'*.[10] They are the result, in short, of *thinking*.

But the sentiments he mentions in the first quotation I cited are just as clearly not—or not in any simple way—the result of thinking. (The sentence runs as follows: 'the sole end of logic is to explain the principles and operations of our reasoning faculty, and the nature of our ideas: morals and criticism regard our taste and sentiments: and politics consider men as united in society, and

6 *Treatise*, Bk I, Pt IV, Sect. iii, pp. 222-3.
7 Ibid., Sect. ii, p. 193. The relevant passage runs: 'For philosophy informs us, that every thing which appears to the mind, is nothing but a perception . . . whereas the vulgar confound perceptions and objects, and attribute a distinct continu'd existence to the very things they feel or see. This sentiment, then, as it is entirely unreasonable, must proceed from some other faculty than the understanding.'
8 *Essential Works*, p. 11.
9 Above, p. 89.
10 *Essential Works*, p. 167 (op. cit., Sect. XII, Pt iii).

dependent on each other'.)[11]

In the concluding section of *An Enquiry concerning Human Understanding* the relationship which he claims to exist among morals, criticism, taste, and sentiment is commented on more fully:

> Morals and criticism are not so properly objects of the understanding as of taste and sentiment. Beauty, whether moral or natural, is felt, more properly, than perceived. Or if we reason concerning it, and endeavour to fix its standard, we regard a new fact, to wit, the general taste of mankind, or some such fact, which may be the object of reasoning and enquiry.[12]

And for Hume, of course, the fundamental problem in moral theory was that of discovering whether our moral attitudes are founded primarily on thought or feeling,

> ... whether they be derived from REASON or SENTIMENT; whether we attain the knowledge of them by a chain of argument and induction, or by an immediate feeling and finer internal sense; whether, like all sound judgments of truth and falsehood, they should be the same to every intelligent being; or whether, like the perception of beauty and deformity, they be founded entirely on the particular fabric and constitution of the human species.[13]

In its crudest form the answer, as Hume saw it, has already been given in his *Treatise*: 'Reason is, and ought only to be the slave of the passions'.[14] A process of ratiocination may help us to determine what we are considering, the facts of the moral situation to which we are responding, but our judgment, our response, is not itself an act of reason but a feeling, that particular species of feeling he called a 'sentiment'.

In his most sceptical moments Hume indeed maintained that there was practically no act of the understanding which could not ultimately be reduced to sentiment. There is a passage in the *Treatise* (which is, of course, generally more extravagant in tone than his later work) where he states:

> Thus all probable reasoning is nothing but a species of sensation. 'Tis not solely in poetry and music, we must follow our taste and sentiment, but likewise in philosophy. When I am convinc'd of any principle, 'tis only an idea, which strikes more strongly upon me. When I give the preference to one set of arguments above another, I do nothing but decide from my feeling concerning the superiority of their influence.[15]

---

[11] *Treatise*, p. xix (quoted above, p. 89).
[12] *Essential Works*, p. 167 (op. cit., Sect. XII, Pt iii).
[13] Ibid., p. 181 (*An Enquiry Concerning the Principles of Morals*, Sect. I).
[14] *Treatise*, Bk II, Pt III, Sect. iii, p. 415.
[15] Ibid., Bk I, Pt III, Sect. viii, p. 103.

Hume, we should note, is referring to *'probable* reasoning'. By this he means reasoning about matters of fact and existence—what he describes elsewhere as 'moral' or 'experimental' reasoning. He is careful to distinguish this from abstract or demonstrative reasoning, which he certainly does not regard as a species of sensation.

> *That three times five is equal to the half of thirty,* expresses a relation between these numbers. Propositions of this kind are discoverable by the mere operation of thought, without dependence on what is any where existent in the universe.[16]

Such propositions are discoverable in this way because they are concerned with 'Relations of Ideas', and our recognition of their truth or falsity does not depend on feeling. Hume would wish to insist, however, I think, that our acceptance of their truth or falsity, and in particular our determination to act on it, does depend on feeling. Hume's fundamental doctrine, as Norman Kemp Smith has said, is that 'the determining influence in human, as in other forms of animal life, is feeling, not reason or understanding, i.e., not evidence whether *a priori* or empirical, and therefore also not ideas'.[17]

But when Hume employs the word 'sentiment' in this manner it has a distinctly different meaning from that which it bears in his discussion of the three theories of existence, or in the statements about his 'philosophical sentiments and principles'. In fact it would be possible, without doing violence to Hume's varying uses of the term, to reword the concluding sentence of the passage from the *Treatise,* quoted above—'When I give the preference to one set of arguments above another, I do nothing but decide from my feeling concerning the superiority of their influence'—as follows: 'When I give the preference to one set of *sentiments* above another, I do nothing but decide from my *sentiments* concerning the superiority of their influence'.

There is, perhaps, nothing odd in the notion that one can have feelings about thoughts or even feelings about feelings. It is odd, however, that Hume should have remained—as he apparently did— quite unconscious of the fact that he was in the habit of using the same word to describe human activities or states of mind which, in general, it was his concern to distinguish carefully. This is particularly remarkable in view of Hume's unusual sensitivity to the role which unacknowledged verbal ambiguities can play in philosophical problems. 'From this circumstance alone, that a controversy has been long kept on foot, and remains still undecided', he observes in

---

16 *Essential Works,* p. 62 (*An Enquiry Concerning Human Understanding,* Sect. IV, Pt i).
17 *The Philosophy of David Hume,* London, 1964, p. 11.

STUDIES IN THE EIGHTEENTH CENTURY

his discussion of 'Liberty and Necessity', 'we may presume, that there is some ambiguity in the expression, and that the disputants affix different ideas to the terms employed in the controversy.'[18] Appendix IV to his *Enquiry Concerning the Principles of Morals* bears the title, 'Of Some Verbal Disputes', and opens with a sentence that has a notably modern ring: 'Nothing is more usual than for philosophers to encroach upon the province of grammarians; and to engage in disputes of words, while they imagine, that they are handling controversies of the deepest importance and concern'.[19] And in his essay, *Of the Standard of Taste,* he asserts that our agreement to use a common aesthetic and moral terminology often conceals profound differences of opinion:

> The sentiments of men often differ with regard to beauty and deformity of all kinds, even while their general discourse is the same. There are certain terms in every language, which import blame, and others praise; and all men, who use the same tongue, must agree in their application of them. Every voice is united in applauding elegance, propriety, simplicity, spirit in writing; and in blaming fustian, affectation, coldness, and a false brilliancy: But when critics come to particulars, this seeming unanimity vanishes; and it is found that they had affixed a very different meaning to their expression.[20]

In morals, he goes on to suggest, the situation is similar: while there is apparent unanimity, this in fact disguises basic disagreement:

> This great unanimity is usually ascribed to the influence of plain reason; which in all these cases maintains similar sentiments in all men . . . So far as the unanimity is real, this account may be admitted as satisfactory: But we must allow that some part of the seeming harmony in morals may be accounted for from the very nature of language.[21]

Hume was alive to the fact that the words which describe particular moral sentiments, or the particular qualities or actions which excite moral sentiments, could mean different things to different people. It seems, however, that he remained totally insensitive to the ambiguity, the inherent duplicity, of the word 'sentiment' itself.

If it can be accepted that Hume used 'sentiment' in this innocently duplicitous manner, a number of questions suggest themselves. Firstly, why did he do so? Why did he not recognise the different ways in which the word could function and distinguish them, as he distinguished different uses of the word 'reason'? Secondly, what

---

[18] *Essential Works,* p. 102 (*An Enquiry Concerning Human Understanding,* Sect. VIII, Pt i).
[19] Ibid., p. 284.
[20] Ibid., pp. 448-9.
[21] Ibid.

implications for Hume's philosophical position does this ambiguity have? And thirdly, what can it tell us, if anything, about the general development of sentimentalism in the eighteenth century?

The simple answer to the first question is that Hume was a man of his age and he spoke the language of his age. 'Sentiment' was a common and an extremely useful term; and when Hume was composing his major works no one seems to have been aware of its basic complexity. As a philosopher he inherited the term from earlier writers, notably Shaftesbury and Hutcheson, and in its French form from Malebranche. But it was never purely a technical term: it was part of the fashionable jargon of the day—especially the fashionable moral jargon. People clearly found it remarkably convenient to have a term which could mean either a 'mental feeling' (*O.E.D.*, sense 7) or 'an emotional thought' (*O.E.D.*, sense 8b); a term, that is, which could be used to describe either thinking or feeling, or a blend of the two, or the attitudes, judgments, theories, notions, convictions—what you will—which resulted from the operations, either singly or together, of these apparently very different processes.

That these processes *were* different Hume, for most of the time at any rate, seems to have been in no doubt: 'Everyone of himself will readily perceive the difference betwixt feeling and thinking',[22] he confidently asserts near the beginning of the *Treatise*. At a later stage in his argument, however, particularly in his consideration of the problem of belief, it becomes clear that he came to regard the question of how we distinguish thinking from feeling as much more puzzling. None the less, this still did not awaken him to the ambiguous manner in which the word 'sentiment' could function. Indeed, as I shall suggest later on, it seems likely that this unacknowledged ambiguity was of some value to Hume in his attempt to cope with two of the most troubling problems in his philosophy: the problem of how we distinguish fiction from belief, and the problem of reconciling the implicit relativism of his moral theory with his conviction that most human beings are innately benevolent. The use of 'sentiment' in each case enables Hume, I believe, to give an apparent solution to each problem while in reality he is sidestepping some of the basic difficulties.

If we are to understand why Hume used 'sentiment' as he did it seems plain then that we shall have to give some consideration to the general question of why the term functioned as it did at the time he was writing. Part of the answer to this may be found if we look at the derivation of 'sentiment', and at the group of words to which it belongs.

22 *Treatise*, Bk I, Pt I, Sect. i, pp. 1-2.

This is not a simple task. As William Empson has remarked, 'This family of words is obviously very difficult; the mere number of them is distracting'.[23] The *O.E.D.* includes in the group over one hundred individual words; and some of these have several different meanings. Thirty distinct uses of the noun 'sense' are noted, for instance, and five of the verb, while ten definitions are given for 'sentiment' itself. The section devoted to the group as a whole occupies fifteen pages of the dictionary; and this does not include combinations such as 'common sense', 'moral sense', and others which are treated separately elsewhere.

The roots from which this large family have sprung are two Latin words: the verb *'sentire'* and the noun *'sensus'*. Apparently simple, these two words are unusually complex. Convincing evidence of their complexity is afforded by the size and diversity of the group of words which has been derived from them: words which in almost every case seem to have been brought into existence in order to limit more precisely certain areas of that extensive field of reference which is covered by *'sentire'* and *'sensus'*. 'Sense' words also seem to be peculiarly susceptible to shifts in evaluative connotation. 'Sentimental' offers the clearest example of this: when the adjective first came into vogue (some time in the 1740s) it seemed—to quote from Lady Bradshaigh's letter to Richardson—that 'everything clever and agreeable [was] comprehended in that word'.[24] By the end of the century, however, it had acquired that suggestion of the shallow, the excessive, and the insincere which it bears today. 'Sensibility' suffered a similar decline; and it is extremely interesting to note that as 'sensibility' went out of fashion 'sensitivity', which apparently had a neutral, scientific (particularly botanical) aura, was brought in to replace it. The adjective 'sensitive' dates back to the fifteenth century; but the first instance of 'sensitivity', the noun, recorded by the *O.E.D.* occurs in 1803 (Jane Austen's *Sense and Sensibility* was published in 1811). At the same time 'sensible' began to lose its meaning of 'sensitive', while the meaning it has today— 'reasonable', 'intelligent', in accord with the dictates of common

---

23 *The Structure of Complex Words,* London, 1951, p. 250 and *passim.*

24 'What, in your opinion, is the meaning of the word *sentimental,* so much in vogue among the polite. Everything clever and agreeable is comprehended in that word; but I am convinced a wrong interpretation is given, because it is impossible everything clever and agreeable can be as common as this word is. I am frequently astonished to hear such a one is a *sentimental* man; we were a *sentimental* party; I have been taking a *sentimental* walk. And that I might be reckoned a little in the fashion, and, as I thought, show them the proper use of the word, about six weeks ago, I declared I had just received a *sentimental* letter' (*The Correspondence of Samuel Richardson,* ed. Anna Laetitia Barbauld, Vol. IV, London, 1804, p. 282 (quoted in *A Study of the Word Sentimental,* p. 22)).

sense—which up till then had been more colloquial than correct,[25] gained in force and respectability.

'Sentire' and 'sensus', the root words, also developed a large range of meanings. 'Sentire', in its most general signification, means simply 'to be aware'. According to Lewis and Short in their Latin Dictionary, it is used primarily in reference to physical awareness: it means 'to discern by the senses; to feel, hear, see, etc.; to perceive, be sensible of'. But it can also refer to 'mental' awareness: it means (with a 'mental' connotation) 'to feel, perceive, observe, notice'; and thus, by transference '(in consequence of mental perception) to think, deem, judge, opine, imagine, suppose'. 'Sensus', the primary meaning of which is given as 'the faculty or power of perceiving, perception, feeling, sensation, sense, etc.' can also be used with either a corporeal or mental connotation. Thus it can refer to a simple physical sensation or perception, or it can refer to a mental feeling—a 'sentiment, emotion, [or] affection'. As 'sensus communis' it acquires the meaning, 'the common feelings of humanity, the moral sense, taste, discretion, tact', and something very like our own 'common sense'. Eventually it comes to denote 'understanding, mind, reason'.

The primary ambiguity in 'sentire' and 'sensus' is that they can be used to refer either to simple physical awareness, to simple mental awareness (if either of these 'pure' states can ever be said to exist), or to an awareness in which elements of both are present. They can refer either to feeling (in the emotional rather than the sensory meaning of the word), or to thinking or to states of consciousness in which both partake. They can refer to the process or power of thinking and feeling, and also to its result—to activities and also to states.

It may be worth noting that the word 'wit' is similarly ambiguous. Nowadays it has the general association of intellectual liveliness— 'always with reference to the utterance of brilliant or sparkling things in an amusing way' (O.E.D.). And indeed it seems (in its substantive form) always to have had thought rather than feeling connotations. The first (and now obsolete) meaning given by the O.E.D. is 'the seat of consciousness or thought, the mind'. But 'wit' also at one time commonly signified corporeal sense—'any one of certain particular faculties of perception, classified as outer (out-

25 This is the last of the eight meanings given by Johnson in his Dictionary. The full set of definitions is interesting, especially (in this context) senses 4 and 5: '1. Having the power of perceiving by the senses. 2. Perceptible by the senses. 3. Perceived by the mind. 4. Perceiving by either mind or senses; having perception by the mind or senses. 5. Having moral perception; having the quality of being affected by moral good or ill. 6. Having quick intellectual feeling; being easily or strongly affected. 7. Convinced; persuaded. A low use. 8. In low conversation it has sometimes the sense of reasonable; judicious; wise'.

ward) or *bodily* and *inner* (*inward*) or *ghostly,* and commonly reckoned as five' (*O.E.D.*). There was also a phrase, 'common wit', which corresponded exactly to 'common sense' in the meaning it once had of 'an "internal" sense . . . regarded as the common bond or centre of the five senses, in which the various impressions received were reduced to the unity of a common consciousness' (*O.E.D.*). This usage of 'wit' survives vestigially in phrases such as 'keeping your wits about you', and 'being scared out of your wits'.

That both 'sense' and 'wit' should exhibit this fundamental ambiguity suggests first of all that whatever it is they refer to is not easy to define. And the questions implicit in the notion of consciousness are admittedly some of the most obdurate in philosophy. The existence of the ambiguity also suggests that at least some of the distinctions we commonly attempt to make between apparently different aspects of consciousness are at best artificial and at worst misleading. Is there in fact a real difference between thinking and feeling? With the problems involved in answering this question Hume inevitably found himself concerned in both the epistemological and the moral areas of his inquiry. And in attempting to grapple with these problems he relied to an extent which has not, I think, been sufficiently recognised on the ambiguities inherent in the word 'sentiment'.

Let us look first at the way in which the word functions in Hume's attempt to explain how we can distinguish fiction from belief.

Hume's notion of belief, while crucial to his general position, is not simple—although it appears to be—and his account of it is not completely consistent. It is not surprising then that it should raise a number of problems. In his attempt to cope with some of these Hume found the word 'sentiment' extremely useful. That he should have done this tells us something not only about Hume's theory, but also about the word.

Hume deals extensively with belief in three places: Book I, Part III, Sections vii-x of the *Treatise*; the Appendix to the *Treatise*; and Section V, Part ii of *An Enquiry Concerning Human Understanding.* Two things, so far as I am concerned, are interesting about the way in which he presents his theory in these three places. First, he becomes to some extent less rather than more confident as he goes on; second, the word 'sentiment' is used with increasing frequency. It does not appear at all in the account of belief given in the main body of the *Treatise*; it is used fairly freely in the Appendix; and it emerges as the key term in Hume's final statement of the problem in *An Enquiry Concerning Human Understanding.*

John Passmore has pointed out that as Hume develops his theory of belief (which he at first asserts is simply a certain kind of feeling),

> belief [comes] to have an honorific meaning, to suggest *reasonableness* . . . Thus, what set out to be a theory of belief, in something like the ordinary sense of the word, [becomes], with no explicit acknowledgement of that fact, a theory of what it is 'rational' to believe.[26]

Since 'sentiment' can suggest rationality as well as feeling it is not surprising that Hume should have come to rely on the word more and more.

In trying to account for belief Hume's difficulty is twofold. First, he faces the problem of giving, within the limits of his own philosophical terminology, a coherent explanation of why we believe in the independent and continuing existence of a world related to but distinct from that which is immediately present to us in our perceptions. Assuming that such a world exists, a second problem arises: how do we explain our ability to distinguish those of our perceptions which are perceptions of the real world from those of our perceptions which are not?

> All the perceptions of the human mind [according to Hume] resolve themselves into two distinct kinds . . . IMPRESSIONS and IDEAS . . . Those perceptions which enter with most force and violence, we may name *impressions*; and under this name I comprehend all our sensations, passions and emotions, as they make their first appearance in the soul. By *ideas* I mean the faint images of these in thinking and reasoning. . . .[27]

Some of our ideas about the world are true, others—hallucinations, illusions, or dreams, for instance—are not. How can we account for the capacity we apparently possess to distinguish true ideas—'beliefs'—from the fictions of the imagination or fancy?

Hume's disposition of the first problem is, finally, to assert that it is in logical terms unanswerable. Theoretically he assents to the phenomenalist position: 'nothing is ever really present to the mind, besides its own perceptions'.[28] But he refuses to accept, as Berkeley did, what appears to be the implication of this assumption, namely, that perceptions and the minds on which they depend for their occurrence are all that exist. Berkeley's arguments, he says in a beautifully economical phrase, *'admit of no answer and produce no conviction'*.[29] Hume has no *psychological* doubt of 'the continu'd existence of external objects when absent from the senses',[30] but he

---

[26] *Hume's Intentions*, Cambridge, 1952, pp. 62-3.
[27] *Treatise*, Bk I, Pt I, Sect. i, p. 1.
[28] Ibid., Pt IV, Sect. ii, p. 197.
[29] *Essential Works*, p. 159, n. 1 (*An Enquiry Concerning Human Understanding*, Sect. XII, Pt i).
[30] *Treatise*, Bk I, Pt IV, Sect. vii, p. 266.

does doubt whether this continued and independent existence can ever be finally demonstrated:

> The sceptic . . . must assent to the principle concerning the existence of body, tho' he cannot pretend by any arguments of philosophy to maintain its veracity . . . We may well ask, *what causes induce us to believe in the existence of body?* but 'tis in vain to ask, *whether there be body or not?* That is a point, which we must take for granted in all our reasonings.[31]

To take this for granted while also accepting the phenomenalist assumption must inevitably lead to dualism, the theory of 'double existence': 'the monstrous offspring of two principles, which are contrary to each other, which are both at once embrac'd by the mind, and which are unable mutually to destroy each other'.[32] But the monstrosity of the situation does not worry us for long: 'carelessness and in-attention'[33] provide the remedy; and if Hume ever allowed the contemplation of the problem to throw him into a 'philosophical melancholy and delirium', he had a simple avenue of escape: 'I dine, I play a game of back-gammon, I converse, and am merry with my friends'.[34]

The second problem is psychological rather than philosophical; and Hume clearly feels that here a solution may be arrived at which, empirically at least, will be more satisfying. 'Nature is obstinate, and will not quit the field, however strongly attack'd by reason'.[35] He therefore appeals to nature, and his appeal, in essence, is as crude and as effective as Dr Johnson's kicking of the stone. Our impressions of the real world, he asserts, just *feel* different from any other process of the understanding; a 'real perception' has a quality, 'call it *firmness,* or *solidity,* or *force,* or *vivacity,* with which the mind reflects upon it, and is assur'd of its present existence'.[36]

Moreover, the 'force or vivacity' which distinctively characterises our perceptions of the real world is communicated to the ideas we form of these impressions. Belief can therefore be defined as 'a lively idea produc'd by a relation to a present impression'.[37] Hume also suggests that the impressions of the real world and the ideas generated by such impressions are observed to fall together in a systematic way, and this system 'we are pleas'd to call a *reality*'.[38] Speaking of the idea which he has of Rome, he says:

31 Ibid., Sect. ii, p. 187.
32 Ibid., p. 215.
33 Ibid., p. 218.
34 Ibid., Sect. vii, p. 269.
35 Ibid., Sect. ii, p. 215.
36 Ibid., Pt III, Sect. ix, p. 106.
37 Ibid., Sect. vii, p. 97.
38 Ibid., Sect. ix, p. 108.

> All this, and every thing else, which I believe, are nothing but ideas; tho' by their force and settled order arising from custom and the relation of cause and effect, they distinguish themselves from the other ideas, which are merely the offspring of the imagination.[39]

The point, of course, as Hume himself asserts, is that the 'settled order', the 'constancy' and 'coherence', belong not merely to the ideas which constitute belief but also to the original impressions from which they are derived. We discriminate amongst our experiences as they occur; and our impressions of reality are not simply feelings, but feelings which are inevitably accompanied by a process of judgment. Belief, as Hume puts it, has something to do with 'the manner, in which we conceive any object'.[40] As a footnote to the paragraph in which this statement occurs, he observes that it is a

> very remarkable error [to divide] the acts of the understanding, into *conception, judgment* and *reasoning* . . . whether we consider a single object, or several; whether we dwell on these objects or run from them to others; and in whatever form or order we survey them, the act of the mind exceeds not a simple conception; and the only remarkable difference, which occurs on this occasion, is, when we join belief to the conception, and are persuaded of the truth of what we conceive. This act of the mind has never yet been explained by any philosopher; and therefore I am at liberty to propose my hypothesis concerning it.[41]

John Passmore has remarked that, 'although it appears in a foot-note, this conflation is of great importance to Hume. It enables him to regard "X exists" as a judgment, although it contains, on his view, no more than the single idea "X".'[42] It also implies, it seems to me, a number of things which Hume had neither the equipment, nor, perhaps, the inclination to follow up. As Antony Flew has observed, 'This is a place where Hume's position is damaged by the deficiencies of the account of thinking which he inherited from his predecessors'.[43] To consider fully the complexity of the process by which we distinguish belief from fiction must lead inevitably to a critical examination of the crudely atomistic model of consciousness from which Hume's impressions and ideas are drawn, and also of the faculty theory of the understanding which he used with such insouciant inconsistency. As well, it could involve one in a radical reconsideration of the general theory of phenomenalism.

39 Ibid.
40 Ibid., Sect. vii, p. 96.
41 Ibid., n. 1.
42 *Hume's Intentions*, p. 21.
43 *Hume's Philosophy of Belief: A Study of his First Inquiry*, London, 1961, p. 102.

Hume recognised the complexity of the process, but was unable to give an account of it which was really satisfying in either logical or psychological terms. Instead he merely asserts that belief is a very special sort of feeling, one with which judgment is inevitably mingled. He does not tell us, as Kemp Smith states,[44] that belief is a passion. The word he finally settles for in the account he gives of belief in *An Enquiry Concerning Human Understanding* is 'sentiment'.

> . . . the difference between *fiction* and *belief* lies in some sentiment or feeling, which is annexed to the latter, not to the former . . . It must be excited by nature, like all other sentiments; and must arise from the particular situation, in which the mind is placed at any particular juncture. Whenever any object is presented to the memory or senses, it immediately, by the force of custom, carries the imagination to conceive that object, which is usually conjoined to it; and this conception is attended with a feeling or sentiment, different from the loose reveries of the fancy. In this consists the whole nature of belief . . .
>
> Were we to attempt a *definition* of this sentiment, we should, perhaps, find it a very difficult, if not an impossible task; in the same manner as if we should endeavour to define the feeling of cold or passion of anger, to a creature who never had any experience of these sentiments. BELIEF is the true and proper name of this feeling; and no one is ever at a loss to know the meaning of that term; because every man is every moment conscious of the sentiments represented by it. It may not, however, be improper to attempt a *description* of this sentiment . . . I say then, that belief is nothing but a more vivid, lively, forcible, firm, steady conception of an object, than what the imagination alone is ever able to attain. This variety of terms, which may seem so unphilosophical, is intended only to express that act of the mind, which renders realities, or what is taken for such, more present to us than fictions, causes them to weigh more in the thought, and gives them a superior influence on the passions and the imagination. Provided we agree about the thing, it is needless to dispute about the terms . . . belief consists not in the peculiar nature or order of ideas, but in the *manner* of their conception, and in their *feeling* to the mind. I confess, that it is impossible perfectly to explain this feeling or manner of conception. We may make use of words, which express something near it. But its true and proper name . . . is *belief*; which is a term, that every one sufficiently understands in common life. And in philosophy, we can go no further than

44 *The Philosophy of David Hume*, p. 11. The passage in full runs as follows: ' "Passion" is Hume's most general title for the instincts, propensities, feelings, emotions and sentiments, as well as for the passions ordinarily so called; and belief, he teaches, is a passion'.

102

assert, that *belief* is something felt by the mind, which distinguishes the ideas of the judgment from the fictions of the imagination.[45]

He sums up, taking in, as he says, 'the whole compass of this doctrine' with a brief recapitulatory definition of 'the sentiment of belief' in which the word 'feeling' does not appear at all.

This is a lengthy passage, but I have quoted it because it seems to me to illustrate two things with remarkable clarity: first, Hume's quite extraordinary (and also, one must admit, very engaging) uneasiness—his account of belief is full of special pleading, and is basically one long appeal to ordinary experience: second, the extent to which 'sentiment' is made to bear the weight of the case he is trying to present. Belief is a process in which feeling and thinking are inextricably bound up: it is, in short, a 'sentiment'.

'Sentiment' comes to play an even more important role in Hume's moral theory. It is also a much more complicated one; and in attempting to deal with it briefly I must inevitably give a crudely and probably unfairly oversimplified account of Hume's position. What concerns me most, however, is not so much the details of his theory as the general tendency of his argument, and the way this seems to me to be reflected, at certain key points, in his use of 'sentiment'.

It will be generally agreed, I imagine, that although the substance of Hume's argument in the *Treatise* and *An Enquiry Concerning the Principles of Morals* is the same, the emphasis in each is different. In the *Treatise* Hume's main concern seems to be to establish the primacy of feeling, to demonstrate that reason is the slave of the passions and that moral sentiments are in essence no different from any other pleasure-pain responses. He discusses the part played by reason in arriving at moral judgments, but it would be fair to say that this is not where the main weight of his argument falls. In the *Enquiry,* however, he pays much more attention to reason. He abandons—or at least does not reiterate—the notion, advanced in the *Treatise,* that what we sometimes take for the determinations of the reason in moral situations are in reality the operation of passions so calm that they seem to excite no emotion. Instead he suggests

> that *reason* and *sentiment* concur in almost all moral determinations and conclusions. The final sentence, it is probable, which pronounces characters and actions amiable or odious,

---

[45] *Essential Works,* p. 79 (op. cit., Sect. V, Pt ii). This is an expanded version of a passage included in the Appendix to the *Treatise* (pp. 628-9).

praise-worthy or blameable . . . depends on some internal sense or feeling, which nature has made universal in the whole species. For what else can have an influence of this nature? But in order to pave the way for such a sentiment, and give a proper discernment of its object, it is often necessary, we find, that much reasoning should precede, that nice distinctions be made, just conclusions drawn, distant comparisons formed, complicated relations examined, and general facts fixed and ascertained.[46]

Hume is careful to insist that 'the final sentence . . . depends on . . . feeling', but the general effect of his argument is to assert that for all practical purposes it is almost impossible for this feeling to arise unless it is preceded or accompanied by a process of reasoning. Thus while a moral sentiment is clearly a feeling, it is a very special kind of feeling; so special, indeed, that its operations become almost indistinguishable from what most people would understand as the operations of reason.[47]

The implications of the moral and aesthetic sense hypothesis are completely subjectivist. There is no quality in the circle, Hume tells us, which makes it beautiful, and no quality in gratitude which makes it good. Beautiful and good are simply words which describe the feelings which the circle and gratitude evoke in the man who contemplates them; and there would seem to be no reason why my feelings should be the same as yours. Hume asserts, however, to put it crudely, that all the best people do in fact have the same feelings:

> The notion of morals, implies some sentiment common to all mankind, which recommends the same object to general approbation, and makes every man, or most men, agree in the same opinion or decision concerning it.[48]

And he also asserts that the main object which arouses this general approbation is the general good: 'every thing, which contributes to the happiness of society, recommends itself directly to our approbation and good will. Here is a principle which accounts, in great part, for the origin of morality'.[49] A man who cannot understand this (by the exercise of reason) or who does not respond with the right feelings, lacks 'humanity'. 'All his sentiments must be inverted,

---

[46] Ibid., p. 183 (op. cit., Sect. I).

[47] Cf. Kemp Smith's comment: 'Hume makes no distinction between belief and judgment, or indeed between judgment and reasoning' (*The Philosophy of David Hume*, p. 87).

[48] *Essential Works*, p. 255 (*An Enquiry Concerning the Principles of Morals*, Sect. IX, Pt i).

[49] Ibid., p. 216 (*An Enquiry Concerning the Principles of Morals*, Sect. V, Pt ii).

and directly opposite to those which prevail in the human species'.[50]
What Hume gives to subjectivism with the one hand by his
doctrine of the primacy of feeling, he takes away with the other by
his assertion that all the right people have the right feelings. He
never seriously considers the notion that the right feelings for some
people may in fact not be aroused by the social virtues; that the
good of the individual may not always coincide with the good of
society.

In this he is at one with Shaftesbury and Hutcheson, the earlier
advocates of the moral sense. Their fine internal feelings responded
with pleasure to benevolence and with pain to ingratitude; by the
exercise of reason they arrived at the conclusion that societies
functioned best when men were benevolent; and empirical observation informed them that men—or at least the best sort of men, those
who were most rational and most sensitive—were naturally benevolent and sympathetic. The moral sense was assumed to function in
the same way in all men, just as the other senses did. A man might
be morally colour-blind, as it were, he might be morally deafened or
blinded; his moral palate might be corrupted by exotic foods, but
he was potentially as incapable of mistaking good for evil as he was
of mistaking red for green—or of thinking that two and two make
five. A man whose moral sense functioned properly could be
expected to act rationally. In fact the more sensitive he was to the
good and ill of himself and his society the more effectively he would
demonstrate his humanity and therefore his rationality—'for of the
reality of such a good and ill', says Shaftesbury, in a most revealing
phrase, 'no *rational* creature can be *insensible*'.[51]

Now this is not what Hume is saying; but in some ways he might
as well be. No normal human being, according to Hume, can have
the wrong sentiments about the things Shaftesbury would assume
to possess the qualities of good or evil. Thus in Hume's ethical
theory, especially as it is presented in the *Enquiry*, 'sentiment'
carries a strong connotation of rationality: a typically human moral
sentiment is always a reasonable feeling.

But it *is* essentially a feeling, not a rational judgment: this Hume

[50] Ibid., p. 222 (*An Enquiry Concerning the Principles of Morals*, Sect. V,
Pt ii). The relevant passage runs as follows: 'A creature, absolutely malicious
and spiteful, were there any such in nature, must be worse than indifferent to
the images of vice and virtue. All his sentiments must be inverted, and directly
opposite to those, which prevail in the human species. Whatever contributes
to the good of mankind, as it crosses the bent of his wishes and desires, must
produce uneasiness and disapprobation; and on the contrary, whatever is the
source of disorder and misery in society, must, for the same reason be regarded
with pleasure and complacency'.
[51] 'An Inquiry Concerning Virtue or Merit', in J. M. Robertson (ed.), *Characteristics of Men, Manners, Opinions, Times* . . . Vol. I, London, 1900, p. 258.
My italics.

emphasised. And in insisting that a sentiment was only a feeling he was, as Thomas Reid pointed out, working against the grain of the language:

> When Mr. Hume derives moral distinctions from a moral sense, I agree with him in words, but we differ about the meaning of the word *sense*. Every power to which the name of a sense has been given, is a power of judging of the objects of that sense . . . the moral sense therefore is the power of judging in morals. But Mr. Hume will have the moral sense to be only a power of feeling, without judging: This I take to be an abuse of a word.
>
> Authors who place moral approbation in feeling only, very often use the word *sentiment*, to express feeling without judgment. This I take likewise to be an abuse of a word. Our moral determinations may, with propriety, be called *moral sentiments*. For the word *sentiment*, in the English Language, never, as I conceive, signifies mere feeling, but judgment accompanied by feeling.[52]

Unlike some of Reid's comments on Hume, this observation seems to me well justified. Hume wished to preserve his hypothesis that all sentiments were essentially feelings; but the more thoroughly he analysed the way in which moral sentiments operate the more convincingly he demonstrated that some process of reasoning is inevitably—or almost inevitably—involved in their operation. In so far as a sentiment is a judgment this seems inescapable.

This confusion is probably inherent in all moral sense theories anyway. Hume merely makes it more obvious (once you see it) because of the vigour, subtlety, and comprehensiveness with which he developed the argument from the position already established by Hutcheson. At the same time he also revealed with unprecedented clarity the extent to which the benevolist and moral sense theory of human behaviour rests on a very simple view of man and society. The weakest point in Hume's ethical theory is its anthropological *naïveté*. By his use of the word 'sentiment', Hume gives an appearance of consistency to his argument: *An Enquiry Concerning the Principles of Morals* is a most lucid and persuasive piece of work. But by using 'sentiment' in this way, he left the word in a peculiarly exposed position. Questions of influence are always very difficult to grapple with, but it seems obvious that he helped to contribute to the latent semantic instability of the word, an instability which was certainly not obvious in 1751 when he published *An Enquiry Concerning the Principles of Morals*. 'Sentiment' and 'sentimental' then carried the most favourable of connotations; but by the end of the century the adjective (which Hume does not seem ever to have

[52] *Essays on the Active Powers of Man*, Vol. V, 1788, p. 7 (quoted in D. D. Raphael, *The Moral Sense*, Oxford, 1947, p. 153).

used) had acquired that suggestion of the sham, the shallow, and the insincere which it bears today; and the noun had also declined considerably in status.

The reasons which lie behind this very fascinating development are highly complex and puzzling. Hume's use of the word 'sentiment' obviously must have played some part in what happened. Whatever he may have been trying to say, the implications of his moral theory are that although moral sentiments are feelings, are the result of individual, pleasure-pain responses, they have the force, in a rational creature—especially an educated, civilised being—of considered (in the vulgar sense, 'reasoned') judgments. This leaves the notion in an apparently powerful but in fact extremely vulnerable position—and it was this vulnerability which became increasingly obvious after the 1760s. It is impossible to assess just how far Hume helped to bring about the decline of sentimentalism. But by the way in which he developed the moral sense theory, and especially by the way in which he employed the term 'sentiment', he made an obviously significant contribution to it.

Johnson's Neglected Muse: The Drama

Roy S. Wolper

Owing to Johnson's bruising language, his antipathies to the drama resound as forcefully today as they did some two hundred years ago. For example:

> On Garrick's showing Johnson a magnificent library full of books in most elegant bindings, the Doctor began running over the volumes in his usual rough and negligent manner; which was, by opening the book so wide as almost to break the back of it, and then flung them down one by one on the floor with contempt. 'Zounds,' said Garrick, 'why, what are you about? you'll spoil all my books.' 'No, Sir,' replied Johnson, 'I have done nothing but treat a pack of *silly plays* in fops' dresses just as they deserve; but I see no *books*.'[1]

Or:

> 'Why, there is no making you read a play,' said Mrs. Thrale, 'neither of your own, or any other person. What trouble had I to make you hear Murphy's *Know your own Mind*! "Read rapidly, read rapidly," you cried, and then took out your watch to see how long I was about it!'[2]

One could, of course, present more examples, but they (as well as the two I chose) can be explained away;[3] it is unfortunate and human, I think, that the tantrum and insult are cherished. Actually, Johnson read and was touched by plays throughout his life, from early boyhood when he was terrified by Shakespeare[4] to his last year when he selected again an old favourite, Euripides.[5] Most of

[1] James Boswell, *The Life of Samuel Johnson, LL.D.*, ed. J. W. Croker, Vol. X, London, 1835, p. 125.

[2] *Diary & Letters of Madame D'Arblay*, ed. Charlotte Barrett, Vol. I, London and New York, 1904-5, pp. 90-1.

[3] Johnson's mistreatment of the books may have been due to his ambivalent affections for Garrick; his reluctance to Mrs Thrale may have occurred at one of the periods in which he did not read plays.

[4] James Boswell, *The Life of Samuel Johnson* (hereafter cited as *Life*), ed. G. B. Hill, rev. and enlarged L. F. Powell, Vol. I, Oxford, 1934-50, p. 70.

[5] *Life*, Vol. IV, p. 311.

the reading was simply for pleasure, when he was devouring books of all sorts. His later judgments—those which we have come to know so well—were nearly always dredged out of the sea of memory. After he had assessed Rowe for his *Lives,* he told Nichols complacently that he 'had not read one of Rowe's Plays for thirty years'![6] In his Life of Congreve he admitted that 'since I inspected them [the plays] many years have passed'.[7] Similarly, quotations from the *Dictionary* reach back to his Oxford days when he went through the plays of Philips and Smith and Addison and others.[8]

The range of his dramatic reading helps reveal his appetite. Although sometimes fond of playing down his knowledge of foreign languages and literatures, he had read considerably in earlier non-English drama. He knew Sophocles, Aeschylus, Euripides, and may have known Aristophanes; he was well acquainted with the Roman comedic dramatists, Plautus and Terence, and the tragedians, Seneca and Menander. He read in the Spanish and French drama; he saw rightly that Corneille, Racine, and Molière were able to 'go round the world'.[9] In his reading of English drama there appear to be some omissions (like the Carolineans Ford, Massinger, Webster), although it is difficult to be certain of this for no one uses all of his reading. None the less, Johnson knew the major plays of the leading dramatists of almost all eras—Kyd, Shakespeare, Jonson, Congreve, Vanbrugh, Farquhar, Dryden, Lee, Otway, Southerne, Rowe, Addison, Goldsmith, Sheridan—as well as the smaller fish—Preston, Granville, Philips, Thomson, Young, Smith, Moore, Mason, and many more like them.[10] Yet a name is not an adequate signpost. To cite a few examples: he had read all of Shakespeare, at the least, fifteen of Dryden's plays, all seven of Rowe's tragedies, all of Congreve's comedies, at least a half dozen of Euripides's plays. One, then, has to be wary of talking about Johnson's shortcomings or gaps in drama. For example, Joseph Epes Brown wrote, 'Johnson's knowledge and love of the classics were profound', and modified it with the note, 'with the notable exception of Greek drama'.[11] Such

[6] *The Works of Samuel Johnson, LL.D.* (hereafter cited as *Works*), ed. A. Chalmers, Vol. X, London, 1810, p. 72.

[7] Samuel Johnson, *Lives of the English Poets,* ed. G. B. Hill, Vol. II, Oxford, 1905, p. 228.

[8] A. L. Reade, *Johnsonian Gleanings,* Vol. V, App. K, London, 1909-52, pp. 213-29.

[9] *Life,* Vol. V, p. 311.

[10] For his reading in the early English drama, see W. B. C. Watkins, *Johnson and English Poetry before 1660,* Princeton, 1936, esp. pp. 58-66; for much of his reading in the Restoration and the eighteenth century, see Johnson's *Lives* and the unpublished dissertation, Cornell, 1939, by Lewis Freed, 'The Sources of Johnson's Dictionary'.

[11] J. E. Brown (ed.), *The Critical Opinions of Samuel Johnson,* Vol. I, Princeton, 1926, p. xxii.

statements, to echo Fanny Burney, are *'too round'*. Johnson's reading gave him a door into comedy, tragedy, tragicomedy, closet tragedy, opera, farce, the history play, the masque, the morality, the scholastic Latin play, the *entr'acte* diversions, the unpublishable play; it enabled him to seize the heart of earlier drama and to write a brief poetic history that is still used by literary scholars[12] (I am, of course, referring to his *Prologue* of 1747), as well as to be familiar with sixteen of the twenty most popular plays appearing at the patent theatres during Garrick's time.

Yet no survey of reading, by itself, can indicate the nearness of the drama. Plays were always at Johnson's fingertips. To illustrate Dryden's profundity, Johnson repeated 'some fine lines on love' from *Tyrannick Love*.[13] To discriminate between characters of nature and characters of manners, Johnson chose as his example Sir Francis Wronghead from *The Provok'd Husband* and 'repeated, very happily, all Sir Francis's credulous account to Manly of his being with "the great men", and securing a place'.[14] He once took Hannah More's hand and quoted many passages from *The Fair Penitent* 'with no small enthusiasm'.[15] And from the Senecan tragedies, *Troades, Hippolytus,* and *Hercules Furens,* came mottoes for his essays.[16]

Lines from plays rain through his conversation. Contemporaries were caught up (and trussed forever) in dramatic verse: Garrick was 'a poor player, who frets and struts his hour upon the stage';[17] Capell, a critic who 'doth gabble monstrously';[18] Miss Aiken, a precocious woman doomed 'To suckle fools, and chronicle small-beer'.[19] In controversy the lines became weapons. Johnson, after having been attacked with coarse raillery, echoed Kent in his answer, 'Sir, your wife, *under pretence of keeping a bawdy-house,* is a receiver of stolen goods'.[20] Arguing with Mrs Knowles about the impossibility of equality among men and women, Johnson quoted Dogberry, 'If two men ride on a horse, one must ride behind'.[21] One is forced to admire the weaponry, if not the logic.

The dramatic lines frequently captured and framed a cherished

---

[12] For one example, see A. S. Downer, *The British Drama: A Handbook and Brief Chronicle,* New York, 1950, pp. 383-4.

[13] *Life,* Vol. II, p. 85 and n. 3.

[14] Ibid., p. 50.

[15] Hannah More, 'Anecdotes', in *Johnsonian Miscellanies (J. Misc.),* ed. G. B. Hill, Vol. II, Oxford, 1897, p. 197.

[16] See the mottoes of *Adventurer* Nos. 40, 62, 111, and of *Rambler* Nos. 130, 178, 205.

[17] *Life,* Vol. II, p. 92 (from *Macbeth,* Act V, Sc. v).

[18] Ibid., Vol. IV, p. 5 (from *The Tempest,* Act I, Sc. ii).

[19] Ibid., Vol. II, p. 408 (from *Othello,* Act II, Sc. i).

[20] Ibid., Vol. IV, p. 26 (from *King Lear,* Act II, Sc. ii).

[21] Ibid., Vol. III, p. 287 (from *Much Ado About Nothing,* Act III, Sc. v).

sentiment of his. The dowry of a religious wife was, he said, stated 'beautifully' by Alcmena to her husband.

Sed pudicitiam, et pudorem, et sedatum cupidinem,
Deum metum, parentum amorem, et cognatum concordiam;
Tibi morigera, atque ut munifica sim bonis, prosim probis.[22]

His belief that there was more to be endured than enjoyed in life found its anatomy in a couplet of *Aureng-Zebe* he 'frequently quoted':

Strange cozenage! none would live past years again,
Yet all hope pleasure from what still remain.[23]

Much of the time the drama was nothing more than a backdrop to fun. Johnson, inviting Boswell to remain with him, used the charming indirection of a Verona girl, 'Get you gone *in*'.[24] He ironically talked of the loss of a wife with a phrase from *Andria*, '*Hinc illæ lachrymæ*'.[25] On the Scotland heath, he parodied the hail of the witches to Boswell-Macbeth: 'All hail Dalblair! hail to thee, Laird of Auchinleck!'[26] And when told that the wind was against a journey, Johnson said 'A Wind, or not a Wind? that is the question'.[27]

Even in his letters, where he most likely would be relaxed, dramatic quotation is plentiful. Often the good-natured man of conversation is revealed. To an indolent Mrs Thrale he echoed Falstaff and chided, 'Call you this backing your Friends?'[28] He put away the thought of tedious nights with Katharine's cheerful 'But a light heart &c [lives long]'.[29] He praised Streatham with the playful hyperbole from *Double Falsehood*: '*None but itself can be its parallel*'.[30] And, too ill and weak to get on his feet for visitors, he ironically quoted *Cato*, '*Painful pre-eminence*'.[31] Since he was aware of his own aging, the letters have a ganglia of quotations concerning mutability: 'So rolls the world away'; 'Omnium rerum vicissitudo'; 'To morrow and to morrow'; 'I am old, I am old'.[32] The death of

22 William Seward, 'Anecdotes', in *J. Misc.*, Vol. II, p. 309 (from Plautus, *Amphytrio*, Act II, Sc. ii).

23 *Life*, Vol. II, pp. 124-5 (from Dryden, *Aureng-Zebe*, Act IV, Sc. i).

24 Ibid., p. 109 (from *Two Gentlemen of Verona*, Act III, Sc. i).

25 G. Steevens, 'Anecdotes', in *J. Misc.*, Vol. II, p. 317 (from Terence, *Andria*, Act I, Sc. i).

26 *Life*, Vol. V, p. 116 (from *Macbeth*, Act I, Sc. iii).

27 Ibid., p. 279 (from *Hamlet*, Act III, Sc. i).

28 *The Letters of Samuel Johnson* (hereafter cited as *Letters*), ed. R. W. Chapman, Oxford, 1952, No. 553 (from *King Henry the Fourth*, Pt I, Act II, Sc. iv).

29 Ibid., No. 536 (from *Love's Labour's Lost*, Act V, Sc. ii).

30 Ibid., No. 616 (from Theobald, *Double Falsehood*, Act III, Sc. i).

31 Ibid., No. 485 (from Addison, *Cato*, Act III, Sc. v).

32 See ibid., Nos. 267 (from *Hamlet*, Act III, Sc. ii), 506 (from Terence, *Eunuchus*, Act II, Sc. ii), 266 (from *Macbeth*, Act V, Sc. v), 552 (from *King Henry the Fourth*, Pt II, Act II, Sc. iv), respectively.

friends often impelled the heightened phrase of a dramatist. Foote's death recalled, 'Life . . . is a shuttle'.[33] After Mrs Williams had died, Johnson wrote to Mrs Thrale of her:

> Thou thy weary task hast done
> Home art gone, and ta'en thy wages.[34]

Johnson was not always concerned about the aptness of the speech; frequently the quotations were an extension of the dramatis personae, and so Foresight and Falstaff and Harpagon and Doodle and Hamlet walk through his letters and conversation. Because the casts were always close to him, Johnson likened his friends to them. To him, Boswell became a faithful Griffith;[35] Foote, a honey-tongued Biron;[36] Dr Levet, a 'scorched up' Portia.[37] He warned Mrs Thrale, 'do not play Agnes',[38] and another time asked, 'Dare you answer me as Brutus answered his evil genius?'[39] Johnson, of course, saw himself in this wise and assumed various costumes himself. A missing book, he admitted, might have made him roar 'as Othello did for his handkerchief';[40] unnecessary and frivolous questions, he said, often made him feel like an enraged Macbeth;[41] in his impatience for spring, he wrote, 'I . . . am ready like Almanzor to bid the Sun *fly swiftly* and *leave weeks and months behind him*'.[42] To Langton he said, 'I think I am like Squire Richard in "The Journey to London", *"I'm never strange in a strange place"*.'[43] He once 'brightened into gay humour' and addressed Mrs Williams and Mrs Hall as Lucy and Polly: 'But two at a time there's no mortal can bear'. 'What, Sir,' said Boswell, who saw Johnson's little drama, 'are you going to turn Captain Macheath?' Boswell went on, 'There was something as pleasantly ludicrous in this scene as can be imagined'.[44]

The easy familiarity should not blind us. Some of his greatest intensity came out of drama, especially the tragedies, since they called forth unnatural worlds congenial to what Boswell called his 'habitual gloomy cast of thought'. Johnson believed that Congreve's

[33] Ibid., No. 561 (from *The Merry Wives of Windsor*, Act V, Sc. i).
[34] Ibid., No. 883 (from *Cymbeline*, Act IV, Sc. ii).
[35] Ibid., No. 329 (from *King Henry the Eighth*).
[36] Hester Lynch Piozzi (Thrale), 'Anecdotes', in *J. Misc.*, Vol. I, p. 265 (from *Love's Labour's Lost*).
[37] John Hawkins, 'Life of Johnson', in *J. Misc.*, Vol. II, p. 111 (from *Julius Caesar*).
[38] *Letters*, No. 558 (from Molière, *L'Ecole des Femmes*).
[39] Ibid., No. 552.
[40] Hawkins, 'Life of Johnson', p. 130.
[41] John Hoole, 'Narrative', in *J. Misc.*, Vol. II, p. 151.
[42] *Letters*, No. 926 (from Dryden, *The Conquest of Granada*).
[43] *Life*, Vol. IV, p. 284 (from Vanbrugh, *The Provok'd Husband*).
[44] Ibid., p. 95.

description of the temple in *The Mourning Bride* was 'the finest poetical passage he had ever read'.[45] Of the world of discord in *Macbeth* where Hecate was celebrated, where 'wither'd murder' prowled, where one feared the prating stones, Johnson wrote that it was 'perhaps the most striking [image] that poetry can produce'.[46] Knowing his continual sense of guilt, one perhaps understands why the only passage that Mrs Thrale ever heard him 'applaud as particularly tender in any common book' was Jane Shore's exclamation, 'Forgive me! but forgive me!'[47] Under 'great pressure of mind' that he might die, Johnson called forth to Dr Brocklesby Macbeth's plea:

> Canst thou not minister to a mind diseas'd; . . .
> And with some sweet oblivious antidote,
> Cleanse the full bosom of that perilous stuff,
> Which weighs upon the heart?[48]

And when he was so concerned with the thought of death that he disdained joining with company and sat by himself, he repeated Claudio's fears:

> Ay, but to die and go we know not where;
> To lie in cold obstruction and to rot;
> This sensible warm motion to become
> A kneaded clod, and the delighted spirit
> To bathe in fiery floods.[49]

But the intense moments are, as they must be, rare: normally Johnson's pleasures were smaller and more constant. As a spectator, he chose comedies, and not distinguished ones at that; yet he enjoyed an Oakley or a Don Felix or a Flora or a Harry Wildair on stage. He was well aware of the sparkle of a performed comedy. *The Jealous Wife*, 'though not written with much genius', was 'so well adapted to the stage, and so well exhibited by the actors, that it was crowded for near twenty nights'.[50] Of *High Life Below Stairs* he said, 'Here is a Farce, which is really very diverting when you see it acted; and yet one may read it, and not know that one has been reading any thing at all'.[51] (It is time we disentangled ourselves from the stereotype of the Johnson 'who neither saw nor heard'— that was an older Johnson.) The comedies enabled him—as he wrote

---

45 Ibid., Vol. II, p. 85 (from Congreve, *The Mourning Bride*, Act II, Sc. ii).
46 'Miscellaneous Observations on the Tragedy of Macbeth', n. xx in *Works*, Vol. II, pp. 89-90.
47 Piozzi (Thrale), 'Anecdotes', pp. 283-4 (from Rowe, *Jane Shore*, Act V, Sc. i).
48 Hawkins, 'Life of Johnson', p. 122 (from *Macbeth*, Act V, Sc. iii).
49 A. Murphy, 'An Essay on the Life and Genius of Samuel Johnson, LL.D.', in *J. Misc.*, Vol. I, p. 439 (from *Measure for Measure*, Act III, Sc. i).
50 *Letters*, No. 138.
51 *Life*, Vol. IV, p. 7.

to Baretti—'to escape' from himself and the hovering Black Dog.[52] For a little, while he was in a patent theatre or in a 'lesser' one or in a converted guild hall, he was able to find 'harmless pleasure'; his contention that this description was 'the highest praise' is inflated and argumentative Johnsonese—as Boswell saw[53]—yet it suggests the gentle and pleasant diversion he found in the grimaces and antics of his Petruchios.

These comedies may be somewhat responsible for his famous conversational style—the retort that shuts off an answer—which reminds one, often, of the verbal encounters of the wits. Some of Johnson's finesse may perhaps be due to Boswellian management; yet from the *Johnsoniana*—of Seward and Mrs Thrale and others— there is no doubt that Johnson's wit and phrasing and timing and delivery were dramatically—even theatrically—effective. Interestingly, Hawkins, in describing Johnson's style, chose a comedian for his comparison: 'In the talent of humour there hardly ever was his equal, except perhaps among the old comedians, such as Tarleton, and a few others mentioned by Cibber'.[54]

In general, he was unable to arouse a suspension of disbelief for a stated tragedy; always he saw the stage, not the wild heath; Garrick, not Macbeth.[55] For the most part, he read his tragedies, letting his powerful imagination create the dramatic world. And it did. For example, Constance's grief in *King John* was 'very affecting'[56] and the pomp of Jane Grey's execution 'terrified' him.[57] Yet moments like these still, I think, suggest emotional waves, when there were, for the most part, ripples. Into his room came 'interesting' fables (like *The Fair Penitent*), fascinating psychological studies (like Iago), 'delightful' scenes (as from *The Conquest of Granada*), 'very pleasing' images (Bernardine is 'As fast lock'd up in sleep, as guiltless labour/When it lies starkly in the traveller's bones'), true pictures of life (like Othello's history of the love between himself and Desdemona (*Othello*, Act I, Sc. iii, ll. 140-70)), 'truly tragical' heroes (like Rhodogune), 'just' observations (like 'Every subject's duty is the king's, but every subject's soul is his own' (*King Henry the Fifth*, Act IV, Sc. i)).

Johnson's spectacles saw into different corners—nay, into different rooms—from those looked into by a modern critic. Yet to say, as one modern scholar has, that Johnson 'did not care particularly

52 *Letters*, No. 138.
53 *Life*, Vol. III, p. 388.
54 Hawkins, 'Life of Johnson', pp. 98-9.
55 *Private Papers of James Boswell from Malahide Castle*, ed., G. Scott and F. Pottle, Vol. IX, New York, 1928-37, p. 265.
56 Notes to Shakespeare, *King John* (Augustan Reprint Society No. 65), Los Angeles, 1957, p. 12.
57 Life of Rowe, in Johnson, *Lives of the English Poets*, Vol. II, p. 76.

for drama as drama'[58] is to be careless of history. Perception and appreciation are largely moulded and determined by the literary traditions one inherits, and can we—with our vocabulary of 'paradox', 'irony', 'ambiguity', 'tension', and so on—say that we see the drama *as drama* or say that we enjoy a play more than a Colman or a Johnson? The wide range of Johnson's response to the drama—and it encompassed mimetic, pragmatic, and aesthetic considerations—helps explain Johnson's path to Drury Lane and his appearance in the handsome waistcoat and gold-laced hat (with, most likely, dreams as golden). It also enables us to see why Johnson and Tetty liked to read plays to each other. He read the tragedies, for she 'always mouthed too much'; she read the comedies 'better than ever he heard anybody'.[59] The reading of plays together must have provided some of the most pleasing interludes in the tangle of their marriage.

One, then, is not surprised that Johnson knew and liked a crowd of actors and playwrights.[60] In this brief paper it is impossible, of course, to see the whole parade, but we can view its larger shapes. His friendships with Garrick, Murphy, Davies, Goldsmith, Savage (to name a few) were among the most enduring and intense he had; he could ask of them favours and love. Other relationships—with the elder Holland, Peg Woffington, Kemble, Kitty Clive, Henderson, Mary Porter, Cradock, Kennedy, Francis Abington, Bickerstaff, Sarah Siddons—were more casual and fragile. At times, though, many of them meant a great deal to him. Kitty Clive was 'a good thing to sit by';[61] Henderson, a pleasant and intelligent visitor;[62] Mrs Emmet, an early love;[63] Cumberland, 'a Million';[64] Hoole, an intimate friend.[65] Each friendship, of course, had its own texture, and Johnson went from Goldsmith's surrogate-father to Thomas Sheridan's verbal duellist, from Davies's man of letters as hero to Garrick's paternalistic persecutor. From his early days in the Green Room (where the flesh was white and exposed) to the later days when the oncoming stars visited him, Johnson was always in touch with dramatic people and 'was much regarded by the players'.[66]

[58] Watkins, *Johnson and English Poetry before 1660,* p. 65.
[59] Hester Lynch Thrale, *Thraliana,* ed. Katharine C. Balderston, 2nd ed. Vol. I, Oxford, 1951, p. 177.
[60] 'In truth, Garrick was a man of many careers', wrote Kalman A. Burnim in *David Garrick: Director,* Pittsburgh, 1961, p. 2, and many of Garrick's contemporaries—both actors and playwrights—had careers of clerk or man of letters or publisher, and so on.
[61] *Life,* Vol. IV, p. 7.
[62] *Gentleman's Magazine,* Vol. LXI, June 1791, p. 500.
[63] *Life,* Vol. II, p. 464.
[64] *Letters,* No. 121.
[65] *Life,* Vol. IV, p. 360.
[66] *Private Papers of James Boswell,* Vol. I, p. 128.

The time was spent with Mur or Kemble or Foote or Goldy, and dramatic matters may well have been pushed aside. Johnson had a taste of mint jelly with Mrs Abington and a cup of weak tea with Peg Woffington, talks with Mary Porter and Kemble, dinners with Davies and Goldsmith; he laughed with Foote and Kitty Clive, walked the streets with Savage and Garrick, stayed up till two or three with Thomas Sheridan and Hannah More. And the talk was of friends or children or political speeches or such daily happenings. Yet because these men and women were of the drama, the talk often went to plays (like *Dido, The Siege of Aleppo, The Recruiting Officer, Oedipus, Othello, Braganza*) and to actors and actresses (like Mary Porter, Kitty Clive, Hannah Pritchard, Garrick) and to theatrical history (like 'Who was the first dramatic writer to introduce genteel ladies upon the stage?'). The umbrella of conversation frequently covered more general dramatic topics: the relationship between an actor and his role,[67] the need of a third patent theatre,[68] the delivery of dialogue on stage,[69] the nature of flattery in drama,[70] and so on; Johnson—needless to say—did not fade into the wings. Because of these friends, he was led to see plays or to a visit backstage where the silk stockings would be tempting or to a tea where an author sang one of the songs in his play. One easily believes Boswell: 'Johnson, indeed, had thought more upon the subject of acting than might be generally supposed'.[71]

Johnson's favourite dainties were a well done leg of pork, a veal pie with plums, and an outside cut of a salt buttock of beef; yet a beefsteak pie the crust of which was made from bad butter still enticed him to a second helping. The drama was not one of his strongest passions. At times he was envious of the actors' salaries and the dramatists' fame; he never tolerated flimsy plays and poor acting; but throughout his life he always went back for second helpings.

[67] See *Life,* Vol. IV, pp. 243-4; Murphy, 'An Essay on the Life and Genius of Samuel Johnson, LL.D.', p. 457.
[68] *Life,* Vol. IV, p. 113.
[69] See *Life,* Vol. I, pp. 168-9; James Boaden (ed.), *Memoirs of the Life of John Philip Kemble,* Vol. I, London, 1825, p. 97; George Anne Bellamy, *An Apology for the Life of George Anne Bellamy,* 2nd ed., Vol. III, London, 1785, pp. 104-5.
[70] *Life,* Vol. II, pp. 233-4.
[71] Ibid., Vol. IV, p. 243.

The Muse of Mercantilism: Jago, Grainger, and Dyer

O. H. K. Spate

Often enough I have begun a paper with an expression of diffidence; never with such desperate sincerity as I do now, feeling myself a minnow among the tritons. What I have to offer is perhaps not much more than comic relief, literary chat rather than literary criticism. By profession I am, in Tickell's phrase, a mere geographer, and some part of my interest in the didactic poems of the century is as sources from which to reconstruct the historical and social geography of England. The other part is simply pleasure, either in good verse or the contortions of bad verse. I think I may have a point or two to make, but probably rather obvious ones.

Most of my subjects, perhaps all of them except John Dyer, are also mere minnows; Dyer a trout at least. There may be no very serious literary reason why a rational man should read Grainger or Jago; but there may be a good historical one. It seems to me that our vision of the past has always the risk of serious distortion if we confine our view, as all but dedicated professional scholars do, to the great figures that have survived. Because they stood, and stand, above their age, they did not necessarily stand outside it—indeed, that sort of genius usually looks a little, or more than a little, mad to his contemporaries. Johnson, for instance, in many ways seems to sum up his age with completeness, even if in some aspects through the distorting mirror of his very imperfect sympathies with romantic beginnings. And yet would Johnson himself mean so much to us without the gallery of obscure men who survive only in his own *Lives of the Poets,* and above all without the crowded stage of Boswell, where what Johnson thought is so often educed by symbiosis with or antithesis to what the ordinary educated man thought?

119

To secure a measure of historical empathy for any age, I think it is essential to realise the 'world-picture' of the average educated man, not professionally interested in the topic immediately in hand, be it Newtonian physics or the Industrial Revolution, but reasonably intelligent and up-to-date in his reading. This average, obviously, will be found more in the minor than the major writers; just as the geomorphologist finds in petty, even minute, features, dips and hillocks not even noticed by the casual traveller, clues to the evolution of landscape quite as important as those derived from towering mountains and deep gorges. The point is elegantly illustrated—not without aid from some of our poets—in the first volume of Chorley and Haggett's *The History of the Study of Landforms, or The Development of Geomorphology*—a nicely Augustan title. Without the background of minor figures the picture may be grand and imposing, but our understanding will be incomplete.

But if minors, why minors in verse? There were obviously other treatises on the wool trade than *The Fleece*; and if one is working specifically on the history of the wool trade these are essential. But not necessarily if what we want is the general view of those not professionally involved in wool; and in our period instruction might often come quite naturally in verse. I shall say more of the habit of didactic verse later, but here I must confess a merely personal taste. Bernard Shaw apologised, if that is the word for any Shavian explanation, for putting *Cashel Byron's Profession* into iambic pentameters by pointing out, with truth, that it is a lot easier to write quickly in bad blank verse than in good prose; and I find even bad verse easier going than bad prose. Though one must admit that Grainger's *The Sugar Cane* does make one sympathise for once with George II in his pathetic query as to why his subjects didn't write 'blain brose'.

So much by way of apology, though more may be needed. I would introduce the main theme by suggesting that the Whig tradition in eighteenth-century poetry is a thesis which may well offer some rewards to further exploration.

It is easy enough—a little too easy—to see the poets of the Augustan age (taking that up to, say, mid-century) as mainly a choir of singing birds nesting in the pleasant gardens of Twickenham and Stowe, with an ugly off-stage chatter of London gutter-sparrows in Grub Street, and a few migrants between the two, such as Gay and Matthew Green and perhaps Bramston. Of course, unless one were so hopelessly old-fashioned as the Countess of Winchelsea, so new-fashioned as Shenstone, or so simply unfashionable as Somerville, one had to have a firm *pied à terre* in Town; but this country house and well endowed rectory sector represented a Tory tradition,

Country Party if not quite Cavalier. This was true whether it was fighting a rear-guard action in defence of traditional values, as in *The Dunciad,* or complacently accepting the comforts of its little world, as in the host of minors collected in Dodsley. Yet alongside was developing a Whig tradition, not so much a Town as a City party. While it is true that my poets themselves are in the fifties and sixties—*The Fleece,* 1757, *The Sugar Cane,* 1764, *Edge-Hill,* 1767— still the movement was there earlier; its first manifestoes were perhaps in the bumptious times of Jenkins's Ear, with Glover and Thomson's *Britannia,* though Young's extraordinary maritime dithyrambs are ten years earlier.

Country, Town, City, were not by any means mutually exclusive. Dissident Whig and Tory, in different ways, plugged the Patriot King, or at least 'poor Fred', and one might even perhaps trace a continuum between the political attitudes of Pope and Akenside, the arch-Whig poet, and a better one than is usually allowed; Thomson in several aspects is an intermediary. However much they verbally disdained the Court and perpetually harked back either to the old church and state idea or to Great Nassau, all groups except the hopelessly compromised, such as Walpole and Hervey, tried to secure some equity in the anticipated take-over of St James's by Leicester House: the dedications to Frederick, Prince of Wales, would make a pretty, but wry, anthology. The point is that not all the poets were strenuously and defensively conservative, as were Pope and Swift, before the forces of modernity, science, and the money power.

In a movement parallel to that assertion of the moral and social worth of the merchantry which we find in prose from Defoe on, some poets actively embraced the new ethos of bougeois dynamism. Few, if any, had the art to control this dynamism and keep it from falling over into unbalanced rhetoric; or, in their resolution to be thorough-paced new men dealing with 'real life' instead of high-flown epic and faded pastoral, into the opposite catastrophe of faithful but flat pedantry. Yet not only Newton but also Commerce demanded the Muse; indeed it is fittingly symbolic that the Hamburg merchant Glover should be the author not only of the phrase 'Newton demands the Muse' but also of *London: or, The Progress of Commerce.* There was common ground also in stalwart and sometimes strident patriotism. Liberty, Property 'that Goddess heavenly-bright', the Power of Trade, the empire of thought in Newton, all were interwoven, all added up to Britannia's Manifest Destiny. Liberty, Newton, and Property (landed) were poetic common property, as it were; but Commerce is specific to the Whig wing. This is explicit enough merely in some of Thomson's titles:

Britannia, Liberty, To the Memory of Sir Isaac Newton: it is introduced even into *The Castle of Indolence*:

> The towns he quicken'd by mechanic arts
> And bade the fervent city glow with toil;
> Bade social Commerce raise renownèd marts,
> Join land to land, and marry soil to soil . . .
> Bade tyrants tremble on remotest shores
> While o'er th' encircling deep Britannia's thunder roars.

It is not so much explicit as exhibitionist—like pretty well everything Young wrote—in *Imperium Pelagi: A Naval Lyric: The Merchant: Ode I on the British Trade and Navigation*:

> 'Tis *property* supports *pursuit*:
> Freedom gives eloquence; and freedom, gain . . .
>
> Britain! behold the world's wide face;
> Nor cover'd half with *solid* space,
> Three parts are *fluid*: empire of the Sea!
> And why? for commerce. Ocean streams
> For *that,* through all his various *names*:
> And, if for commerce, ocean flows for thee . . . .

This leads on to a description of winds, seas, constellations, and (by what, for Young, is a natural transition) the praise of Sir Isaac Newton.

The title of this paper is, I think, warranted by this brief survey; the poets with whom I am most concerned—Jago, Grainger, Dyer—were all mightily impressed by the Power of Trade, though they must have disappointed Adam Smith by writing in blank. This, however, was a perfectly natural mode for didactic and topographic verse after the success of *The Seasons*, though the avowed didacts stem rather from John Philips.

It is difficult nowadays to take such an avowedly didactic title as *The Art of Preserving Health* quite seriously; indeed only too often the pomp of the diction and the commonplace of the detail produce bathos. However, before laughing at these poets we should be quite sure that they are not laughing themselves now and then. Most of the didactic poets, except the egregious Grainger and the flat Jago, however stiff and rhetorical they were, had some sense of style. And they had a tradition behind them, the tradition of the Georgics, which Johnson seems to have forgotten when he said, 'The subject of *The Fleece*, Sir, cannot be made poetical. How can a man write poetically of serges and druggets?' Virgil had done just that of sheep-scab and dung, but it took a nice touch. Cowper could manage it, with a little quiet pleasure in the conscious incongruity of the

notes on raising cucumbers set in the easy yet firm descriptive moralising of *The Task*; Grainger, as we shall see, came a mucker.

It is worth harking back to Philips's *Cyder* of 1706. Philips, after
Virgil the father of the didacts, had a talent for semi-serious work,
and knew it; his love for Milton seems to have been the poetic passion of his life. It is true, as Sutherland says, that 'to burlesque
Milton *at such length* as Philips does he must have a curious want
of confidence in himself or in his readers',[1] though I think it is
going a little too far to say that 'he never does anything else'. From
the cautious lead-in with *The Splendid Shilling* and the more ambitious follow-up of *Cyder* (not to mention *Blenheim*), one may suspect
that it was not his own skills but reader reaction which worried
Philips; indeed one gets the impression that to strict contemporaries
it was rather a daring thing to write blank on such a scale and with
such deliberation.

But after *The Seasons* there was no reason for such a prudential
attitude; yet the half-apologetic mode persists. The game was played
according to strict rules and a standard form; announcement of
subject, invocation to Muse, apostrophe to Patron, and then the
technical body-work, interlarded with picturesque description and
touching moral anecdotes. An apostrophe to 'Pomona's bard' was
proper form, and half a century after *Cyder* its formal opening reappears in *The Hop-Garden* and *The Sugar Cane*. Thus Philips:

> What soil the apple loves, what care is due
> To orchards, timeliest when to press the fruits,
> Thy gift, Pomona, in Miltonian verse
> Adventurous I presume to sing . . . .

Now Smart, just fifty years later:

> The land that answers best the farmer's care
> And silvers to maturity the hop:
> When to inhume the plants; to turn the glebe;
> And wed the tendrils to th' aspiring poles:
> Under what sign to pluck the crop, and how
> To cure, and in capacious sacks infold,
> I teach in verse Miltonian . . .

and so on with advice on soil and aspect in the Philips manner.
This is not plagiarism, any more than the century's numerous and
often admirable 'Imitations of Horace' are plagiarism: it is adaptation. There is an element of play: in a way these things were
literary competitions; and if they seem elaborate compared to a
New Statesman or *Spectator* competition, the reward for a lucky hit
might be a literary career. Moreover, I do not think it likely that a

---

[1] J. Sutherland, *A Preface to Eighteenth Century Poetry*, Oxford, 1948, p. 152.

man of Smart's poetic temper would mistake this agreeable verse of discourse for the real thing; and I may add that in speaking of his poetic temper I am thinking not only of the Smart of *A Song to David,* but of some of the odes and ballads, and even some flashes in the Seatonian poems.

It is adaptation, also, only proximately of Philips, ultimately of Virgil; beneath that aegis any Augustan might dwell secure. The business of poetry was to instruct and delight: the instruction was quite as much in the proper province of poetry as the delight. And so we find Johnson giving *Cyder*

> this peculiar praise, that it is grounded in truth; that the precepts which it contains are exact and just; and that it is therefore, at once, a book of entertainment and of science. This I was told by Miller, the great gardener and botanist, whose expression was, that *there were many books written on the same subject in prose, which do not contain so much truth as that poem.*

But this is in part a digression, though a rather material one; *revenons à nos moutons,* a phrase particularly appropriate to *The Fleece,* the most considerable of the three poems I wish to discuss. As I have said, Jago, Grainger, Dyer were all much concerned with commercial expansion; so much so that one could use them as the peg for a Marxist thesis on the world market in literature. This is so even of Jago, very much a stay-at-home compared with the other two.

Richard Jago was a member of the Shenstone group, which may not unfairly be considered the prototype of the (later) Georgian 'Week-end school'; his *Edge-Hill,* 1767, is perhaps at once the type-specimen of topographical verse and its nadir. Chalmers justly remarked that though it had 'some passages not destitute of imagination, it is so topographically exact, that to enjoy it the reader must have a map constantly before him';[2] to a modern reader even cartography is not much aid to Jago's pedestrian Muse. The design is of a devastating symmetry: the view from Edge Hill in four directions at four times of the day; in one respect at least Jago is not destitute of imagination, since his range of eyesight apparently extends to Birmingham and Tamworth, some thirty miles away. It has the usual embellishments—panegyrics on improving landlords, rhetorical rhapsodies on the superiority of rough—I had almost said home-spun—British iron to corrupting foreign gold, an affecting tale of a blind young lover, various digressions into natural philosophy, 'Rot amongst the sheep, General thoughts on the vanity and disorders of human life', and so on, leading up to a faithful but

2 Alexander Chalmers, *The Works of the English Poets,* Vol. XVII, 1810, p. 283.

tepid description of the battle of Edge Hill. Jago's geomorphological views are very interesting evidence of the extent to which notions of geology, in this protohistoric phase of the science, had seeped into the consciousness of an ordinary educated clergyman, but are irrelevant to our main theme.

The usual ruck of the book is thuswise:

> Of Alcot's swelling lawns, and fretted spires
> Of fairest model, Gothic or Chinese,
> Of Eatington's, and Tolton's verdant meads
> And groves of various leaf, and Honington
> Profuse of charms and attic elegance . . . .

The Gothic and Chinese spires strike an interesting period note, but the point of all this is, I fear, more sordid. Each of the places mentioned has a footnote to tell you whose seat it is; there are about fifty of these, which ought to have brought in two score subscriptions . . . .

Local as he is by intent, the spectacle of the Black Country and Birmingham industry draws him on to wider horizons. He starts tamely enough:

> Nor does the barren soil conceal alone
> The sable rock inflammable. Oft-times
> More pon'drous ore beneath its surface lies,
> Compact, metallic, but with earthy parts
> Incrusted. These the smoky kiln consumes . . . .

There follows a detailed description of smelting, rolling bars, the manufacture of wrought iron, until

> How the coarse metal brightens into fame
> Shap'd by their plastic hands! what ornament!
> What various use! See there the glitt'ring knife
> Of temper'd edge! The scissar's double shaft,
> Useless apart, in social union join'd,
> Each aiding each! Emblem how beautiful
> Of happy nuptial leagues! The button round,
> Plain, or imbost, or bright with steely rays!
> Or oblong buckle, on the lacker'd shoe,
> With polish'd lustre, bending elegant
> In shapely rim . . . .

and so on, like a manufacturer's trade catalogue, with an exclamation mark for every item. So much, to adapt Bagehot on *Enoch Arden,* has not often been made of ironmongery. The point of it is to lead up to a striking display of the advantages of industrial imperialism, and here Jago rises to what with him passes for a height:

> Would ye your coarse, unsightly mines exchange
> For Mexiconian hills? to tread on gold

As vulgar sand? with naked limbs to brave
The cold, bleak air? to urge the tedious chase
Through gloomy forests, where the sounding axe,
To the sun's beam, ne'er op'd the cheerful glade,
Nor culture's healthful face was ever seen?
In squalid huts to lay your weary limbs,
Bleeding and faint, and strangers to the bliss
Of home-felt ease, which British swains can earn
With a bare spade; but ill, alas!, could earn
With spades of gold? Such the poor Indian's lot!
Who starves midst gold, like misers o'er their bags,
Not with like guilt! Hail, native British ore!
For thine is trade, that with its various stores
Sails round the world, and visits ev'ry clime,
And makes the treasures of each clime her own,
By gainful commerce of her woolly vests,
Wrought by the spiky comb; or steely wares,
From the coarse mass, by stubborn toil, refin'd.
Such are thy peaceful gifts! And war to thee
Its best support, and deadliest horror, owes,
The glitt'ring falchion, and the thund'ring tube!
At whose tremendous gleam, and volley'd fire,
Barbarian kings fly from their useless hoards,
And yield them all to thy superior power.

British swains in the age of enclosures were less impressed by their
bliss of home-felt ease; but that is what the Industrial Revolution
looked like to an educated man living not far away. Jago is an
innocent, of course, but the far more travelled Grainger and the far
more intelligent Dyer reacted in the same way.

Grainger took himself even more seriously than Jago, and, having
higher pretensions, crashed even more disastrously. As the famous
story of the transformation of rats into 'the whisker'd vermin-race'
shows, the excuse of a half-humorous intent will not hold water.
It is true that Grainger tried to pass off the episode as mock-heroic
comic relief; but he forgot that for the relief to be comic the body
of the work must not be so, and there is just too much bathos
throughout his book. He never does his own dirty work but always
bullies his poor Muse, perpetually inciting her to do the oddest
things:

> Shall the Muse celebrate the deep dark mould
> With clay or gravel mix'd?
>
>   *   *   *   *   *
>
> Of composts shall the Muse disdain to sing
> Nor soil her heavenly plumes?
>
>   *   *   *   *   *

> There are, the Muse hath oft abhorrent seen,
> Who swallow dirt; (so the chlorotic fair
> Oft chalk prefer to the most poignant cates):
> Such dropsy bloats . . . .

The translation of the *Georgics* to the West Indies must be allowed to have a certain boldness of approach; but Grainger cannot carry it through on the level of *The Hop-Garden*. Insect life has a fascination for him, and his documentation is thorough: it is unlikely that cockroaches were altogether unknown in Augustan kitchens, but there is a footnote of twenty-ones lines to tell you what they are. The climax of anti-climax is, of course:

> And pity the poor planter, when the blast,
> Fell plague of heaven! perdition of the isles!
> Attacks his waving gold. Though well manur'd,
> A richness though thy fields from nature boast,
> Though seasons pour, this pestilence invades:
> Too oft it seizes the glad infant-throng,
> Nor pities their green nonage: Their broad blades,
> Of which the graceful wood-nymphs erst compos'd
> The greenest garlands to adorn their brows,
> First pallid, sickly, dry, and withered show;
> Unseemly stains succeed; which, nearer view'd
> By microscopic arts, small eggs appear
> Dire fraught with reptile life; alas, too soon
> They burst their filmy jail, and crawl abroad,
> Bugs of uncommon shape . . . .

All the same, the age found instruction in it, and there is any amount of useful source-material on West-Indian sugar; Grainger had lived there and put in some solid research, though why he thought he had to be a poet and couldn't write honest prose remains a mystery: Anderson remarks, quite solemnly, that

> Much praise is due to him for the liberal and diffusive pains he has taken in his *Notes* to enlarge the knowledge of the West-Indian botany. They may indeed be considered, both in their medical and botanical capacity, as a very valuable part of the work; and possibly there are few parts of it more entertaining.[3]

The technical details—soils, tillage, culture, machinery, choice and treatment of slaves, and so on—are meticulously described; as a technical treatise *The Sugar Cane* might well have been required reading for young planters.

There is a lot of medical detail, and while Grainger was doubtless sincere enough in his wish that the tender Muse might be able to

> knock off the chains
> Of heart-debasing slavery,

3 Robert Anderson, *The Works of the British Poets,* Vol. X, 1795, p. 894.

as a doctor and a good man of business he makes the best of a bad job; the usual apologies for the system are mingled with very practical hints on how to choose the best—in tribes where all field drudgery is left to the women,

> Be these thy choice:
> They, hardy, with the labours of the cane
> Soon grow familiar; while unusual toil,
> And new severities their husbands kill.

Just like that: we have still two decades to wait for Cowper.

Grainger is very firmly in the mercantilist tradition. 'False Gallia's sons' mix sand with their sugar, a practice reprobated not only on moral grounds but because it is easily found out. Though the Thames is hardly an Amazon or a La Plata, still 'Delighted commerce broods upon [her] wave'. The book ends with a hurricane of rant to the glory of George and Britain:

> She shall not crouch; if these cane ocean-isles,
> Isles which on Britain for their all depend,
> And must for ever; still indulgent share
> Her fostering smile: and other isles be given,
> From vanquish'd foes.—And, see, another race!
> A golden era dazzles my fond sight!
> That other race, that long'd-for era, hail!
> THE BRITISH GEORGE NOW REIGNS, THE PATRIOT KING!
> BRITAIN SHALL EVER TRIUMPH O'ER THE MAIN.

The implication that previous Georges had been neither British nor Patriot was of course far from displeasing in 1764, whatever the Pittites might think. Mercantilist as he is, perhaps we should not claim Grainger as in the Whig line; he is no great loss.

It is a relief to turn to Dyer, fleecy bleaters and all. *The Fleece* is the high point both of the Georgic and the mercantilist strain; unlike the other two, Dyer does not have to shout. Book I indeed is pure Georgic, and there is plenty of pedestrian didactic: 'The infectious scab' should be treated with oil

> Dispersive of Norwegian tar, renowned
> By virtuous Berkeley . . . .

Yet even here Dyer manages things with more art: within fifteen lines of

> All arid soils, with sand, or chalky flint,
> Or shells diluvian mingled

we find ourselves on

> the spacious plains
> Of Sarum, spread like Ocean's boundless round,

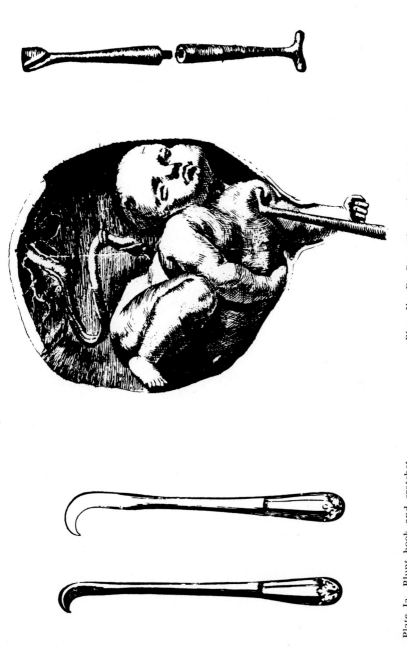

Plate Ia Blunt hook and crotchet, from *The Diseases of Women with Child*, 1668, by François Mauriceau

Plate Ib Dr Burton's crotchet with detachable crutch used to push a foetus back into the womb, from the *Essay Towards a Complete New System of Midwifry*, 1751

Plate IIa Dr Burton's extractor, from the *Essay towards a Complete New System of Midwifry*, 1751

Plate IIb Mauriceau's squirt, from *The Diseases of Women with Child*, 1668

Plate IIc Forceps of the Chamberlen type, from the *Essay towards a Complete New System of Midwifry*, 1751

> Where solitary Stonehenge, gray with moss,
> Ruin of ages, nods . . . .

The account in Book II of the various types of wool and the growth
of the woollen industry since the Dark Ages is good enough to be
quoted with appreciation in Lipson's *History of the English Woollen Industry,* and ends with 'The advantages of trade, and its utility
in the moral world'.

With Book III we have once more the Industrial Revolution as
it struck a contemporary. Much of this is heavy going; Dyer gets
into horrid contortions with Paul's new spinning machine:

> We next are shown
> A circular machine, of new design,
> In conic shape: it draws and spins a thread
> Without the tedious toil of needless hands.
> A wheel, invisible, beneath the floor
> To every member of the harmonious frame
> Gives necessary motion . . . .

One feels that Dr Johnson was right enough at this point; and one
could also wish to have his comments on the complacency with
which 'Houses of labour, seats of kind restraint'—in other words,
county workhouses—are elevated into philanthropic mansions, to
be viewed 'with wonder and with silent joy'. All is joy, too, when
Dyer contemplates

> The ruddy roofs and chimney-tops
> Of busy Leeds, up-wafting to the clouds
> The incense of thanksgiving . . .
>   So appear
> The increasing walls of busy Manchester,
> Sheffield, and Birmingham, whose redd'ning fields
> Rise and enlarge their suburbs.

This euphoria again was not to last beyond Cowper.

The argument of Book IV is a complete mercantilist survey of
the economic geography of the wool trade: 'Our manufacture
exported . . . Our woollen manufactures known at Pekin . . . View
of our probable improvements in traffic and the distribution of our
woollen manufactures over the whole globe'. It is true that although
'Guinea's sultry strand' is a good market for light Norwich cloths,

> yet the valued trade
> Along this barbarous coast, in telling wounds
> The generous heart, the sale of wretched slaves.

Dyer consoles himself by alleging that they are criminals otherwise
condemned to death, but hints that there may yet be vengeance for

129

cruelty and avarice in the trade. Other Africans have only themselves to blame, the

> savage Hottentots,
> Whose hands unnatural hasten to the grave
> Their aged parents: what barbarity
> And brutal ignorance, where social trade
> Is held contemptible!

The conclusion, as with Grainger and Jago's third book, is once
more a vision of Britannia's commercial empire; it must be said
that not only the verse but the temper and the patriotism of Dyer's
version are far purer. Indeed *The Fleece* has been described by
Dobrée as 'in many ways the greatest patriotic poem in the language, bursting with the energy which characterised the country',[4]
and yet modulated not infrequently to a pure pastoral—

> Could I recall those notes which once the Muse
> Heard at a shearing, near the woody sides
> Of blue-topp'd Wreakin! Yet the carols sweet
> Through the deep maze of the memorial cell
> Faintly remurmur.

Dyer fulfils his program with vigour and assurance, and not without
a good deal of elegance; one picks up the book to check a point,
and finds oneself reading on. In Australia, still carried as regards
exports on the sheep's back, a geographer may be pardoned for yet
another quotation, almost the end of the book:

> That portion too of land, a tract immense,
> Beneath the Antarctic spread shall then be known,
> And new plantations on its coast arise.
> Then rigid winter's ice no more shall wound
> The only naked animal; but man
> With the soft fleece shall everywhere be clothed.

The merchant as hero, the industrial town as unmixed triumph
and blessing, did not long survive as a theme for respectable verse.
In the same year as Grainger published *The Sugar Cane,* in which
'every quarter of this sea-girt globe' pays due tribute to the Thames,
'but chief the world By great Columbus found', Churchill in his
slashing way pricked the bubble:

> The man who finds an unknown country out,
> By giving it a name, acquires, no doubt
> A gospel title, though the people there
> The pious Christian thinks not worth his care.
> Bar this pretence, and into air is hurl'd

---

[4] B. Dobrée, *English Literature in the Early Eighteenth Century 1700-1740,*
Oxford, 1959, p. 518.

The claim of Europe to the *western world* . . .
Our vices, with more zeal than holy pray'rs,
She teaches them, and in return takes theirs;
The worth of freedom strongly she explains,
Whilst she bows down, and loads their necks with chains.

Two decades later the change in climate is almost complete, and the change is perfectly displayed in *The Task*. Yet the ethos of mercantilist England is also perfectly displayed in *The Fleece,* an ethos not without some sense of grandeur.

,

The Birth of Tristram Shandy: Sterne and Dr Burton

Arthur H. Cash

Imagine to yourself a little, squat, uncourtly figure of a Doctor *Slop,* of about four feet and a half perpendicular height, with a breadth of back, and a sesquipedality of belly, which might have done honour to a serjeant in the horse-guards. (p. 104)[1]

The citizens of York in 1759 recognised in this grotesque caricature Dr John Burton, founder and quondam surgeon of the York Public Hospital, man-midwife, antiquary, and rabid Tory partisan. Dr Slop waddles through the pages of *Tristram Shandy,* dealing out advice to the Widow Wadman about Uncle Toby's groin, destruction to the nose of Tristram, and plastic surgery to either end of that diminutive character. His importance to the novel, however, is more profound than his ludicrous appearance suggests: Dr John Burton and his obstetrical writings underprop the first four volumes of the novel. The key ideas represent his actual theories, the key events are tragicomical extensions of his practices, and the key objects are the instruments of Dr Burton's own proud invention.

Dr Burton was excellently trained in his art. He completed the M.B. degree at St John's College, Cambridge, studied with the great Boerhaave at Leyden, and at Paris with Grégoire and Dusée, both eminent obstetricians. He received his M.D. degree from the university at Rheims and settled in York about 1736, where he quickly established a large practice among the poor, influencing them to vote with his Tory party.

It is not likely that the mature Sterne satirised Dr Burton because

[1] Quotations from *Tristram Shandy* are taken from the James Aiken Work edition, New York, 1940.

of the political antagonism of their youth.[2] Sterne's treatment of
Burton as Slop is not at all political. It has, however, a very personal tone, strongly suggesting that Sterne had been perennially
amused by the irascible temper, papist sympathies, and portly, short
figure of the doctor.

What really inspired Sterne, however, was Burton the 'scientifick
operator', who

> had expressly wrote a five shillings book upon the subject of
> midwifery, in which he had exposed, not only the blunders of
> the sisterhood itself,—but had likewise superadded many curious
> improvements for the quicker extraction of the foetus in cross
> births, and some other cases of danger which belay us in getting
> into the world. (p. 44)

The reference is to Burton's *Essay towards a Complete New System
of Midwifry*, 1751, the first of his indiscretions in the literature of
science. It was followed two years later by a second and even
greater blunder, *A Letter to William Smellie, M.D.*

To appreciate the foolishness which Sterne found in Dr Burton,
we must visualise the doctor as a promising and prominent man in
a burgeoning science. It was a great age for obstetrics. In 1733
Edmund Chapman had published the first full account of the
obstetrical forceps, which offered a new and inspiring hope for the

---

[2] They opposed each other in the York by-election of 1741/2, when the young
Sterne edited a newspaper and wrote pamphlets for the Whigs. Sterne, however,
had sold his services for a prebend stall at York Minster, and his heart was not
in politics. When Walpole resigned in 1742, Sterne publicly apologised for his
part in the recent campaign and quit politics for good. Thereafter Burton and
Sterne found themselves sharing an unenviable position as the two men most
hated by that maniacal Whig, the powerful Archdeacon of Cleveland and
Precentor of York, Dr Jaques Sterne, the uncle of the novelist. One would
think that the persecutions each suffered at the hands of this terrible man
would have created a bond of sympathy between them.

In *The Politicks of Laurence Sterne*, London, 1929, p. 18, L. P. Curtis
suggested that Sterne had a hand in Burton's imprisonment during the revolution of the Pretender of 1745/6. Burton was arrested by Dr Jaques Sterne, who
was also a Justice of the Peace and second in command of the defences of York,
after he was captured and released by the rebels (as he maintained), or met with
them by assignation (as Dr Sterne said). In Burton's published defence (*British
Liberty Endanger'd*, 1749), he spoke of a letter written by a 'relation' of
Jaques Sterne which had accused him of inviting the rebels to York. Curtis
surmised that Laurence Sterne was the author, but I cannot agree. A more
likely person is Thomas Pulleyn, Clerk of the Peace for the West Riding, a
nephew of Jaques Sterne by marriage, who is frequently mentioned in Burton's
book. There is something suspicious in Burton's inadequate account of his
capture. Nevertheless, no formal charge was ever brought against him, though
he was incarcerated for more than a year and forced into bankruptcy. Jaques
Sterne, on the other hand, was guilty of inciting false witness against Dr Burton
while the man was in prison (Leeds City Library, Temple-Newsam Papers
PO/3C: ff. 143, 162). On the whole Burton seems more sinned against than
sinning, a candidate for the compassion of Sterne, who was waiting out the
revolution, so far as I know, at his rural parish.

science.[3] The forceps had been invented a century before by the Chamberlen family, who unscrupulously guarded them as a secret for three generations. At length Hugh Chamberlen defrauded the faculty of the University of Amsterdam by selling them what he said was his 'nostrum'—one blade only of the forceps. However, the full secret was soon out, and the surge of experimentation which followed made of obstetrics the most advanced branch of medicine of the time. It was the age of Hendrik van Deventer, Richard Manningham, Fielding Ould, André Levret, William Gifford, Benjamin Pugh—the pioneers of the science. The greatest of all, by common consent, was that friend and countryman of Tobias Smollett, Dr William Smellie, who modified the forceps to the various sizes and shapes still used, devised the lock still standard, and taught the world how to use the instrument.

At the beginning of 1751, John Burton had in hand a half-finished manuscript of the *Essay towards a Complete New System of Midwifry* when he heard of a number of distressing developments. Brudenell Exton, William Clark, George Counsell, and Benjamin Pugh were all publishing or preparing works on midwifery. André Levret, the very great French tocologist, was soon to bring out a description of some long, curved forceps. Most worrisome of all, William Smellie, whose reputation was then immense, was preparing to release the first volume of his monumental *Treatise on the Theory and Practice of Midwifery*. Burton, the historians are agreed, could no longer stand the anxiety: he took his unfinished manuscript to the printer.

The *Essay* is certainly not devoid of merit, but it is deficient in the standards and spirit of the new science. Burton is unreasonably hostile to the discoveries of his contemporaries and smug about his own. He writes well about matters in which he has had much

3 For my facts about the history of obstetrics here and throughout the article I am indebted to a number of medical historians: J. S. Fairbairn, 'The Development of Obstetrics from the Embryonic State', *St. Thomas's Hospital Gazette*, Vol. XIX, 1909, pp. 163-81; John Byers, 'The Evolution of Obstetric Medicine', *British Medical Journal*, 1912, Vol. I, pp. 1345-50; H. R. Spencer, *The History of British Midwifery from 1650 to 1800*, London, 1927; I. H. Flack (pseud. Harvey Graham), *Eternal Eve: the History of Gynaecology and Obstetrics*, Garden City, N.Y., 1951; D. T. Atkinson, *Magic, Myth, and Medicine*, Cleveland, 1956; L. S. King, *The Medical World of the Eighteenth Century*, Chicago, 1958; B. L. Gordon, *Medieval and Renaissance Medicine*, New York, 1959.

I especially appreciate several studies of Dr Burton by medical men: J. Glaister, *Dr William Smellie and his Contemporaries*, Glasgow, 1894, Ch. 16; A. Doran, 'Burton ("Dr Slop"): His Forceps and His Foes', *Journal of Obstetrics and Gynaecology of the British Empire*, Vol. XXIII, 1913, pp. 3-24, 65-86; R. W. Johnstone, *William Smellie, the Master of British Midwifery*, Edinburgh and London, 1952, Ch. 13; W. Radcliffe, 'Dr John Burton and his Whimsical Contrivance', *Medical Bookman and Historian*, Vol. II, 1948, pp. 349-55.

experience, but insists upon erroneous anatomy and untested techniques. He is not quite able to separate his antiquarian self from the scientific, parading his learning ostentatiously and seriously vending the teachings of seventy writers on midwifery from the most ancient times, which he lists in a Preface. The Appendix alone would have secured for Burton an unenviable niche in the history of medicine even if Sterne had never written *Tristram Shandy*. In the Appendix he recommends a new forceps of his own devising, 'better than any yet contrived'. The historians, who treasure this instrument as the most odd, impractical, whimsical device ever suggested for insinuation into womankind, usually quote the words of Sir Alexander Simpson: 'an ingenious but very unserviceable forceps, working like a lobster's claws'. The laity are apt never to forget this curious forceps as the machine which crushed the infant Tristram Shandy's nose.

The inevitable happened: Burton was all but ignored, while Smellie won universal acclaim. Imagine the chagrin of the fiery little doctor when he read in the *Monthly Review* of September that his was

> a performance, which we cannot think will greatly illuminate or entertain any adepts in midwifery; some cautionary parts of which, however, and some of the cases, may be worth the perusal of beginners.

Tristram Shandy might never have been born had Burton let the matter rest there. But the hot-tempered, egoistic little doctor could only rage. He must have raged for a full two years: he did not take comfort until he published, in 1753, *A Letter to William Smellie, M.D. Containing Critical and Practical Remarks Upon his Treatise.* . . . This unprovoked attack, sometimes supercilious, sometimes vitriolic, could have been motivated by nothing but Burton's consuming envy. To be sure, he makes two or three good points,[4] but they are lost in the mass of sarcastic and picayunish sallies. He quibbles over minutiae—the ambiguous use of *sometimes* and *often*. He unjustly teases Smellie about his 'favorite instrument', his 'beloved forceps'. Ignoring the fact that Smellie had already caught a silly error (probably by some careless assistant) and corrected it in the second edition, Burton haughtily reprimands him for taking the words *Lithopaedii Senonesis Icon* to be the name of a writer when they had actually appeared under an illustration to which the words referred: 'a picture of a petrified child'. Sterne burlesqued

---

[4] Glaister, Doran, and Radcliffe (see note 3) evaluate Burton's criticism in detail. His most telling points seem to have been (1) that the uterus includes a muscle structure, and (2) that the blades of the forceps should not be wrapped in leather, as Smellie believed.

the correction to make the most amusing footnote in *Tristram Shandy* (p. 150).[5] On the whole, Burton failed to detract from the great *Treatise,* and Smellie never deigned to reply, though his student, Giles Watts, calmly devastated Burton in a book called *Reflections upon Slow and Painful Labours.*

Just when or how Burton came to recognise his own errors I do not know. He never again published a medical treatise. Henceforth he channelled his creative energies into the antiquarian studies for which he was better suited, publishing his *Monasticon Eboracense* before Sterne had created Dr Slop, and winning thereby some measure of renown.[6]

Sterne found in Dr Burton and his books a new and inspiring vision of foolishness, one which impinged upon the most fundamental human experiences—generation, nativity, infanticide, and hopeless surrender. Sterne read Burton pronouncing upon copulation and conception, and the vitality of the animal spirits. He considered Burton's ovular theory of generation against the animalcular theory of Smellie. He read Burton's warnings about possible damage to the nose or the genitals of a child during parturition (*Essay*, pp. 190-3; *Letter,* p. 108), and his defence of the Caesarean operation. He was fascinated to discover the danger of the cerebrum's pressing against the cerebellum in a strait delivery, but the harmlessness of the cerebellum's pressing against the cerebrum. He read a defensive argument that man-midwives preserve the heirs of gentry families (*Essay*, pp. 254-5). He was horrified with the vision of a woman dying, the severed head of her offspring lost in her womb. He learned of the dread operation whereby the too-large head of an unborn infant is opened so that it will pass and free the mother of her deadly burden. That such questions of life, and such actual decisions of how and when to take or save life should be left to John Burton! Ordinary fools, driven by passions and lusts, blundered across the surfaces of life. Dr Burton's foolishness was profound. It was the inspiration of Sterne's great comedy.

The extensive digressions of the first four volumes of *Tristram Shandy* are held together by the central episode, the birth of Tristram. Tristram must turn back to explain the history which preceded his birth—his conception (of course), his father's theories,

---

[5] Sterne's name for Smellie in this joke was 'Adrianus Smelvgot', a corruption of a name Sterne found in Burton's *Letter*: listed among the 'moderns' of midwifery whom Smellie should have studied is one 'Joh. Adriani Slevogt'.

[6] Vol. I of the *Monasticon Eboracense, or The Ecclesiastical and Monastic History of Yorkshire* appeared in 1758. Soon afterwards Burton was made a Fellow of the Society of Antiquaries of London. He had not completed the second volume when he died in 1771.

his parents' marriage contract, and the stories of the players in his drama—Uncle Toby, Parson Yorick, the midwife. He must also move ahead to the events brought on by the manner of his birth—his misbaptism and his father's plea to the divines at the visitation dinner.

No child was ever more carefully planned. Tristram was as much the product of his father's intellect as of his loins. No father was ever less successful. From the very moment when Tristram, born and baptised, set out upon his life (p. 336), the family of which he was the intended bulwark was doomed. His uncle had refused to marry, his brother was at the brink of death,[7] and he himself had been condemned already by his begetting and birth to a life of impotence and an early death.[8]

Dr John Burton provided Sterne with the materials, not only for the central birth episode, but also for the genetic[9] and obstetrical theories of Walter Shandy which determined the circumstances of the birth.

Even the locus of Tristram's birth, a Yorkshire country house, was fixed obstetrically. The contract which Walter Shandy had been forced to sign when he married Elizabeth Mollineux gave to her the privilege of bearing her children in London, where she sought

[7] T. Baird, 'The Time-scheme of *Tristram Shandy* and a Source', *Publications of the Modern Language Association of America*, Vol. LI, 1936, pp. 803-20. Brother Bobby died in 1719, a short while after Tristram's birth on 5 November 1718. Uncle Toby's courtship of the Widow Wadman had taken place earlier, in 1713, albeit the narrative of that frustrated love concludes the novel. As Baird showed, the events of the novel are exactly arranged within the military and political history of England. Within medical history, however, the birth of Tristram makes no chronological sense. In 1718, the year of Tristram's birth, forceps were unknown in England and Dr John Burton was only 8 years old.

[8] My general idea about the structure of the novel is taken from W. B. Piper, *Laurence Sterne*, New York, 1966. Piper convincingly argues that all the digressions are related to a core plot having to do with the frustrated attempts of the Shandy family to prolong their line.

[9] Sterne went far beyond Burton's few comments on genetic theory. See L. A. Landa, 'The Shandean Homunculus: the Background of Sterne's "Little Gentleman"', in Carrol Camden (ed.), *Restoration and Eighteenth-Century Literature: Essays in Honor of Alan Dugald McKillop*, Chicago, 1963, pp. 49-68. Sterne's interest in generation theory, however, may have been sparked by the remarks of Burton and Smellie. Especially curious is an amusing exchange between Burton and one Kirkpatric, the reviewer of Burton's *Essay* for the *Monthly Review*, Vol. V (Sept. 1751), pp. 286-92. Kirkpatric, deriding Burton's speculations about how the semen stimulated the ovum, made a joking implication about Burton's masculinity which left the doctor fairly sputtering in print: 'For where is the Conclusion that mine is a defective Birth, because I leave the Use of the Semen Masculinum (which is here a Thing merely speculative) to be discussed by some abler Hand?' (*Letter*, p. 242). How Sterne must have laughed at that! Is it possible that this banter about a congenital impotence, occurring as it does within a dialogue about conception, could have suggested to Sterne Walter Shandy's idea about 'due care' in propagation? Tristram, who lost the benefit of such care because of his mother's unhappy association of ideas, was later plagued with impotence (see pp. 517-18).

the care of Dr Richard Manningham (p. 44), the physician who founded the first lying-in ward in England.[10] However, if Mrs Shandy were ever taken to London at her own desire but on false tokens, she would forfeit her privilege for the next pregnancy. It happened that Mrs Shandy had been carried to London the year before only to discover that it was all wind and water.[11] Consequently, as Walter announced to his wife minutes after Tristram's conception, she must bear her child in Yorkshire (p. 43). There are many reasons for Walter's decision, including an elaborate theory about the pernicious effects of migrations towards the capital. They are all chimerical but one: 'Of all men in the world, Dr. *Slop* was fittest for my father's purposes' (p. 153).

The exact reasons why Walter Shandy and Dr Slop had become 'two such allies in science' (p. 153) depended ultimately upon the squire's very liberal moral doctrine—liberal no less in our day than in his—the equality of man.

> Now, as it was plain to my father, that all souls were by nature equal,—and that the great difference between the most acute and the most obtuse understanding,—was from no original sharpness or bluntness of one thinking substance above or below another,—but arose merely from the lucky or unlucky organization of the body, in that part where the soul principally took up her residence. . . . (p. 147)[12]

The moral philosophy demanded a physiological prop. Walter read Coglionissimo Borri; he read the great Metheglingius; and he read Descartes (from whom Sterne surely took his idea, giving it an appropriate twist). The *sensorium* of the soul, he concluded, was 'in, or near, the cerebellum,—or rather some-where about the

[10] Established in Jermyn Street, 1739, the ward became eventually Queen Charlotte's Hospital. A second ward was opened at Middlesex Hospital in 1747, and 1749 saw the establishment of the British Lying-In Hospital (later called the British Hospital for Mothers and Babies). Although the greatest contribution of Sir Richard Manningham was the founding of his ward, he is more often remembered as the man who exposed in 1721 the 'rabbit breeder', Mary Tofts, who had convinced much of the world that she gave birth to rabbits. Manningham was a conservative operator—too conservative, one suspects, for Walter Shandy's purposes.

[11] 'There are natural great Bellies, containing a living Child, and these we call true; and others against Nature, in which instead of a Child, is engendered nothing but strange Matter, as Wind mixed with Waters . . . they are called false Great-Bellies'—François Mauriceau, *The Diseases of Women with Child* (first published Paris, 1668), trans. Hugh Chamberlen, edition of 1752.

[12] Comically, but consistently, Walter is assuming an ideal equality among embryos as he (or Tristram speaking for him) had already assumed among *homunculi* (pp. 5-6). In the earlier instance, Tristram referred to Cicero's *De Legibus* and Pufendorf's *De Jure Naturae et Gentium,* thus aligning Walter's spermatozoic ethic with the great latitudinarian legal tradition which culminated with Jefferson and the Declaration of Independence.

139

medulla oblongata'. Ergo, Walter's first duty as a father was to preserve in his child

> this delicate and fine-spun web, from the havock which was generally made in it by the violent compression and crush which the head was made to undergo, by the nonsensical method of bringing us into the world by that part foremost. (p. 149)

He was greatly distressed to discover that the force of the mother's efforts created a 'weight of 470 pounds averdupoise acting perpendicularly'.[13]

> But how great was his apprehension, when he further understood, that this force, acting upon the very vertex of the head, not only injured the brain itself or cerebrum,—but that it necessarily squeez'd and propell'd the cerebrum towards the cerebellum, which was the immediate seat of the understanding.—Angels and Ministers of grace defend us! (pp. 150-1)

Walter's ideas about the jeopardy of the cerebellum during labour Sterne took directly from John Burton, who was at pains to explain how 'the Danger to the Child increases, as the Cerebellum is the more compressed'. True, he wrote about the danger, as Sterne says of Slop, 'not with a view to the soul's good . . . as was my father's system,—but for reasons merely obstetrical' (pp. 153-4). Obstetrically speaking, prolonged pressures on the cerebellum could bring on convulsions in the new-born infant which were often fatal.

> When, therefore, the Child's Head is . . . large . . . let the Force of the Mother's Effort, that propells the Child, be ever so strong or weak, the Cerebellum will, in such Proportion, become pressed; because Action and Re-action are, in this Case, equal; whence it follows, that the more the Head is squeezed . . . the more the Brain [cerebrum] is forced towards the Cerebellum, and consequently, the Mischiefs abovementioned will ensue. (*Letter*, p. 123)

Walter's first solution to this terrible problem had the simplicity of genius—he could maintain the cerebellum intact if the child were delivered by Caesarean section. He casually mentioned this one day to Mrs Shandy, no doubt remarking upon what he had been thinking, that certain towering geniuses—notably Julius Caesar, Hermes Trismegistus, Scipio Africanus, Manlius Torquatus, and Edward the Sixth—all came sideways into the world; 'but seeing her

---

[13] I have not found the source of this interesting statistic, though I suspect it was taken from André Levret, *L'Art des Accouchemens démontré par des principes de physique et de mécanique*, Paris, 1753, a copy of which I have been unable to obtain.

turn as pale as ashes at the very mention of it, as much as the operation flattered his hopes, he thought it as well to say no more of it' (p. 153).

Well might Mrs Shandy pale, for the operation in the eighteenth century was always fatal. An Irish woman had survived it, though performed by an ignorant midwife, only to die a few weeks later. Fielding Ould, the first British obstetrician to mention the Caesarean in writing, called it an 'unparalleled Piece of Barbarity'. John Burton, interestingly, is the first Englishman to say a word in its favour. He did not believe a woman would be apt to survive it, but he cogently argued that it must be performed anyway if it were her last chance. In this he was vindicated by Smellie in the *Treatise,* who took a similar stand. It is apparent where Sterne got his idea for Walter's admiration of the operation, though Sterne gave it a unique turn. British obstetricians of this period always valued the life of the mother over that of the child. Burton and Smellie sanctioned the Caesarean only to save the mother's life. Walter has the honour of being the first Englishman to advocate it as a benefit to the child.[14]

Unable to convince his wife that she should deliver sideways, Walter put his hopes in a technique which today is called the 'podalic version':

> . . . when a child was turn'd topsy-turvy, which was easy for an operator to do, and was extracted by the feet . . . instead of the cerebrum being propell'd towards the cerebellum, the cerebellum, on the contrary, was propell'd simply towards the cerebrum where it could do no manner of hurt. (p. 151)

It seems that Dr Slop 'had scattered a word or two in his book, in favour of the very thing which ran in my father's fancy' (p. 153)— as indeed he had. The very dangerous podalic version, widely practised in the early years, had been falling rapidly into disuse because of the forceps.[15] Dr Burton, however, out of his hatred for Smellie's clever forceps, vastly overstated the virtues of version in his *Letter.* In the course of his protest, he made Walter Shandy's argu-

14 So far as I know, continental writers did not openly approve the Caesarean, but they reveal that another attitude sometimes prevailed. Mauriceau, in *The Diseases of Women with Child,* has this to say of it: 'I know very well they palliate it with a pretence of baptizing the Infant, which else would be depriv'd of it. . . . But I do not know that there ever was any Law, Christian or Civil, which doth ordain the martyring and killing the Mother, to save the Child: 'Tis rather to satisfy the Avarice of some People, who care not much whether their Wives die, provided they have a Child to survive them' (p. 236).

15 During the sixteenth century, when it was taught by Ambrose Paré, it had been the only hope for the child's life in preternatural cases. Burton, though he recognised its dangers, was wrong to advocate it over delivery by forceps. Walter Shandy stands alone in recommending it for births which might be normal.

ment: 'the more Liberty there is for the Brain to be squeezed from (instead of towards) the Cerebellum, the less . . . Danger'. He supported his contention with the following theory:

> . . . by turning and extracting the Child by the Feet . . . the Child's Head is only compressed by the Bones of the Pelvis, and that too in such a Manner, as to do the least Injury to the Cerebellum, for the Pressure then is from the lower Part of the Head, next to the Neck, towards the Os Bregmatis and Os Frontis, both which will yield and give Way; so that when the Head is squeezed on the Sides, the Cerebrum is pressed towards these Parts, and consequently does less Injury to the Cerebellum than when the Apex comes first. (*Letter,* p. 124)

The theory is sound enough in what it indicates about the structure of the brain and cranium, but it shows poor understanding of the mechanisms of parturition. In fact, there is very grave danger to the cerebellum of any child born with the head coming last. Walter's ultimate hope that this child might enter the world feet first was founded upon a very bad argument.

Because of this hope, little Tristram suffered a rural birth sponsored by a 'coalition' between the philosophic squire and the foolish doctor.

Walter, as well as the doctor, is a fool: he too expressed the mistaken ideas of Dr Burton. Yet Sterne created them as vastly different fools. Slop was Sterne's obstetric clown; Walter his confused philosopher. Walter remained the consummate father image—determined to beget, bring forth, and rear his child judiciously. His hypotheses, though mistaken, reflect the more respectable ideas of Burton's books. The neurological theory of the various functions of cerebrum and cerebellum did not originate with Burton, but was learned by him from the admirable Boerhaave.[16] Consequently, as late as 1912 Dr W. H. Allport, in an appreciative essay called 'Tristram Shandy and Obstetrics',[17] announced that 'Shandy *père* . . . had views which would have done full credit to many of our present day obstetricians'. He thought that Walter's fears for the cerebellum were in accord with the most modern theories, and he especially admired Walter's intuition that delivery by Caesarean was less prejudicial to the child than natural delivery. One might add that Walter adumbrated a point of Freudian theory in suggesting that the foetal experience affected the psyche of the child. As a consultant obstetrician, Walter was foolish. As a philosopher of the life sciences, he was advanced.

Alas, neither his sound philosophy nor his questionable program

[16] See King, *The Medical World of the Eighteenth Century,* pp. 103-4.
[17] *American Journal of Obstetrics,* Vol. LXV, pp. 612-17.

was to be realised. Dr John Burton had advocated podalic version only so long as he was quarrelling with Dr William Smellie and Dr Smellie's forceps. His attitude was rather different when he spoke of his own invention. Likewise, Dr Slop had 'scattered a word or two in his book' in favour of version, yet 'his new-invented forceps was the armour he had proved, and what he maintained, to be the safest instrument of deliverance' (p. 153). Poor Walter, who could better manipulate ideas than people, was destined to be disappointed.

Walter Shandy, caught up as he was in sapience about the cerebellum and theories of the preponderate influence of Christian names and noble noses, was insulated from the raw truths of human birth. He could not understand his wife's dread of Dr Slop. Yet birth in the eighteenth century was a fearful thing, and the sight of a man-midwife struck terror in the hearts of most women. Dr Slop entered the house as an Angel of Death among the hobby-horsical muses of the Shandy brothers—a suggestion Sterne planted at Slop's rap upon the door:

> ANALOGY, replied my father, is the certain relation and agreement, which different—Here a devil of a rap at the door snapp'd my father's definition (like his tobacco-pipe) in two,—and, at the same time, crushed the head of as notable and curious a dissertation as ever was engendered in the womb of speculation. (pp. 102-3)

Throughout its history, man-midwifery had been looked upon as an art of the abnormal. Men were seldom called in until the mother was in mortal danger and the foetus doomed. Such a grisly business drove away the more sensitive physicians and attracted such crude men as that described by Deventer:

> . . . a Man in Liquor, almost void of the use of his Senses, both void of Pity and Compassion, furnished with a Knife, a Hook, an Iron Forceps, and other Instruments horrible to Sight . . . come to the Assistance of one in Agony . . . commonly first begins, with rash Oaths to hurt the Mother, then kill the living Infant, then with a great deal of Pain to draw it out in Pieces, and at last to think no Reward satisfactory for such an extraordinary Piece of Work.[18]

Elsewhere Deventer gave an even more horrifying description of a man-midwife drawing out an infant with hooks while it was still

18 H. van Deventer, *The Art of Midwifery Improv'd*, English edition of 1746, p. 14. See also p. 325.

alive and moving. Professional standards were certainly climbing rapidly by the middle of the century when obstetricians began to be accepted by the upper classes as a fashion. Still, the books on the subject by the most reputable practitioners, which circulated among the gentry, were hardly able to quiet the old fears since they were written without the merciful disguise of scientific language. Even the dispassionate Smellie knew not how to hide the drama when he told about doctors who, having turned the infant to bring it by the feet, 'pull at random with all their strength; so that the neck is stretched and separated, and the head left behind' (Vol. I, p. 362). As a consequence of the fears so aroused, the men of the profession resorted to deceptions. Smellie advised doctors to hide their instruments in their pockets and to tie two corners of the bed-sheet about the waist or neck so that the instruments could be manipulated without being seen. When the child is delivered and handed to the nurse, 'the next care is to wipe the blades of the forceps, singly, under the cloaths, slide them warily into your pockets, and deliver the *Placenta*' (Vol. I, p. 271).

The fears of expectant mothers, so naturally aroused, were reinforced by a constant, bitter antagonism of midwives toward the man-midwives. As early as 1668 Mauriceau reprimanded the sisterhood for maliciously putting

> . . . Terror and Apprehension of the Chirurgeons in the poor Woman, comparing them to Butchers and Hangmen, that they chuse rather to die in Travail with the Child in their Womb, than to put themselves into their hands.[19]

The slander was still going on in 1751 when Smellie spoke of 'a general outcry . . . raised against gentlemen of the profession, as if they delight in using instruments and violent methods' (Vol. I, p. 242).

The women who raised this fuss were dismally trained in their work. They were licensed, if at all, by the bishop of the diocese without any regard for their medical knowledge. A letter of 1705 survives at the York Minster Library written by eleven women of Preston to the Archbishop of York recommending for a licence one Mrs Hannah Savage because she is 'a Woman of good fame and credit & due Frequenter of the Church. And one that hath been helpful to severall poore Women & their Labour in case of necessity.'[20] No more. Although Sterne sympathised with the taciturn, motherly midwife of *Tristram Shandy*, with whom he sided against

---

[19] Mauriceau, *The Diseases of Women with Child*, pp. 155-6.
[20] York Minster Library MSS., Ad. A 4 (3) b.

Dr Slop, he did not hide the fact that she had no medical training (p. 11).[21]

The prolonged attack of this ignorant group of women upon the practitioners of the new science was reprehensible, but effective. The woman who made the most noise of all was Mrs Elizabeth Nihell, the Haymarket midwife, who published in 1760 *A Treatise on the Art of Midwifery,* in which she lambasted all 'he-practicers', whose ranks are filled, she said, with

> broken barbers, tailors, or even pork butchers, for I know one myself of this last trade, who, after passing half his life in stuffing sausages, is turned an intrepid physician and man-midwife.[22]

As if the women were incapable of carrying on their own campaign of fright, two unscrupulous men joined their ranks. Frank Nicholls, a well known man-midwife, turned traitor to his profession, had accepted from a midwife, Mrs Kennon, £500 for writing and publishing in 1751 *The Petition of the Unborn Babes to the Censors of the Royal College of Physicians.* Of all physicians, he wrote,

> the men midwives alone (as such) give no test of their learning, dexterity, or integrity; and yet these men are permitted on their single opinions avowedly and professedly to kill our children, and to treat our wives in such a manner, as frequently ends in their destruction, and to have such intercourse with our women, as easily shifts itself into indecency, from indecency into obscenity, and from obscenity into debauchery. (p. 6)

The most scurrilous attack of all, however, was that of Philip Thicknesse in *Man-Midwifery Analysed,* 1764, which must be read to be believed. Typical of its quality is Thicknesse's explanation of examination by 'touching', which is done, he said, 'to see if any emotions arise in the *touched* lady's breast, that the Doctor may take advantage of' (p. 8).

The attempts to frighten the women by painting the doctors as lechers reveals a puritanical attitude about the human body which we do not usually associate with the eighteenth century. We can only admire Sterne's taste in refusing to capitalise upon this irrational and embarrassing fear. His one reference to it comes through Uncle Toby, who was trying to help his brother understand why Mrs Shandy would not see Dr Slop:

21 She had been licensed by Didius, a Commissary of the Archbishop. Didius was Sterne's satiric portrait of Dr Francis Topham, who indeed held among his many offices the Commissaryship of the Exchequer and Prerogative Courts of the Archbishop of York.
22 Quoted by Flack, *Eternal Eve,* p. 292.

—Then it can be out of nothing in the whole world, quoth my uncle *Toby*, in the simplicity of his heart,—but MODESTY:— My sister, I dare say, added he, does not care to let a man come so near her ****. (p. 100)[23]

The most insidious and knavish altercation of the midwives and their allies was on the danger of obstetrical instruments.

> That multitude of disciples of Dr. Smellie, trained up at the feet of his artificial doll, [wrote Mrs Nihell] see the whole pack open in full cry: to arms! to arms! is the word; and what are those arms by which they maintain themselves, but those instruments, those weapons of death!
> ... crotchets, knives, scissors, spoons, pinchers, fillets, speculum matrices, all of which and especially their forceps whether Flemish, Dutch, Irish, French or English, bare or covered, long or short, straight or crooked, windowed or not windowed, are totally useless or rather worse than good for nothing, being never but dangerous and often destructive.[24]

We should not be deaf to the funereal overtones when Dr Slop lays his hands upon his green baize bag.

When Dr Slop was dumped into the mud from his diminutive pony by the roaring past of Obadiah on the great coach-horse, he had only intended a casual call at Shandy Hall, not knowing that Mrs Shandy's labour had begun.

> ... what canst thou do?—Thou has come forth unarm'd;—thou has left thy *tire tête*,—thy new-invented *forceps*,—thy *crotchet*,— thy *squirt*, and all thy instruments of salvation and deliverance behind thee.—By heaven! at this moment they are hanging up in a green bays bag, betwixt thy two pistols, at thy bed's head! (pp. 109-10)

Sterne's irony is unmistakable: only one of the instruments in this 'tokological armamentarium', as Dr Allport called it, had anything to do with 'salvation'. The others were instruments of death.

The crotchet was a very ancient and very dangerous weapon, a hook used to destroy and extract a foetus which would not pass. No doubt Slop carried several forms of it, as did Burton. The most widely used types are seen in Plate Ia, taken from François Mauri-

---

23 Radcliffe, in 'Dr. John Burton and his Whimsical Contrivance', suggests that Sterne's asterisks become more meaningful when we know that Burton placed his patients in an unusual position, thereby risking a heightening of their feelings of shame. 'In France the left lateral position in delivery is still known as Burton's position, for he was an ardent advocate of its use on all occasions. . . . It will be remembered that the custom was to deliver in the supine position, or a modified lithotomy position.'
24 Quoted by Flack, *Eternal Eve*, p. 292.

ceau, *The Diseases of Women with Child*, 1668. The more merciful instrument on the left was often called the 'blunt hook'. That on the right, more properly spoken of as the 'crotchet', was merely a hooked knife. Dr Burton, however, was a great inventor. The green baize bag would have contained also the crotchet of his own design seen in Plate Ib. If it lacked the pretty silver handle of Mauriceau's, it sported an ingenious detachable handle complete with cross-member, a device Burton called his 'crutch'. Dr Burton used the crutch, he said, to push a foetus back into the womb, in the manner illustrated, when an arm presented first.[25] That particular presentation was one of the most feared, for the child could progress no further. The old procedure had been to amputate the arm.

The most common preternatural case was that of a child, presenting the head naturally, which could not pass because the head was too large. Consequently, a great deal of ingenuity was expended upon devices which would destroy the child by opening the head, and extract by attaching the head from within the cranial vault. For this dread operation, the most commonly used instrument was the *tire tête* of Mauriceau. Sterne, by speaking of the *tire tête* in the bag, was teasing Dr Burton, who had elaborately criticised that instrument. What was really in the bag was Burton's improvement upon the older device, which he was always careful to call his 'extractor'. That it was an improvement was attested by William Smellie, who spoke in praise of it (Vol. I, p. lv). The extractor (Plate IIa) was really two instruments. The portion on the right, seen in various stages of assembly, was used by Burton to open the foetal head. The three figures on the left show the instrument used to grip the head and extract the dead foetus. Tristram Shandy comes within a hair's breadth of entering the world with the help of this terrifying implement.

The third deathly device is the 'squirt', the syringe used to baptise the unborn infant when it is doomed. Sterne had already introduced his readers to the squirt in that magnificent joke about baptising 'all the HOMUNCULI at once, slap-dash, by *injection . . . par le moyen d'une* petite canulle, and *sans faire aucun tort au père'* (p. 62). Baptism by syringe had been practised at least as early as 1668, when Mauriceau spoke of it.[26] Sterne, however, got his information about this expedient from the *Observations* of Hendrik van Deventer, who had quoted his question about the sacrament to

[25] This illustration, as the others from Burton's *Essay* (Plates IIa, IIc, III), was made for the doctor by George Stubbs (1724-1806), later famous as a painter of horses and lions.
[26] First noted by Dr John Ferriar in 'Comments on Sterne', *Manchester Philosophical and Literary Transactions,* 1793, republished in the *Annual*

the theologians of the Sorbonne. Had Sterne read their original reply, he would not have missed one very interesting detail: the efficacy of the rite would be enhanced, said the good doctors of the Sorbonne, if the opening in the nozzle were in the form of a cross.[27] Alas, Mauriceau's squirt, the only one I could find in a plate (Plate IIb), lacks that particular advantage.

Sterne's remarks about the squirt, as well as his bald statement that Slop was a papist, amounted to a very serious charge against Dr Burton, for the infiltration of the Roman Church into Yorkshire was still feared. Probably Burton had Catholic sympathies; obviously he was rumoured to be a Catholic. Nevertheless, his obstetrical works contain strong evidence of the Protestantism he always claimed. He took the moral stand typical of Protestant man-midwives: the life of the mother was to be saved before that of the child (*Essay*, p. 208; *Letter*, p. 117). Had he been a Catholic, he very likely would have avoided such statements, as did most continental writers; for the Church had long before laid down a doctrine that a child should be saved at the expense of the mother's life, if necessary, so that it can have the benefit of baptism which she already enjoys.[28] Burton mentions no squirt in his books.

The one instrument which offered some hope for the life of Tristram was the forceps.

In the course of his career, Dr Burton used three forceps. His earliest instrument, for which he gave instructions in the body of the *Essay,* was a crude forceps of a type invented by the Chamberlens. The curved blades had no lock. They were placed at the sides of the foetal head and articulated, if at all, by holding the shanks together with the fingers of one hand. In Plate IIc we see Burton's plate, but a side view only of unmatching blades. The left one, when paired with an identical blade, made up the forceps. That on the right, a hooked blade, is one of a pair called the 'double crotchet', which could deliver only a dead foetus.

Register, 1793, pp. 379-98. Dr Ferriar used the 1681 edition of *Maladies des Femmes Grosses,* from which he quotes: "il n'y a pas d'occasions ou on ne puisse bien donner le baptême à l'enfant, durant qu'il est encore au ventre de la mere, estant facile de porter de l'eau nette par le moyen du canon d'une seringue jusque sur quelque partie de son corps . . . et il seroit inutile d'alleguer que l'eau n'y peut pas etre conduite, à cause que l'enfant est envelopé de ses membranes, qui en empêchent; car ne sçait-on pas qu'on les peut rompre tres aisement, en cas qu'elles ne le fussent pas, apres quoi on peut toucher effectivement son corps' (p. 394).

27 This information is from Flack, *Eternal Eve,* p. 328. Flack dated the original document 30 March 1733. Sterne, in his note to *Shandy,* pp. 57-8, dated the document he quoted from Deventer 10 April 1733. I cannot explain the discrepancy. Philip Peu also discussed baptism by squirt in 1694; see Radcliffe, 'Dr. John Burton and his Whimsical Contrivance', p. 354.

28 Glaister, *Dr. William Smellie and his Contemporaries,* p. 263. Also see the quotation from Mauriceau in note 14.

In his third and last period, Dr Burton used a more modern forceps of the sort designed by his old master, Dusée. This instrument, now at the York Medical Society, has long, straight, unfenestrated blades articulated with a removable pin—a passable instrument, though decidedly inferior to the several forceps designed by William Smellie. This instrument was found among his things at Burton's death. Apparently he had learned the truth about the forceps he designed, but had refused to the very last to admit the worth of the forceps invented by Dr Smellie.

If either of these devices is in the green bag, neither is withdrawn from it. The instrument which delivered Tristram Shandy was Slop's 'new invented forceps'. The three references to their newness (pp. 110, 153, 186) make it abundantly clear that Sterne meant the instrument of Burton's own invention described and illustrated (Plate III is Burton's plate) in the Appendix hastily tacked to the *Essay* of 1751—so hastily added, in fact, that the implement is not mentioned in the text itself. The arguments Burton advanced in its favour were brief in the original Appendix, but long in the *Letter to Dr. William Smellie* appearing two years later (pp. 141-3). It could be placed in one operation, said Burton; and the blades could be fixed in a rigid position once the set screw at the bottom was tightened.

> This Instrument is less prejudicial to the Child's Head, because the wings can be fixed, at any determinate Degree of Expansion, as not to compress the Head more than necessary; whereas, with other Forceps, the more you pull, the more you squeeze. . . .
> (*Essay*, pp. 389-90)

For all that, the machine is not well designed, as we can see in the photograph of the actual forceps, now at the obstetrical museum of the University of Edinburgh (Plate IV).[29] The blades are too narrow and the curve poorly designed for a child's head. The major objection is to its bulk. 'A very whimsical contrivance', commented Dr Lowder in 1782, which requires 'more room than we expect to have when we use forceps'.[30] To these criticisms I would add a point discovered by Dr Margaret Rowbottom and myself when she recently demonstrated for me the facsimile forceps at the Welcome Medical Museum in London. So great is the magnification of force between the screw handle and the claw-like blades, that the operator has no sense of the pressure being exerted by the blades. The discovery was made, to my sorrow, upon the bones of my hands, which,

---

[29] The photograph is reproduced from R. W. Johnstone, *William Smellie, the Master of British Midwifery*, Edinburgh and London, 1952. I wish to thank the publishers for permission to use the photograph.

[30] From a manuscript lecture quoted by Doran in 'Burton ("Dr. Slop")', p. 20.

like those of Uncle Toby's, were nearly broken as Dr Rowbottom casually turned the handle.

Imagine to yourself now the scene in the back parlour. Dr Slop has been washed up, after his fall into the mud, and rubbed down and fitted out, or into, a pair of Obadiah's pumps. Obadiah has returned from his second trip upon the great coach-horse, this time to get the green baize bag, which he has placed before Dr Slop and Uncle Toby and his master. But Obadiah, so that he could hear himself whistle as he trotted home, had quieted the 'terrible jingle' in the bag by taking cord and tying and cross-tying the bag with many roundabouts and hard knots. 'A sudden trampling in the room above' and a groan from Mrs Shandy startles Dr Slop into action. He cannot undo the knots. Now the 'most virtuous way' would be to take fingers and teeth to them.

> Dr. *Slop* had lost his teeth—his favourite instrument, by extracting in a wrong direction, or by some misapplication of it, unfortunately slipping, he had formerly in a hard labour, knock'd out three of the best of them, with the handle of it:— he tried his fingers—alas! the nails of his fingers and thumbs [in accordance with Burton's instructions in the *Essay*] were cut close. (p. 168)

Dr Slop borrows a penknife and cuts his thumb to the very bone. 'Curse the fellow . . . I am undone for this bout.' Thereupon Walter Shandy lifts down his copy of Bishop Ernulf, and Dr Slop stands anathematising Obadiah as above the innocent unborn moves closer to the point which will determine his life or death.

Susannah runs downstairs.

> Bless my soul!—my poor mistress is ready to faint,—and her pains are gone,—and the drops are done,—and the bottle of julap is broke,—and the nurse has cut her arm,—(and I, my thumb, cried Dr. *Slop*) and the child is where it was. (p. 184)

But more: 'the midwife has fallen backwards upon the edge of the fender, and bruised her hip as black as your hat'. Perhaps she was tugging hard at a fillet when it slipped off. (A fillet is a slit linen sling placed over the head.)

> . . . the midwife would gladly first give you an account how things are, so desires you would go up stairs and speak to her this moment . . . No, replied Dr. *Slop,* 'twould be full as proper, if the midwife came down to me.—I like subordination, quoth my uncle *Toby*. (p. 184)

The midwife has come down subordinately to make her report.

Dr Slop does not feel rushed. He first must demonstrate his forceps to the gentlemen.

> Upon my honour, Sir, you have tore every bit of the skin quite off the back of both my hands with your forceps, cried my uncle *Toby*,—and you have crush'd all my knuckles into the bargain with them, to a jelly.
> . . . the points of my forceps have not been sufficiently arm'd, or the rivet wants closing—or else the cut on my thumb has made me a little aukward,—or possibly—'Tis well, quoth my father . . . that the experiment was not first made upon my child's head piece. (p. 187)

Slop discounts the suggestions, explaining that the head of a foetus is 'naturally as soft as the pap of an apple;—the sutures give way'—a point Burton had frequently made in his books.

'And besides,' continues the doctor, 'I could have extracted by the feet after', to which the old midwife standing by comments eloquently, 'Not you'. Walter, of course, pricks up his ears: 'I rather wish you would begin that way'.

The doctor, beginning to enjoy his power, turns to the midwife. 'Will you take upon you to say, it may not be the child's hip, as well as the child's head?' ' 'Tis most certainly the head, replied the midwife' in the second and final speech of that delightful character.

> Because, continued Dr. *Slop*, (turning to my father) as positive as these old ladies generally are,—'tis a point very difficult to know,—and yet of the greatest consequence to be known;—because, Sir, if the hip is mistaken for the head,—there is a possibility (if it is a boy) that the forceps   *   *   *
> *   *   *   *   *   *   *   *   *   *

Thereupon Dr Slop picks up the green baize bag and trips 'pretty nimbly, for a man of his size', across the room and up the stairs.

From these few hints we can know exactly Mrs Shandy's condition. Her labour has been short, stopping two hours and ten minutes after it began.[31] It was a critical labour from the first, as evidenced by Susannah's sudden, fearful flight for the old midwife. The short, violent labour indicates that Mrs Shandy's waters had suddenly broken. Consequently, the baby has moved well down towards the pelvis. The head presents, as the midwife well knows, for she has

---

31 Two hours and ten minutes lapsed between Slop's entrance and his tripping upstairs (p. 188). Labour had begun when Susannah went for the midwife and Obadiah for Dr Slop (p. 99). If we allow about ten minutes for Obadiah's fetching of the horse, his accident with Slop at the corner of the garden wall, and Slop's dragging himself to the house, then the labour began two hours and twenty minutes before Slop goes upstairs. But by then the labour had been stopped for about ten minutes—from the time Susannah first ran downstairs (p. 184).

been attempting some sort of manual extraction and has had a grip, which did not hold, upon the head. The difficulty is clear: Tristram's head is too large for the opening. The case is a common one, to be found described in every eighteenth-century obstetrical treatise, including Burton's *Essay* (pp. 191, 215) and *Letter* (pp. 118-19). As the midwife knows, in such an advanced stage there is no chance at all for the podalic version Walter wants so badly, Dr Slop's bragging notwithstanding. The possibilities have been narrowed to two: Tristram *must* be delivered by the forceps or by the *tire tête*.

A calm falls upon the Shandy household. At least a quiet falls, for the two gentlemen in the parlour fall asleep. When they awake Dr Slop is in the kitchen preparing for a brave attempt at plastic surgery. ' 'Tis a bridge for master's nose', reports Trim.

> In bringing him into the world with his vile instruments, he has crush'd his nose, *Susannah* says, as flat as a pancake to his face, and he is making a false bridge with a piece of cotton and a thin piece of whalebone out of *Susannah's* stays, to raise it up. (pp. 214-15)

Thus, too, is crushed another hope of the father, for in Walter Shandy's opinion a good, generous nose (next to a proper begetting, a birth feet first, and an inspiring Christian name such as Trismegistus) is the most important asset a man can have.

The forceps, as Dr Burton's *Essay* (p. 217) or any obstetrical work of the time will explain, are to be placed over the foetal head at or close to the temples, the exact position being determined by the operator's first feeling the ears. The instrument could slip. But slipping from the narrow dimension, side to side, to the longer dimension, front to back, is out of the question—especially for Dr Burton's forceps, the blades of which will not move once the set screw has been fixed. As bungling as Slop appears, it is hard to believe he could misplace the forceps out of sheer stupidity. His error was caused by the cut on his thumb. The gash having robbed his hands of their sensitivity, he misjudged the location of the ears.[32] When he tightened down the blades, the device being made as it was, he could not feel any resistance.

Worse still, the delivery was too slow. The head had remained under pressure in the narrow pelvic passage. While Dr Slop haughtily called down the midwife and foolishly questioned her, while he

[32] Tristram tells us (p. 166) that had Nature set up a race with Dr Slop to see if she could deliver before Slop untied all the knots made by Obadiah, Tristram's nose would not have been depressed. The passage might be taken to mean that Nature could have decided to deliver the boy normally, but that reading would not fit with the facts of Mrs Shandy's condition. The passage means, rather, that had Dr Slop untied the knots instead of cutting them (thus cutting his thumb), he would have delivered Tristram whole.

demonstrated his forceps on Uncle Toby's fists, the cerebellum, or soul, of the infant (depending on the point of view) was being slowly pressed above. Hence the evening of Tristram's birth:

> There is not a moment's time to dress you, Sir, cried *Susannah* —the child is as black in the face as my—As your, what? said my father, for like all orators, he was a dear searcher into comparisons—Bless me, Sir, said *Susannah,* the child's in a fit. (p. 287)

Fit was a good medical term in those days, one used to describe the convulsions in the new-born, often fatal, brought on by too great and too prolonged pressures upon the cerebellum. The baby, black in the face and presumed dying, is rushed to the silly curate, while Walter is trying to climb into his breeches, and misbaptised with the name Tristram—of all Christian names, the very one his father thought the worst. All of Walter's fears, without exception, have been realised in the birth of his son.

> It might have been worse, replied my uncle *Toby*—I don't comprehend, said my father—Suppose the hip had been presented, replied my uncle *Toby,* as Dr. Slop foreboded.
> My father reflected half a minute—looked down—touched the middle of his forehead slightly with his finger—
> —True, said he. (pp. 280-1)

Tristram's birth was utterly circumstantial and accidental—the exact opposite of his father's inspired ideal of planned, rational creation. Dr Slop did save the life of the Shandy heir, but not because his ideas were sound or his inventions clever. Tristram survived, the 'sport of small accidents' (p. 166), of an odd marriage contract, a too-large head, a clumsy machine, and a cut thumb. Not reason, but Fate, gave to Tristram Shandy his life and his inadequate configuration.

Slop reappears from time to time to play the medical clown, farcically in the cataplasm-throwing fight with Susannah over the prone Tristram after the falling window sash had circumcised the small hero (p. 413); more subtly in his prediction that the wound 'will end in a *phimosis*' (p. 401), although a phimosis is cured by circumcision, not caused by it.[33]

Dr Slop's real role in the story, however, was finished once Tristram was born. In the birth episode, he and Walter Shandy had

---

[33] A phimosis is a narrowing of the preputial orifice. Robert James, in *A Medical Dictionary*, Vol. III, London, 1743-5, explained its causes as either a too-long foreskin, or 'impure coition'. Its cure, he said, if medication failed, was circumcision. There remains, however, some argument in favour of Dr Slop's prognosis. If only a small part of the prepuce were amputated and mangled by the sash, irregular scar tissue might form, resulting in a phimosis.

represented truthfully the theories and practices of Dr John Burton. In these Sterne had discovered his profound comic vision of man's utter foolishness before the mysteries of life and death.

The melancholy literature of midwifery gave to Sterne a paratactical life-death image, his informing symbol, his own myth. The image remained with him to the last. Speaking of the *Sentimental Journey,* he wrote to George Macartney three months before his death,

> I am going to ly-in; being at Christmas at my full reckoning—and unless what I shall bring forth is not *press'd* to death by these devils of printers, I shall have the honour of presenting to you a *couple of as clean brats* as ever chaste brain conceiv'd —They are frolicksome too, *mais cela n'empeche pas.*

That life should begin with a threat of death. For an age which assumed a reasonable world, this was the most nonsensical of mysteries. It was the germ of Sterne's great frolic.

Research for this paper was supported by a grant from Colorado State University Research Funds. I wish to thank John B. Blake of the History of Medicine Division, National Library of Medicine, for his help in locating materials, and Dr Robert J. Bliss for checking my surmises about the exact manner of Tristram's birth.

Some Eighteenth-Century Attempts to Use the Notion of Happiness

S. A. Grave

The eighteenth century engaged in obsessional talk about happiness. This paper will consider three proposals, one or more of which are to be found in many eighteenth-century philosophical writers: firstly, to use the desire for happiness as a fundamental principle in explaining human conduct; secondly, to use this desire to mould conduct into virtue; thirdly, to use a tendency to promote the general happiness as the criterion of right conduct. Happiness was commonly thought of as the combination of contentment and pleasure,[1] the word 'pleasure' covering everything from the most spiritualised delight to the simple pleasures of sense. There was often in eighteenth-century writing a casualness about the distinction between happiness and pleasure. I shall not be making anything of this distinction, and also, for brevity, I extend 'the desire for pleasure or happiness' to include 'aversion from pain or misery'. These imprecisions might not give trouble in a study which is concerned with very wide generalities. The doctrine that we can desire only our own pleasure or happiness, some gratification of ourselves, I shall refer to as 'self-love theory'.

The idea of Newtonian achievements in a science of human nature, built up by 'the experimental method', was in the eighteenth-century air. A gravitational drive towards pleasure was spoken of, but no theory of hedonic gravitation was constructed having, like the physical theory, experimentally testable predictive powers. We need a moral science which is experimental like physics, Helvétius said.[2] And he makes a gesture towards another Newtonian model:

---

[1] The article 'Bonheur' in the *Encyclopédie* (ed., D. Diderot and J. le R. d'Alembert), for example, defines happiness as 'un état tranquille, semé çà et là de quelques plaisirs . . . .'

[2] C. A. Helvétius, *De l'esprit*, 1758, Préface (*Oeuvres*, Vol. II, Paris, 1784, pp. 5-6).

'Si l'univers physique est soumis aux lois du mouvement, l'univers moral ne l'est pas moins à celles de l'intérêt'.[3]

Taken seriously, as more than a verbal flourish, the suggested analogy is wholly misleading. From the laws of motion, together with a specification of the particular circumstances, the movements of a body can be deduced and are thus explained. But anything that anyone might do, and any evaluations he might make, are necessarily compatible with the law of universal determination by self-interest. Since this law excludes no possibilities, it explains no particular occurrences. An attempt to put down the incalculability of men's behaviour, not to the emptiness of the law of self-interest as a premise but to our inability to specify the relevant circumstances, would still have to acknowledge that this law does not stand or fall by its relation to empirical facts, as scientific laws ultimately do. The appeal which Helvétius makes to experience for confirmation of his law prescribes what is to be found. Will anyone who turns an honest scrutiny upon himself fail to perceive, he asks, *'que c'est uniquement à la manière differente dont l'intérêt personnel se modifie, que l'on doit ses vices & ses vertus? que tous les hommes sont mus par la même force? que tous tendent également à leur bonheur? . . .'*[4] It will not be within the powers of experience to present a counter-instance to determination by self-interest for anything appearing to be such will be determination by some 'modification' of self-interest.[5]

As deductively sterile, the postulated law of self-interest is quite unlike the laws of physical science. But though the law cannot explain why this rather than that occurs, it does not follow that it must be without explanatory value of any kind. Suppose that self-interested actions are thoroughly understood and that apparently disinterested ones are baffling; then if the second class could be reduced to the first, even though no predictions would be possible, intelligibility would have been spread over the whole field.[6] Advocates of the law on these grounds would, however, have two tasks to perform. They would have to effect the reduction: they would

[3] Ibid., Discours II, Ch. 2, pp. 69-70. Helvétius's use of the plural (*'celles de l'intérêt'*) is, I think, purely rhetorical: *laws* of motion, so *laws* of self-interest.
[4] Ibid., pp. 68-9.
[5] Two remarks made by Helvétius on method are worth placing side by side, along with a comment of Diderot's on the second. 'C'est la méditation qui seule peut nous révéler ces vérités premières, générales, les clefs & les principes des sciences' (*De l'homme*, Sect. II, Ch. 15 (*Oeuvres*, Vol. V, p. 173)).
'Il faut s'avancer à la suite de l'expérience, & jamais ne la précéder' (Sect. II, Ch. 20, p. 199). Diderot's comment: 'L'expérience n'est-elle pas souvent précédée d'une supposition, d'une analogie, d'une idée systématique que l'expérience confirmera ou détruira?' (*Réfutation suivie de l'ouvrage d'Helvétius intitulé l'Homme (Oeuvres*, Vol. II, Paris, 1875-7, p. 349)).
[6] This consideration was mentioned to me by Dr R. L. Franklin.

also have to make it clear that there is something improbable, impossible, or impenetrably opaque in the idea of a disinterested action. One of the reasons, perhaps, for the *naïveté* of so much self-love theory is the extent to which it was taken as obvious that there is something impossibly wrong with this idea.

In spite of aspirations towards Newtonian models, the characteristic eighteenth-century method in the science of man was genetic, the construction of a theoretical history deriving present complexities of mind from primitive simplicities of experience.[7] This rationalistic empiricism guided the construction of the mental life of Condillac's animated statue[8]—quite the most important piece of sculpture in the century. Under a marble exterior the statue has our organic structure. It has a mind which is at first completely blank. It is given senses so that it might have the sensations we have, and it needs nothing else in order to become all that we are. The development of its faculties makes great progress even while it has only the sense of smell. Thus with its awareness of succession in itself when a sensation dies away leaving a residual 'idea', it distinguishes between present and past, and has acquired memory. When its attention is divided between different ideas it compares— this divided attention is comparison—and as soon as there is comparison there is judgment, which is merely the perceiving of a relation between ideas when these are compared.

It is, however, only through the sense of touch that it emerges from a solipsistic existence to a knowledge of things other than its own variously modified being. Pleasure or pain begins with the first sensation. Desire is delayed until transition from one to the other has been experienced; desire arises from present pain contrasted with remembered pleasure. As generating desire and aversion, pleasure and pain energise the whole psychological development of the man Condillac is creating and move him to whatever he does.

The genetic method rejects the notion, so to speak, of fixity of species in the psychological world, substituting for it a doctrine of transformation, and it is inherent in the method to try to get as much from as little as possible. (Its constant tendency is either to have the new species appear by saltation, or to offer as a new species what is quite obviously the old one redescribed.) We shall now glance at a formidable undertaking in genetic economy: an attempt

---

[7] This approach to the understanding of man was in part due to Locke's great influence—though at times one is tempted to think that Locke would have had as great an influence if he had never existed, since so much of what is in him is already to be found elsewhere.

[8] E. B. Condillac, *Traité des sensations*, 1754 (*Oeuvres philosophiques de Condillac*, ed. G. Le Roy, Vol. I, Paris, 1947).

to explain how the disinterested approbation of virtue can arise in men whose ultimate end is their own individual good.

John Gay[9] allows it to be a 'matter of fact' that with most men moral approbation or disapprobation operates 'immediately', not waiting upon any calculation of personal interest; that even if they do take their personal interest into consideration and find it damaged by what they approve of, their moral judgment is un-affected. There is, however, he argues, no need to suppose in explanation a moral sense and 'public affections' implanted in us by nature; we have both, but both are acquired. 'Virtue is the conformity to a rule of life, directing the actions of all rational creatures with respect to each other's happiness. . . .'[10] We learn virtue largely by imitation. In so far as self-conscious reflection is involved, virtue—our own and that of others—recommends itself to each of us as a means to our happiness; for this in great part depends on how other men behave towards us, and their behaviour to us depends on ours to them. Now, by association, a means to an end may so borrow desirability from its end as to appear to have it in its own right. And it is in this way that virtue (with the moral sense and dispositions essential to it) may emancipate itself from the motive of self-interest which was for each of us its only rationale.

The contrast between the notion of a law of self-interest that is never superseded and a notion of the development of disinterested-ness and benevolence in men born wanting only their own happiness but dependent on each other for its realisation, brings out an am-biguity in the reference of all human action to self-love. It may be meant firstly that self-love is the perpetual determinant of all our actions. What is thought of as done selflessly would be only appar-ently so, would really proceed from hidden self-love. It may be meant secondly that self-love is the original source of all our actions but that derivatively other principles of action have arisen which operate autonomously. Genuine selflessness exists, though it has developed from an alien origin. It should be emphasised that a writer is quite likely to hold inconsistently both these views (ex-pressions such as the 'transformation of self-love' perhaps concealing their difference from him). In the rest of this paper I shall limit myself to comments on the first view, to which general considera-tions are more readily applicable than to the second, and shall be using the expression 'self-love theory' only in reference to this view. The second view is committed to telling a story of origin and

9 John Gay, *Concerning the Fundamental Principle of Virtue or Morality.* This dissertation was prefixed anonymously to the English translation of Archbishop King's *Essay on the Origin of Evil,* 1731. It is included in Vol. II of L. A. Selby-Bigge's *British Moralists,* Oxford, 1897, to which the page number refers.
10 Gay, *Concerning the Fundamental Principle of Virtue,* p. 272.

change and is not very profitably talked about apart from the story, which needs to be carefully detailed before its probabilities can be assessed. Gay's narrative, for instance, is a token performance.

In connexion with the suggested analogy between the laws of motion and the law of self-interest I remarked, transferring a philosophical commonplace to this context, that the law of self-interest could explain no particular occurrence since it is compatible with whatever is done. The possibility was left open that the law might, nevertheless, have explanatory value of another kind. It must now be asked, and again the general consideration is of a type that has become very familiar, whether there is any meaning at all in an assertion that all our behaviour proceeds from self-interest. We call an action 'self-interested' as opposed to one which is 'disinterested'. The assertion that all behaviour is self-interested seems to take away the possibility of our making this contrast. It cannot allow that the contrast is exhibited in any actual instances: all actions are self-interested. How, then, do we frame the notion of a (really) disinterested action; how do we know what we are looking for and never find? There may be an answer which does not borrow a specious plausibility from the fact that we do have both the opposed notions. But if the assertion that *all* actions are self-interested does take away the possibility of our making the contrast, it deprives itself of meaning; it deprives of meaning the description of *any* action as self-interested.

The philosophers who asserted that 'self-love is the principle of all our actions' were very unwilling, as a rule, to be taken as turning us all into egotists. The word 'self-love', in this assertion, has been misunderstood, Helvétius said. He goes on to explain its meaning:

> *Il étoit cependant facile d'appercevoir que l'amour-propre, ou l'amour de soi, n'étoit autre chose qu'un sentiment gravé en nous par la nature; que ce sentiment se transformoit dans chaque homme en vice ou en vertu....*[11]

Self-love is only the desire for our happiness. But though the word 'self-love' might have been imperfectly understood, the purport of the assertion in which it figures was not obscure. What was being said is that we can desire only our happiness.

The remarkable thing about the belief that all our actions are determined by self-love, self-interest, the desire for our own pleasure or happiness is that it came to get such a grip on so many minds. I shall not touch on historical explanations for the prevalence of this belief in both the seventeenth and eighteenth centuries. I shall quote a passage from the first of Joseph Butler's sermons, 'Upon the

11 Helvétius, *De l'esprit,* Discours I, Ch. 4 (*Oeuvres,* Vol. II, p. 50).

love of our Neighbour', which suggests a reason for its persuasiveness at any time.

> Every particular affection, even the love of our neighbour, is as really our own affection, as self-love; and the pleasure arising from its gratification is as much my own pleasure, as the pleasure self-love would have, from knowing I myself should be happy some time hence, would be my own pleasure. And if, because every particular affection is a man's own, and the pleasure arising from its gratification his own pleasure, or pleasure to himself, such particular affection must be called self-love; according to this way of speaking, no creature whatever can possibly act but merely from self-love. . . .[12]

It is easy to slide from the truth that the gratification of any of my affections or desires is my own into the error that all I ever want is my own gratification. If it be not error, if all I ever want is my own pleasure, then I want something, Butler argues, that I can never have; for pleasure arises from the satisfaction of desires and affections set on things other than one's pleasure:[13] on food and drink, for example, on other people's ruin, or their happiness.

The error into which it is easy to slide from the trivial truth that the gratification of any of my desires is always mine, is a strange one. It sees us as setting our desires on one of two opposed alternatives, where in fact there is no duality at all. A distinction is made, consciously or implicitly, between wanting a thing for its own sake and wanting it for the sake of the pleasure it gives us; and the declaration is added that nothing but pleasure is ever wanted for its own sake, every other object of desire being sought only as a means to pleasure. Now there is a difference between, say, engaging in an activity for pleasure and engaging in it for profit, but none between engaging in it for its own sake and for the pleasure of it. We should not understand the question if we were asked whether we wanted our children around us for the sake of their presence, or for the pleasure we get from it. When we take pleasure in an activity, or in an object that delights us, or in another man's pleasure, there is no logical room for the means-end distinction.[14] If the eighteenth century had had a better opinion of Aristotle, attention to considerations set out in the *Nicomachean Ethics*[15]

---

12 Joseph Butler, *Works*, ed. W. E. Gladstone, Vol. II, Oxford, 1896, p. 188.
13 Ibid., p. 190. Butler has overstated his good case, as Henry Sidgwick points out: many pleasures—pleasures from sights and scents, for instance—arise 'without any perceptible relation to previous desires' (*The Methods of Ethics*, 6th ed., London, 1901, pp. 44-5).
14 Cf. G. Ryle, *Dilemmas*, Ch. 4, Cambridge, 1954, and A. Kenny, *Action, Emotion and Will*, Ch. 6, London, 1963.
15 *Nicomachean Ethics*, 1174a-1176a ('. . . each of the pleasures is bound up with the activity it completes' (1175a, 29-30)).

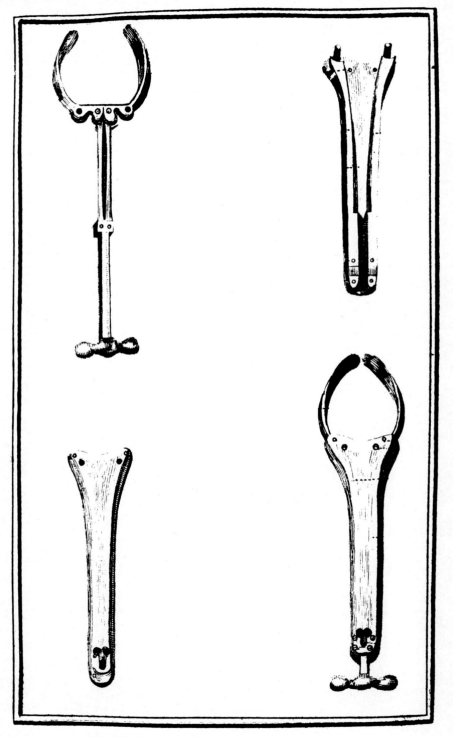

Plate III   Dr Burton's forceps, from the *Essay towards a
Complete New System of Midwifry*, 1751.

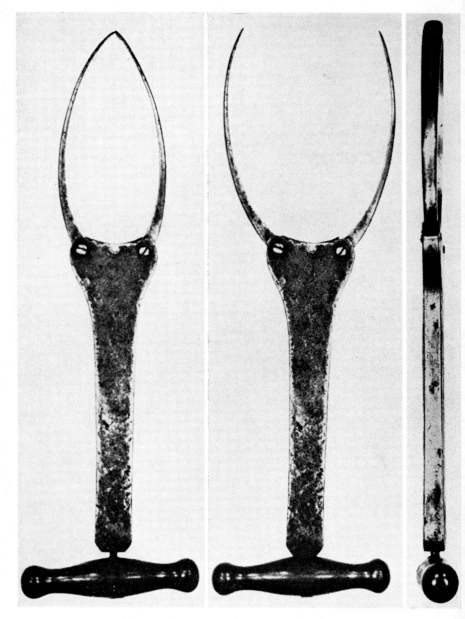

Plate IV   Dr Burton's forceps, now in the obstetrical
museum, University of Edinburgh

might have put a brake upon what appears to have been a strong, unnoticed tendency to regard pleasure in anything as a feeling which we happen to get from a thing, but which is detachable from it in thought and might conceivably have been derived from something else.

I must now quote from Rousseau's *Confessions* a passage which presents an experience that is in complete conflict with an account of pleasure or happiness tying them conceptually to objects or activities.

> *Je me levois avec le soleil et j'étois heureux; je me promenois et j'étois heureux, je voyois maman et j'étois heureux, je la quittois et j'étois heureux, je parcourois les bois, les coteaux, j'errois dans les vallons, je lisois, j'étois oisif, je travaillois au jardin, je cueillois les fruits, j'aidois au ménage, et le bonheur me suivoit par tout; il n'étoit dans aucune chose assignable, il étoit tout en moi-même, il ne pouvoit me quitter un seul instant.*[16]

This feeling of happiness no doubt had its physiological or psychological causes, but it was in a way independent of objects and activities—one was as good as another. I think that an experience of this kind tells decisively against any attempt to make an 'Aristotelian' account cover every state of pleasure or of being happy. It does nothing to show that such an account never holds. It is, indeed, as impossible to wedge apart in idea pleasure and happiness from the things in which we take pleasure or which make us happy, as it is to weld on to anything Rousseau's objectless happiness.

Drawing some threads together, I shall say that self-love theory seems to move into unintelligibility from two directions. Firstly, it might intend to let such words as 'self-love' have more or less their ordinary meanings. But these meanings presuppose in each case a distinction which the theory looks as though it destroys in maintaining that everything is done from self-love. It cannot simply stipulate a new meaning for the words, since its purpose is to disabuse us of the belief that we can ever act except for our own gratification, so it is forced to oscillate between the old meanings and no meaning. Secondly, in order to have us always acting only for our own gratification, it is also necessary to invent a distinction, in cases where no such distinction is possible, between wanting something for its own sake and wanting it for the sake of the pleasure it gives.[17]

---

[16] J. J. Rousseau, *Confessions*, Bk VI (at the beginning).
[17] Many things that we want to have or to do for their own sake can also, of course, be sought for or done as a means to something else. We might want to relieve a man's distress simply in order to make him happy, or we might want

If the principle that all our actions are dictated by self-love, self-interest, the desire for our own pleasure or happiness, carries only the illusion of meaning, it is not surprising that it should have had no explanatory value.

We shall now watch self-love at work in the production of virtue. The principle of self-love does not look favourable to virtue which, however moderately it is defined, is going to require some subordination of one's own interests to the good of others. I propose to take for consideration a definition in which virtue appears with rapacious demands: self-love might turn out to have unsuspected capacities for self-transcendence. This definition comes after Mandeville's description of the way in which natural man was, 'or at least might have been', broken in. It was agreed, he says,

> to give the Name of VIRTUE to every Performance, by which Man, contrary to the impulse of Nature, should endeavour the Benefit of others, or the Conquest of his own Passions out of a Rational Ambition of being good.[18]

Is virtue, as Mandeville defines it, possible? We might suppose that we had a notable example of it in the parson[19] who is living on oatmeal and water, sleeping on straw, and doing everything in his power to make his people happy. He makes his appearance as an answer to clergymen claiming that they had to live in some style to keep up respect for their order, but he ends ambiguously: there is some question of his allowing himself, unreasonably under the circumstances, to want a wife. More importantly, had he been unfaltering in self-denial, he would still have fallen short of virtue as Mandeville conceived of it. To see why, let us look at Mandeville's account of the origin of virtue and at his characterisation of virtuous men.

The civilisers of natural man had somehow to persuade him that 'it was more beneficial for every Body to conquer than indulge his Appetites, and much better to mind the Publick than what seem'd his private Interest'. He was unlikely to be persuaded unless he could be provided with 'an Equivalent to be enjoy'd as a Reward for the Violence' he was being asked to do to himself. It was not possible to provide each individual with a real recompense for acts of self-denial. Instead, an 'imaginary' one was devised, which cost

to relieve his distress to remove our own at the sight of his. That there is a real difference between the two cases is shown by the fact that in the first we might have no noticeable feelings at all. Only in the second can we meaningfully be said to act from self-love.

18 Bernard Mandeville, *The Fable of the Bees*, ed. F. B. Kaye, Vol. I, Oxford, 1924, pp. 48-9.

19 Ibid., pp. 156-60.

nobody anything but which was most acceptable to those who received it: the pride included in our 'very Essence' was got at; the self-deniers were paid in praise, called 'the true Representatives of their sublime Species', and contrasted with the self-indulgent 'Dross of their Kind'. There were also obvious practical benefits for everyone in coercive rules of morality: men were made less of a nuisance and more useful to each other.[20] So it was agreed to preach down as vicious any self-gratification that might have the least tendency to harm others or even make a man less useful to others, and to preach up the demands of virtue as they are stated in Mandeville's definition.

The virtue defined and the virtue whose origin has been described do not appear to be the same thing. The virtue that men have been induced to practice is self-centred. The virtue defined requires a selflessness that human nature, as expounded by Mandeville, cannot make available. Even in the best of men the love of goodness is flawed.

> . . . such Men, as without complying with any Weakness[21] of their own, can part from what they value themselves, and, from no other Motive but their Love to Goodness, perform a worthy Action in Silence: Such Men, I confess, have acquir'd more refin'd Notions of Virtue than those I have hitherto spoke of; yet even in these (with which the World has yet never swarm'd) we may discover no small Symptoms of Pride, and the humblest Man alive must confess, that the Reward of a Virtuous Action, which is the Satisfaction that ensues upon it, consists in a certain Pleasure he procures to himself by contemplating on his own Worth: which Pleasure, together with the Occasion of it, are as certain Signs of Pride, as looking Pale and Trembling at any imminent Danger, are the Symptoms of Fear.[22]

If pride is essential to human nature, the virtue of the definition is beyond our accomplishment. But one wants to know how Mandeville has made this discovery about human nature. The method by which he does reveal to us disturbing things about ourselves is by contrasting what we say with what we do, or would do, in easily imaginable circumstances. He is well aware of this method.

> I expect to be ask'd why in the Fable I have call'd those Pleasures real that are directly opposite to those which I own the wise Men of all Ages have extoll'd as the most valuable. My Answer is, because I don't call things Pleasures which Men say are best, but such as they seem to be most pleased with; how

[20] Ibid., pp. 42-9.
[21] That is, they are not overcome by the passion of pity, which is a mere 'Impulse of Nature'.
[22] Mandeville, *The Fable of the Bees*, Vol. I, p. 57.

can I believe that a Man's chief Delight is in the Embellishments of the Mind, when I see him ever employ'd about and
daily pursue the Pleasures that are contrary to them?[23]

According to this method, the presence of pride in a man is to be
established by his behaviour, from signs of pride as unmistakable
as the signs of fear. In any particular case, then, Mandeville will
need the evidence of behaviour to show that someone's satisfaction
in a virtuous action is not just that but is really self-satisfaction,
pleasure in contemplating his own worth; and in any particular
case he may succeed in showing it. But to get a universal truth here
Mandeville implicitly discards this empirical method—for though
there may be no signs of pride he will not allow it to be absent—and
he has implicitly to define the pleasure in virtue as self-congratula-
tory pleasure. It is a definition that tells us nothing about ourselves.

We should be going too far afield to take up in any detail the
associated questions whether Mandeville framed an ironical definition of virtue, and whether his doctrine, 'Private Vices, Publick
Benefits', was intended to effect a utilitarian change in our notions
of what is vicious. The evidence is conflicting and vague. On the
first of these questions I shall merely say that I think Mandeville
wanted to have virtue making demands that could never be met
because he could not bring himself to allow *merit*. (Thus interpreted, his position would have secularised resemblances to the
theology which taught both total depravity and an inexorable
moral law.) As regards the second question, it seems to me that
Mandeville really wanted to maintain paradox.

To assert that we can desire nothing but our pleasure or happiness commits one to denying that we can desire virtue for its own
sake, even if virtue is not thought of as requiring teeth-gritting
struggle towards self-suppression. If the purpose of virtue is totally
the good of society and one's own good as a member of society, this
perhaps need not matter. I shall end this section of the paper with
a remark on the confidence felt by many eighteenth-century writers
that the virtue necessary to the well-being of society could be
ensured by being made to pay.

The self-lover is eminently the manipulable man. Efficiently
handled, he can be expected to learn to find his happiness in ways
that do not diminish, and often promote, the general happiness;
vice can be made too costly and virtue worth his while. Mandeville
gives (cynically) one account of the manner in which his conduct is
moulded into the sort of virtue society cannot do without. The
accounts vary, the principle is the same. Moralists, Helvétius says,
should occupy themselves in discovering how to use rewards and

23 Ibid., p. 151.

punishments to bind self to social interest. '*Si les citoyens ne pouvoient faire leur bonheur particulier, sans faire le bien public, il n'y auroit alors de vicieux que les fous; tous les hommes seroient nécessités à la vertu. . . .*'[24]

There is, of course, much to be said for making virtue pay and vice have to be paid for. It is dangerous, though, to give instruction in this system of profit and loss (at least if you let it be thought there is no God to be feared). Told to be virtuous *because* it pays, an apt pupil might think of circumstances in which only a fool would be virtuous.

We have now to consider the utilitarian proposal to make a tendency to promote the general happiness the criterion of right action. I shall take Bentham as the representative of utilitarianism partly because his name is so especially associated with it, and partly in order to mention some neglected arguments of his in justification of this criterion.

'NATURE has placed mankind under the governance of two sovereign masters, *pain* and *pleasure*. It is for them alone to point out what we ought to do, as well as to determine what we shall do.' These sentences begin the first chapter of Bentham's *Introduction to the Principles of Morals and Legislation,* 1789.[25] Bentham is not maintaining that Nature has arranged things so that what we do and what we ought to do coincide. The pain or pleasure determining our actions is our own; the pain or pleasure which ought to regulate them is that of everyone affected by our actions. We have to be '*made*' to do as we ought by the 'sanctions' with which a rule of conduct is invested. These sanctions constitute the 'binding' character of obligation.[26] We do as we ought when we act in conformity with the 'principle of utility'. This principle requires that every action be approved of or condemned 'according to the tendency which it appears to have to augment or diminish the happiness' of those whose interests are involved.[27] In the *Fragment on Government,* 1776, an earlier statement of the principle of utility uses the phrase now so familiar: '*It is the greatest happiness of the greatest number that is the measure of right and wrong*'.[28] In the *Constitutional Code* (unfinished when Bentham died in 1832) the

---

24 Helvétius, *De l'esprit,* Discours II, Ch. 22, (*Oeuvres,* Vol. II, p. 246).

25 Jeremy Bentham, *Works,* ed. J. Bowring, Vol. I, 1838-43 (reprinted New York, 1962), p. 1.

26 *Principles of Morals and Legislation,* Ch. 3, Sects. i-ii, p. 14. Cf. *Fragment on Government,* Ch. 5, Sect. vii (*Works,* Vol. I, p. 293), where Bentham represents political, moral, and religious duty as 'created' by the penalties attached as sanctions to laws of the state, moral rules, and divine commands.

27 *Principles of Morals and Legislation,* Ch. I, Sect. ii (*Works,* Vol. I, p. 1).

28 Preface (*Works,* Vol. I, p. 227).

'proper end of government' is stated to be 'the greatest happiness of all, or, in case of competition, the greatest happiness of the greatest number'.[29]

The utilitarian principle, Bentham says in the first chapter of the *Principles of Morals and Legislation,* seems to be incapable of 'direct proof' (that is of being established by inference from some other truth). But he sets out a number of arguments[30] addressed to those who are disposed to reject it. Most of them, I think, fit into a pattern if they are seen as designed to show that rejection of the principle leads to various kinds of incoherence.

1. Arguments against the principle presuppose it.[31] In so far as they prove anything, they prove that it is being given some mis-application.

2. Divorced from a 'reference to utility', the words 'right' and 'wrong' and 'ought' and 'ought not' become meaningless. There is the merest hint of a reason for this assertion in a different argument nearby.[32] Taking up this hint, we can at least attribute to Bentham a reason he would not have refused: apart from the tendency of actions to produce happiness or unhappiness, there is no criterion, at any rate no public criterion or rule, for the application of such words as 'right' or 'wrong'.

3. What alternative to the utilitarian principle is there other than 'sentiment'? If sentiment is to be made the standard of right or wrong, are despotic privileges to be claimed for one's own feelings or is equal validity to be allowed to every man's feelings? On the second supposition, the same thing will be both right and wrong; on both suppositions, there is no possibility of moral argument.

4. As a result of 'the natural constitution of the human frame', everyone does in fact defer to the principle on many occasions. Let anyone who proposes to put limits on its application ask himself why he accepts it 'in part' and why he does not accept it altogether.

Bentham was writing towards the end of a great period in British moral philosophy. I shall draw on an earlier eighteenth-century writer for some of the considerations that might be used in meeting these arguments.

The most serious moral objection that the utilitarian principle has to face does relate to possible consequences of the principle, but it is not a utilitarian objection to utilitarianism. It is that the

[29] Bk I, Introduction, Sect. i (*Works,* Vol. IX, p. 5).
[30] Ch. 1, Sects. x-xiv (*Works,* Vol. I, pp. 2-4).
[31] This is Bentham's example. ' "The principle of utility (I have heard it said) is a dangerous principle: it is dangerous on certain occasions to consult it". This is as much as to say, what? that it is not consonant to utility, to consult utility; in short, that it is *not* consulting it, to consult it.'
[32] Ch. 1, Sect. xix, 3.

principle could sometimes require us to call right what we can't help believing to be wrong. Butler thought that the worst mistake a moralist could make was to represent virtue as consisting entirely in benevolence directed towards the temporal happiness of mankind and all vice as doing what is, or might be, foreseen as likely to produce unhappiness.

> For it is certain [he says] that some of the most shocking instances of injustice, adultery, murder, perjury, and even of persecution, may, in many supposable cases, not have the appearance of being likely to produce an overbalance of misery in the present state: perhaps sometimes may have the contrary appearance.[33]

Anyone who urges considerations of this type against monopolistic claims on behalf of happiness will be able to explain, in answer to Bentham's oddly worded question, why he accepts the utilitarian principle only 'in part'. Asked why he accepts it even in part, he would be speaking sensibly if he replied that the probable effect of an action on the happiness of everyone closely or remotely concerned might very well have to be taken into account in determining whether it was right or wrong. The action and its circumstances would have to be fully specified. And then it might become clear that the effect on the happiness of everyone in any way concerned was the decisive consideration because no one had any particular title to be counted as more than one. In other cases the effect of the action on the happiness of all would have diminished relevance because the agent stood in some special relation to a person (owed him a debt of gratitude, perhaps, or was his son), so that those concerned could no longer be summed as units. In still other cases the general consequences of an action might be held altogether morally irrelevant; for example, when it was being proposed to wring information from a prisoner by torture.

As reflection on actual moral disputes shows, the criteria used for determining rightness or wrongness will vary with different cases. Of course doubts are not always settled or disputes resolved. Nor would they be if everyone could be persuaded to adopt exclusively the utilitarian criterion. The difficulty is not merely that of calculating the direct consequences of an action on the happiness of what may be an indefinitely large number of people with indefinitely varied interests. The indirect effects of an action in weakening respect for a morally useful rule of behaviour may also have to be taken problematically into account.

In the Preface to the *Fragment on Government* Bentham dis-

---

[33] Dissertation II, appended to the *Analogy of Religion*, 1736 (Joseph Butler, *Works*, Vol. I, p. 410).

tinguished between two points of view in jurisprudence: that of the 'Expositor', who undertakes to say what the law is, and that of the 'Censor', who undertakes to say what it ought to be.[34] To object to the utilitarian principle on the ground that it has, potentially, consequences that are morally intolerable is, it might be argued, to appeal questions-beggingly to *de facto* morality against a censorial principle for morality.

Bentham's censorial principle for morality is, however, itself a moral principle and therefore itself exposed to moral scrutiny. There are ways of testing a moral principle. They are more effective in refuting than in establishing it, though there are none that can guarantee success even in refutation, if the measure of success is that the advocate of the principle gives it up. The procedure I shall mention here is suggested by the reference made by both Butler and Bentham to the 'constitution' of human nature. A principle cannot be a moral one unless it is put forward with a claim on everyone's acceptance, for it is to direct all men's behaviour in the appropriate circumstances. And whatever emphasis is put on the distinction between a claim as of right and its acceptance as mere matter of fact, there is no use in advocating as a first principle in morals one which cannot be reconciled with the solid convictions of the bulk of mankind; its rightness (if it is right) will not be able to be made apparent and its advocacy will seem idiosyncratic—the expression of an individual's mere 'sentiment'—and perverse.

> The fact . . . appears to be [Butler says] that we are constituted so as to condemn falsehood, unprovoked violence, injustice, and to approve of benevolence to some preferably to others, abstracted from all consideration, which conduct is likeliest to produce an overbalance of happiness or misery.[35]

Butler and Bentham do not have to be left in blank confrontation. A utilitarian philosopher could first attempt to defend Bentham's principle against moral censure by arguing that the 'supposable cases' in which it might seem to have morally intolerable consequences collapse when thought through: because the actions condemned have been mistakenly inferred from the principle, or if correctly inferred, can be seen to have been mistakenly condemned when compared with other possibilities of action in the same situation.[36] He might then be able to recommend the principle by arguing that it unifies and makes morality self-consistent, and that it has

---

[34] Bentham, *Works*, Vol. I, p. 229.
[35] Butler, Dissertation II (*Works*, Vol. I, p. 408).
[36] Seen by whom? Both the critic of the principle and its defender are implicitly appealing to the judgment of everyone who thinks over the matter carefully.

practical utility in guiding our decisions on at least some occasions where we would have been otherwise at a loss.

The details of Bentham's account of the way in which men, moved only towards their own happiness, can be brought to do what tends towards the general happiness, are of no great interest. Briefly, the bad man is a bad calculator. There is an obvious tension between the opinion that we ought to act so as to promote the general happiness and the opinion that all our actions are determined by the desire for our own happiness. No improbable congruity is to be looked for between utilitarian and self-love theory. Bentham brought to his moral philosophy what seemed to him, as to so many others in the eighteenth century, an obvious truth about human nature.

The Augustan Mode in English Poetry

Ralph Cohen

Since I wish to define the common features of the poetry written from 1660 to 1750, a period sometimes called Augustan, it will perhaps be best to proceed empirically towards a definition by examining varied poetic examples from the generally considered 'neo-classical' or 'sublime' periods, otherwise known as the Age of Dryden and the Age of Pope.[1] My procedure shall be to examine representative and valued works in genres that have quite different formal ends in order to inquire whether sufficient similarities exist to warrant generalisations that would distinguish this poetry from what might be considered the earlier Elizabethan 'mode' or the later Romantic 'mode'.[2]

[1] For a discussion of the terms 'Augustan' and 'neo-classic' see J. W. Johnson, *The Formation of Neo-Classical Thought*, New Jersey, 1967, pp. 3-30. I do not share his preference for 'neo-classical', especially since I am describing what modern critics call 'the mode of existence' of a work or works, rather than their mere sources or ideas.

[2] The attempt to describe the features of a group of works, such as poems, in any given period of time is considered capable of success by R. Wellek and A. Warren in *Theory of Literature*, New York, 1949, although they recognise the difficulties involved: 'If we can describe the style of a work or of an author, there is no doubt that we can also describe the style of a group of works, of a genre: the Gothic novel, the Elizabethan drama, the Metaphysical poem; that we can also analyze stylistic types such as the Baroque style of seventeenth-century prose' (p. 188). This position is also argued by many of the writers referred to below—as will be apparent from their definitions of the 'Augustan mode'.

But a contrary position is taken by L. T. Milic, 'Against the Typology of Styles', in *Essays on the Language of Literature*, ed. S. Chatman and S. R. Levin, Boston, 1967, p. 450, who writes that 'the proper study of stylistic speculation is the individual writer'. His reasons include the belief that every writer has his own 'style' and generalisations about group features imply that writers are alike. But no such inference need be drawn. I do not deny that a poet's work shows variations; I insist upon them. I do deny that such variations are incompatible with shared uses of rhetorical, grammatical, lexical, and organisational features.

I begin with two passages from Dryden: the opening of the didactic *Religio Laici*, 1682, and a representative passage from the satiric *MacFlecknoe*, 1682.

> Dim, as the borrow'd beams of Moon and Stars
> To *lonely, weary, wandring* Travellers,
> Is *Reason* to the *Soul*: And as on high,
> Those rowlling Fires *discover* but the Sky
> Not light us *here*; So *Reason's* glimmering Ray
> Was lent, not to *assure* our *doubtfull* way,
> But *guide* us upward to a *better Day.*
> And as those nightly Tapers disappear
> When Day's bright Lord ascends our Hemisphere;
> So Pale grows *Reason* at *Religions* sight;
> So *dyes,* and so *dissolves* in *Supernatural Light.* (ll. 1-11)

This passage shows Dryden converting a number of metaphysical images of supernatural light, of the relation between heaven and earth, reason and belief into a new constellation. The passage is governed by the imagery of spatial wandering; dim and limited reason, by fainting and dying and seeing the true religious light, becomes part of a supernatural illumination. The innovative quality of this poetry is that the typically limited rational progress of reason is described in process terms—'borrow'd beams', '*wandring* Travellers', 'rowlling Fires', 'glimmering Ray'—that suggest momentary and fragmented experience. And this fragmentation is compared with the paradox of the fortunate dissolution—the dissolving into supernatural light. The implications of uneasy and fragmented action are carried by participles, and they connect this sense of a changing, moving, limited world with the shifting imagery of reason, first a 'glimmering Ray', a dim light image, and then a personification that grows pale, dies, and dissolves into '*Supernatural Light*'.

This spatial-process innovation is connected with the conduct of the argument in consecutive terms, that is, the repetitions develop the argument, as do the images, by indicating a gradual transformation. Rachel Trickett describes the procedure as follows:

> The repetition of the same constructions ['Dim, as', 'as on high', 'but the Sky', 'Not light us', 'So *Reason's* Ray', 'not to *assure*', 'But *guide*', 'And as those', 'So Pale', 'So *dyes*', 'so *dissolves*'] interspersed by modifying clauses is as syntactically lucid as any piece of prose. It also stresses the periodic rhythm which Dryden emphasized by the other rhythm of the heroic couplet and its variations of triplet and alexandrine. The movement is as much a part of the beauty of the passage as the imagery, and the movement depends on a syntactical sense of

discourse or argument as much as the imagery depends upon a general framework of simile, or overt explicatory comparison.[3]

The particularly Drydenian use of spatial process—abstract imagery being transformed to personification—and the use of repetition to form part of an antithetical argument developing by steps into heavenly resolution of the contrasts—can be recognised again in the satire of *MacFlecknoe.*

> This is thy Province, this thy wondrous way,
> New Humours to invent for each new Play:
> This is that boasted Byas of thy mind,
> By which one way, to dullness, 'tis inclin'd,
> Which makes thy writings lean on one side still,
> And in all changes that way bends thy will. (ll. 187-92)

This passage begins with a line that seems to be a form of compliment put in spatial language, just as the opening of the poem puts the theme in a seemingly serious proverbial line about the process of disintegration: 'All human things are subject to decay'. But just as the opening leads to the decay of the monarch of nonsense, so the 'wondrous way' becomes, by addition, the process of creating new 'unknown' traits in man, 'New Humours'. The 'way' becomes the spatial incline to dullness and the puns on 'way', 'incline', 'lean', and 'bend' convert spatial terms into images of movement sliding the wrong way. This is not the best Dryden can do in satire, but it is the characteristic method in which spatial process and repetition lead to a unified resolution despite change. 'And in all changes that way bends thy will.' This resolution comes from the world that can be seen as serious or comic depending upon the kind of direction that is taken both syntactically and ideationally.

This spatial imagery of process becomes, in Augustan poetry, connected with the past through the imitative assumptions of art. The imitation of features of Latin poetry, the imitation, translation, and parody of Latin or other poems, demands that the reader have a knowledge of the original, in order to group the distinctions introduced in the modern work, distinctions of tone as well as those of subject and form. Often Augustan poetry shifts from serious to comic in the same work (*The Seasons*), or converts serious features of Latin poetry to mock or comic effects. This practice appears in Swift's application of the epic conventions to a housemaid as well as in Pope's rewriting of Horace's *Epistle to Augustus,* so that King George becomes the butt instead of the model of the poem.

3 Rachel Trickett, 'The Idiom of Augustan Poetry', in F. Murphy (ed.), *Discussions of Poetry: Form and Structure*, Boston, 1964, p. 118.

STUDIES IN THE EIGHTEENTH CENTURY

This is Swift's mock-heroic technique:

> Brisk *Susan* whips her Linen from the Rope,
> While the first drizzling Shower is borne aslope,
> Such is that Sprinkling which some careless Quean
> Flirts on you from her Mop, but not so clean.
> You fly, invoke the Gods; then turning, stop
> To rail; she singing, still whirls on her Mop.
> Not yet, the Dust had shunn'd th' unequal Strife,
> But aided by the Wind, fought still for Life:
> And wafted with its Foe by violent Gust,
> 'Twas doubtful which was Rain, and which was Dust.
>
> (ll. 17-26)

The brisk household warriors move with speedy action to fulfil their tasks disregarding the consequences to the unfortunate bystander in the same way that the dust becomes engaged in unequal battle with the rain. Recognisable in this mocking tone are the conventions of the present participles to convey fragmentary process—'drizzling Shower', 'turning', 'singing'—to support the spatial motion of whipping off the linen and the shower 'aslope'. These are contrasted with the mock-epic simile of the battle between the rain and the dust. The allusive quality derides the bystander's comic helplessness, overwhelmed as he is by the dirt and rain beyond his control.

Swift shares with Dryden a serial or successive approach to his subject, Dryden's argument or satire turning on the additive repetition of details, Swift's on the fragmentariness of such details. For Dryden the resolution or harmony is a form of absorption into oneness, in a tradition based on the metaphysical resolution of opposites, but in Swift, the resolution or harmony becomes a blending—that is, a joining together of complementary features—as in the following mock harmony image from the conclusion of 'A Description of a City Shower', 1710:

> Sweeping from Butchers Stalls, Dung, Guts and Blood,
> Drown'd Puppies, stinking Sprats, all drench'd in Mud,
> Dead Cats and Turnip-Tops come tumbling down the Flood.
>
> (ll. 61-3)

Swift's use of the series—dung, guts, blood, drowned puppies, and so on—blending in space provides a harmony of dismembered objects, and this is his particular use of the spatial technique. The harmonious process by which the dismembered fragments are joined in the shower is an analogy to a society that may be capable of resembling natural beauty but is, in a grotesquely naturalistic way, a harmony of garbage. The spatial process conveying fragmentation, the use of participles—'sweeping', 'Drown'd', 'stinking', 'drench'd',

174

'tumbling'—governing a series of vulgar terms ironically relates the grubby present with a classical past. And as the flood gathers all the garbage together, the typical harmony image is placed in a triplet, the last line of which is elongated by an Alexandrine that grotesquely blends what, in Dryden, had been dissolved in super-natural light.

Even in Swift's poem of personal affection, 'On Stella's Birth-day', 1719, the Augustan characteristics of serial development, of process, of allusion, and of a first-person speaker as a social role-playing observer—form the skeletal structure on which Swift's typical dis-memberment version is built.

> On Stella's Birth-day
> Stella this Day is thirty-four,
> (We won't dispute a Year or more)
> However Stella, be not troubled,
> Although thy Size and Years are doubled,
> Since first I saw Thee at Sixteen
> The brightest Virgin of the Green,
> So little is thy Form declin'd,
> Made up so largely in thy Mind.
> Oh, would it please the Gods to split
> Thy Beauty, Size, and Years, and Wit,
> No Age could furnish out a Pair
> Of Nymphs so gracefull, Wise, and fair
> With half the Lustre of Your Eyes,
> With half thy Wit, thy Years, and Size:
> And then before it grew too late,
> How should I beg of gentle Fate,
> (That either Nymph might have her Swain.)
> To split my Worship too in twain.

In this playful poem of dismemberment, first the increase or multiplication of Stella takes place and then, in the second part, she is teasingly divided into two nymphs:

> No Age could furnish out a Pair
> Of Nymphs so gracefull, Wise, and fair

Swift's approach to Stella's birthday is an aspect of the serial or successive technique because Swift plays with the relation of Stella's doubling in time and space—'Although thy Size and Years are doubled'. And complimenting and teasing Stella, he compares the continuing ideal 'form' of the mind with the rather changing 'size' of the body. The process, therefore, relates past and present through physical change, and the second stanza converts this, through dis-memberment as an ideal, to the creation of two ideal nymphs from one, and the humour and playfulness are turned against the speaker

who, with his total admiration given to the one Stella, is not sure
that he can become the total worshipper of two ideals:

> And then before it grew too late,
> How should I beg of gentle Fate,
> (That either Nymph might have her Swain.)
> To split my Worship too in twain.

The two stanzas are structured on the mathematical images of multiplication and division, using the techniques of the series and of
repetition to suggest the extended beauty of the world which will
take place when two nymphs exist instead of the somewhat over-
sized one.

In identifying dismemberment as the specifically Swiftian version
of Augustan harmony or fragmentary images, one can point to the
nymph disjoining herself in 'A beautiful Young Nymph Going to
Bed', or to the 'Verses on the Death of Dr. Swift', the unfolding of
which depends upon a separation or disengagement of character,
parts, or speakers. To contrast this version of Augustan additive
technique with that of Pope is to recognise that despite their shared
organisational and imagistic strategy, Pope uses the serial, additive
view to distinguish art from artificiality, gracefulness from gross-
ness. Both poets operate within the view of spatial extension, but
Swift sees a competitive world in which the parts remain separate
and inharmonious, even grotesque. Pope recognises the appearance
and power of seeming harmony and, depending upon the range of
the poem, playfully undermines the false appearance or derides its
grotesqueness.

In the Augustan mode this view of addition becomes a version of
spatial extension and it illustrates a poetic practice that can be
called the 'prospect view'. Augustan poetry converts inherited poetic
features or conventions by relating them to scientific spatial assumptions, to philosophical assumptions regarding the acquisition of
knowledge by experience, experiment, and observation, and by
asserting a relation between local observation and God's presence
in infinity. The purpose of this conversion is to reflect the variety of
objects, people, and situations enclosed within a universe dominated
by movement and change. Such a poetic universe connects patriotism with peace, plenty, and property, and it becomes a common
feature of Augustan poetic practice implying, especially after 1688,
the harmonious power of the landed squires as supporters of
country and God. This technique can occur in the mock-heroic as
in the descriptive poem.

If we consider the Augustan features I have been describing as
evolving after the Restoration, then we can perhaps suggest that the
prospect feature provides an organising procedure that replaces the

Augustan version of metaphysical analogy still detectable in Dryden and Swift. The relation between man, nature, and God is not the analogy between physical progress and eternal oneness but the progress from physical space to infinite space. As an example of a prospect view, I offer a passage from the 1704 section of *Windsor Forest*:

> Here in full Light the russet Plains extend:
> There wrapt in Clouds the blueish Hills ascend:
> Ev'n the wild Heath displays her Purple Dies,
> And 'midst the Desert fruitful Fields arise,
> That crown'd with tufted Trees and springing Corn,
> Like verdant Isles the sable Waste adorn.
> Let *India* boast her Plants, nor envy we
> The weeping Amber or the balmy Tree,
> While by our Oaks the precious Loads are born,
> And Realms commanded which those Trees adorn.
> Not proud *Olympus* yields a nobler Sight
> Tho' Gods assembled grace his tow'ring Height,
> Than what more humble Mountains offer here,
> Where, in their Blessings, all those Gods appear.
>
> (ll. 23-36)

The prospect from Windsor reveals in full light the russet plains, blueish hills, purple heath, and green isles. This harmony of colour is joined with the fruitfulness of plain and desert, and the sight becomes connected with patriotic power by comparison with the lush Indian trees, for English oaks and English power control what these trees adorn. The description moves from the plain to the mountain; the natural details become the signs of God's blessedness. Thus the colour, trees, plain, hills, and mountains are seen as local phenomena indicative of political power and heavenly blessing as a form of harmony.

Another somewhat later variant of this procedure can be observed in John Dyer's *Grongar Hill*, 1726:

> Ever charming, ever new,
> When will the landskip tire the view!
> The fountain's fall, the river's flow,
> The woody vallies warm and low;
> The windy summit, wild and high,
> Roughly rushing on the sky
> The pleasant seat, the ruin'd tow'r,
> The naked rock, the shady bow'r,
> The town and village, dome and farm,
> Each give each a double charm,
> As pearls upon an Aethiop's arm. (ll. 103-13)

177

As the poet sees the prospect from Grongar Hill, the movement and exciting contrasts create a harmony of particulars. The living force of the landscape is the consequence of the random order that seems to create unison by contrast: the woody valleys, the windy summit, the pleasant seat and ruined tower, the naked rock and shady bower—light and darkness become as harmonious as bright pearls upon a black arm. The technique of details and process in a spatial world suddenly ordered by blending—these in Pope led to nation and God; in Dyer, nature itself is the harmonious whole composed of contrary fragments. The stylistic procedure permits, even demands, that the different shared uses be discriminated—and poets who share techniques clearly do not exploit them in the same way. (I point out parenthetically that the very term 'prospect' becomes identified in this period in such a poem as 'On a Distant Prospect of Eton College' with a view of time as well as space, and simultaneously with the economic idea of 'prospect'.)

To observe how a convention of enumeration becomes transformed in the Augustan mode, I wish to examine the well known passage of the 'sacred Rites of Pride' in *The Rape of the Lock,* 1714, a model of wit that has as one of its features a parody of the prospect technique. For the prospect is, as I have indicated, a way of recognising God's presence through his spatial diversity. Since the passage substitutes narcissistic Belinda for God, it wittily reverses the prospect:

> Unnumber'd Treasures ope at once, and here
> The various Off'rings of the World appear;
> From each she nicely culls with curious Toil,
> And decks the Goddess with the glitt'ring Spoil.
> This Casket *India's* glowing Gems unlocks,
> And all Arabia breathes from yonder Box.
> The Tortoise here and Elephant unite,
> Transform'd to *Combs,* the speckled and the white.
> Here Files of Pins extend their shining Rows,
> Puffs, Powders, Patches, Bibles, Billet-doux.
> Now awful Beauty puts on all its Arms;
> The Fair each moment rises in her Charms,
> Repairs her Smiles, awakens ev'ry Grace,
> And calls forth all the Wonders of her Face;
> Sees by Degrees a purer Blush arise,
> And keener Lightnings quicken in her Eyes. (ll. 129-44)

The tone of the passage is the speaker's tracing of Belinda's self-admiration revealing the process by which her art and beauty are transformed into artificiality. The movement is an inverted prospect from the farthest reaches of the world to the dressing-table to the very face, cheeks, and eyes. If the prospect view moves from the small local detail to infinite extension combining extent with God and order, Belinda's rites proceed from the ceremonial opening to the smallest dimensions of self-adornment, beauty being enhanced and then made purer than nature's blush and keener than natural lightning. The ceremony, which is an inverted religious ceremony, is described as a process developing by degrees. And the gems are 'glowing', Arabia 'breathes', pins *extend* their rows—the action grows and rises with the preparations and the conclusion of the process is a painted goddess, powerful in her beauty, but the grace she has snatched is, indeed, far beyond the reach of art, an artificial harmony.

Within the same poem, there is a straightforward description that exemplifies the prevalence of the prospect view. I refer to the meeting of the sylphs:

> Some to the Sun their Insect-Wings unfold,
> Waft on the Breeze, or sink in Clouds of Gold.
> Transparent Forms, too fine for mortal Sight,
> Their fluid Bodies half-dissolv'd in Light.
> Loose to the Winds their airy Garments flew,
> Thin glitt'ring Textures of the filmy Dew;
> Dipt in the richest Tincture of the Skies,
> Where Light disports in ever-mingling Dies,
> While ev'ry Beam new transient Colours flings,
> Colours that change whene'er they wave their Wings.
>
> (Canto II, ll. 59-68)

This description deals with what I mean by 'process'—here the changing effect caused by the sun's rays striking the wings of the sylphs, combining the aerial movement of unfolding, wafting, sinking, flowing, glittering, changing, with the beauty of colours. This delicate description of the sylphs reflects their grace and beauty while it indicates their insubstantiality. Yet it is constructed on the same premise as the description of the colours of the rainbow in Thomson's ode *To the Memory of Sir Isaac Newton,* 1727, even though Pope's passage has as its end the responsiveness of the sylphs to eternal forces, whereas Thomson's has as its end Newton's disclosure of God's internalised subtle beauty.

The prospect view invades the poetry of science as it invades the mock-heroic. Here is the description of the colours of the rainbow in Thomson's ode:

> [While the last Gleamings of refracted Light
> Dy'd in the fainting Violet away.]
> These, when the Clouds distil the rosy Shower,
> Shine out distinct adown the watry Bow;
> While o'er our Heads the dewy Vision bends

Delightful, melting on the Fields beneath.
Myriads of mingling Dyes from these result,
And Myriads still remain—Infinite Source
Of Beauty, ever-flushing, ever-new! (ll. 110-18)

Thomson uses spatial imagery of process and change, governed by verbs and verbals to imply transformation, the isolated details of which lead to a general statement, here of renewal or newness. This prospect view leading to a harmony of apparent or actual unity reflects the Augustan principle of a spatial world observed through successive details, the embracing unity of which is a form of spatial blending, that is, one detail fitting next to another like colours in a rainbow. And this blending leads to a momentary insight that gives the sense of a harmony that normally is limited by the fragments from which a whole must be inferred.

My illustration of the prospect technique in descriptive, satiric, or scientific poetry is not intended merely to define and identify a poetic practice, but to suggest that it makes Augustan poetry a very particular mixture. The two primary poetic forms of this period were satire and the Georgic-descriptive poem, both forms that in Augustan Rome were mixed, relating poetry to politics and to varied formal features. The English Augustans use these mixtures for the same purposes and add a version of a spatially shifting, varied world in change. From this world is derived a belief that either supports religious anthology, satirises its neglect, or embraces its denial.

The prospect view is not the only descriptive feature appearing in different genres; retirement imagery is omnipresent too. Maynard Mack has argued that the retirement tradition, normally assumed to have been reserved for non-satiric poetry, plays 'rather a larger role than has been appreciated in the complex of attitudes, reminiscences, assumptions, and value symbols (everything that constitutes a sensibility and habit of mind) on which his [Pope's] poems draw from first to last'.[4]

The mixtures that I have been discussing are merely a few of the features that are contained in the two major Augustan poetic genres. Other mixtures include a speaker with multiple voices, whether this is the Dean in the *Verses on the Death of Dr. Swift* or the sophisticated and innocent speakers of Gray's *Elegy*. The mixture combines satiric 'character' portraits with Biblical history in *Absalom and Achitophel* or with personal references in the *Epistle to Dr. Arbuthnot*; it combines burlesque with elegies and descriptions in *The Seasons*. The mixture is apparent in the general

4 M. Mack, '*Secretum Iter:* Some Uses of Retirement Literature in the Poetry of Pope', in E. R. Wasserman (ed.), *Aspects of the Eighteenth Century*, Baltimore, 1965, p. 209.

antithetical development of the Augustan poem, a development of what might be called the procedure of contrary contexts. The same person, place, or action is seen from more than one perspective in order to convey the changes in nature and to contrast, in a spatial and special way, the transitoriness of things human with those eternal.

There is a relation between the satiric and non-satiric poetry of the period not merely in rhetorical contrasts, but in organisational contrasts and antitheses. In the structure of such a poem as *The Seasons,* Alan D. McKillop points out, for example, that contrasts and antitheses underlie its total order.

> Throughout there is likely to be a loose employment of the principle of contrast—the beautiful over against the ugly, the delightful against the terrible, the generative forces of nature over against violence and destruction.[5]

The dominant genres permit a ready expandability, and the mode I am defining has as one of its imaginative assumptions the connexion of comprehensiveness with artistry. 'Newton', wrote Thomson in his ode to Newton, 'untwisted all the shining Robe of Day'. And in untwisting the light—Keats referred to this disdainfully as 'unweaving' the rainbow—Newton laid it out to extensive view. 'To know' meant to extend knowledge, not to control it with greater economy. When Johnson began *The Vanity of Human Wishes* with the couplet:

> Let observation, with extensive view,
> Survey mankind, from China to Peru;

he was summarising a general Augustan assumption about how knowledge was acquired. To know meant to observe, to experience, to experiment; it meant to unravel God's secret working, to make extensive and visible what was knotted in obscurity. In this respect the Augustan poem was, in its wholeness, a poem by accretion. When Pope revised *The Rape of the Lock* and *The Dunciad,* although he made revisions of diction and rhyme, the primary revision was additive. This is the history of *The Seasons* as it is the history of Akenside's *The Pleasures of the Imagination,* for when Akenside revised the poem there were more pleasures than before.

I relate the mixed form to expansiveness because poetic mixture and artistic expansiveness imply a special kind of unity. If my assumptions about the features of the mixed form are correct, then character portraits, prospect views, eulogies and elegies, and the other features of the genres can best be described as completed fragments that combine into a whole. Unity in the Augustan poem

[5] A. D. McKillop, *The Background of Thomson's Seasons,* Minneapolis, 1942, p. 130.

depends upon the interaction of the fragments, upon their contrast, upon their opposition, climactic succession, upon any possible associational connexions. The diverse completed fragments have within them a high degree of the repetition of words and actions. Although scholars are familiar with the repetitions of 'wit' and 'nature' in the *Essay on Criticism,* verbal repetitions are a characteristic of the Augustan mode. Such repetitions are organising strategies of discrimination, the variations of the terms forming a basis for graded distinction of the parts, paralleling the procedure of antithetical development.

The following figure of repetition, for example, becomes converted to specifically Augustan practice by Rochester:

> For Hunger, or for Love *they* [animals] bite or tear,
> Whilst wretched Man is still in Arms for Fear:
> For Fear he arms, and is of Arms afraid;
> From Fear, to Fear, successively betray'd.
>
> (*A Satyr against Mankind,* ll. 139-42)

The man who is 'still' in arms for fear runs to the 'arms' of his beloved, although by being still in arms he is not a very active lover. And when he puts on his armour, he does so out of fear, and he does not know how properly to use the arms he has or—returning to the previous meaning—how to accept the arms of his beloved. The repetition that I wish to emphasise is that of *successive* movement, each action (whether of fear or love) being a betrayal of the other. The technique is to use the same term to express antithetical ideas so that repetitive succession reveals the intensified betrayal of important values.

The use of repetition as a form of process and spatial extension can be recognised in Thomson's lines,

> Snows swell on Snows amazing to the Sky;
> And icy Mountains high on Mountains pil'd.
>
> (*Winter,* ll. 905-6)

The swelling of the snows is a process defined by height and extent in the same way as the 'icy Mountains' are 'pil'd' on other mountains. The principle of degree noted in Rochester is operative here too.

Some contemporary critics divide the features I have been describing into an Augustan mode and a sublime mode, identifying the first with satiric poetry and the second with descriptive poetry. Such critics assume that balance, counterstatement and decorum exist in the first, but not in the second, or that they are substantially different in the second. Josephine Miles, whose *Eras and Modes in English Poetry* (Berkeley, 1964) is one of the few works to grapple with the problem of modes, separates the dominant 'classical mode', 1660-1700, from the dominant 'sublime mode', 1700-70. For her, the classical poets are Marvell, Dryden, Addison, Pope, Parnell, Johnson, Goldsmith; the sublime poets include Shenstone, Akenside, Thomson, Collins, and the Wartons. The 'classical' mode is a special moderation of the Latin style:

> Two sets of vocabularies, sound patterns, sentence structures, as different from each other as we have ever had in English poetry, partly blended and combined for one or two generations of poets at that time which we called neoclassical, with the result of poise: a poise of metrical and sentence forms in the pentameter couplet and the balance of adjective and verb per pentameter line; a poise of diverse materials, native, Biblical, classical in a harmony at once social and cosmic. (pp. 45-6)

She distinguishes the poem of the 'sublime' mode as follows:

> First of all, by its cumulative phrasal sentence structure, its piling up of nouns and epithets, participles and compounds, with a very minimum of clausal subordinations and active verbs. Second, by its vocabulary of cosmic passion and sense impression. Third, by its internal rather than external patterning of sound, the interior shadings and onomatopoeias of its unrhymed verse. In combination, these three major traits make for an exceptionally panoramic and panegyric verse, emotional, pictorial, noble, universal, and tonal, rising to the height of heaven and of feeling in the style traditionally known as the grand or sublime. (pp. 56-7)[6]

These distinctions of diction, sentence structure, versification and subject-matter are, as I have been pointing out, two variations of common syntactical, organisational, and ideational patterns. The vocabularies, as we shall see, are governed by the common allusive principle, the poise and cosmic passion are variants of a shared way of building parts into wholes that are inevitably incomplete, the interior shadings and the interior poise are governed by the essential duality of the mode. Poise or balance are qualities that are wedded to this common poetic habit of thinking and feeling, and

[6] Other equally distinguished critics agree on separating the satiric and sublime modes. W. K. Wimsatt jun., in 'The Augustan Mode in English Poetry', *ELH*, Vol. XX, 1953, p. 9, formulates the proper 'Augustan mode' as follows: 'The peculiar feat of the Augustan poet was the art of teasing unreality with the redeeming force of wit—of casting upon a welter of unreal materials a light of order and a perspective vision'. To this view, he opposes another type of Augustan poetry that expresses the 'sublime view of the world': 'a way of facing and comprehending evil by assimilating it—the part into the grander whole, the definite ugly detail into the larger mystery' (p. 12). My objection to this way of putting the matter is that it overlooks the fact that the different attitudes stem from common poetic assumptions and practices.

this habit or procedure was shared by the descriptive poets as well as by the satirists. The attitudes to this double view, the actuality of evil and the faith in God's goodness, resulted in Augustan poets either mounting a satiric attack on man's wickedness or exhorting man to turn to God and goodness (sometimes both) while acknowledging that pain and suffering are often the unaccountable mortal payment for virtue. The assumption that wit poetry, because of its double view, is constructed on ironies different in kind from those of the descriptive poets can be examined in Pope's well known couplet about Lord Hervey:

> Beauty that shocks you, Parts that none will trust,
> Wit that can creep, and Pride that licks the dust.
> *(An Epistle from Mr. Pope to Dr. Arbuthnot*, ll. 332-3)

Here is the balanced relationship between beauty and ability, between 'Wit' and 'Pride' (here personal respect), and contrasted with these balances are the antitheses of shocking beauty and despicable pride. The personification of general qualities, whether beauty, wit, or pride, is seen through positional behaviour (shocking, creeping, licking) that ridicules Hervey's vulgar status in the social world. The adjective clauses modifying each noun provide, in the first line, a consistent and extended temporal attitude increasing in degree: 'Beauty' that *immediately* 'shocks' and that no one, after the shock, will trust. And the second line provides an intensification of degree—of creeping and then of creeping by licking the dust. The Augustan features of spatial imagery, of process, of degree invade the rhetorical balance and create a progression despite balance. If one were to diagram the couplet it would be

> noun (adj. clause) noun (adj. clause)
> noun (adj. clause) conjunction noun (adj. clause)

Each line seems equally paired and balanced, but the imagery conveys intensified degradation, a progress of corruption.

Pope converts paradox into his special Augustan vision of a ceremonial social world connected in these lines to a natural world by unnatural social attributes. The so-called traits of satiric poetry are used by Pope in didactic poetry, too. In the *Essay on Man* he writes of the great power of God,

> That, chang'd thro' all, and yet in all the same,
> Great in the earth, as in th' aethereal frame.
> *(Epistle* I, ll. 269-70)

The phrases 'thro' all' and 'in all', though balanced, indicate the variety or process by following the modifier in the first half of the line and preceding it in the second—the change preceding the emphatic sameness or oneness. And the second line uses the two apparently balanced phrases to contrast the greatness of power 'in the earth' with that in the higher sphere, the 'aethereal frame'. One can detect here Pope's sense of a ceremonial world in which minute alterations become the basis for subtle and important changes of meaning. And this idea of degree within tradition is contrasted in the terms 'earth' and 'aethereal frame' that imply God's power over the solid and mortal as well as over the equally ordered, framed, and commanded 'aethereal realm'.

In the Augustan mode, traditional rhetorical features (including even such conventionalised figures as personification and repetition) become converted to spatial imagery of extension and of process. The following examples from Pope and Thomson are based on connecting personification with social man and extended nature, relating these to the public virtues of peace, plenty, and patriotism:

> Rich Industry sits smiling on the Plains,
> And Peace and Plenty tell, a STUART reigns.
>
> (*Windsor Forest*, ll. 41-2)

> O Vale of bliss! O softly-swelling Hills!
> On which the *Power* of *Cultivation* lies,
> And joys to see the Wonders of his Toil.
>
> (*Summer*, ll. 1435-7)

Regardless of the difference between the heroic couplet and blank verse, between the exclamatory and the indicative mood, these images provide a similar way of treating personification. The allegorical 'Industry' or '*Power* of *Cultivation*' hovers between personification and natural description. For the 'Rich Industry' that smiles on the plains, in imitation of a Virgilian image, becomes the grain that effort and labour sowed. The effort can perhaps be seen as a metonymical figure of action standing for its consequence. And so, too, the hills that swell because of cultivation, do so because the '*Power* of *Cultivation*' fuses the sowing and growing. This type of image that moves between personification and natural description is a typical Augustan conversion technique. It creates a figure that mingles image with actuality, that blends the human with the natural.

I have noted the kind of conversion Augustan poetry gives to rhetorical figures; I wish now to argue that satire and Georgic description present the same poetic awareness of a universe in which man is limited and belief is essential. Satirists and non-satirists alike took for granted the partial, fragmented state of man's knowledge. The satirists directed their attack against what they considered extravagant claims made for merely 'partial' knowledge; the non-satirists used scientific knowledge as another serviceable tool in describing the bounded world.

For the satirists this view has been amply described as the recognition of suffering and human limitation caused by man's behaviour to man. The similarities between their poetry and that of the nature poets, however, have been ignored or minimised. In 'Elegy to the Memory of an Unfortunate Lady', 1717, Pope writes:

> Poets themselves must fall, like those they sung;
> Deaf the prais'd ear, and mute the tuneful tongue.
> Ev'n he, whose soul now melts in mournful lays,
> Shall shortly want the gen'rous tear he pays. (ll. 75-8)

Gray, in the sonnet that is an elegy to Richard West, 1742, writes:

> My lonely anguish melts no heart but mine,
> And in my breast the imperfect joys expire, (ll. 7-8)

and concludes the same sonnet:

> I fruitless mourn to him, that cannot hear,
> And weep the more, because I weep in vain. (ll. 13-14)

Both passages deal with limitations of the speaker in terms of processes that are limited and fragmentary. Falling and melting are not reciprocated; they are changes that reveal their hopelessness. It is nature's resistless power that causes suffering—although it may, in another world, prove 'universally good'. In neither is there a denial or minimising of the reality of suffering. Pope's ceremonial and allusive language—'prais'd ear' and 'tuneful tongue' and melting lays—brings to the fore the incapacity of ceremony to make the momentary permanent. Gray's more personal tone indicates the incapacity of nature to substitute for personal loss. And the imagery of 'fruitless' and melting becomes with him part of the universe of plenty in which, however, the growth of nature does not reciprocally create growth in the poet, nor is pain in the poet's heart reciprocated by nature.

A representative sublime passage from *The Seasons* can illustrate that it, like the satiric poetry, not only recognises human suffering caused by natural forces as evil, but also uses shared Augustan techniques to express this suffering. In narrating Sir Hugh Willoughby's fatal trip to the polar regions, Thomson writes:

> Miserable they!
> Who, here entangled in the gathering Ice,
> Take their last Look of the descending Sun;
> While, full of Death, and fierce with tenfold Frost,
> The long long Night, incumbent o'er their Heads,
> Falls horrible. Such was the Briton's Fate,
> As with *first* Prow, (What have not Britons dar'd!)

> He for the Passage sought, attempted since
> So much in vain, and seeming to be shut
> By jealous Nature with eternal Bars.
> In these fell Regions, in *Arzina* caught,
> And to the stony Deep his idle Ship
> Immediate seal'd, he with his hapless Crew,
> Each full exerted at his several Task,
> Froze into Statues, to the Cordage glued
> The Sailor, and the Pilot to the Helm. (*Winter,* ll. 920-35)

This passage deals with the death of good, noble, and patriotic men, but contrary to the claim that their suffering is assimilated into 'the larger whole', their suffering is ironically enshrined in the very ice they sought to conquer. The men become, like Job, the playthings of God, the sport of 'jealous Nature'. The Augustan grammar of modification through adjectives, participles, and adjective phrases is strongly present to suggest the gradualness of the falling dusk and the suddenness of death, 'immediate seal'd'.

Implicit in the Augustan mode is a traditional view of human limitation, but this limitation is apprehended in spatial terms of the new science, in terms of social and natural change. I have indicated how the mode blends fragments into a unity, the past into the present, how its allusiveness extends from classical imitation of forms to Latinate sentence structure and diction. The periphrastic, Latinate, scientific, and Biblical language of description and the colloquial language of satire form two aspects of a single lexical procedure: the satiric aspect that vexes the present by mocking once-heroic language and genres, and the Georgic-descriptive aspect that incorporates the past into the present by encompassing it in allusions and terms of expanding nature. The language of Augustan poetry, therefore, complements the spatial procedures by implying extension in time of a linguistic tradition. This practice is noted in Dryden's poetry by Reuben Brower, who finds that in the characteristically best poems the 'irony is most concentrated in a word of classical origin which is rich in literary and historical connotations and which suggests the Roman oratorical tone'.[7] And referring to unexpected contexts of scientific terms in the so-called 'post-Augustan mode', Bertrand Bronson quotes Thomson's 'And *ventilated* states renew their bloom', or Matthew Green's engaging '*Tarantulated* by a tune', and declares: 'Perhaps, then, on one side, this trait is affined to the impulse to recover the Past, the same force that caused poets to break out in a rash of Allegro-Penserosiads and Spenseriantics'.[8]

[7] R. A. Brower, *The Poetry of Allusion,* Oxford, 1959, p. 7.
[8] B. H. Bronson, 'The Pre-Romantic or Post-Augustan Mode', *ELH,* Vol. XX, 1953, p. 25.

Between the beginning and the end of the mode, from Dryden to
Johnson, there occurs a considerable variation in the manipulation
of the couplet. From Dryden's enjambment within the couplet,
which he sometimes makes into triplets, the form can be manipu-
lated so that it becomes a variant of the quatrain. In Johnson's
well known and characteristic passage, this later use can be observed:

> With fatal heat impetuous courage glows,
> With fatal sweetness elocution flows,
> Impeachment stops the speaker's pow'rful breath,
> And restless fire precipitates on death.
> *(The Vanity of Human Wishes,* ll. 17-20)

The first and fourth lines support each other, as do the second and
third, in terms of cause and effect. The entangled couplets, like each
line in the couplets, suggest a view in which any form of order or
blessing brings with it suffering or disorder. In the first couplet the
phrase expressing fatality precedes the elemental images of coura-
geous fire and elocutionary flow, but the second reverses the order,
for the stopping of breath and ending of life conclude the lines.
Such reversal is typical of the Johnsonian poetic idiom in which,
despite the shifts of emphasis, each wish is carried by an afflictive
dart.

Critics have noted that the couplet, in the Augustan mode, tends
to be end-stopped, and it can, perhaps, be interpreted as a completed
fragment containing harmonies and contrasts of the known world.
The blank verse of the mode with its phrasal balance and emphatic
verbs and participles also tends toward end-stopping for the same
reason.[9] Within the couplet the effects of zeugma, paradox, internal
and end-rhymes have been studied, and Josephine Miles is surely
right in explaining that Augustan blank verse has 'internal rather
than external patterning of sound', 'interior shadings and onoma-
topoeias'. The only correction to offer is that the heroic couplet
shares these characteristics.

The relation between the earlier and the later version of
Augustan poise—not to be confused with equilibrium—can be noted
in Pope's

> Plac'd on this isthmus of a middle state,
> A being darkly wise, and rudely great:
> *(Essay on Man,* Epistle II, ll. 3-4)

[9] P. Fussell jun., in *Poetic Meter and Poetic Form*, New York, 1965, p. 117,
quotes *Winter* (1746), ll. 17-26 and writes: 'The technique of the Thomson
passage is very close to that of the end-stopped heroic couplet: we are moved
forward by line units and almost by syntactical units of predictable length and
weight, and the effect is one of closure, of taking up a thing only when the thing
preceding it is entirely finished. The view is analytic: the materials are being
accumulated, like mosaic, piece by piece.'

and Johnson's

> Yet still he fills affection's eye,
> Obscurely wise and coarsely kind.
> (*On the Death of Dr. Robert Levet*, ll. 9-10)

Both are spatial, visual images, although Pope's is more distanced than Johnson's. Both use paradoxical descriptions, yet Pope's is of generic 'man', who is progressively seen as 'darkly wise' and 'rudely great', whereas Johnson's is of Dr Levet, who is 'obscurely wise and coarsely kind', a man not in the heroic but the humane tradition, affectionately showing wisdom and kindness through unrefined manners and untrained mind. Pope's lines imply prophetic wisdom and rough heroism, whereas Johnson's imply small triumphs over circumstances that wound.

There is, as critics have noted, an increasing attitude of stoicism to the inherent limitations of man as the mode moves to mid-century. Although the poets do not abandon Christian orthodoxy, there is an increase in modification and qualification, of religious assurance, in recognition of the unresolvably complicated world. As an example of this subtle change one can use a revised passage:

> Ill fares the Bark, the Wretches' last Resort,
> That, lost amid the floating fragments, moors
> Beneath the Shelter of an icy Isle;
> (*Winter*, 1726, ll. 337-9)

> Ill fares the Bark, with trembling Wretches charged,
> That, tossed amid the floating fragments, moors
> Beneath the Shelter of an icy Isle.
> (*Winter*, 1744, ll. 1004-6)

The revision shows an increase in participial modification, to create the sense of anxiety that stoicism confronts, and by its spatial imagery—from 'lost' to 'tossed', from 'Wretches' to 'trembling Wretches'—it conveys the fragmentation of action in which the security of 'moors' belies the actuality of tossing, trembling, and the ironic shelter of an 'icy Isle'.

When Goldsmith, echoing Thomson's line, wrote:

> Ill fares the land, to hastening ills a prey,
> Where wealth accumulates and men decay;
> (*The Deserted Village*, 1770, ll. 51-2)

he shared the spatial imagery and its implication of movement implying anxiety, for although wealth increases and it seems to be balanced by men declining, both rise and decline are images indicating ruin. And so, too, the repetition of 'ill' and 'ills' creates distinction by degrees in which a process is hastened into a product. These passages, and those of Johnson, use stylistic features to connect spatial movement, anxiety, and inevitability with stoicism or resistance, and in this respect they are typical expressions of the elegiac aspect of the mode.

The features of the Augustan mode formed part of a consistent theory of the mimetic imagination. This theory made it possible for the Augustans to argue that it was the function of art to approximate the vitality and vividness of the world it imitated. One theory assumed that such vividness could never fully be achieved, and the other that it could, by selecting some details and ignoring others. Both views assumed that art used the fragmentary details of the visual world, but the first view conceded the impossibility of attaining God's vividness in sight, sound, smells, and so on, whereas the second claimed to improve upon the confused welter of the observable world.

If we examine these distinctions it is apparent that both views accept an interpretation of art that is based on the observed and observable world. I use two quotations from the *Epistle to Mr. Jervas* to illustrate the interrelatedness of apparently contradictory positions. The first,

> Beauty, frail flow'r that ev'ry season fears,
> Blooms in thy colours for a thousand years. (ll. 57-8)[10]

implies the permanence of art and the frailty of life. The second, the conclusion of the poem, indicates how little of life even the ideal of art preserves:

> Alas! how little from the grave we claim?
> Thou but preserv'st a Face and I a Name. (ll. 77-8)

The relation between art and nature is, at the end, reversed. What is preserved is not the bloom but the colour, not the vivid life but the mere appearance. The quotation connects social grace ('Beauty') with transitory nature and personifies it as enduring art. But what endures in art is a mere appearance of the actuality, and it is characteristic of the Augustan mode that it should stress the anxiety resulting from the inevitable changes in human life. The artist is governed by limitations greater than those imposed upon the

---

10 This passage is quoted by T. R. Edwards jun., in *This Dark Estate: A Reading of Pope,* Berkeley and Los Angeles, 1963, p. 5. He equates 'Augustan mode' with the finest of Pope's early poetry. He writes of this couplet with subtle understanding: 'The ominous oppositive "frail flow'r" is restrained by the hopeful predicates; "ev'ry season" yields to "a thousand years" and yet remains to qualify the latter phrase ironically. Phrase against phrase, line against line, couplet against couplet—the poem typically develops through statement and counter-statement, achieving a final effect of poise. The tone mixes moral elevation with the decorum of good manners, "seriousness" with "wit".'

ordinary human being because the living person is involved in the sounds, smells, sights of the world that can only be faintly secured by the artist.

> But who can paint
> Like Nature? Can Imagination boast
> Amid its gay Creation, Hues like hers?
> Or can it mix them with that matchless Skill,
> And lose them in each other, as appears
> In every Bud that blows? (*Spring,* ll. 468-73)

The life, force, and beauty that are the mimetic basis of Augustan art place a premium upon the moving, changing, active human experience, not upon rules of art. The references to sculpture and painting are to their capacity to become warm, to approximate the vivacity of human life. The arts remain approximations to the world that God has created, in its variety and in its quality. The Augustan poet can embody only fragmentarily the world he knows because that is all he knows of it; the rest is faith. The Augustan mode assumes, therefore, that there is nothing that the poet can imagine which God has not already created. The shift by which metaphors become literal and literal terms become metaphoric is the poetic technique by which God's creation and omniscience are suggested. The Augustan poet is no God-like creator, but a man who seeks, within the limitations of his craft, to suggest the relation between the known and the unknown, the literal and the metaphoric, the actual and the ideal.

I have sought in this paper to define the 'Augustan mode' so that it would provide a basis for reliable generalisations about poetic habits of thought and expression in the poetry from 1660 to 1750. The Augustan mode includes:

1. The recognition of the two dominant poetic genres, satire and the Georgic-descriptive poem, that share a body of common features, similarly used.

2. The composition of the Augustan poem by accretion with revisions as additions, implying a view of knowledge as extended and detailed observation and experience.

3. The rhetorical techniques of prospect views, spatial imagery, figures of extension, implying a world locatable in Newtonian successive space and time, leading (though not necessarily) to an infinity beyond man's comprehension.

4. The organisational strategy of the inherited mixed form, with its varied tones or varied speakers, varied poetic features, varied political and social attitudes, implying a social and natural world in exhilarating, anxious, or dangerous change.

5. A unity often using the original Latin or English poem as

191

referent in an undeclared simile and providing in translations, imitations, and parodies a relation between the present and the past.

6. The grammatical principle of modification in adjectival and adverbial words, phrases, and clauses, implying a precise tradition improved by degree and by qualification.

7. The use of the heroic couplet and blank verse as preferred metres in the primary forms, containing subtle shadings and rhymings that imply harmonies and contrasts in these completed fragments.

8. The gradual shifts towards greater syntactic qualifications and intermingling of verse techniques, implying an increasing awareness of the unresolvably complicated world of man and nature.

9. The analogy between man and nature and God, implying a faith that the transforming world is a whole, though only partially known because of the fall or the corruption of a past paradisal or golden age.

10. The subsuming of these techniques under hypotheses of imitative imagination, in which the controlling 'life' in art can approximate but never equal the 'life' God created.

These habits of expression and thought form the basis for what I call the Augustan mode. By this term I mean no more than a range of special poetic uses of conventionalised figures, images, ideas, and syntactical, metrical, or organisational structures in the poetry of 1660-1750.

Plate Va Elevation of
St Peter's, Rome, from
Vitruvius Britannicus,
Vol. I, p. 6

Plate Vb Design for a new
church in Lincoln's Inn Fields,
by Colin Campbell, from
Vitruvius Britannicus,
Vol. I, p. 9

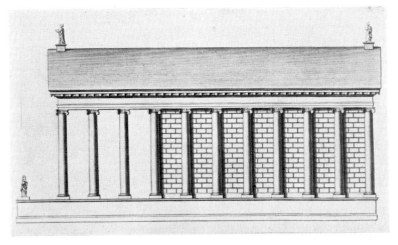

Plate VIa   Elevation of a church 'in the Vitruvian Stile', by Colin Campbell,
from *Vitruvius Britannicus*, Vol. II, p. 27

Plate VIb   The Maison Carrée at Nîmes, completed 16 B.C.

'From a Fable form a Truth': A Consideration of the Fable in Swift's Poetry

C. J. Horne

Many collections of fables and related kinds of moral tales had been published in England by the end of the seventeenth century, often with a prefatory recommendation of their value in providing palatable instruction. The popularity of the fable spread throughout the eighteenth century and, following the example of La Fontaine, Gay and others exploited the mode as a minor literary form. Addison set his approval upon the genre. 'Fables', he wrote in the *Spectator* (No. 183, 29 Sept. 1711), 'were the first Pieces of Wit that made their Appearance in the World, and have been still highly valued, not only in times of the greatest Simplicity, but among the most polite Ages of Mankind'. A year later (*Spectator* No. 512, 17 Oct. 1712) he returned to the subject to emphasise the universality of their appeal: 'among all the different Ways of giving Counsel, I think the finest, and that which pleases the most universally, is *Fable,* in whatsoever Shape it appears'. The fable, it was considered, could take many forms. Dryden, for instance, had in 1700 given the collective title of *Fables Ancient and Modern* to his superb translation of narrative pieces from Homer, Ovid, Boccaccio, and Chaucer, each chosen for the 'instructive Moral' it contained.

In Swift's time the most popular collection of the ancient simple type was L'Estrange's *Fables of Æsop and Other Eminent Mythologists: with Morals and Reflections,* 1692, to which a second part was added in 1699. The minor role that L'Estrange is known to have played as a victim of Swift's contempt in *A Tale of a Tub* has recently been enlarged by Mr Rosenheim: L'Estrange, in his prefaces and fables, was for Swift, it would seem, the principal representative of those Grub Street authors who, in Rosenheim's words, 'soberly attach inordinate wisdom to the tales of Aesop and other fableists of antiquity'.[1] When the Grub Street author in *A Tale of a Tub* lists a number of fables and proceeds to interpret them in a fantastic, pompous, and mystical way, I cannot agree that Swift's intention is primarily to ridicule L'Estrange's doctrine that the fable is an entertaining and instructive form of writing.

It was the pretentiousness of hack writers that raised Swift's gall. The fable itself he respected when rightly used as an apt and witty instrument of satire and morality; he was well acquainted with fables and employed them with skill in his writing. Much later, in 1732, when Gay was preparing a sequel to the very successful set of *Fables* that he had published in 1727, he had the uneasy suspicion that Swift did not approve. In self-justification he wrote: 'Though this is a kind of writing that appears very easy, I find it the most difficult of any that I ever undertook'.[2] Swift replied with the warmest encouragement.

> But you have misunderstood me, for there is no writing I esteem more than Fables, nor any thing so difficult to succeed in. which however you have done excellently well, and I have often admired your happyness in such a kind of performance, which I have frequently endeavoured at in vain. I remember, I acted as you seem to hint, I found a moral first, & then studied for a Fable, but cou'd do nothing that pleased me, & so left off that scheme for ever.

He recalls one unsuccessful attempt he had made

> to represent what Scoundrels rise in Armys by a long War, wherein I supposed the Lyon was engaged, & having lost all his animals of worth, at last Serjeant Hog came to a Brigadeer, & Corporall Ass a Colonell, &c.[3]

In suggesting that he had himself never succeeded in writing a fable, Swift was either depreciating his own efforts as a way of encouraging Gay, or else he was incredibly forgetful. Not only did he in that very same year, 1732, perhaps as a consequence of this correspondence, write the finest of his verse fables, 'The Beasts Confession to the Priest'; his career as a writer had begun with two of the most brilliant of his fables (as the term was then understood), the dispute of the Spider and the Bee in *The Battle of the Books* and the parable of the three brothers in *A Tale of a Tub*. Is not Gulliver's encounter with the Houyhnhnms, moreover, the most searching and memorable extension of the fable form in a manner that Swift had by then made characteristically his own? If it was

1 E. W. Rosenheim jun., *Swift and the Satirist's Art*, Chicago, 1963, p. 88.
2 16 May 1732 (*The Correspondence of Jonathan Swift*, ed. H. Williams, Vol. IV, Oxford, 1965, p. 22).
3 10 July 1732 (ibid., pp. 38-9).

the verse fable only that he was thinking of when writing to Gay, he was equally unmindful of his own poems, which include about a score of pieces that are either fables themselves or in some way employ fable material in the form of analogy, parable, myth, and simple allegory, all of which were then regarded as types of fable, as indeed they are when designed to convey a moral. Seven at least of these poems, sometimes with acknowledgment, are derived from the fables of Aesop and similar writers. Though it cannot be claimed that L'Estrange's collection is the source of them, all seven of the original fables are nevertheless to be found in it.

Swift's attraction to the fable form throughout his career will not surprise us. His early mentor, Sir William Temple, had got himself into trouble and precipitated the controversy with Bentley over the Epistles of Phalaris and the Fables of Aesop by instancing both in support of his contention that 'the oldest Books we have, are still in their kind the best' (*An Essay upon Ancient and Modern Learning*, 1690). It was in support of Temple that Swift first emerged as a writer and he cannot have been unimpressed by his patron's predilection for fables and his regard for Aesop as 'the greatest Master in his kind'. Even without that early prompting, Swift would inevitably have been drawn to the potential of the fable for a moral satirist. Though his writing, as often remarked, is singularly bare of metaphorical imagery, he was a master of the surprising similitude and the pert analogy, always applied with wit and ingenuity to surprise, delight, and above all to convince the reader of some apparently incontestable truth. It was skill of this kind that made *The Conduct of the Allies* such a devastatingly successful political pamphlet. Often in Swift the supposed truth is by no means incontestable, and his purpose then is to disguise his special pleading under cover of a convincing analogy. His poems, almost ingenuous and direct by comparison with his prose, are frequently used to point a moral, usually a specifically political or social one, without much concern to adorn the tale. Castigating the folly of the young men who had been stripped of their estates by the bursting of the South Sea Bubble, he finds a telling parallel in the legend or fable of Icarus:

> A Moralist might here explain
> The Rashness of the *Cretan* Youth,
> Describe his Fall into the Main,
> And from a Fable form a Truth. (ll. 41-4)

It is sometimes much less than a whole truth that Swift promotes by his ingenious application of such fables, but an essential truth is inescapably at the centre of them all.

The fable has never been restricted to the apologue with speaking animals, not even in Aesop. The distinctive feature is always that of a simple tale, patently fabricated, often fantastic, and intended by the implication of allegory to convey a useful lesson. The two main sources for Swift are Aesop and the *Metamorphoses* of Ovid. He had, moreover, an originality of his own in devising fables, as he did for the earliest of them, the dispute of the Spider and the Bee in *The Battle of the Books*. Though the brilliantly conceived incident appears to have been his own creation, the model is, of course, Aesop. As appropriate to the occasion of a battle between books, it is Aesop in person, as one of the contending books, who is made to deliver the moral in a long and ingenious application to the contest of the Ancients and Moderns. Every parallel is expounded, up to the demonstration that the Bee is the precise equivalent of the ancient author, 'furnishing Mankind with the two noblest of Things, which are *Sweetness* and *Light*'. The trappings of the fable are elaborated in appropriate mock-heroic form; but the core of it is in the dialogue, and that is not heroic in manner at all. It is delivered in coarse, cutting, vulgar speech on the Spider's part, parried by the urbane colloquialism of the Bee in his ironic twitting of his blustering adversary. In the ingenuity of the parallels, even more in the lifelikeness, the cut and thrust of the dialogue, Swift had already discovered his *métier*. His adroitness in both was his special contribution to the art of the fable. By these means, constantly employed, he renewed the fable as a poetic art. The element of burlesque is always present but it is an art as serious in its intention as it is engaging in its assumption of a brisk, familiar manner.

For the first of his verse fables Swift turns to Ovid. In praising Ovid (along with Chaucer) for the graphic reality of his 'Descriptions of Persons, and their very Habits', Dryden had selected the tale of Baucis and Philemon as an instance for translation. In 1706 Swift wrote his own imitation of the legend. It is a playful piece in the manner of other poems he was writing at the time, such as the pieces on Vanbrugh's modish little house. Behind the general commendation of the humble, contented life of the pious old couple, there seems in the choice for the central figures of a parson and his wife in Rixham or 'a small Village down in *Kent*' some private jest that defies elucidation. Perhaps more than the charming rural fantasy, it is the style of the poem that keeps it fresh. For two main features Swift elaborates on Ovid.

The first is the rollicking description of the inhospitable villagers and their demotic speech when repulsing the two strolling saints, gods in Ovid but in Swift's version

> Two Brother-Hermits, Saints by Trade
> Taking their Tour in Masquerade. (ll. 7-8)

As is everywhere evident in his prose, Swift had an acute ear for the
nuances of the spoken language and it is by this means that he gives
a new sharpness to poetry. The suggestive intonational patterns of
his sentences account for much of the effect of a personal, intimate
communication in his writing. Thus, disguised as beggars, the
vagrant saints appeal to the charity of the villagers:

> They call'd at ev'ry Dore; Good People,
> My Comrade's Blind, and I'm a Creeple
> Here we ly starving in the Street
> 'Twould grieve a Body's Heart to see't:
> No Christian would turn out a Beast
> In such a dreadful Night at least. (ll. 15-20)

In speech that is even more dramatic, the suspicion and violent
hostility of the villagers are conveyed by an adjustment of tone to
idiom that is amazingly real:

> One swore he'd send 'em to the Stocks,
> A third could not forbear his Mocks,
> But bawl'd as loud as he could roar,
> You're on the wrong side of the Door.
> One surly Clown lookt out, and said,
> I'll fling the P[iss] pot on your head;
> You shan't come here nor get a Sous
> You look like Rogues would rob a House. (ll. 33-40)

A second main feature of the poem is the concreteness of Swift's
fancy and his charming inventiveness in depicting the metamor-
phosis of the furnishings of the cottage into those of the church.
Before our eyes the lowly chimney is smoothly transformed into a
spire and the kettle into a bell; by more elaborate graduations the
roasting jack becomes the movement of the church clock, while,
more grotesquely,

> The groaning Chair began to crawll
> Like a huge Insect up the Wall,
> There stuck, and to a Pulpitt grew,
> But kept it's Matter and it's Hue,
> And mindfull of it's antient State,
> Still Groans while tatling Gossips prate. (ll. 105-10)

Swift had a rare ability to observe physical objects as in themselves
they are and to depict them in all their physicality—it is not infrequently a cause for offence in his work. Though he despised and
often ridiculed the scientists, he fully shared their interest in
physical processes, their curiosity about the way things worked; but
none of the scientists of the day could match his skill and precision
in describing such processes. This is a kind of enrichment that we

come to expect in his poetry, and the fable, to which it is most pertinent, gave him admirable scope for it. In 'Baucis and Philemon' he was obviously writing with enjoyment and good humour.

When one considers the details of these passages they are both found to be in fact additions to Ovid, and they are just the parts that Swift deleted or made more respectable in his 1708 version, apparently at the prompting of Addison. The ingenuity of the changes in the old couple and their house remains, but most of the dialogue and the lively rendering of the strollers' cant are removed, while the prevailing air of colloquialism is toned down. Yet these were the most distinctive and sparkling qualities of the first version, and it is to this manner, though with more concentration and with more pithy urbanity, that Swift returns in his later fables. In his Preface to a translation of the *Metamorphoses* in 1717, Garth was to single out as most characteristic of Ovid 'the propriety of our author's similes and epithets, the perspicuity of his allegories, the instructive excellence of the morals, the peculiar happy turns of his fancy'.[4] These were the qualities that appealed to Swift and which, with the addition of sprightly dialogue, he most happily exploited from now on in his own fables.

The 'confinement to the present object', which Garth also notes in Ovid, gives point to Swift's next Ovidian poem, 'The Fable of Midas', 1712. On 30 December 1711 the Duke of Marlborough had been stripped of his military appointments. As part of the campaign of vilification against him and the Whigs there appeared early in January of the next year 'A Fable of the Widow and her Cat', in which Swift seems to have had a share. This fable of the pampered cat who got above himself and cheated his mistress can also be found in L'Estrange's collection. It may have been at this time also, or during his preceding campaign in the *Examiner* against the prolongation of the War of the Spanish Succession, that Swift had tried to compose the fable representing 'what Scoundrels rise in Armys by a long War'—an Aesopian imitation obviously. However that may be, the legend of Midas as related by Ovid fitted his purpose better.

In the famous No. 28 of the *Examiner* (1-8 Feb. 1711) Swift had pilloried Marlborough's supposed peculations and his undoubted avarice by representing him as the Roman general, Marcus Crassus. For the latter failing, that of greed, which Swift genuinely detested in Marlborough, though in other ways he believed he was too hardly used by his political opponents, Midas provided the perfect analogy. With this choice Swift is at the same time parodying the use of classical gods and heroes in contemporary panegyrics. Later Addison in the *Spectator* (No. 523, 30 Oct. 1712) protested that 'when we

4 Ovid, *Metamorphoses*, trans. Dr Garth *et al.*, London, 1812, p. 10.

would write a manly Panegyrick, that should carry in it all the Colours of Truth, nothing can be more ridiculous than to have Recourse to our *Jupiters* and *Junos*'. Was he making a dig at Swift with his further observation?

> Many of our Modern Authors, whose Learning very often extends no farther than *Ovid*'s *Metamorphosis,* do not know how to celebrate a great Man, without mixing a parcel of School-boy Tales with the Recital of his Actions.

This aspect of parody is only incidental in Swift's 'The Fable of Midas'. Equally dividing the poem between a tendentious rendering of the classical legend and his invitation 'To think upon a certain *Leader*', Swift concentrates his derision on 'the *Chymick* Power' and the ass's ears that have descended to Marlborough from his proto-type. The details from the original are perfectly chosen and manipu-lated to make a laughing-stock of Marlborough, in a manner that seems more sportive than malicious. In Ovid, when Midas plucked ripe ears of corn, when he tried to eat bread, his unfortunate gift turned all to gold. In Swift,

> Whene'er he chanc'd his Hands to lay,
> On Magazines of *Corn* or *Hay,*
> *Gold* ready Coin'd appear'd, instead
> Of paultry *Provender* and *Bread.* (ll. 14-18)

After an official inquiry, Marlborough had been convicted by Parlia-ment of taking a commission on the contracts for the supply of bread and forage to the army. Swift's cool jibe is neatly made and his racy phrases about laying hands on the corn and the 'paultry *Provender*' must have produced involuntary and derisory laughter in readers daily primed on the political scandal. With his ass's ears and his preference for Pan, Midas-Marlborough is stupid as well as greedy, 'And there's the Jest, for *Pan* is ALL'. The burlesque of Ovid, like this punning, is not merely playful. While amusing the reader, Swift is deliberately debasing the subject through his buffoonery with the figure of Midas as part of his denigration of Marlborough.

> His empty Paunch that he might fill,
> He suck't his Vittels thro' a Quill:
> Untouch't it pass't between his Grinders,
> Or't had been happy for *Gold-finders.* (ll. 9-12)

The colloquial 'Grinders' is both ludicrous and sinister. Gold is equated with filthy excrement, fit only to be gathered up by the scavenging nightmen of an insanitary city, the slang term for whom was 'gold-finders'. The allusion is picked up again in the latter part of the poem with the mocking reference to Marlborough's virtue in 'turning *Dung* itself to *Gold*' (l. 48). By a reversal as it were of the natural process, Marlborough has found out the great secret of the alchemists. None of the more generous feelings for Marlborough recorded in the *Journal to Stella* are admitted into the lampoon. Midas had had the grace to ask to be freed of his hateful boon; the irony of the poem is that Marlborough is being stripped of both the power and the spoils that he would wish to retain. By a dazzling piece of poetic virtuosity, punning, elusive, deftly importing key words from the official charges ('*Pensions, Bribes,* and *three per Cent*'), Swift leaves Marlborough stripped of every vestige of honour and dignity, 'With *Asses Ears* and *dirty Hands*'. The verdict is politically unjust, as Swift well knew, but as poetry it is decisive.

Thereafter it was usually the Aesopian type of fable that Swift employed on occasion to make a political point. Specific application, not a general moral, was his usual motive. These are truly occasional poems. 'The Faggot' of 1713 opens with Aesop's fable of the dying father who tries to reconcile his factious sons by demonstrating with a bundle of sticks the strength of unity and friendship. More urbane than in most of his fables, Swift is here endeavouring to heal the breach between Oxford and Bolingbroke by means of friendly admonition. The simple fable with which the poem briskly opens is briefly concluded:

> Keep close then Boys, and never quarrel.
> Here ends the Fable and the Moral. (ll. 13-14)

The application that follows is several times longer than the fable, still brisk, epigrammatic in manner, but in more elevated style as it goes on to draw the parallel with the Roman Consul's fasces, the office of White Rod, the Lord Chancellor's mace, and so on. This has its own conclusion, which brings the poem back to the original fable, now seen with its political purport:

> You'll then defy the strongest *Whig*,
> With both his Hands to bend a *Twig*;
> Though with united Strength they all pull,
> From *Sommers* down to *Craigs* and *Walpole*. (ll. 49-52)

Dialogue is more central to the effect of two other fables of the Aesopian type that Swift wrote, 'The Fable of the Bitches' (from Abstemius) in 1715 and 'The Dog and the Thief' in 1726. The originals of both are again given in L'Estrange. Both have political and religious applications, the first to the treachery of the Dissenters at a time when one of the many attempts was being made to repeal the Test Act; the second, drawing on a fable that had already been expounded along similar lines by L'Estrange with reference to the politics of the former age, is a satire on self-seeking politicians and their bribery at elections. It is aimed at the Whig stock-jobbers and the moneyed men who were seeking to oust the landed interest:

> Who'd vote a Rogue into the Parliament-house,
> That would turn a Man out of his own? (ll. 19-20)

I must pass over many other instances of Swift's employment of the fable and give attention to the two poems that constitute, along with 'The Fable of Midas', his finest handling of the genre in a way that was specially his own. Written at the height of the frantic speculation in the South Sea project at the end of 1720, when the market for the grossly inflated shares was about to slump, 'The Bubble' is a poem built almost entirely out of a series of similitudes. If the manner is jaunty and popular, the range of Swift's similitudes is so widely diversified as to catch at the interests of almost all elements in the community. Folklore, new scientific discoveries, Biblical incidents, and fables of the popular as well as the Ovidian kind, each is wittily and dextrously turned to the indictment of the knavery and deceit and malpractice of the South Sea directors and stock-jobbers; nor are the investors, more greedy than wise, immune from Swift's scorn. The incidental fables, each set at a key point in the poem, are my present concern, and here the two kinds Swift had been practising are mingled in the one poem. First (ll. 33-48) comes the Icarus legend from Ovid earlier referred to, as attached to the profligate 'young Advent'rer' who has rashly bought the now useless shares:

> On *Paper* Wings he takes his Flight,
> With *Wax* the *Father* bound them fast,
> The *Wax* is melted by the Height,
> And down the towring Boy is cast. (ll. 37-40)

At another point (ll. 73-89) the common crowd of investors are seen as the yokels of a folk-tale, the origin of which I cannot trace. According to the tale, they thought an ass had swallowed the moon when its reflection in the stream where the animal was drinking disappeared as the moon passed behind a cloud. But as Swift acidly comments with the profiteering directors in view, 'The Moon lay safe behind the Cloud'. Similarly the illusion of wealth that has enticed the investors to their ruin is portrayed (ll. 125-32) by the fable of the Fool who, mistaking the reflection of the moon and stars for coins, jumped into a brook and came out 'All cover'd o'er with Slime and Mud'. The Midas legend reappears as the archetype for the directors with the golden touch:

> Oh! would these Patriots be so kind
> Here in the Deep to *wash their Hands*,

201

> Then like *Pactolus* we should find
> The Sea indeed has *golden Sands*. (ll. 109-12)

Marlborough comes to mind and Swift is in fact adapting the image
he had used on the former occasion. It is all superbly, exhilaratingly
apt, and does not need the italics of the original to make its point.
For the directors also, the fable of Antaeus and Alcides is employed
(ll. 181-8) as emblem of their miraculous powers of recovery after a
fall. With a visual transmutation of the image, Swift caps his stroke
by the delicious *double entendre* that they too, like Antaeus, should
be 'Suspended for a while in Air'. The poem even has that proverbial expression of a commonplace moral much favoured by the
fabulist: 'Alas! all is not Gold that glisters' (l. 107). In the context of
Swift's poem the commonplace is recharged with meaning; it has
the shock of an actual occurrence.

Jocular but biting, colloquial in syntax and rhythm, simple in
manner, but scarifying in its exposure of folly and knavery, the
impact of the poem is undeniable. Though unmistakable in meaning and intent, it is yet a truly sophisticated piece of poetic writing
where the unelaborate similitude provides the excitement and the
nexus of meaning for which other poets rely on imagery and elaborately intellectual conceits. For this kind of precision, exact, full of
surprises, uncontradictable, yet perfectly easy and natural, there is,
it seems to me, hardly another poet to compare with Swift.

The final poem that I want to consider, unlike most of Swift's
fables, is neither personal nor political in reference, but, as befits
his post-Gulliver period, is an indictment of all mankind and in
particular the representative professions of Church and Law and
Politics. It is called 'The Beasts Confession to the Priest, on Observing how most Men mistake their own Talents', and it triumphantly
refutes the admission that he made in his letter to Gay that same
year, 1732, that he had never succeeded in writing a fable.

> The following Poem [so goes the Advertisement] is grounded
> upon the universal Folly in Mankind of mistaking their
> Talents; by which the Author doth a great Honour to his own
> Species, almost equalling them with certain Brutes.

It is Swift's favourite subject, the pride and self-deception of man,
and as it recalls to our minds the fourth book of *Gulliver's Travels*,
so it is scarcely inferior to it in the pungency and ironic *naïveté*
of its style. The poem, like several others I have mentioned, has its
slender original in one of Aesop's fables, as Swift acknowledges in
lines 197-202. The fable is No. 217, 'A Plague among the Beasts',
in the second part of L'Estrange's collection.

In a time of plague, as Aesop relates, the Lion, consulting history, finds that plagues were a punishment for wrong-doers. All the animals are summoned to confession with the intention of sacrificing the most guilty. The Lion begins with his own confession, followed by the Fox, the Bear, the Wolf, the Tiger, etc., but each turns his crime to his credit, even priding himself on the basest of his traits. The Ass confesses to the most venial fault of all, but the rest make it out to be the worst of sins, an act of sacrilege. Swift converts the fable to imply that men are more hypocritical, more given to self-deception and exculpation than the beasts. To this end he substitutes for the supposedly nobler animals the very worst beasts, the Wolf, the Ass, the Swine, the Ape, the Goat, each denying his true nature or commending what is worst in it or supposing himself to have the very opposite of his true talents. The Ass, for instance, believes that he is a wit.

> Apply the Tale [says Swift], and you shall find
> How just it suits with human Kind. (ll. 73-4)

So he proceeds to extend the confessions to the classes and professions of human beings, the Lawyer, the Place-seeker, the Chaplain, the Doctor, the Statesman (the longest and most ironical confession), and the Sharper. Though he uses *oratio obliqua* throughout in place of direct dialogue, it marvellously retains the raciness of colloquial speech. For Swift, the moral when it comes will not do: 'fabling *Esop*' has libelled the '*Four-foot* Race' because

> Creatures of ev'ry Kind but ours
> Will comprehend their nat'ral Powers;
> While We, who *Reason* ought to sway,
> Mistake our Talents ev'ry Day. (ll. 203-6)

Swift puts Aesop right and concludes the poem with an ironic reversal of Aesop's fable:

> For, here he owns, that now and then
> Beasts may *degen'rate* into Men. (ll. 219-20)

There is a footnote reference to 'Gulliver *in his Account of the Houyhnhnms*'. Its appositeness to the last two paragraphs of Swift's greatest satire is obvious:

My Reconcilement to the *Yahoo*-kind in general might not be so difficult, if they would be content with those Vices and Follies only which Nature hath entitled them to. I am not in the least provoked at the Sight of a Lawyer, a Pick-pocket, a Colonel, a Fool, a Lord, a Gamester, a Politician, a Whore-munger, a Physician, an Evidence, a Suborner, an Attorney, a Traytor, or the like: This is all according to the due Course of Things: But, when I behold a Lump of Deformity, and Diseases

203

both in Body and Mind, smitten with *Pride,* it immediately breaks all the Measures of my Patience; neither shall I be ever able to comprehend how such an Animal and such a Vice could tally together.

A powerful poem, perfectly rational and detached in tone, and rising to a pitch of irony not elsewhere encountered in his poetic fables, 'The Beasts Confession' in its smaller compass is comparable to Swift's achievement in *Gulliver's Travels,* to which it serves as a fitting coda.

The figure of Aesop appears in the first fable that Swift wrote, and in the last. There is no doubt that in the character of Aesop Swift is speaking with his own voice in *The Battle of the Books* when he opposes to the dirt and poison in the breast of the Spider the sweetness and light that the Bee furnishes to mankind. For the younger Swift the two possibilities were still open to men. When, late in his career, he reformulated the truth in the fable of 'The Beasts Confession', there was no choice left.

There is much contention about the position that Swift is taking up in the last book of *Gulliver's Travels* because in it all is being delivered in the person of Gulliver. In 'The Beasts Confession' there is no such concealment and the verdict is unambiguous. Swift pushes Aesop aside to speak again in his own voice, to form his final truth from fable: Aesop's 'Tale is false in Fact' because it is designed to compliment mankind. The one final truth for Swift is that man, proud man, by the corruption of his talents has set himself below the beasts.

Milton and the German Mind in the Eighteenth Century

J. H. Tisch

A section of Fritz Strich's *Goethe und die Weltliteratur*[1] bears the characteristic title, '*Empfangender Segen. Die weckende Macht der englischen Literatur*'. The 'English revolution' in German letters had already been spoken of by Borinski.[2] It was a revolution that deeply affected the intellectual life of the German-speaking regions in the eighteenth century; and in it Milton rose to the position of an exemplary aesthetic program, an almost religious creed.

And yet, in the sphere of literature in the German language the influence of Milton is widely regarded as having been eclipsed by that of Shakespeare. The question of what Shakespeare actually meant to German literature—the forces underlying his reception as well as those released by it—was raised and examined by F. Gundolf in *Shakespeare und der deutsche Geist*.[3] The allusion to Gundolf in the title of this paper is intentional, and it would seem justified by the fact that in his view the German enthusiasm for Milton and —as Gundolf sees it—for his model, Shakespeare, were closely related, Shakespeare serving for the Germans mainly as a means of finding Milton.

Milton has often been placed beside Shakespeare as the type of the modern 'Genie'—witness Dennis, Addison, or Young—and literary historians in England have advanced the claims that Milton's influence on the German literature of the eighteenth century was hardly inferior to Shakespeare's, that Milton was the first English poet 'to inspire respect and win fame for our literature on the continent' (Robertson) and that the rise of both Shakespeare and Milton from obscurity to acceptance on the continent followed largely parallel lines.

One common trait of the advance of Shakespeare and Milton in

1 Berne, 1957, Ch. 2, Sect. 7.
2 K. Borinski, *Die Antike in Poetik und Kunsttheorie*, Vol. I, Leipzig, 1914, p. 137.
3 Berlin, 1922, pp. vii, 102.

Germany is its involvement with crucial literary and aesthetic issues of the period. Their names become shibboleths dividing clashing factions, opposed schools of thought; and they begin to mark progressive, indeed revolutionary positions; they grow near-synonymous with powerful emotional and aesthetic experiences, with the liberation from classicist domination, with startling new departures, with the dawn of a new era of poetic taste.

From this point of view, *Paradise Lost* and the 'Miltonic'[4] do constitute an artistic, even a spiritual, religious force in Germany. Is it a coincidence that Schiller in *The Robbers* plays off Lucifer against Hamlet? Milton was, beside Shakespeare, one of the magnets (to use Korff's metaphor) that deflected the needle of German literature away from French Classicism. His relevance during the decades 1730-70 reaches far beyond the critical discussions on the theory of the epic, into questions involving the very principles of poetry, and touching upon the interpretation of the world by the writers concerned.

But whereas Shakespeare, still often called the third German classic, was welcomed by the Germans like a fellow-countryman born in exile, Milton did not become an integral part of the German literary heritage. No Wieland, let alone a Schlegel or Tieck, took up his cause. And it is perhaps paradoxical that the German-speaking cultural era, though with a deeper appreciation of Milton's art than the French, did not match this understanding by a Milton translation that was in any way superior to French renderings of the poet, or comparable to the German translations of Shakespeare.

In the Shakespeare anniversary celebrations in 1964, Walter Muschg pointed out that Germany in the eighteenth century did not discover the real Shakespeare, but a myth to which people attached Shakespeare's name. Perhaps we should ask ourselves whether this does not hold good for Milton, too. We should investigate the extent to which discoverers of and apologists for Milton, in their response to and pleas for *Paradise Lost,* speak *pro domo,* as it were, as the young Goethe did in his exuberant *Rede zum Shakespeare-Tag.* Did every German poet and critic that was stirred by *Paradise Lost* form a Milton after his own image, as W. Witte has attempted to show with regard to Shakespeare?[5]

The Background
It would lead too far to more than hint at the phenomena that formed the background of the enthusiastic discovery of English

4 *O.E.D.*, 1708. On 'miltonisch' see P. F. Ganz, *Der Einfluss des Englischen auf den deutschen Wortschatz 1640-1815*, Berlin, 1957, p. 144.
5 'Deus absconditus. Shakespeare in 18th Century Germany', in *Papers mainly Shakespearian*, Edinburgh, 1964.

literature and the reception of Milton in Germany. Perhaps I may just touch upon a few of the most relevant factors.

There is Anglomania, *Anglomanie*, that European-wide admiration for England's political, philosophical, scientific, and cultural achievements, often little more than an intense but vague enthusiasm for an absolute idea of England, as the chosen country, the divine island to which the lovers of political liberty and freedom of thought must undertake a pilgrimage and to which many young German poets of the time pay homage in tones of almost religious veneration.

Klopstock—to adduce the example of an author directly influenced by Milton—at one stage worships England with a fervour matched by few of his German contemporaries: in *'Auf meine Freunde'* (probably 1747) he sings of *'Britanniens Göttereilande'*—

> . . . *Göttercolonien*
> *Sendet vom Himmel Gott den Briten*
> *Wann er die Sterblichen dort beseelet.*

Klopstock's youthful attitude towards England later underwent a radical change, reflected for instance in his ode, *'Wir und Sie'*, 1777.

Apart from the traditional cultural centre, Holland, there were four major places from which early in the eighteenth century English influences began to radiate into Germany and Switzerland: Hamburg, predestined for its mediatory role by its commercial and maritime links with England; as was Göttingen by Hanover's union with the English crown; Zürich; and, following at a somewhat sceptical distance, owing to Gottsched's censorship of taste, Leipzig.

Many scholars have come to realise that Hohlfeld's[6] theory of the three successive waves of English influence—Augustan, Miltonic (including Young and Richardson), and Shakespearian—is far too rigid to marshal the complex material adequately.

It is sobering but instructive for the comparativist to investigate to what extent the original language of a literature that is being warmly received by another country is known to its admirers. In the case of English in eighteenth-century Germany, the actual linguistic knowledge even in educated circles must not be over-estimated. Despite the increase in prestige that English culture enjoyed in the *siècle des lumières* as distinct from the seventeenth century, English literature still was more of a legend than a reality and comparatively few people were capable of reading Milton in the original, even if they had access to a text, then still quite a rarity on the Continent.

The eighteenth century was the great hour of England in Ger-

---

6 See L. M. Price, *Die Aufnahme englischer Literatur in Deutschland, 1500-1960*, Berne-Munich, 1961, p. 56; Ganz, *Der Einfluss des Englischen* (quoting Price, with some reservations), p. 17.

many, and English literature and taste made a powerful impact on German letters. The poet Uz observes in 1754:

> 'Der englische Witz scheint auf dem deutschen Parnass ebenso vielen Einfluss zu haben, als die englischen Kriegsheere und Schätze auf das Gleichgewicht von Europa. . . .'[7]

Herder more than once contends that Milton, Shakespeare, Ossian, Thomson, Addison have been welcomed in Germany with a warmth and respect they would hardly have encountered in their own country. Even Gottsched admits as early as 2 May 1739 in a letter to Bodmer, 'Es scheint, als wenn die Engländer die Franzosen bald aus Deutschland verjagen wollten'.

German writers turned the more eagerly to English models because the social basis of their own literature at the time was acutely and notoriously unsatisfactory and the 'bürgerliche Lebens-struktur' (H. Mayer) had been more clearly and effectively developed across the channel than within German frontiers. But there were also other less rational forces at work that proved conducive to the literary Anglomania—for instance the widespread feeling of cultural and racial affinity. According to Herder, the German regards the Englishman as 'bone from his own bone', as a German transplanted to an island; Bodmer believes the heart that is susceptible to the power of Milton to be of the same kind amongst the Germans and the English; and the Milton translator, Zachariä, while defending the alignment of German literary taste with England, fervently maintains:

> Aber noch brennt auch in unserem Deutschland das heilige Feuer, Das von germanischen Barden auf brittische Barden gekommen. . . .[8]

Perhaps more than in the case of any other poet, the German enthusiasm for Milton was tinged with non-literary, non-aesthetic elements, including the religious-theological one, an important feature of the English literary influence. Here *Paradise Lost* takes pride of place as a source of spiritual edification. In fact, in the influence of Milton, two decisive factors in the development of eighteenth-century German literature are said to have coalesced— the impact of English letters and the religious, irrational revival.

If we leave aside the pietist Pyra and the theologian Herder, this religious undertone of the admiration for Milton is nowhere more audible than in Switzerland, especially in the circle of Milton's champion, J. J. Bodmer, who practically single-handed disseminated

---

[7] Quoted by G. Jenny, *Miltons 'Verlornes Paradies' in der deutschen Literatur des 18. Jahrhunderts,* St Gallen, 1890, p. 41.
[8] Quoted by Price, *Die Aufnahme englischer Literatur,* p. 43.

a knowledge of and a respect for Milton in the German-speaking regions.

His endeavours should be viewed against the wider background of the eighteenth-century Swiss contribution to the cultural and literary discovery of England, the stimulation of an awareness and understanding of English taste and thought. This contribution reaches from Beat Ludwig Muralt's *Lettres sur les Français et les Anglais* (1725, but circulating long before in manuscript) to the achievements of the group around the standard-bearer of English literature, Bodmer. This *'Bruthenne der Talente'* (Goethe) turned Zürich, a city of around 10,000 inhabitants, into a cosmopolitan intellectual centre of European importance, and proceeded, together with other sons of clergymen, to create a new type of didactic secular but morally edifying literature.

We can witness a similar aliveness to English literature in Basle,[9] in particular among the theologians and mathematicians whose intellectual *milieu* was saturated with English influences. These processes were aided by affinities the republican Swiss felt with the 'free Britons' as well as by Protestant sympathies and theological connexions reaching back several centuries. While the legend of the incomparable freedom, of the idyllic happiness of Switzerland, was losing status in the eighteenth century, especially amongst enlightened writers disillusioned with the political reality of the country, these notions were gradually being ousted by the cult of the *'britische Freiheit'*. There were also ties between English and Swiss Protestants dating back to the time when English religious refugees found shelter in Switzerland in the reign of Queen Mary, and contacts in the field of theological and devotional literature were frequent.

Milton exercised a profound direct and indirect influence on the 'emergence of German as a literary language', to use Blackall's phrase. The new poetic ideals that had been distilled from his work cried out for more adequate forms and media. German translators of Milton, Bodmer in particular, wrestled with the challenge of providing a German counterpart to Milton's stupendous handling of words. They strove to forge a language that would eschew, like Milton's, all that is hackneyed and common, and would aspire to a sublime mode of expression; they grappled with the sophisticated stylistic devices, the mighty vocabulary and the syntactical freedom of their great model. The sonorousness and dignity of Milton's style constitute one of the roots of the new German poetic diction that

---

9 Haller, for instance, discovered his literary models, not during his visit to England, but in Basle; see H. Küry, *Simon Grynäus von Basel,* Basle, 1935, pp. 4, 35, 76.

was born during this period. The nature of this Miltonic element is clearly reflected by lexicographical evidence, too. The Miltonic loan words—such as *ätherisch* or *empyreisch*—largely belong to an elevated stylistic level and tend to become favourite expressions, the use of which borders on fetishism; small wonder that such lofty words are criticised and ridiculed by rationalist reactionaries like Schönaich. While Milton's *Pandämonium* and *Myriade(n)* already occur in the first published German translation of *Paradise Lost* by Berge, 1682, the bulk of the borrowing belongs to the eighteenth century: *ätherisch, Elfe, empyreisch, Fahre wohl!, hyazinthene Locken* (all first recorded in 1732, the year of publication of Bodmer's first translation of *Paradise Lost*); *Empyreum* and *Miltonisch* follow in 1752. One can hardly open the *Messias,* for instance, without discovering confirmation of the fact that *ätherisch* was cherished by Klopstock.[10]

The reception of Milton was also closely linked with, indeed was the main cause of, the revival of interest in the epic. Eighteenth-century Germany was swept by enthusiasm for this genre that the Germans had so sadly neglected. Herder makes a special point of appreciatively comparing Milton with Homer and the other epic poets of first magnitude. If Lessing regards *Paradise Lost* as the *'zweite Epopöe nach Homer',* Haller considers Milton Homer's equal, and both Bodmer and Klopstock rate him above Homer. Indeed, for many German writers on this subject the Biblical epic and its mythological machinery form an issue that looms large in the feud between Zürich and Leipzig. *Paradise Lost* embodies the very idea of the epic; the work of the Christian Homer is admired as the realisation of the genre's most rigorous formal and thematic requirements. In short, the progress of Milton's art and thought in Germany is a focal point for heated exchanges of opinion on several then vital problems of aesthetics and poetics, and coincides with a chapter in the history of literature and ideas.

Let us now turn to Bodmer, Klopstock, Goethe, and Schiller, authors vastly different in stature and sensibility, but together constituting a representative and historically fairly coherent pattern of Milton's impact on the German mind in the eighteenth century.

Bodmer
If the name of Milton came to evoke literary rather than political-historical associations in eighteenth-century Germany, this was largely due to the endeavours of one man, who virtually rediscovered *Paradise Lost* decades after it had first been translated into German: J. J. Bodmer (1698-1783), a vicar's son, Professor of History at the

10 E.g. Canto I, ll. 205, 309; Canto II, l. 275; Canto III, l. 17.

Civic Gymnasium in Zürich, the 'Milton impresario' (Korff), a 'veritable apostle of Milton' (Ibershoff). The exact nature and date of his first contact with Milton's work and the detailed genetics of his translation remain shrouded in some obscurity. We do know, however, that Bodmer, who in the winter of 1720 began to study the English language, was carried away by Milton, the fellow republican and Protestant, and on a sudden decision tackled the original with the aid of a Latin-English dictionary, using the Tonson edition of Milton's work, then a rare book in Switzerland.

Underneath the barren dates of the chronology of Bodmer's various prose translations of *Paradise Lost,* there lies a lifetime—from the twenties into the eighties of the century—of self-critical polishing, a determined effort of 'incredible revisional labour' (Ibershoff).

Bodmer starts with Book VIII, only to experience the frustration of seeing some eight years elapse between completion and publication of his rendering, having offended the religious censors in Zürich, who regarded the work as too romantic a treatment of a sacred theme. At last in 1732, the year of Haller's *Versuch Schweizerischer Gedichten* and of Gottsched's *Cato,* the first version (A) appeared in Zürich—Bodmer had finally found a publisher—as Johann Miltons *Verlust des Paradieses. Ein Helden-Gedicht. In ungebundener Rede übersetzt.* But the response appears to have been lukewarm. Other versions followed: B (1742), C (1754) (based on the annotated Newton edition which Bodmer obtained from Hagedorn), D (1759), E (1769), and F (1780).

The recent facsimile reprint in the *Deutsche Neudrucke* series should rehabilitate Bodmer's achievement as a translator of Milton, an achievement that had been grossly underrated from his antagonist Gottsched down to modern critics. The reprint is based on the B text of 1742 which was chosen owing to its bridging position between clumsiness and polish, or in Bodmer's terms, as the 'German' translation as distinct from the 'Swiss' effort of 1732 on the one hand, and the 'poetic' translation of 1754 on the other; but the *Neudrucke* volume also allows rewarding but tantalisingly brief glimpses of most other editions.

A (1732) with its rambling syntax manifests Bodmer's struggles with Milton's almost untranslatable emphatic compactness, stylistic concentration, and creativeness, and his desire to render Milton as accurately as possible—Gottsched actually scoffs at him for doing so. Bodmer finds the imaginative element, the emotional appeal he postulates in his theories, fully realised in Milton's epic. Here he discovers a vital poetic vocabulary and he attempts to apply the points made by Addison in the well known *Spectator* essay 285

(26 Jan. 1712) to German poetry, because he regards some essential linguistic devices of Milton as suited to the spirit of the German language. The subsequent editions indicate how Bodmer is working towards greater lucidity and a smoother flow of language.

What makes B, the edition in which Bodmer introduces footnotes, such captivating reading is the fact that it is so clearly an attempt at a poetic realisation of the theoretical endeavours of the Zürich critics. The copious annotation, frequently polemical and apologetic in nature and liberally drawing on Addison, is clearly meant to buttress Bodmer's case. In his defence of Milton, for instance, against Voltaire and Constantin Magny, Bodmer furnishes evidence of his penetrating intellect, cosmopolitan reading, and responsive sensibility, as well as of rationalist didacticism. After his victory over Leipzig, the notes are omitted, having no doubt become redundant.

Bodmer anticipates an era when Milton will be the delight and wonder of the Germans who, he thinks, are yet unaccustomed to such unusual and sublime beauty. Milton occupied a position[11] of paramount importance in Bodmer's life and thought, and supplied him with an overwhelming, indeed triumphant, justification of his critical views. From these sources Bodmer, basically an Enlightenment rationalist like Gottsched, derived his insights into the nature of poetry and poetic imagination. It was this exclusive knowledge which, perhaps in conjunction with the still baroque colouring of Leibniz's spacious and creative world view, gave Bodmer a formidable edge of superiority over his Leipzig opponent and inspired the dramatic liberation of taste from Gottschedian rule.

The quarrel between Gottsched and his disciples and the Swiss critics Bodmer and Breitinger, who hailed Milton and the 'Miltonic Klopstock' as revelations, as godsent embodiments of their literary ideals, ostensibly revolved around questions of principle highly relevant to the development of German poetry. It was aggravated, however, by resentment and personal antipathies. But the question has often been posed: what was the real bone of contention in this bitter feud between Zürich and Leipzig?—a feud that might seem almost incomprehensible in view of the solid ground of Enlightenment philosophy and aesthetics common to both parties, the wide areas of agreement, for instance, in the condemnation of the excesses of baroque style and the respect for the seventeenth-century classicist Opitz. For whatever reason, Milton, enthusiastically received by the one side, scornfully rejected by the other, is the touchstone, the only

11 For Milton as 'die Lust und das Wunder der Deutschen', see S. v. Lempicki, Geschichte der deutschen Literaturwissenschaft bis zum Ende des 18. Jahrhunderts, Göttingen, 1920, p. 296. On Milton's importance for Bodmer, see Jenny, Miltons 'Verlornes Paradies', p. 17.

tangible criterion that separates the sheep from the goats. But was the battle then fought at the theological and religious level, a struggle over basic differences, differences which appear disguised as 'literary' issues? Was Bodmer's whole life's work nothing but 'applied poetry' (Schöffler), secularised literature for edification? Were these the deeper roots of the forces that activated the Swiss to inaugurate a new era of literature?

Whilst I would not subscribe to the extreme view that the new aesthetics arose purely from the dictate of theology (Gundolf), one can hardly overlook the marked didactic, moral, and Christian elements in the attitudes of the Swiss critics. If it is true, as Pascal says, that 'the great mass of criticism in Germany was religious and moralistic', then this becomes particularly manifest with regard to Milton.

There is evidence that the rise of the literary Zürich of the eighteenth century should be understood as a direct continuation of the 'theological Zürich', and the theological bias of Bodmer's aesthetics largely accounts for the mutual aversion between him and Gottsched, who, despite an equally strong theological background, in practice was irredeemably secularised. In the work of the Zürich circle, theology and aesthetic theory sustain each other. Bodmer, who shows an early preference for Biblical subjects and is deeply concerned with the freedom of religious imagination, produces theories made to measure for the defence of the religious epic, of poetry as latent theology, of sacred poetry that celebrates deeds 'more heroic than the wrath of stern Achilles'. 'His recommendation of imaginative poetry remains in the service of Christian doctrine, of a religious didacticism' (Wellek). Bodmer regards the religious epic in unrhymed verse as the highest realisation of poetry and proclaims, in the context of defending the didactic passages of *Paradise Lost,* that the poet has as his avowed main objective *'die Wege Gottes gegen den Menschen zu rechtfertigen'*.

It is hardly surprising then that Bodmer in his *Charakter der deutschen Gedichte,* 1734, allots a special niche to the poet who in Bodmer's view sings only the praise of God: B. H. Brockes (1680-1747), like Bodmer one of the pioneers of English literature in Germany. Brockes's actual indebtedness to Milton in his major work, the *Irdische Vergnügen in Gott,* an overgrown, schoolmasterly, yet delicately poetic physico-teleological theodicy in rhyme, is a matter of dispute but should not be overrated. But of Brockes's early interest in Milton and in translating *Paradise Lost* there can be little doubt. One of the two excerpts published in 1740 in Brockes's translation of Pope's *Essay on Man,* in catalectic trochees of eight feet, covers *Paradise Lost,* Book V, lines 1-272, comprising Milton's description of the sunrise that entranced the German poets and the morning hymn of Adam and Eve, Milton's 'true poetic version of the Psalms' (Hanford), the superb manifestation of God's glory through created nature. Herder originally intended to include this passage in his essay, '*Vom Geist der ebräischen Poesie*', where he is concerned with illustrating the Biblical tone of praise he also finds 'woven into' Milton's 'immortal poem'. Eventually he chose a briefer example, Milton's address to light from *Paradise Lost*, Book III, of which he provides a sympathetic rendering. It was this text that was ridiculed by Klopstock in a translation making fun of the numerous non-Germanic words ('*des Eternellen coeterneller Strahl*' for 'of th' Eternal coeternal beam'). Klopstock's crudely nationalistic attitude to language in this context has rightly been called 'almost racialist' (Blackall).

But back to Zürich. Here the conventional notion of 'imitation' is transformed into 'the imitation of nature in the realm of the possible' (Breitinger), into a theory of creation. Unlike Gottsched's conservative *Critische Dichtkunst*, a practical manual for would-be poets and poetasters, J. J. Breitinger's (1701-76) treatise of the same title comes genuinely to grips with the creative aspect of poetry. The two staid Swiss professors attribute to the poet the status of a creator which the term etymologically implies. It was in the Bodmer circle, too, that the noun *Schöpfer* acquired the additional human connotations (a being that is artistically productive) that were frowned upon by the clergy and derided by Schönaich.

Closely related to the discussion about Milton are the notions of the plausible or the probable (*das Wahrscheinliche*), the possible (*das Mögliche*) and the miraculous (*das Wunderbare*). The miraculous in particular is pervasive in Bodmer's notes on *Paradise Lost* and in other relevant writings; and it was especially this *Wunderbare*, also for Herder *conditio sine qua non* for the epic, and a concept of crucial importance for the future of German aesthetics, that endowed the Zürich party with dynamic force. What it entails might be summed up as follows: the concept of the world is expanded beyond the sphere of the coldly empirical, by the distinction between possible and real, visible and invisible worlds. Unlike the historian, the poet for his 'imitation' draws on the world of possible things. While the Enlightenment lineaments still stand out clearly (enthusiasm must remain under rational control, and Breitinger defines the miraculous as a 'disguised probable'), the *Wunderbare* (which also embraces the 'novel' and the 'extraordinary') soars to a dominating position in Bodmer's and Breitinger's views. It opens a loophole for the imagination and its irrational attributes in the jealously guarded edifice of Enlightenment thinking. Thus

214

the *Wunderbare*—in conjunction with Milton—becomes a focal point of both religious and aesthetic issues, as a peculiar synthesis of Protestant dogma of English-Swiss mould and a new flair for the enigmatic side of poetic imagery.[12]

Bodmer defends Milton's use of pagan mythology and allegorical figures in his 'poetic theology' (he goes rather beyond Addison on this issue). One has to remember that many far from devoutly Christian critics of the age vehemently attacked Milton's Biblical-Homeric machinery on theological grounds. On this front Bodmer has an ally in Herder, who, like Pyra, shows an intensive awareness of the subordination of the artistic to the religious aspects of Milton's work. Herder brilliantly refutes Klotz, who takes religious poets to task for employing pagan mythology, and he emphasises that such classical devices merely possess an ancillary, ornamental function, serving to exalt religion and enhance the sacred message.

Much has been made of the imitations of and borrowings from *Paradise Lost* in Bodmer's *Noah,* one of his verbose and sentimental Biblical epics. But to hunt for Milton parallels in these self-conscious verses is to distort Bodmer's *Miltonbild* for us; Bodmer is intoxicated by Milton, but his admiration is coupled with perception and understanding.

While he takes Satan's might in *Paradise Lost* rather seriously and is not blind to the relics, however tarnished, of former glory and greatness among the fallen angels, he recognises their powerlessness in relation to the divine sovereignty, their pseudo-nobleness and specious grandeur; he puts the finger on the discrepancy between outward appearance and inward falseness and perversion, and warns his readers against taking Satan's proud utterances at face value.

Unlike the Storm and Stress authors, who, fascinated by Satan, sense a kindred heroic and revolutionary spirit in him, Bodmer repeatedly underlines that Adam, not Satan, is the hero of Milton's specifically Christian poem (Gottsched jibes that the poem should bear the title *Sataneis*). But Herder, too, is not taken in by the 'splendour of hell' and decides that the true sublime resides in the total structure of *Paradise Lost*. In applying structural arguments to *Paradise Lost* Bodmer shows a grasp of its total composition, and an awareness of the architectural notion of a unifying point of view, of a 'centre'. This, as Wehrli has pointed out, is reminiscent of the Renaissance and baroque predilection for presentation through central perspective. The seventeenth century even interprets the

12 E.g. B. Markwardt, *Geschichte der deutschen Poetik,* Vol. II, Berlin, 1956, p. 90; Bodmer, *Critische Abhandlung von dem Wunderbaren in der Poesie,* Zürich, 1740; H. Straumann, *Miltons Epos von den Abtrünnigen,* Zürich, 1963, p. 10.

multiple threads of a complicated courtly novel, as handled by the omniscient author in accordance with a focal point of view, as a mirror of divine providence—Catharina von Greiffenberg sketches this in her dedicatory poem to the third volume of Duke Anton Ulrich of Brunswick's *Aramena*. But at the same time Bodmer and also Pyra here seem to be at the very source of modern thought regarding tectonic integration, the structural identity of a work. *'Aber o was vor eine recht göttliche Übereinstimmung herrschet in dem Paradiese'*, Pyra exclaims, admiring the harmony of *Paradise Lost*, its lucid causality and its radial structure that converge in the disobedience and fall of mankind as its governing centre.

Klopstock

Although Klopstock (1724-1803) commenced his lyrical epic *Der Messias* with an almost frenzied exaltation in 1748, it was not completed until 1773. However, it was hailed in its earlier stages as the fulfilment of the seemingly utopian program and the new ideal of style, the 'grand manner' proclaimed by the Zürich critics to whom Klopstock was invaluable as the embodiment of their aesthetics. In the opposite camp, amongst the Gottschedians, he was resented and attacked as a thorn in the flesh.

Klopstock, then very much a young people's, a young poets' poet, was greeted in feverish, idolatrous terms (Voss: if we weren't Christians, Klopstock would deserve our adoration) by admirers. Schubart, who wept and trembled at his public readings of the epic that earned Klopstock the title 'The German Milton', speaks of him as an angel who has strayed amongst mortals; Bodmer, to whom Klopstock owes much of his fame, is thrilled that such a poetic messiah should have arisen in the country of the Gottscheds, and the young Wieland places Klopstock above Homer and Milton.[13]

Klopstock's followers 'were no less followers of Milton because they received their inspiration from him indirectly' (Boyd), but there is something paradoxical about what has been called 'Milton's replacement by Klopstock' as an example for German writers. Lessing and others actually find access to Milton through Klopstock. And although Hölderlin (1770-1843) may have known Zachariä's translation of *Paradise Lost* (1760) during the 1780s, his formative years, he read and imitated not Milton but Klopstock, who claimed

13 On Klopstock and Milton see Jenny, *Miltons 'Verlornes Paradies'*, p. 43; E. Pizzo, *Miltons Verlornes Paradies im deutschen Urteile des 18. Jahrhunderts*, Berlin, 1914, p. 26 (both treatments are largely obsolete). On Klopstock enthusiasm see G. Kaiser, *Klopstock, Religion und Dichtung*, Gütersloh, 1963, p. 158. On *'der deutsche Milton'*, see Price, *Die Aufnahme englischer Literatur*, p. 113.

to have achieved for Germany what Milton had done for his own country.

But if growing numbers of modern critics feel justified in according *Paradise Lost* a more or less central position in the English baroque, then Klopstock's contemporaries can hardly be blamed if they, friends, and particularly foes, sensed a direct affinity between the grandeur of the *Messias* and the seventeenth century. Gottsched and his myrmidons decried Klopstock's style as an alarming resuscitation of baroque bombast, a relapse into tasteless overembellishment unchecked by rational control. In these accusations, interestingly enough, Klopstockian and Miltonic become virtually interchangeable.[14]

To his own age, Klopstock must have appeared as the German Milton; and it was Bodmer's translation that provided the decisive impulse for the young Saxon poet and student of theology, who, in his valedictory speech at the famous Schulpforta in 1745, praised the formal accomplishments of the 'unseeing' pagan poets Homer and Virgil but fervently celebrated Milton (whom he proposed to emulate and surpass). Klopstock admired Milton as the founder of sacred Christian heroic poetry, as the genius who contrived to combine formal and thematic perfection and, as Klopstock's supporter Pyra put it, had led poetry from the heathen Parnassus into Paradise. In a Latin letter of 10 August 1748 Klopstock confessed to his fatherly adviser, Bodmer:

> When finally Milton, whom without your translation I would not have discovered until it would have been too late, came unexpectedly into my hands, he fanned the fire within me which Homer had kindled and lifted my soul towards Heaven, towards religious poetry.

And Bodmer endorsed the first cantos (which the no doubt slightly dazed editors of the *Bremer Beiträge* published on his advice) by announcing 'The spirit of Milton has descended upon the poet'.[15]

Klopstock's epic indeed is unthinkable without Milton. His whole work rests on Miltonic foundations, *Paradise Lost* serving as its main

14 On Klopstock and the baroque, see J. H. Tisch, 'Baroque', in *Periods in German Literature*, London, 1966, p. 20; H. O. Burger, 'Deutsche Aufklärung im Widerspiel zu Barock und "Neubarock"', in *Formkräfte der deutschen Dichtung*, Göttingen, 1963, p. 80 (disagrees with K. L. Schneider, *Klopstock und die Erneuerung der deutschen Dichtersprache*, Heidelberg, 1960, pp. 35 and 116); Kaiser, *Klopstock, Religion und Dichtung*, p. 11 (critical). On *Paradise Lost* and English baroque, see R. Stamm, 'Englischer Literaturbarock?', in R. Stamm (hg.), *Die Kunstformen des Barockzeitalters*, Berne, 1956, p. 403; an extreme view is that of R. Daniells, *Milton, Mannerism and Baroque*, Toronto, 1963.
15 On Klopstock's Schulpforta address see P. Böckmann, *Formgeschichte der deutschen Dichtung*, Vol. I, Hamburg, 1949, p. 555; M. Freivogel, *Klopstock, der heilige Dichter*, Berne, 1954, p. 16; R. Grimm, 'Christliches Epos?', in *Strukturen. Essays zur deutschen Literatur*, Göttingen, 1963, p. 118.

source besides the Bible. It provides the framework and overall pattern which Klopstock fills with a wealth of Miltonic elements ranging from subject matter to epic conventions and structure, from vast complexes of motifs and expressions to subtle allusions and minute verbal borrowings (*'Donners Narben'*, Canto II, l. 484; 'deeps scars of thunder', Book I, l. 601) which it would be tedious to quote in any detail. Particularly Klopstock's description of the infernal scene and his narrative of the battle in heaven betray the lasting impression Milton made on him. Herder comments with regard to Klopstock's hell: *'Hier hätte kein Milton vor Klopstock sein sollen'*. *Paradise Lost,* at least as Klopstock conceived it, became part of the very fibre of the *Messias,* so much so that Klopstock's own poetic substance has been seriously called in doubt in Freivogel's provocative *Klopstock, der heilige Dichter.*

Even stylistically Klopstock (who, as Herder says, practically transformed poetic diction) appears to have derived some inspiration from Milton, even though up to 1752 he knew *Paradise Lost* only through Bodmer's prose translation. But Bodmer had adopted some of Milton's stylistic principles and had lovingly striven to reproduce some salient features of the original.

What Klopstock found particularly attractive was Milton's masterly combination of the seemingly discordant and incompatible worlds of Homer and the Bible, and, like Milton, Klopstock consequently exposed himself to attacks from literary as well as from theological quarters for his epic use of Biblical subjects and for resorting to an anthropomorphic Christian mythology.

The most obvious common denominator of *Paradise Lost* and the *Messias* was, of course, that both works could be taken to have arisen out of the notion of divine inspiration, and to illustrate the concept of the *poeta vates,* the seer poet (and its corollaries, the Christian muse and the absolute supremacy of religious poetry over all secular literature). Klopstock's verses certainly reverberate with his uninhibited trust in his inspiration; although Milton is more humbly reticent on these matters, Klopstock openly declares himself to be the mouthpiece of higher revelations.

It was under Milton's influence that Klopstock adopted the idea of the poet-prophet. He differs, of course, markedly from Milton in the often obtrusive, explosive subjectivism that pervades his work. Klopstock's unfortunate tendency to view himself in absolute terms, as chosen and irreplacable, is not matched or sublimated by the political and religious reality that saves even Milton's most personal pronouncements from sounding hollow or conceited. While few would deny the devotional aspect of the *Messias,* Klopstock's religious inspiration has long been suspect, and recent zealous attempts to rehabilitate him as a great theological poet may have confirmed rather than allayed these doubts.[16]

The reception of Milton in Germany is overhung by a massive irony, however fruitful it may have turned out to be artistically. The work of Klopstock, the most gifted follower to respond imaginatively on a large creative scale to Milton, is in the last analysis worlds apart from Milton's epic in tone and particularly in spirit. Nothing could more vividly illuminate the fundamental misunderstanding upon which the cult of the German as well as the English Milton was grounded than the fact that the *Messias,* a basically un-Miltonic work, and not *Paradise Lost* itself, led the Miltonic school to victory. To a large extent, then, Milton in Germany, like Shakespeare, was a myth. This was not so much the Milton who emerged from the painstaking activities of the translators but the one who was projected so forcefully into German literary and emotional life through the agency of Klopstock who, having shaped a Milton after his own image, underwent a remarkable alienation from the real Milton. This becomes evident in his self-conscious efforts, from about 1750 onwards, to gloss over or to belittle, after exuberant initial acknowledgment, his indebtedness to *Paradise Lost.* Klopstock's silences and denials, his evasive and contradictory statements that even tamper with the proven chronology of Milton's influence on the *Messias,* his laboured references to heavenly inspiration, to a sudden visionary conception of the plan, with which the painfully protracted poetic execution is oddly at variance—all these things embarrass biographers, who tend to play down Milton's influence on Klopstock. There are in any case ample factors in Klopstock's work to establish his own identity as a major poet—without such subterfuges. Miltonic diction, applied to Klopstock, is a vague blanket term that obscures the real stylistic divergencies between the two poets. The dissimilarities far outweigh any general resemblances. The very metrical form Klopstock chooses, the hexameter, is a deliberate departure from Milton's art, and in turn it colours the artistic image of Milton that imprints itself on the German mind, through Zachariä's cumbersome hexameter translation of 1760; this version depended on the more expansive metre for keeping to the number of lines of the blank verse original, and in Herder's opinion greatly offended against Milton.

But the contrasts between Milton and Klopstock go far deeper.

---

[16] For attempts to rehabilitate Klopstock, see, e.g., Kaiser, *Klopstock, Religion und Dichtung* (who claims for Klopstock a unique synthesis of religion and poetry, but fails to do justice to Milton). For doubts, see, e.g., Freivogel, *Klopstock* (with whom Kaiser takes issue); W. Muschg, *Tragische Literaturgeschichte*, Berne, 1953, p. 135; M. Wehrli, 'Sacra Poesis', in *Festschrift F. Maurer,* Stuttgart, 1963, p. 281.

Critics from Benkowitz (1797) to Kaiser in our day have commended
Klopstock for piously avoiding Milton's type of anthropomorphic
representation. There is indeed a vast dissimilitude between the
substantiality, clarity, and concreteness of *Paradise Lost* and Klopstock's poem. In the *Messias,* with its fusion of narrative and devout
reflection, all contours, even spatial movements and time relationships, dissolve into emotive inwardness and the haze of unsensuous,
incorporeal diffuseness. Schiller observes that Klopstock divests all
he describes of its physical body, as it were, and Herder drily regards
Klopstock's God as too sublime even to thunder.

Milton's symbolic-medieval world picture in *Paradise Lost,* reflect-
ing a time 'halted between two opinions' (Gilbert) and subordinat-
ing the scientific issues to the thematic warning against sinful
hubris and immoderate thirst for knowledge, was not completely out
of place in eighteenth-century Germany. The poetry of the time
still largely operated with a ptolemaic-medieval cosmology, and the
great scientist J. J. Scheuchzer as late as 1721 had to delete Copernican formulations in a work at the behest of the Zürich censor
(who, what with Bodmer's *Paradise Lost* translation, seems to have
had a field-day).

Klopstock none the less was carried away by such facets of
Paradise Lost as he could appreciate by virtue of heightened
emotions. In an era susceptible to *Rührung* Klopstock not unreasonably demands from the masterpiece that it should stir the whole of
the human soul. He is bent on audience participation, as it were, on
Wirkung, on the emotional effects on the *Herz* (a key concept of
Empfindsamkeit)—that is why Schiller, himself a master of pathos
and the emotive effect, calls him a musical poet. But even
Klopstock's rhetoric is different from Milton's in function and
technique.

In a brilliantly sustained comparison of Milton and Klopstock,
Herder explodes the myth of the German Milton and expresses the
wish that the two poets had never been bracketed together, indeed
that Klopstock had never known Milton. Herder compares them to
Moses and Christ, the Old and the New Testament; and in fact,
despite the overlap in subject matter and characters, Klopstock's
'pseudo-epic' (Muncker) is separated from *Paradise Lost* by a whole
gulf of '*Unübernehmbares*' (Freivogel), by a wealth of incommensur-
able and incompatible elements, and it has little affinity with
the religious and intellectual climate in which Milton wrote.

Emotionally, Klopstock is more attuned to the sentiments of the
Night Thoughts of Young, the 'divine poet' (Klopstock, 1748) with
whom he briefly corresponded and whose popularity, like Thomson's, profited from the general Milton enthusiasm. Young's influ-

ence (through the German translation of 1751) is discernible for instance in Klopstock's choice for his sentimental drama *Der Tod Adams*.[17] Its theme is characteristic of Klopstock: death, the premonition, growing awareness and increasing certainty of dying. These literary impulses were fused with and strengthened by the eschatological mood of pietism which Klopstock shared, at least indirectly through sentimentalism. Milton's drastic allegories of sin and death seem remote indeed to the reader confronted with the sombre dignity of Klopstock's *Todesengel*.

Klopstock's preoccupation with immortality is only the other side of this persistent concern with death. He views the life beyond as a continuation and enhancement of earthly life. Conversely, 'bliss' is already in man's reach in the course of his days on earth. This immanent component, Klopstock's insistence on *'Glückseligkeit'* (a neologism!) is strangely similar to Gottsched's unmetaphysical, pedestrian cogitations on the subject in his Wolffian *Weltweisheit* and it indicates the strong Enlightenment stratum in Klopstock's outlook.

Freivogel's formula about Klopstock—the immortality of grace is replaced by the self-made salvation through fame—while polemically overstating its case, has a grain of truth in it. From the Schulpforta speech onwards, to the spectacular state funeral in Hamburg, Klopstock's whole life and poetry are dominated by the longing for glory, recognition, and splendour. The drive to erect an enduring monument for himself shapes his basic idea of the poet's mission, and he untiringly exalts literary greatness, the deathless quality of song. If the young Klopstock's aspirations in this respect are still akin to the expectations of fame that swayed the Milton who had yet to accept the message of *Lycidas,* this resemblance does not extend to the mature works. There, particularly in *Paradise Regained,* Milton with homiletic severity expounds the danger of the Satanic temptation of secular fame and self-love and extols the fame in Heaven for which man can only wait patiently and in submission to the divine will.

In Klopstock there is no perceptible merging, no reconciliation of the religious and the literary spheres; on the contrary, the obsessive regard for the honour that is due to the poet makes a bid to

17 The impact of Milton and the enthusiasm for Young not infrequently coalesced. This author discovered an item in the David Nichol Smith collection in Canberra (W. J. Cameron and D. J. Carroll (eds.), *Short Title Catalogue,* Canberra, 1966, entry No. 8359) that is interesting in this context, and also in view of the affinities between Klopstock and Gessner: Salomon Gessner's (1730-88) sentimental, Klopstockian-Miltonic epic, *Der Tod Abels,* 1758, translated into English by Thomas Newcomb 'in the Stile of Milton' and dedicated to 'the Reverend and Very Learned Dr. Edward Young'—*The Death of Abel: A Sacred Poem,* London, 1763.

eclipse the *Gloria Dei*. The struggle for literary and the belief in personal immortality, as Blume has shown, lead an uneasy existence side by side. Milton's admonition:

> Yet so much bounty is in God, such grace
> That who advance his glory, not their own
> Them he himself to glory will advance

would not have been in harmony with the spirit of Klopstock.

Goethe

For Goethe the 'wakening' breakthrough of the Swiss critics opened up vistas into the world of English literature. Naturally, Shakespeare played an important part in Goethe's early development, and Goethe was never able to free himself from viewing the dramatist who had overwhelmed him as a young Storm and Stress author, in mythical, absolute terms. But Milton, too, already mentioned in his correspondence from Leipzig in 1766, belongs to these formative influences. Goethe jots down for *Poetry and Truth*: 'The effect of the English models. At first Milton, Young. Later especially novels. At last Shakespeare'. Milton appeals to him, and the student and young lawyer is filled with 'a feeling approaching reverential awe' (Boyd); and this admiration never completely falters. Without *Paradise Lost,* Goethe's poetic cosmos and world view would be the poorer.

Goethe read Milton at an early stage, and at least partly in the original. But in the sphere of Herder, then a commanding and influential figure, Goethe was inevitably brought also into indirect contact with Milton—through the medium of Macpherson's Ossianic poems that thrived on the soil of sentimentalism. The Germans, too, surrendered to the wave of enthusiasm for Ossian's splendid lachrymose gloom that engulfed Europe, and Milton is amongst the major ingredients of the Ossianic alloy of styles and moods, from Old Testament and Homer to Pope and Young.

In experimenting with the epic in the wake of the revival of the genre, largely triggered off by the growing interest in Milton, the young Goethe paid some tribute to the poet of *Paradise Lost* who had been acclaimed as the Christian Homer. But he follows neither Milton nor Klopstock, but Hans Sachs's rugged mode of expression and homely metre for his *Ewiger Jude*.[18]

Goethe's titanic heroes are no doubt more closely linked with Milton: Mahomet, Prometheus, Faust. But Goethe himself is acutely aware that Satan's subaltern destructiveness differs from the defiant creativeness of Prometheus. He denudes Milton's Satan of

[18] See E. Staiger, *Goethe*, Vol. I, Zürich, 1957, p. 125.

his theological connotations and treats him as a sentient, attractively poetic figure: 'What we admire in Milton's Satan is the human being'. To him, Milton appears as the 'literary ancestor' of his inimitable idol, Byron.

Goethe is more concerned with the emotions and experiences of the human soul than with *Weltanschauung,* and characteristically his lively interest in Milton is not prompted by a religious, meta-physical, or ideological message. It is aroused and fostered by the captivating individual, the unique personality, the *'interessante Mann',* and by respect for a mind capable of soaring towards grandeur, the sublime. Goethe shows esteem for the 'true poet', in whom, however, he sees a fellow craftsman rather than the *poeta vates,* and whose sheer stylistic and intellectual eminence he acknowledges.

As his criteria in regard to Milton are predominantly aesthetic, Goethe is candidly unsympathetic towards the subject-matter and plot of *Paradise Lost* which he assails with some acerbity as improbable, 'hollow', and as containing some painfully lame and false motifs. Even such an ardent admirer of Milton as Herder occasionally hints that the religious system of *Paradise Lost* is detrimental to the poem. And the distinguished Swiss historian Johannes von Müller, who was acquainted with Goethe and Herder, has to draw on Milton's 'gigantic greatness' to be able to forgive him his choice of subject.

But sceptical though the 'classical' Goethe may appear towards the contents and thought of Milton's major work, it is at least likely that the young Goethe's world view has been enriched by the very object of his later criticism. The distinct possibility remains that impulses from *Paradise Lost* may have been absorbed into the young Goethe's cosmogony. It seems surprising that Milton, to my knowledge, has not been mentioned in the literature on the subject. Perhaps more so, as traces of the philosophy of Jacob Boehme (in whose thought the origin of evil and the fall of Lucifer occupy a central position) abound in *Prometheus* and *Faust.* Boehme, whose complete writings were published in England and in English between 1644 and 1662, in some cases before there was a German edition, may have influenced Milton, and so the pattern becomes one of multiple strands, and intricate enough to warrant a more thorough investigation.

Whether it is true that *Faust* has to be connected with *Hamlet* rather than with Marlowe's play is a matter for debate. But it is fairly obvious that a good deal of the poetic world of *Faust,* with its heavenly exposition, its visionary longings, its cosmic splendour, its stark manifestation of evil, is impregnated with Miltonic—as distinct from Shakespearian—inspiration.

From 10 August to 16 October 1799 Goethe had Zachariä's hexa-meter translation on loan from the Weimar library. This simple fact even bears on the much discussed chronology of his work on *Faust,* since some scenes are so imbued with Miltonic touches, so interspersed with Miltonic phrases that Goethe seems to have kept the Zachariä text at his elbow at the time of writing. It goes without saying that Goethe tends to echo Zachariä's turns of phrase rather than Milton's, but even though much of the influence of *Paradise Lost* on *Faust* may have been filtered by translation, the results are remarkable indeed.

Whether the striking mixture of Ptolemaic and Copernican traits in the Prologue points back to Milton is impossible to decide. But is it pure coincidence that Goethe elsewhere sums up the side effects of the Copernican revolution as the loss of 'a second Paradise, a world of innocence, poetry and piety'? Milton, one might say, helped Goethe to solve some problems of exposition, but the relationship is partly one of contrast, in the sense that Goethe's Prologue is thrown into relief by the implicit comparison with *Paradise Lost.* Milton's work serves as an indispensable foil to *Faust,* for instance, as far as Mephisto's 'legitimate' position is concerned —we know that the problem of freedom in Milton exercised Goethe's mind. Has the theological framework of *Paradise Lost,* within which Satan is an instrument of Providence against his will, been trans-formed into more human, more intimate terms?

The literary similarities between Milton's and Goethe's 'humor-ous God'—a notion absent from Dante's or Klopstock's epics—have been over-emphasised by some critics, who overlook the common Biblical background of ironical divine superiority which already Bodmer recognised.

In the Prologue, the Archangels sing in festive, hymnal words of cosmic harmony and totality. Into these magnificent verses Goethe, with Protean adaptability, has worked his Milton material so suc-cessfully that he temporarily appears to abandon his own identity and to become, as Zachariä did, a kind of *'Miltonrhapsode'* (Mommsen) commanding a resounding richness of tone.

Faust bears the stamp of the monumental and sublime as well as of the lyrical (*'Schwindet ihr dunklen Wölbungen droben'*), and last but not least, of the 'dramatic' Milton. Mephistopheles owes much to Satan, all basic divergencies notwithstanding. Goethe had eagerly turned to Milton, by then the canonical poet of Satan, for clarification of Mephisto's position in the hierarchy of infernal spirits (which subsequently underwent some change)—Goethe's

Plate VII   Comparative drawing by Sir John Soane of the Circus at Bath and the Colosseum in scale elevation.
By courtesy of the Trustees of Sir John Soane's Museum.

Plate VIIIa   The garden front of Kedleston, by Robert Adam, *c.* 1761.
A. F. Kersting photograph.

Plate VIIIb   The Arch of Constantine, Rome

human interpretation of Milton's Satan, a fruitful misconception of Milton, certainly contributed to the far-reaching humanisation and secularisation of Mephistopheles; but Goethe is also alive to the more sinister, threatening sides of Satan, to the violent clash of light and darkness.

In a continuation of the *Walpurgisnacht* he intended to introduce Satan as a fiery colossus towering on a mountain peak, with a whole firework of Miltonic effects, and to depict him against the huge canvas of a homage and worship ceremony of Aristophanic obscenity on the Hartz Mountain—a full-scale parody of the Last Judgment, a day of reckoning for literary sinners such as Klopstock and Nicolai. And the first known plan for the Epilogue of the whole work was to have 'Chaos on the way to Hell' as its location, possibly with an appearance of Sin and Death and of Mephisto, aided by Satan, struggling with the victorious Christ for Faust's soul. Here, too, we are 'on Miltonic ground' (Morris).

But Goethe also gained access to other parts of Milton's creative range. As late as 1829 he read *Samson Agonistes*—with Crabb Robinson, a young Englishman studying in Jena—and he expresses a modern classicist's warm appreciation of how perfectly Milton recaptures the tradition and atmosphere of Greek tragedy. He re-iterates 'written in the spirit of the Ancients like no other play by any modern writer'. But his utterances convey that once more his interest is focussed upon any human, personal, autobiographical, confessional qualities the drama may have, on the insight *Samson Agonistes* affords him into Milton's mind. Here, as elsewhere, the man rather than an ideology or a belief invites Goethe's attention. What he had written to Schiller (31 July 1799) with regard to *Paradise Lost* would appear to be appropriate in this context too:

> *Auch bei diesem Gedichte, wie bei allen modernen Kunstwerken, ist es eigentlich das Individuum, das sich dadurch manifestiert, welches das Interesse hervorbringt.*

Schiller

The seventeenth-century affinities of a good deal of Schiller's work are well known;[19] in particular the style, content, and atmosphere of his early plays are steeped in Biblical-eschatological elements. In a language of metallic musicality, Schiller recreated baroque religious drama in terms of secular moral heroism, and the tone and form of his verse recall the sonorous poetry of Andreas Gryphius. Besides Gryphius (1616-64), Schiller is perhaps the German poet who

---

[19] See W. Rehm, 'Schiller und das Barockdrama', in *Götterstille und Göttertrauer*, Berne, 1949, p. 62; E. Läuchli, *Schiller und das Barock*, Basle, 1952; W. Keller, *Das Pathos in Schillers Jugendlyrik*, Berlin, 1964, p. 107 and *passim*; G. Storz, *Der Dichter Friedrich Schiller*, Stuttgart, 1959, p. 112.

is most akin to Milton in regard to his ardent ethical seriousness, the often misunderstood uncompromising rigour of his message, the fusion of the didactic with the sublime.

Readers of Milton and Schiller may be struck by the general resemblance between the two figures—in their insistence on the morally blameless character of the poet, in their notions of musical harmony as a symbol of the function of art in human life, in the prominence and implications of their light imagery.

But there are far more solid bridges leading from Milton to Schiller, in whose portrait Jean Paul, 1795, saw a 'cherub with the germ of revolt'. For the Storm and Stress Schiller, *Paradise Lost* held a curious fascination, and we can discern a genuine affinity of imagination which may also extend to the cosmic-rhetorical *Jugend-lyrik*. Schiller's early plays, down to details of their vocabulary, are dominated by the polarities heaven-hell, angel-devil, ethical reality-deceptive appearance, humble submission-rebellious *hubris*; polarities which determine the poetic and theological structure of Milton's epic. Schiller's volcanic first drama, *The Robbers*, 1781, is embedded in a whole cluster of Milton references, associations and echoes. They occur in the Preface as well as in the text—in Karl Moor's monologue on time and eternity modelled on 'to be or not to be', Hamlet and Lucifer (Satan) are played off against one another by implication—in Schiller's amazingly detached review of his own play in the *Wirttembergische Repertorium* as well as in the encomiastic poem, 'Monument of Moor, the Robber'.

Schiller is visibly impressed with the suggestive force, the heroic stature of Satan, 'the man without his equal', 'the extraordinary "Genie" who could not suffer anybody to be above him'. Satan shares with Schiller's own heroes the kind of amoral, natural, colossal greatness the Storm and Stress so fervently admired.[20] While Franz may appear to be hardly more than an infernal villain, an ingenious, grotesque Jago caricature with theological overtones, his noble brother Karl—who is sympathetic with Satan—is to a certain degree himself presented as a fallen angel in almost romantic terms, as one would imagine a humanised interpretation of Satan by Füssli or Goethe.

Schiller's interest in Milton was not confined to *Paradise Lost*, it seems. A decisive scene of *Fiesco* (*Buchfassung* 1783, Act II, Sc. 19) is impregnated with Miltonic touches indicating acquaintance

---

[20] See H. A. Korff, *Geist der Goethezeit*, Vol. II, Leipzig, 1955; H. Mayer, 'Schillers Vorreden zu den Räubern', in *Von Lessing bis Thomas Mann*, Pfullingen, 1959, p. 147; H. Sudheimer, *Der Geniebegriff des jungen Goethe*, Berlin, 1935, p. 81.

with *Paradise Regained,* in which Milton with almost medieval ascetic severity condemns sinful worldly glory.

Schiller tends to sublimate Satan, or Lucifer as he calls him, into a fully heroic character; he disregards the ironical unmasking by the poet of Satan's pretence, self-love, superbia, and false values. This creative, subjective misunderstanding of Milton's intentions is carried over into Schiller's philosophical writings. In a context that in itself throws light on what Milton meant for the eighteenth-century German mind, he cites Satan as an aesthetic example of sublimity, *'Erhabenheit der Fassung',* and admirable strength of character. There is a distinct line leading back from this essay—a high-water mark of German prose—*Vom Erhabenen* (1793, later, *Über das Pathetische*) to Karl Moor (the sublimity of the moral world is thrown into relief by the fall of the noblest). Also Blankenburg in his *Versuch über den Roman,* 1774, mentions Milton's Satan in connexion with the sublime when he deals with the *'Höchstböse',* the use of great qualities for evil purposes.

Whether Schiller's *Jungfrau von Orleans,* a modern version of the fall and rehabilitation of God's chosen representative, was inspired in any way by Milton's *Samson Agonistes* is a matter for speculation. But an inward similarity with the texture of Milton's thought never completely disappears in Schiller's oeuvre.

In his analysis of basic poetic types, *Über naive und sentimentalische Dichtung,* Schiller celebrates Milton's 'magnificent' depiction of Adam and Eve and the state of innocence in Paradise as

> *die schönste mir bekannte Idylle in der sentimentalischen Gattung. Hier ist die Natur edel, geistreich, zugleich voll Fläche und voll Tiefe, der höchste Gehalt der Menschheit ist in die anmutigste Form eingekleidet.*

Schiller's intuitive awareness of a nostalgic, idyllic aspect of *Paradise Lost* may induce us to regard him as the Milton for whom the poet Matthisson had yearned after the subjugation of the old Swiss Confederation by France, a Milton to sing 'Europe's lost Eden' after the legendary Swiss liberty had disappeared from the face of the earth (one of Schiller's reasons for writing *Tell*).

The Sublime

More than once Schiller's references to Milton point to the realm of that concept that divides the factions, constitutes a kind of synonym for 'Miltonic', and, like a focal point, gathers various aspects of the reception of Milton in Germany—the sublime. His admirers almost unanimously confer this epithet upon Milton; his resonant diction is hailed as an ideal medium for the sublime, and even his uncongenial arch-enemy, Gottsched, in whose view bombastic neo-baroque obscurity and the sublime were connected, scornfully speaks of Milton's 'horribly sublime nature'.

For many writers the sublime, closely linked with the notion of sacred poetry, stood out as an integral characteristic of Milton and his work. The history of the Milton enthusiasm in eighteenth-century Germany overlaps to a large degree the rise of the sublime as an artistic and emotional category, an *ars dicendi,* an aesthetic-philosophical notion, from Wernicke, Bodmer, Haller, Pyra, and Klopstock to Herder, Schiller, and Kant.

Milton is admired as the mightiest realisation of the ideal of a sublime poetic imagination as conceived by Bodmer, who emphatically postulated the *Erhabene,* and planned to write a treatise on it (the impact of Burke comes comparatively late in Germany). It is in particular in the writings of the Zürich critics, whose aesthetics derived their essential energies from Milton's work, that the sublime is closely bound up with the marvellous, the quintessence as it were of all the irrational qualities, the abundance of which in *Paradise Lost* Bodmer and Breitinger discovered with pleasure, Gottsched with irritation.

In the course of our selective survey, Milton's reception and influence has emerged as a phenomenon of great diversity. For Gottsched *Paradise Lost* was a distasteful riot of baroque bombast. But it towers as an influential model behind a variety of works in which it is mirrored in widely different facets—in the sublime defiance of Schiller's heroic criminals as well as in the seraphic emotionalism of Klopstock, in the pastoral and infernal highlights of Bodmer's stodgy Biblical epics, in the cosmic grandeur and spaciousness of *Faust,* to give a few examples. The heroic, the didactic, the idyllic-lyrical, the 'classical' Milton—they all left their significant marks on the thought, style, and sensibility of the period. Different authors formed different Miltons after their own images, but through this very process *Paradise Lost* enriched the eighteenth-century German mind as few other books have done.

Shakespeare for many of his German disciples became a revelation and inner fulfilment, a glimpse of a heightened, enlarged existence. Milton, however, evokes, in a disenchanted world, a feeling of reverence, the lasting impression of almost unprecedented greatness and moral integrity. *Paradise Lost* is cherished as an intimation of human goodness and salvation, as the realisation of poetry in its loftiest and most anti-rationalist form. It is not fortuitous that Milton's fame in Germany owes much to theological and pietist circles, that Miltonic came to signify sublime. Milton in a way was received under the auspices of Longinus, and the ideas of the latter in the context of Milton become fraught with transcendental, pious connotations. *Paradise Lost,* to put it drastically, was Bodmer's polemical, secret weapon with which he triumphed over his intellectual half-brother Gottsched and the whole phalanx of Early Enlightenment classicism.

In the sense outlined here, Milton, for many, became just as overwhelming, exalting, and transforming an experience as the Shakespeare of the great tragedies. And Bodmer, raised by his devoted love for Milton to transcend his own personal and nationalistic limitations, speaks with moving sincerity for many of his contemporaries when he asserts that there is hardly a higher peak to which the human mind can elevate itself than Milton, *'kaum ein höherer Gipfel . . . auf welchen sich das Gemüthe des Menschen erheben kann'.*[21]

SELECTED BIBLIOGRAPHY

E. A. Blackall, *The Emergence of German as a Literary Language 1700-1775,* Cambridge, 1959.
B. Blume, 'Orpheus and Messiah: The Mythology of Immortality in Klopstock's Poetry', *German Quarterly,* Vol. 34, 1961, pp. 218-24.
J. Boyd, *Goethe's Knowledge of English Literature,* Oxford, 1932.
A. H. Gilbert, 'Milton and Galileo', *Studies in Philology,* Vol. 19, 1922, pp. 152-85.
J. H. Hanford, *A Milton Handbook,* New York, 1946.
C. H. Ibershoff, 'Bodmer and Milton', *Journal of English and Germanic Philology,* Vol. 17, 1918, pp. 589-601.
H. A. Korff, *Voltaire im literarischen Deutschland des 18. Jahrhunderts,* Vol. I, Heidelberg, 1917.
M. Mommsen, 'Zur Entstehung und Datierung einiger Faust-Szenen um 1800', *Euphorion,* Vol. 47, 1953, pp. 295-330.
M. Morris, 'Mephistopheles', *Goethe Jahrbuch,* Vol. 22, 1901, pp. 150-91.
F. Muncker, *Friedrich Gottlieb Klopstock,* Berlin, 1900.
W. Muschg, 'Deutschland ist Hamlet', in *Studien zur tragischen Literaturgeschichte,* Berne-Munich, 1965.
R. Pascal, *The German Sturm und Drang,* Manchester, 1953.
J. G. Robertson, 'Milton's Fame on the Continent', *Proceedings of the British Academy,* 1908, pp. 319-40.
H. Schöffler, *Deutscher Geist im 18. Jahrhundert,* Göttingen, 1956.
M. Wehrli, *Johann Jakob Bodmer und die Geschichte der Literatur,* Frauenfeld-Leipzig, 1937.
R. Wellek, *History of Modern Criticism,* Vol. I, New Haven, 1955.

[21] To Zellweger, 1724, quoted in *Johann Miltons Episches Gedichte, Deutsche Neudrucke,* Stuttgart, 1965, p. 5.

The Grand Tour and the Rule of Taste

Joseph Burke

In 1914 the first author of a serious history of the Grand Tour, the American scholar, W. E. Mead, defined its combined program of study and travel as 'an indispensable form of education for young men in the higher ranks of society'.[1] A carefully planned outward journey through France and Italy, and a return journey through France and the Low Countries, it usually required three years. Its goal was Rome. There were two reasons for the choice of this destination. Firstly, it had been inherited from the Middle Ages and confirmed by the splendours of the Italian Renaissance. Secondly, Greece had been overrun by the Ottoman Turks after the fall of Constantinople in 1453, and the conquerors had lowered an iron curtain which was penetrated only by the most ardent travellers, until the Turks partially relaxed their policy of obstruction in the second half of the eighteenth century.

Because the history of travel to Rome is unbroken from the earliest days of Christian conversion of the barbaric invaders of the Roman Empire, it is difficult to assign a date for the commencement of the Grand Tour except by distinguishing between a predominantly religious and a predominantly secular purpose. The Reformation marks a turning-point, for the Protestant nobility, gentry, scholars, and artists of the north certainly did not travel to Rome in order to pay their devotions at the shrine of St Peter's. When Roger Ascham quoted the Italian proverb, *un Inglese italianato è un diavolo incarnato,* he did so to criticise the corruption of morals

1 *The Grand Tour,* Boston, 1914, p. 3. This pioneer treatise has been super-seded by the monumental work of Ludwig Schudt, *Italienreisen im 17. und 18. Jahrhundert,* Wien-München, 1959. The sections on 'Die Engländer' and 'Die Kunst' contain by far the best account of the activities of English Grand Tourists in the eighteenth century, and are supported by a bibliography of primary sources.

and manners, not a change of faith.[2] Nor can a precise date be given for its conclusion. It did not fade out after the Napoleonic Wars; Byron in Italy was immediately recognised as standing in the authentic tradition of the English Milord on his splendid travels.[3] It is, however, possible to propose a symbolic date for the terminus of its golden age: the year 1841, when Thomas Cook, who was born in Melbourne, Derbyshire, in 1808, organised the first cheap railway excursion from Leicester to Loughborough in aid of a temperance cause.[4]

'And no man understands Livy and Caesar', wrote Richard Lassels in one of the first English Grand Tour guide books, *The Voyage of Italy*, 1670, 'like to him who hath made exactly the Grand Tour of France and the *giro* of Italy.' Unlike the French term, *le voyage d'Italie*, and the German, *die Italienische Reise*, the English one does not specify a country of destination. But there was never any doubt about where that journey led. When William Cowper ridiculed the Grand Tourist, he made use of a pun which must have been immediately recognised by most of his readers:

> Returning, he proclaims, by many a grace,
> By shrugs, and strange contortions of his face,
> How much a dunce, that has been sent to roam,
> Excels a dunce, that has been kept at home.[5]

Because the Grand Tourist stood in a tradition of travel to Rome, his activities were strongly influenced by the interests of his predecessors. Three in particular left their mark on his program: the medieval cult of *mirabilia* or ancient marvels, the ideal of good government or *ratio gubernatoris*, and the humanist goal of completing a classical education by studying the monuments of antiquity. To the eighteenth century a further interest was bequeathed by the seventeenth century, the age of noblemen and artists who were also *virtuosi*: the collection of rare works of art.[6] The tracing of these different strands not only throws light on the Rule of Taste and its artistic expression, but accounts for certain features which at first sight might appear to contradict its aims.

The oldest surviving medieval guide, the *Einsiedeln Itinerary*,

---

[2] In *The Schoolmaster*, Bk I, 1570. See *The Whole Works of Roger Ascham*, ed. J. A. Giles, Vol. III, London, 1864, p. 156. I have given the modern spelling of the proverb. Despite his stricture, Ascham did full justice to the advantages to be gained from Continental travel.

[3] Cf. Peter Quennell, *Byron in Italy*, London, 1941, for the state in which Byron lived in Italy, and the impression that he made.

[4] J. A. R. Pimlott, *The Englishman's Holiday: a Social History*, London, 1947, p. 91.

[5] 'The Progress of Error', in *Poems*, 1782.

[6] Cf. W. E. Houghton, 'The English Virtuoso in the Seventeenth Century', *Journal of the History of Ideas*, Vol. III, pp. 51-73, 190-219.

compiled by a Swiss monk in the eighth century, lists the pagan and Christian marvels to be seen along the route, and was probably illustrated by a circular map of Rome.[7] In the twelfth century the great medieval guide to Rome, the *Mirabilia Romae,* set a pattern traces of which can even be found in the guide books of the eighteenth century. The tradition of the circular plan survived in the circular view, which was already ubiquitous by the fifteenth century. Two famous examples are the illumination in the *Très Riches Heures de Jean de France, Duc de Berry,* 1412-16, and the painting by Taddeo di Bartolo in the Chapel of the Palazzo Pubblico in Siena, 1413-14; both are conveniently reproduced in Miss Scherer's book.[8] In the latter Old St Peter's, Old St John Lateran and St Paul's Outside the Walls figure as Christian marvels; the Colosseum, Pantheon, Hadrian's Mausoleum, the Columns of Trajan and Marcus Aurelius, and the Horse Tamers of the Quirinale as ancient ones. The Christian monuments or ancient basilicas were to be eclipsed by the new St Peter's and St John Lateran, but the main wonders of ancient Rome were fixed, with the exception of a few statues which aroused universal admiration after their excavation.

During the Renaissance the classical goal became the rival of the Christian pilgrimage. Brunelleschi drew and measured the ruins of antiquity, the first in importance of a long line of artist studies culminating in Palladio's codification of Roman architecture and its Renaissance interpretations in the sixteenth century. Palladio's two guide books grew out of the old *Mirabilia,* which he characteristically described as 'full of strange lies'. *Le Antichità di Roma,* 1554, described the classical ruins and their history for travellers, whereas the *Descritione de le Chiese, Stationi, Indulgenze & Reliquie dei Corpi Sancti, che sonno in la Città de Roma,* published in the same year, was addressed to pilgrims. In thus distinguishing between the classical traveller and the Christian pilgrim, the secular and the religious, Palladio announced one side of the Grand Tour, which came into existence at that moment when travellers from the north set out for Italy to study both the ancient marvels and the modern wonders of the Italian Renaissance.

> By the middle of the eighteenth century [writes Wittkower of the former guide] Palladio's little work had gone into more than 30 editions, and helped to form the conception of ancient Rome which travellers carried home for 200 years.[9]

It did more than form the conception of Rome, it added to the

[7] Margaret R. Scherer, *Marvels of Ancient Rome,* New York and London, 1955, p. 3.
[8] Ibid., Fig. 2 and Plate 8.
[9] R. Wittkower, *Architectural Principles in the Age of Humanism,* London, 1952, p. 56.

prestige of Palladio as an authority on taste as well as antiquity. 'Were a modern architect to build a palace in Lapland, or the West-Indies,' wrote Hogarth in 1753, 'Palladio must be his guide, nor would he dare to stir a step without his book'; as indeed he had already been to the sights of Rome.[10]

By contrast to the medieval legacy of sightseeing, the program of travel as a form of education for responsibilities in government was largely the consolidated achievement of northern scholars after the Reformation. In 1594 Nathan Chyrtaeus, Poet Laureate and Professor in the Academy of Rostock, published a compilation from manuscript and other sources, *Variorum in Europa itinerum deliciae,* in which he mentioned his own journey through Germany and Switzerland in 1567.[11] Monuments (*Opera*), divided into *Publica Sacra, Publica Profana,* and *Privata* (the last including gardens, pictures, and statues), occupy only one, the fifth, out of his six headings. Both ancient and modern names are given in the sections on geography, ethnography, and topography. The last and culminating section is on the *ratio gubernatoris.* Its list of contents covers assemblies; senators, and leading families; institutions of education and learning, scholars and libraries; and popular customs, necessaries of life, costumes and handicrafts or manufactures.

In 1625 a greater spokesman of northern humanism, Francis Bacon, published the classic statement of travel as a branch of education for the *élite* of a governing class. His essay, 'Of Travel', has many striking parallels with Chyrtaeus, and it is difficult to resist the conclusion that he had read the Latin treatise by the Protestant scholar. What distinguishes Bacon's essay is that he was solely concerned with general principles; he was not compiling a guide book. The Aristotelian ideal of good government as the product of education shines through the pages of the essay, and supports the claim that Bacon was the oligarch's Machiavelli in the non-pejorative sense. His injunctions were given a new lease of life in the eighteenth century and a special application to the Grand Tour by the self-identification of the Whig oligarchy with the senators of republican and imperial Rome. Many of his ideas were taken up by the moralising essayists of the Augustan Age, so that if Palladio was the Englishman's guide to Rome, Bacon was the ultimate preceptor on his wider travels.[12]

[10] William Hogarth, *The Analysis of Beauty with the Rejected Passages from the Manuscript Drafts and the Autobiographical Notes,* ed. J. Burke, Oxford, 1955, p. 62.

[11] Schudt, *Italienreisen im 17. und 18. Jahrhundert,* p. 38n., p. 139.

[12] Those Englishmen who did not bother to learn Italian, not a difficult task for those who had been taught Latin, would still be conducted round Rome by *ciceroni* who knew Palladio's guides.

It is against this wider background of political and social education that the artistic activities of the Grand Tourist, so easily misconstrued as recreational, must be viewed to ensure a sense of proportion. In a surprisingly large number of eighteenth-century diaries and journals the references to works of art are only incidental. As with the frivolous, like Boswell at this stage of his life, so with the serious. When the agriculturalist Arthur Young published his *Travels in France and Italy during the Years 1787, 1788 and 1789,* he had behind him a long line of countrymen who had written their travel books to improve and guide their readers in other matters than artistic taste.[13]

After allowing for these wider and long-established interests, it is still true to say that the distinctive contribution of the Georgian Age to the Grand Tour was its artistic program. In the course of the century this assumed such dimensions that no less than three key diplomatic representatives of the British government in Italy became famous for their artistic activities and guidance. These were, in order of residence, Joseph Smith, Consul at Venice, whose unrivalled collection of Canalettos was later acquired by George III;[14] Sir Horace Mann, who took up an appointment at Florence under the British Minister in 1738 and became 'Resident to the Great Duke of Tuscany' in 1740;[15] and Sir William Hamilton, British Ambassador at Naples from 1764 to 1800.[16] Negotiations for the purchase of works of art had become a recognised function of high diplomacy in the seventeenth century, and had been a major concern of Rubens on his diplomatic missions. From the Arundel Marbles through the Townley Marbles to the Elgin Marbles, to cite

---

[13] The scientific interests, however, are rather more marked in the seventeenth century. Cf. John Ray's *Observations topographical, moral and physiological,* London, 1673, with its catalogue of plants not native to England, and Edward Brown, *A Brief Account of Some Travels,* London, 1673, which is especially informative on mines and mineral waters. One of the most popular guides was Maximilien Misson's *Nouveau Voyage d'Italie, faite en l'année 1688,* La Haye, 1691. This was considerably enlarged and became a standard guide, e.g., the fifth English edition, *A New Voyage to Italy, with Curious Observations on several Other Countries,* London, 1739, although described as in two volumes, had to be bound as four substantial ones. It was virtually useless for Grand Tourists seriously interested in art and antiquities. Joseph Addison, in the Preface to *Remarks on several Parts of Italy,* London, 1705, mentioned the excellent books available on religion, governments, natural history, and geography as a justification for his own concentration on antiquities.

[14] According to the *Dictionary of National Biography,* Joseph Smith (*c.* 1675-1770) engaged in commerce at Venice at the age of eighteen, and was Consul from 1744 to 1760. George III purchased his works of art for £20,000, his library for £10,000.

[15] He continued in office until his death in 1768. His will specified 5 Poussins to be left to Horace Walpole.

[16] The British Museum purchased the first of his great collections of Greek vases in 1772, with a parliamentary grant of £8,400.

classical sculpture alone, many of the most valuable treasures that came to England were secured either by diplomats or with their assistance. The fact that envoys and agents from other countries were equally active only added to the zest of the game. Consul Smith in particular had to compete with the formidable Count Algarotti, acting on behalf of King August of Saxony. In Rome art dealing became inextricably interwoven with espionage and counter-espionage. In a fascinating study Lesley Lawrence has recently un-ravelled from two once highly confidential sources, 'State Papers Foreign' in the Public Record Office, London, and *'Gesandtschafts-archiv Rom/Vatican'* in the Haus-, Hof-, and Staatsarchiv, Vienna, an almost incredible story of secret agents who were connoisseurs. Because England was not represented at the Vatican, and the Jacobites were only too ready to add to the confusion, the notorious Philip von Stosch had unrivalled opportunities to play one side off against the other.[17]

In 1734 the Society of Dilettanti was founded as a kind of Old Boys' Club of Grand Tourists.[18] Its aim, according to a note addressed to the reader in a later archaeological publication spon-sored by the Society, *Ionian Antiquities*, 1769, was to encourage at home 'a Taste for those Objects which have contributed so much to their Entertainment abroad'. Three toasts were originally pro-posed and adopted by the Society: *'Viva la Virtù'*, 'Grecian Taste and Roman Spirit' and 'Absent Members'. Only the second half of the second toast had any reference to an ideal of good government. To quote Adolf Michaelis,

> the idea . . . that the 'grand tour', through the continental countries, particularly France and Italy, was the necessary complement to a refined training and gave it a final polish, and that art was an essential element in this higher culture, does not appear to have been very generally realised before the beginning of the eighteenth century.[19]

By the fourth decade of the eighteenth century a society had been formed to give priority to art and entertainment. Two reservations must be made before accepting these aims as representative. Not all Grand Tourists shared the Dilettanti's enthusiasm for *virtù* and conviviality. Horace Walpole described the Society as 'a club, for

[17] L. Lawrence, *Connoisseurs and Secret Agents in Eighteenth Century Rome,* London, 1961, Ch. 3, 'Stosch in Rome'.

[18] There had been informal meetings since 1732/3, but the Society later adopted 1734 as the official date of foundation. See L. Cust and S. Colvin, *History of the Society of Dilettanti*, London, 1898, p. 37, for the original toasts, to which a fourth, to the King, was later added.

[19] A. Michaelis, *Ancient Marbles in Great Britain*, Cambridge, 1882, p. 56.

which the nominal qualification is having been in Italy, and the real one, being drunk', and went on to comment that the two chiefs, Lord Middlesex and Sir Francis Dashwood, were seldom sober the whole time they were in Italy.[20] Others whose habits were convivial were uninterested in the arts. In the event the Society quickly advanced beyond the stage of rococo playfulness, and played a pioneer and outstanding part in promoting the rise of archaeology during the neo-classical period.[21]

By 'Grecian Taste' the Society meant the taste that was formed by a study of classical architecture and sculpture, at a time when many of the ancient marbles in Rome were believed to be Greek originals, and Roman art itself simply an extension of Greek: *Graecia capta ferum victorem cepit.*[22] The toast expressed the orthodox view that Greece as *fons et origo* set the purest standard, and did not anticipate the argument of Winckelmann that the 'noble simplicity and calm grandeur' of the Greeks was a secret unknown to the Romans. Antiquity itself had evolved the theory of a cycle of rise, peak, and decline; but far more important was the belief that a universal standard had been set and could be attained by later ages, so that departure from this standard was viewed rather as an aberration from the norm than an historically conditioned drive to other and antithetical values. Pheidias, Raphael, and Poussin were thus as homogeneous for eighteenth-century connoisseurs as the architecture of Athens under Pericles, Rome under Augustus, and the Italian Renaissance had been for Palladio. The simplicity and unhistorical nature of this belief should not blind us to those Augustan connotations that give the Georgian Rule of Taste its distinctive character, and were decisively promulgated by theorists in the second decade of the century.

In 1711, 1715, and 1719 a poet, an architect, and a painter published independently manifestoes for a classical reformation of English literature, architecture, and painting respectively. Each took his standards from the three main phases of the classical tradition: antiquity, the Renaissance, and seventeenth-century classicism. For each of these phases a hero was nominated. In his *Essay on Criticism,* 1711, Pope chose Homer for antiquity, Vida for the Renaissance, and Dryden for seventeenth-century classicism. The importance of his epistle lies partly in the fact that he was the only

20 To Horace Mann, 14 April 1743.
21 Michaelis, *Ancient Marbles in Great Britain,* p. 63.
22 As early as 1766, however, Richard Chandler brought back a marble from the frieze of the Parthenon, later lent to the Royal Academy and finally presented to the British Museum to join the Elgin Marbles. See Cust and Colvin, *History of the Society of Dilettanti,* p. 105.

one of the three to codify for all the arts, and constantly stress the parallel:

> A Raphael painted, and a Vida sung.
> Immortal Vida: on whose honour'd brow
> The poet's bays and critic's ivy grow.[23]

Vida was an inescapable choice by the logic of a strict parallelism, even if his writings were unfamiliar to most English readers. In 1715 Colin Campbell published an attack on the Roman baroque in the Preface to Volume I of the *Vitruvius Britannicus,* dedicated to George I. His three heroes were Vitruvius, who wrote the only treatise on architecture that survives from antiquity; Palladio, yet to be detached from the Renaissance and placed in the category of Mannerism; and Inigo Jones. Jonathan Richardson the elder first prescribed for painting in *The Theory of Painting,* also published in 1715, but it was the *Two Discourses on the Art of Criticism as it relates to Painting and the Science of a Connoisseur,* 1719, that inaugurated the era of connoisseurship as distinct from that of *virtù* in the previous century. Antiquity left him without an alternative for his first nomination, Apelles, although none of his work had survived. His other two were Raphael and Van Dyck. The third may come somewhat as a surprise, until it is realised that all three theorists nominated a national hero for the third category. Richardson must have been well aware that Poussin, in his own words 'justly stiled the French Raffaele',[24] had stronger claims on strictly classical grounds, but patriotic fervour led him to champion the Flemish artist who had become Court Painter to Charles I and died in the country of his adoption. The trinity of national heroes thus reads: Dryden, Inigo Jones, and Van Dyck. Of the three theorists Richardson was faced with the greatest difficulties. No one could object to Pope's choosing Dryden instead of Milton if classical correctness were the standard, but there was no seventeenth-century native painter who could be ranked with the architect Inigo Jones, or could be regarded as the heir to Raphael. It was also unfortunate that Apelles was only a name, but this weakness Richardson and his learned son set out to remedy by publishing their guide to ancient marbles in Italy.[25] In the event the painters of the century took their

---

23 *Essay on Criticism,* ll. 704-6.

24 *The Works of Jonathan Richardson,* Strawberry-Hill, 1792, p. 87. In the same passage he defended his bias by singling out Van Dyck's excellence as a portrait painter, a category which required other gifts besides a mastery of the ideal.

25 Jonathan Richardson the elder and Jonathan Richardson the younger, *An Account of Some of the Statues, Bas-reliefs, Drawings and Pictures in Italy, &c.,* London, 1722.

classical standards from sculpture, an important consideration for understanding the practice of Reynolds and other painters.[26]

The Georgian Rule of Taste, the program of which was outlined so clearly for literature, architecture, and painting in three publications appearing in the same decade, may be defined as a tripartite canon of antiquity, the Renaissance and seventeenth-century classicism, modified by a predilection for the national achievements in the third phase and governed by the moralising 'good sense' of the Augustans. The escape-clause that did so much to foster originality in interpretation was the licence to admire national achievement even when it showed affinities with the continental baroque, or involved romantic and anti-classical associations. It also helps to an understanding of the interaction of the sister arts, at a time when the Horatian tag *Ut Pictura Poesis* was frequently quoted, as well as the marked divergences between them.[27] Last but not least, the survival of anti-classical tendencies was guaranteed by the cult of the national past. Pope admired Shakespeare and Milton as well as Dryden. Colin Campbell denounced Bernini, Borromini, and Carlo Fontana, but praised Wren, Vanbrugh, and Hawksmoor. James Gibbs was to owe as much to Wren as to Palladio, and Robert and James Adam eulogised Vanbrugh after their neo-classical studies on the Continent. On his second visit to the Low Countries Reynolds made a special study of Van Dyck's master, Rubens.

The popular conception of the Georgian Rule of Taste is largely derived from architecture and the domestic arts.[28] Its governing principle in architecture was mathematical proportion, the revival of which became the theoretical obsession of the age.[29] There is an essential difference between this revival and the doctrine of antiquity and the Renaissance. The symbolic associations of mathematical proportion with the cosmos and the divine order were dropped, or barely mentioned.[30] Whereas for the age of Leonardo the Vitruvian Image was invested with the most solemn meaning,

[26] Cf. the masterly analysis in E. Wind, 'Humanitätsidee und heroisiertes Porträt in der englischen Kultur des 18. Jahrhunderts', in *Vorträge der Bibliothek Warburg*, Leipzig and Berlin, 1930-1.

[27] Cf. R. Lee, '*Ut Pictura Poesis:* the Humanistic Theory of Painting', *Art Bulletin*, 1940, pp. 197-263.

[28] The background of the architectural phase is admirably presented in J. Steegmann, *The Rule of Taste from George I to George IV*, London, 1936.

[29] A key figure in the dissemination of proportional theory was Robert Morris, who wrote in *Lectures on Architecture*, 2nd ed., London, 1759, p. 78: 'Beauty in all objects, springs from the same unerring Law in Nature, which, in *Architecture*, I would call Proportion'.

[30] The quotation in note 29 is as close as the architectural theorists came to acknowledging a cosmic significance.

proportion was now equated with good taste.[31] The peace of the Augustans was seldom disturbed by mystical analogies, and Reynolds spoke for the Age of Reason when he stated that it had been 'the fate of the arts to be enveloped in mysterious and incomprehensible language'.[32] Second only to proportion in importance was the classical ideal of *simplex munditiis*.[33] This in turn has led to a modern cult of what Horace Walpole noted as a distinguishing excellence of England, 'the middling house', that is the Georgian country squire's house, the merchant's house, the rectory, and the farmhouse, with their legacies of Queen Anne silver and furniture, and the kind of parlour so charmingly commemorated in the conversation pieces of Anthony Devis.[34]

This modern image is based on a pleasing by-product, and does not correspond with the high aims of the promoters, who were chiefly concerned with the elevated categories. Behind the writers of the manifestoes lies the immensely influential figure of Anthony Ashley Cooper, third Earl of Shaftesbury, who provided the high philosophical background of the Rule of Taste by an acute, copious, and graceful discussion of the property within a neo-Platonic system.[35] The first popular writer unequivocally to advocate a Rule of Taste was Joseph Addison: 'the Taste is not to conform to the Art, but the Art to the Taste'.[36] 'Strength with Politeness', 'Ornament with Simplicity', and 'Beauty with Majesty' were the merits claimed by Campbell for the Banqueting House.[37] They were also the merits to which Augustan prose aspired in its elevated forms. Because the age took its highest standards from tragedy, epic, and pastoral in literature, from religious oratorio in music, from the grandiose sepulchral monument in sculpture, and from history painting, turning to the Bible and antiquity for its themes, it is by studying these that the interrelationship between the Grand Tour and the Rule of Taste is most clearly established. A comprehensive investigation is outside the scope of this paper, but an examination of certain trends in architecture will serve to bring out the fundamental unity of purpose in both.

31 Cf. Pt IV, Sect. 7, 'The Break-away from the Laws of Harmonic Proportion in Architecture', in Wittkower, *Architectural Principles in the Age of Humanism*, pp. 124-35.

32 R. R. Wark (ed.), *Discourses on Art*, San Marino, California, 1959, p. 118. The context is appropriately a discussion of taste.

33 See Stephen Switzer, *Iconographica Rustica*, 1718, p. xv et seq., where the ideal of *simplex munditiis* is discussed as complementary to proportion.

34 To Horace Mann, 13 Sept. 1741.

35 For the importance of Shaftesbury in this context, see Christopher Hussey's Introduction to Margaret Jourdain, *The Works of William Kent*, London, 1948.

36 *Spectator* No. 29, 3 April 1711.

37 *Vitruvius Britannicus*, ed. Colin Campbell, Vol. I, London, 1717, p. 4.

In the classical reformation of English elevated architecture three manifestations of the influence of antiquity, or modes of imitation, may be distinguished: classical revision, classical reproduction, and classical quotation.[38] Before describing these a relevant distinction may be drawn between the situations in art and literature respectively. Whereas the writer had at his elbow texts which were complete, the architect, painter, and sculptor had to construct their picture of antiquity from isolated monuments, ruins, and fragments. The archaeological discoveries that followed the excavations under Alcubierre at Herculaneum from 1738 and extended in the second half of the century to Greece upset the canon in art but not in literature. So immeasurably superior was the literary evidence that it can be argued that Winckelmann's analysis of the difference between Greek and Roman art had its origin in his early mastery of the existing corpus of both literatures, a mastery which opened his eyes to the separateness of the two worlds.[39] The Roman bias of Georgian elevated architecture, particularly before the Greek discoveries made their impact, gives it a distinctive stamp and makes it at once a dignified background and a foil to the variety and liveliness of the Rule of Taste in literature.

Of the three manifestations of influence or modes of imitation, the first owed least to the Grand Tour and to Rome. It was initiated by Colin Campbell, whose early life is obscure. In his Preface he made no mention of having ever been to Italy, and there is nothing in his theory or designs before Burlington's second visit of 1719 that could not have been acquired from architectural publications. That Campbell conceived his program as a classical revision of baroque models is made clear by the first three buildings illustrated in *Vitruvius Britannicus*, Volume I, 1715, and the accompanying text. These are St Paul's Cathedral by Wren, St Peter's, Rome, and his own design for a new church in Lincoln's Inn Fields. In an inscription below the elevation of St Peter's (Plate Va), which is the only foreign building illustrated in any of the volumes, he drew attention to the baroque additions of Carlo

---

[38] I have taken the term 'quotation' from Horace Walpole, who used it in a comparable sense to describe the borrowed attitudes of Reynolds: 'Where a single posture is imitated from an historic picture and applied to a portrait in a different dress . . . this is not plagiarism, but a quotation: and a quotation from a great author, with a novel application of the sense, has always been allowed to be an instance of parts and taste; and may have more merit than the original'.
See Horace Walpole, *Anecdotes of Painting in England*, ed. J. Dallaway, rev. R. N. Wornum, Vol. I, London, 1888, p. xvii, n. 2.
[39] For the literary sources of Winckelmann's criticism at a formative stage see H. Zeller, *Winckelmanns Beschreibung des Apollo im Belvedere*, Zürich, 1955.

Moderno and Bernini, and it was as a correction of a baroque plan and elevation that his own design (Plate Vb) was presented. 'The Plan was reduced to a Square and a Circle, which, in my weak opinion, are the most perfect Figures.' In other words, he had restored the geometric plan of the Vitruvian Image, which the elongation of St Peter's by the addition of a baroque nave had marred. The hexastyle portico, which commands the front, is regular, that is based on authentic models. The parts are all 'in certain Measures of Proportion'; and these parts are carefully distinguished in opposition to the baroque principle of merging or coalescence, the flanking towers being removed 'at such a distance that the great Cupola is without any Embarrass'. The whole is 'dressed very plain, as . . . most comfortable to the Simplicity of the Ancients'. By a single design Campbell both corrected what the Baroque Age had made of St Peter's and demonstrated the four basic principles or cornerstones of classicism: a regular or correct imitation of classical forms; the observance of geometric proportion; the order or harmony of 'staccato' or distinct parts; and ancient simplicity.[40]

In other designs he illustrated a similar revision of English baroque models, for example his own Wanstead House, Essex, which is essentially a correction of Vanbrugh's Castle Howard.[41] But there is no need to proliferate examples. Series after series of great houses and villas by Campbell and others have been traced back to their seventeenth-century English prototypes.[42] In each case all the four principles of classical revision are observed. The porticoes are now regular, mathematical ratio has been reinstated, the parts are distinguished, and the exuberance of baroque ornament is carefully avoided.

The second volume of *Vitruvius Britannicus* came out in 1717, and opened like the first with older buildings, in this case all from the English seventeenth century. Again the first modern design to appear is by Campbell, and again it belongs to the most elevated of all the categories of architecture, the sacred. His second or *Maison Carrée* design for a church is the first known reproduction of an entire classical building for modern use in the history of European architecture (Plate VIa). The Ionic order has been substituted for the Corinthian, and a Venetian window inserted at the

40 *Vitruvius Britannicus*, Vol. I, pp. 3-4.
41 For the three designs of Wanstead see *Vitruvius Britannicus*, Vol. I, Plates 21-7; Vol. III, Plates 39, 40. If the central cupola of the second design had been retained, and the flanking towers of the third design built, the derivation from Castle Howard would have been unmistakable.
42 Notably by Sir John Summerson in his three Cantor Lectures on 'The Classical Country House in 18th-Century England', *Journal of the Royal Society of Arts*, Vol. 107, July 1959, pp. 539-87.

east end. Externally, nothing distinguishes this church, which was dedicated to the Archbishop of Canterbury, from the classical temple (Plate VIb) except this substitution, the window, the prophets and martyrs on the acroteria, and the pedimental relief of the Baptism of Christ. The Church of England was not enamoured of the proposal to worship in a pagan temple with a Christian iconography, for neither was the church built nor one like it. But like the first design, it announced a whole series, of which the Assembly Rooms at York (1731-2), by the Earl of Burlington himself, are the most famous example.[43] This reconstructed in its entirety the Egyptian Hall or *oecus* of Vitruvius, with details taken from Palladio's reconstruction of the ancient basilica where the Latin text was insufficient.[44] The others are all garden or other ornamental buildings, for there was an obvious difficulty in finding modern uses for ancient models. Strangely enough, a choice of Napoleon and a change in historical circumstances resulted in Campbell's idea being realised on an even grander scale in France during the nineteenth century. The Emperor chose Pierre-Alexandre Vignon, or rather imposed him on the judges of the competition of 1806, as architect for the Temple of Glory to be raised in honour of the soldiers of the *Grande Armée*.[45] 'His project', he commented when the designs were submitted, 'is the only one which fulfils my intentions. It was a temple I asked for, not a church. . . .'[46] But a church in due course the temple became, when it was restored to Catholic worship as La Madeleine.[47]

The third mode of classical quotation may be described as the central insertion of a classical model, formula, or motive in an alien or unclassical construction or setting.[48] When John Wood the elder began the Circus at Bath in 1754, he took as his model the Colosseum (Plate VII). It can be read in two ways. To Matthew Bramble in Smollett's *Humphrey Clinker*, 1771, it looked 'like Vespasian's amphitheatre turned inside out'. This is exactly what it was, although the circle became an ellipse in the process. The second

[43] Cf. R. Wittkower, 'Burlington and his Work in York', in W. A. Singleton (ed.), *Studies in Architectural History*, London and York, 1954.

[44] For the Vitruvian source see Bk VI, Ch. 5 in Joseph Gwilt's translation, 1826, p. 176, and Bk VI, Ch. 3 in M. H. Morgan's translation, 1914, reprinted 1966, p. 179. For Palladio see Bk II, Ch. 10.

[45] P. Lavedan, *French Architecture*, Harmondsworth, 1956, p. 143.

[46] Ibid.

[47] The original proposal had been for a church dedicated to the Magdalen. but Napoleon cancelled this until the Battle of Leipzig and the loss of Spain led him to change his mind. See H. Russell-Hitchcock, *Architecture: Nineteenth and Twentieth Centuries*. The Pelican History of Art, Harmondsworth, 1958 p. 11.

[48] Many examples have been conveniently gathered in F. Saxl and R. Wittkower, *British Art and the Mediterranean*, Oxford, 1948.

way, which is the relevant one here, is as an inscription of the three identically superimposed orders of the Colosseum on the elevation of terrace houses. 'Perhaps it will occur to some mad Englishman', Winckelmann observed sarcastically in a letter to Muzel-Stosch, 'to have even Trajan's column transported to London.'[49] In the event it was a greater masterpiece, the sculptures of the Parthenon, that came to London. Rome was better guarded than Athens, and *faute de mieux* the English fell back on the substitutions that had been made by Burlington and Wood. Classical quotation on this grand scale can, like the other modes, be traced back to the great originator of the Burlington circle, Colin Campbell. His first design for Houghton shows the body of a Roman temple placed centrally between Palladian wings.[50] Like the Archbishop of Canterbury, the Prime Minister was not convinced, and proceeded with an alternative scheme.

Perhaps the most striking example of classical quotation in architecture is the 'idea' of the garden or south front of Kedleston 'taken from' the Arch of Constantine by Robert Adam (Plates VIIIa, VIIIb).[51] Copies of the Flora Farnese and Antique Bacchus occupy the niches, and copies of the Medicean and Borghese Vases ornament the steps that lead to the Pantheon-interior of the Saloon, in a scheme which owes everything to Rome and nothing to Spalatro.

There is a variant of the third mode which can be paralleled extensively in painting and sculpture. This is the borrowing of a classical model, formula, or motive, which may or may not be given a modern dress, and its insertion in a romantic context. In architecture it may be illustrated by the Palladian bridge erected by Roger Morris at Wilton for the Earl of Pembroke in 1737 and copied by Wood and others (Plate IXa). The source of its most unusual feature, an open colonnaded gallery without a pediment above the arches, was Plate 50 in Giacomo Leoni's *Alberti*, 1726 (Plate IXb). This is altogether different in its scheme from Palladio's bridge, which carried three streets flanked by shops and followed in its elevation the palace-front formula of a temple-front centrepiece linked by colonnaded wings to end pavilions. A juster title would therefore be the Albertian bridge, but Morris copied the end units from the entrances to Palladio's flanking pavilions, and the name of Palladio was irrevocably attached.

---

49 26 Feb. 1768. Cited by Michaelis, *Ancient Marbles in Great Britain*, p. 87. Plate VIIa shows the comparative reconstruction by Sir John Soane, first published by Sir John Summerson in *Heavenly Mansions*, London, 1949.

50 In *Vitruvius Britannicus*, Vol. II, 1717, Plates 83-4.

51 *A Catalogue of the Pictures, Statues, &c., at Kedleston, with some account of the Architecture*, printed by W. Bemrose and Sons, Derby, 1861, gives a lengthy list of the Roman repertory of sources at Kedleston.

The exquisite invention was at once a landscape object and a scenic platform, and it would be difficult to decide whether the bridge at Prior Park or Stowe were the more romantically situated. In painting and sculpture the detection of the classical source is simplified by the fact that both painters and sculptors drew exclusively on ancient marbles. A whole literature has grown around these borrowings, which range from Sir Joshua Reynolds's use of the Apollo Belvedere for the pose of full-length portraits to the group of paintings and statues that derive ultimately from the Marble Faun in the Capitoline sculpture-gallery.[52] The latter first appears in England in Giovanni Battista Guelfi's Monument to James Craggs in Westminster Abbey, 1727 (Plate Xa), the main changes being the crossing of the bent leg before instead of behind the straight one and the elbow instead of the hand of the leaning arm resting on the support.[53] It was taken up by fashionable portrait painters ubiquitously. Gainsborough used it for the portrait of David Garrick, 1769, commissioned by the Corporation of Stratford-on-Avon (Plate Xb). The setting is a romantic corner of a landscape garden with a view of the Palladian bridge at Prior Park deliciously inserted in the distance. Allan Ramsay was the first to use the Apollo Belvedere pose in his portrait of 'Norman, 22nd Chief of Macleod', 1748, striding in his tartans against a desolate sea-shore.[54] Reynolds followed with *Commodore Keppel*, 1753, in which the hero is shown after shipwreck in similar desolation, but this time the romantic effect is heightened by the storm-tossed sea. He was to use it several times later, always splendidly and in either a baroque or romantic context, most notably for *Omai*, 1776, the Noble Savage walking among the exotic palms of his native Tahiti.[55]

The change of context, not the disguise of costume, is the key to the artistic uses to which the variant was put. These did not depend on altering or disguising the classical model. Henry Hoare, some time in or after the 1750s, placed a copy of the Vatican Ariadne (Plate XIa) in the heart of the grotto he constructed at Stourhead.[56]

[52] The most important study is by Wind, 'Humanitätsidee und heroisiertes Porträt in der englischen Kultur des 18. Jahrhunderts'. An interesting article by A. N. L. Munby, 'Nathaniel Hone's Conjuror', in *Connoisseur*, December 1947, shows how exhaustive a contemporary could be in detecting borrowings.
[53] Margaret Whinney, in *Sculpture in Britain 1530 to 1830*, The Pelican History of Art, Harmondsworth, 1964, pp. 80-1, notes that the monument was designed by James Gibbs, who, like Guelfi, had had opportunities to study the cross-legged statues of antiquity. The precise classical source has not yet been identified.
[54] E. K. Waterhouse, *Painting in Britain 1530 to 1790*, The Pelican History of Art, Harmondsworth, 1950, p. 152.
[55] Reproduced in E. K. Waterhouse, *Reynolds*, London, 1941, Plate 171.
[56] O. Siren, *China and the Gardens of Europe in the Eighteenth Century*, New York, 1950, p. 49.

A single shaft of light penetrates the gloom of the dark interior, and illumines the lines by Alexander Pope inscribed on the floor:

Nymph of the Grot, these sacred Springs I keep,
And to the Murmur of these Waters sleep;
Ah spare my Slumbers, gently tread the Cave!
And drink in silence, or in silence lave.[57]

As if the eighteenth century ever did drink in silence! The grotto is a fake grotto; the statue is a copy of a Roman version of a decadent Hellenistic original; the poet's verses are only a translation. But the spirit of poetry obeys mysterious laws, and may invade even a world as artificial as this.

'The members of the English Parliament', observed Voltaire after his return from England to France, 'are fond of comparing themselves to the Old Romans.'[58] All three modes of classical revision, classical reproduction, and classical quotation are dignified by Roman associations, among which the *ratio gubernatoris* is paramount. In the Stone Hall by William Kent at Houghton (Plate XIb) a collection of Roman imperial portrait busts stamps the august character of the room. The level alignment is broken only once, by Rysbrack's bust of the Prime Minister placed centrally and in a higher position on the mantelpiece, so that Sir Robert Walpole takes precedence over a regimented company of Roman emperors. The bas-reliefs by Rysbrack illustrate sacrifices and other scenes from Roman life, for example the Sacrifice of the Bull, a theme appropriate to a landowner who bred cattle, from Montfaucon's *L'Antiquité Expliquée*, 1719.[59] The place of honour above Walpole's bust is occupied by the Sacrifice to Diana, the tutelary goddess of a virtue of which he had no high opinion, but whose identification with Queen Elizabeth I he may have respected. On his bust in Roman drapery is proudly displayed the Star of the Garter, which is repeated in the spandrels of the ceiling, separated from the rest of the room by Artari's *putti*, a baroque device for distinguishing between the celestial and terrestrial spheres. At the summit of the celestial sphere, in the place traditionally reserved for the apotheosis, appears in full splendour the Walpole Coat of Arms.

The meaning of this somewhat confident iconography is explained outside the room by the sculpture on the pediment over the central window, originally designed by Colin Campbell as an entrance

[57] *The Twickenham Edition of the Poems of Alexander Pope*, Vol. VI, Minor Poems, ed. N. Ault and J. Butt, London, 1954, p. 248.

[58] D. Flower (ed.), *Voltaire's England*, London, 1950, p. 37.

[59] M. I. Webb, *Michael Rysbrack, Sculptor*, London, 1954, p. 128. For the Stone Hall at Houghton see the same authority, pp. 127-9, and Margaret Jourdain, *The Works of William Kent*, pp. 63-4.

to be approached by a flight of steps.[60] Neptune and Britannia, reclining in positions not unreminiscent of Michelangelo's Medici tombs, flank a cartouche of the Walpole Coat of Arms adorned by the Star of the Garter. The elderly Neptune, who in antiquity merely presided over the Mediterranean and its outlets, gazes with admiration at the young Britannia, who now rules the waves of wider oceans.

The Prime Minister's son Horace is sometimes dismissed by the uninformed as a dilettante Gothicist, but the Roman message of Houghton, which is also the message of Holkham and other great houses of the period, was one he never forgot. Strawberry Hill was among other things a museum of relics of British history. But when he commissioned Sir Joshua Reynolds to paint his portrait in 1755-6 (Plate XIc) it was with his Roman imperial eagle that he chose to be commemorated.[61] The reference to Rome may be compared with those in a swagger portrait of a Grand Tourist recently acquired by the National Gallery of Victoria in Melbourne (Plate XII). It was painted by Pompeo Batoni in Rome in 1767, and shows Sampson Gideon, later Earl Eardley of Spalding, with his *cicerone* Signor Basti.[62] The young heir to an immense fortune was the son of the Anglo-Portuguese banker who bore the name of the greatest of all the judges of Israel, Gideon; and he was about to marry into an ancient English family, for he shows his tutor a miniature of his fiancée, Maria, daughter of Chief Justice Sir Eardley Wilmot. On the table at his side stands a bust of Athena, reproduced from the famous Roman figure of Minerva Guistianini standing with a spear; and in the background is glimpsed what was then called the Temple of the Sybil, now usually identified as the Temple of Vesta, situated at Tivoli on the outskirts of Rome.[63]

[60] The great staircase inside made their function mainly ornamental. According to the legend of a print of Houghton published by W. Watts, Chelsea, 1 September 1782: 'The Entrance was originally in the principal storey, by a grand Flight of Steps in Each Front, but is now confined to the Basement (similar to Holkham), the Steps having been lately pulled down, in consequence of their being considerably decayed'.

[61] It was found in the gardens of Boccapadugli, in the precinct of Caracalla's Baths, in 1742, and was the subject of an extensive correspondence with Horace Mann before it arrived in Strawberry Hill. See *The Yale Edition of Horace Walpole's Correspondence*, ed. W. S. Lewis. Vol. XIX, *Correspondence with Sir Horace Mann*, London, 1954, p. 66, n. 10.

[62] Unfortunately Signor Basti has not been identified. Perhaps the old but not contemporary inscription, now removed, was a corruption. Filippo Barazzi, a merchant friend of Batoni, has been suggested. In the 1770s the *primo custode* of the Uffizi was Signor Bastianelli. The history of the portrait is given in a learned article by Harley Preston, 'Two Portraits by Pompeo Batoni', in the *Annual Bulletin of the National Gallery of Victoria*, Vol. VI, Melbourne, 1964, pp. 11-19.

[63] Harley Preston, 'Two Portraits by Pompeo Batoni'. The painting was apparently finished in Rome after Gideon had returned to England.

The Georgian Rule of Taste was originally conceived as a program for all the arts. It is not suggested that the Grand Tour, with its goal in Rome, was decisive for literature; the writers who were classically educated had received a similar message from the Latin texts they studied at school and University. But a concluding reference may be made to one writer who made the Grand Tour and exemplifies its influence on the Rule of Taste: the poet Thomas Gray. A remarkable number of the grander images of Gray's *Elegy* can be paralleled in the Roman associations with which returning Grand Tourists who had the means surrounded themselves. The *ratio gubernatoris* as an identification of the two empires and their history is clearly stated:

> Th' applause of list'ning senates to command,
> The threats of pain and ruin to despise,
> To scatter plenty o'er a smiling land,
> And read their hist'ry in a nation's eyes.

The sources here are literary, but other images can be paralleled precisely from Lord Cobham's seat at Stowe. This is not surprising, if we recall that the poem might never have been written but for the author's friendship with the Cobham family. 'When Lady Cobham resided at her house at Stoke, Mr Gray was at no great distance in the same parish.'[64]

> On his return from Stoke House, which he constantly visited, the poet was obliged to pass by the churchyard, which was almost close to the house, and he would sometimes deviate into it and there spend a melancholy moment.[65]

There must have been a frequent exchange of news between the Dowager at Stoke House and her family at Stowe in the same county, Buckinghamshire, and the gardens were a topic likely to interest Gray keenly. Like Cowper, he often had a private audience in mind as well as the world outside, and during the formative years of the *Elegy* his most personal contacts were with 'Lady Cobham and her friends'.[66]

The same spirit of Whig liberalism breathes over garden and poem. In the Temple of British Worthies the heroes of the Whig Pantheon are divided into the national representatives of the Active Life and the Contemplative Life. As a leader of the historic struggle to overthrow absolutism Hampden is paired with Milton, just as in the poem. The line, 'Some Cromwell guiltless of his country's blood',

[64] 'The Life of Gray', by J. Mitford, in *The Eton Edition of the Poetical Works of Thomas Gray*, London, 1863, incorporates the recollections of Jacob Bryant, his Eton schoolfellow, from whom these quotations are taken.
[65] Ibid., p. 95.
[66] Ibid.

explains why the great Protector was left out at Stowe. Gray's central antithesis between the mausoleums and memorials of the great and the graves of the poor in a country churchyard receives at Stowe the essential weight on the side of 'Grandeur' and 'Ambition' which is lacking at Stoke Poges, where the grandiose monuments, storied urns, and animated busts of the eighteenth century are sought in vain. Moreover, the gardens at Stowe are essentially elegiac; the images of the illustrious dead are conjured up at every turn, so that a French visitor could actually prefer it to *'le temple auguste de Westminster'*.[67] Those who have attended a service in King's College Chapel at Gray's university read with an enhanced awareness the lines:

> Nor you, ye Proud, impute to These the fault,
> If Mem'ry o'er their Tomb no Trophies raise,
> Where thro' the long-drawn isle and fretted vault,
> The pealing anthem swells the note of praise.

To visit Stowe after Stoke Poges similarly prepares the mind for a heightened reception of the poem's meaning by freshly stocking it with most of the images that Gray evoked to contrast the lot of the humble and underprivileged with that of the great and famous.

The *Elegy* is sometimes interpreted as an early document of radicalism. Gray, in the penultimate stanza of his poem, 'A Long Story', reveals that Lady Cobham was criticised by conservative opinion for her democratic tendencies. No doubt some of those who returned from the Grand Tour deserved the taunts of Ascham and Cowper, and Gray, who parted company with the Prime Minister's son at Reggio on his own Grand Tour, had good reasons to associate it with social distractions and perhaps with pride. It is to the credit of Horace Walpole that he later took the blame on himself for the separation.[68]

Both the Rule of Taste and the Grand Tour, the influences of which are so inextricably interwoven, deserve to be judged by the brighter as well as the darker side, by the serious and humane as well as the superficial and affected. Each was based on the great inheritance of antiquity and its later interpretations; the roads of the second led out from Rome as well as to it. The Grand Tourist went to Rome with a totally different purpose from that of the Christian pilgrim, but inherited the delight in incidental *mirabilia*. The objects of his

[67] *L'Art de former les jardins modernes,* Paris, 1771, a translation from Thomas Whately, *Observations on Modern Gardening,* London, 1770, contains as an Appendix a long, detailed, and important description of the gardens at Stowe, written by the anonymous translator, who clearly knew the gardens at first hand, for he makes many original observations.

[68] W. S. Lewis, *Horace Walpole,* London, 1961, pp. 49-51.

wonder had now changed. To the medieval pilgrims the Christian basilicas provided the norm, the ancient relics of paganism the strange marvels. For the generation of Gray the position was reversed; they took their standards of normality from antiquity, and it was the Gothic cathedrals they saw *en route* in France that were the curious relics, just as the baroque in Rome seemed eccentric. The perceptive admired the architecture of the Middle Ages, and were thrilled by Alpine *terribilità* as well as soothed by *il riposo di Claudio* in the Roman Campagna. Rome was the source of every Western *renovatio* or revival of antiquity in the Middle Ages; in 'the Golden Age of Classic Dilettantism', the apt title coined by Adolf Michaelis, the voyage to Rome helped to nourish a love of Gothic and open men's eyes to the beauties of wild nature. The Grand Tour, both by its historical continuity and its opportunities, widened the interests and susceptibilities of those who made it, and at once strengthened and undermined the Rule of Taste on the threshold of romanticism.

Johnson's London: *The Country Versus the City*

John Hardy

The Oxford edition of Johnson's *Poems,* of which the late Professor David Nichol Smith was senior editor, stands as one of the greatest contributions to Johnson scholarship during the first half of this century.[1] On this occasion, when we meet to honour the memory of David Nichol Smith and pay tribute to his scholarship, it is therefore appropriate that we turn once again to Johnson's poetry. The present paper will invite a reconsideration of *London,* Johnson's first great poem. Although published anonymously in May 1738, when Johnson was only twenty-eight, this work so caught the attention of the literary world that the reigning poet Pope predicted its author would soon be *'déterré'.*[2]

Today, however, many critics tend to refer rather slightingly to *London.* Except in T. S. Eliot's famous essay,[3] Johnson's imitation in the Augustan manner of Juvenal's third satire on Rome has generally received less than its due. Naturally enough perhaps, it is overshadowed in discussions of Johnson's poetry by the praise rightly bestowed on the later, impressive *Vanity of Human Wishes,* a work which can properly be said to exist independently of its Latin original. Yet even Johnsonians seem unwilling to recognise the merit of the earlier poem. Boswell, though perhaps without any derogatory intent, styled it 'Johnson's juvenile poem',[4] and recent

---

[1] *The Poems of Samuel Johnson* (hereafter cited as *Poems*), ed. D. Nichol Smith and E. L. McAdam, Oxford, 1941. (All quotations from *London* are taken from the text of this edition.) My grateful thanks are due to Miss Mary Lascelles, who, though she cannot be held responsible for any errors of interpretation, contributed greatly to this paper by her prompt and stimulating comments on questions raised in correspondence between us.

[2] *Boswell's Life of Johnson* (hereafter cited as *Life*), ed. G. B. Hill, rev. and enlarged L. F. Powell, Vol. I, Oxford, 1934-50, p. 129.

[3] *London: A Poem and The Vanity of Human Wishes with an Introductory Essay by T. S. Eliot,* London, 1930, esp. pp. 15-17.

[4] *Life,* Vol. I, p. 131.

critics have, so to speak, given his words the force of a value-judgment. In his highly praised book on Johnson, J. W. Krutch dismisses *London* as merely 'a skilfully executed exercise';[5] while Sir Sydney Roberts, too, regards it as 'in form . . . a Latinist's exercise'.[6] The assumption behind this and much other criticism of the poem is that the youthful poet made unoriginal, uninspired use of a rather Procrustean model.

What seems to critics especially unimaginative or uncharacteristic is Johnson's treatment of that contrast between city and country which is central to the structure of both poems. According to Boswell *London* exemplified Johnson's 'prejudices as a "true-born Englishman", not only against foreign countries, but against Ireland and Scotland'.[7] Yet this is, to say the least, a curious reading of the couplet,

> For who would leave, unbrib'd, Hibernia's land,
> Or change the rocks of Scotland for the Strand?

Later critics, though rightly reading these lines at their face value, have nevertheless been perplexed that this sentiment should have been uttered by one who found the metropolis such a congenial home. In his book on English satire and satirists Hugh Walker, who is obviously influenced by biographical considerations, overlooks the subtlety and complexity of Johnson's role of poet. 'With the knowledge', he writes, 'we now have of Johnson's opinions and likings, we are disturbed in *London* by praises of the country as a setting for life far preferable to the Strand.'[8] Similarly Professor Krutch finds 'the conventional contrast between the country and the city . . . little short of fantastic coming as it does from a man who was as completely and contentedly urban as any one who ever lived'.[9] Other critics, too, openly assume that the young poet was slavishly following his Latin model. The Yale editor of the poetry, referring to Boswell's comment on Johnson's early lines, notes that these express 'only the standard contrast between the poor but simple rural life and the vicious and dangerous life of the city'.[10] Likewise, in a paper read to the Johnson Society of London on 'Johnson and the Classics', H. M. Currie has recently stated that the poet '. . . adopted in his *London* a pose and advanced views alien to his own, following, for example, the denunciation of the

5 J. W. Krutch, *Samuel Johnson*, New York, 1944, p. 64.
6 S. Roberts, *Samuel Johnson*, London, 1954, p. 8.
7 *Life*, Vol. I, pp. 129-30.
8 H. Walker, *English Satire and Satirists*, London, 1925, p. 230.
9 Krutch, *Samuel Johnson*, p. 63.
10 *Samuel Johnson: Poems,* ed. E. L. McAdam jun., with G. Milne, New Haven, 1964, p. 48n.

town which he had found in the Latin original'.[11] Yet the truth is not so simple as this. Johnson's attitude to the country is, as I shall try to show, very different from Juvenal's. The critic must ultimately ask himself what creative use the English poet made of the contrast he found in his original.

As Mary Lascelles has noted in her article, 'Johnson and Juvenal', the Latin poem assumes the form of a dialogue between friends in which Umbricius, the 'friend', 'playing the part of Juvenal's well-wisher, takes leave of him with the advice: "Do as I am doing. Cut loose from Rome, and live by yourself in the country".' Yet, as she rightly observes, 'we are sensible of an unspoken commentary', for the poet himself has no intention of taking this advice:

> His real theme is not country pleasures but the mingled attrac-tion and repulsion exercised by the great cosmopolitan city, and Umbricius' leave-taking is merely an occasion for a denun-ciation of all that displeases him in Roman life.

Thus Miss Lascelles plausibly suggests that Juvenal's pose is ironical, expressing the poet's 'inmost certainty that, if life in Rome is disagreeable, dangerous, degrading, outside Rome there is nothing to be called life, at all'.[12] The irony seems pervasive from the outset: *'ego vel Prochytam praepono Suburae'*. There is no place *'tam miserum, tam solum'* [so dismal and so lonely]—not even the deso-late little island of Procida—which the poet does not pretend to prefer to one of the chief though noisiest streets of Rome.[13] Because of this irony, Juvenal's city-country antithesis is not a simple one. Despite its discomforts and dangers the metropolis acts like a magnet on the poet, who is for this reason unable to exalt a life of retirement in the country as a real and whole-hearted alternative to life in the city.

Johnson, on the other hand, whole-heartedly condemns the corrupt city and praises the country. His poem is free of Juvenal's irony, and has, in fact, its own individual theme. Indeed, it is this theme, developed in terms of the implied contrast between country and city, which differentiates *London* so obviously from Juvenal's third satire. The critic should forget that Johnson was later the great city-dweller, and recognise that the poem's contrast between country and city is rhetorical, with its own special validity and point. As poet Johnson shows good reasons, both moral and politi-cal, for depicting life in the country as a desirable and even necessary alternative to life in the city.

[11] *New Rambler*, June 1965, p.15.
[12] Mary Lascelles, 'Johnson and Juvenal', in F. W. Hilles (ed.), *New Light on Dr Johnson*, New Haven, 1959, pp. 41-2.
[13] *Juvenal and Persius*, trans. G. G. Ramsay, Loeb Classical Library, London, 1918, p.33.

As a poem on the evils of city life, *London* exploits a common theme. From the outset the city is described as a place of 'malice, rapine, accident', of physical danger and moral corruption and decay. Yet, as the poem proceeds, Johnson gives individual expression to this theme by setting it in a particular context. *London* is not a topical poem merely in the sense that it describes fires, falling houses, fell attorneys, female atheists, and those other social evils to be found in the eighteenth-century capital. It is also a topical poem in the further sense that it satirises the measures of a particular government and the corruption which that government could be said to have fostered. In reading the poem we are gradually made aware of Johnson's specifically *political* prejudices as a true-born Englishman, and these were prejudices widely enough shared at the time to give his work the breadth and significance of political satire.

The composition of *London* coincided, in Boswell's words, with 'that ferment against the court and the ministry, which some years after ended in the downfall of Sir Robert Walpole'.[14] Thus the editors of the *Poems* point out that Johnson's

> antipathy to Walpole's administration is given free scope in the allusions to excise, the abuse of pensions, the tyranny of the licensing laws, and the servitude of a thoughtless age.[15]

As Donald Greene remarks in his book on Johnson's politics, such allusions were 'the merest commonplaces of opposition propaganda'.[16] Yet their presence is important to the poem's overall theme. Aptly citing Sir Sydney Roberts's phrase, M. J. C. Hodgart notes that Walpole was accused by Johnson and others of 'corruption at home and appeasement abroad'.[17] In the domestic sphere Johnson deplored both excise and a system of political pensions which, he feared, would inevitably lead to a corrupt system of government through dependants. In this way Britain would be reduced to a nation of sycophants. Moreover, Walpole's foreign policy could be imagined to have similarly dangerous consequences, pursuing as it did a servile attitude towards Spain and France. These countries were Britain's traditional enemies. With the Seven Years' War still unfought, the threat of France especially, as Britain's natural rival, was perhaps never far from Johnson's thoughts. He made the point emphatically, not only in his poem, by picturing a capital overrun with Frenchmen, but also in his

---

14 *Life,* Vol. I, p. 129.
15 *Poems,* p. 2.
16 D. J. Greene, *The Politics of Samuel Johnson,* New Haven, 1960, p. 90.
17 M. J. C. Hodgart, *Samuel Johnson and his Times,* London, 1962, p. 28.

Marmor Norfolciense of the following year,[18] in his report of the Lords debate (13 Feb. 1741) on the motion to remove Walpole,[19] and in his *Introduction to the Political State of Great-Britain,* published in the first number of the *Literary Magazine* for 1756.[20]

Thales, the poet's 'friend' in *London,* gives expression to this aspect of Johnson's own John Bullism when he sets up the country in opposition to the corrupt city. A 'true Briton', he refuses to live in the capital under an administration which adopts a servile policy towards Britain's traditional rivals. Unable and unwilling to compete in lies and flattery with a 'fasting Monsieur' or 'supple Gaul', he is described as 'injur'd'—a word which Johnson's *Dictionary* allows us to gloss as not only 'wronged' but 'annoyed, affected with inconvenience'. Thales has, as a 'true Briton', been wronged by the loss of that freedom which was his birthright. And so, with a backward glance at the 'neighb'ring town', he addresses the poet in words of righteous indignation:

> Here let those reign, whom pensions can incite
> To vote a patriot black, a courtier white;
> Explain their country's dear-bought rights away,
> And plead for pirates in the face of day;
> With slavish tenets taint our poison'd youth,
> And lend a lye the confidence of truth.
> Let such raise palaces, and manors buy,
> Collect a tax, or farm a lottery,
> With warbling eunuchs fill a licens'd stage,
> And lull to servitude a thoughtless age.

This passage serves to illustrate one important structural principle to which we shall later return, namely, that rhetorical patterning by which Johnson connects those vices meriting his censure. Although to one eminent modern critic and Johnsonian the strictures on city life read like 'a masterpiece of the higgledy-piggledy',[21] the poet in presenting these goes a long way towards satisfying Dryden's preference for 'unity of theme, or subject' in satire. While Dryden had allowed that the etymology of 'satire' spelt 'variety', he thought that this might 'arise naturally from one subject, as it is diversely treated, in the several subordinate branches of it, all relating to the

[18] *The Works of Samuel Johnson, LL.D.,* Oxford and London, Vol. VI, 1825, pp. 91, 103-4.

[19] Ibid., Vol. X, p. 166. For a revealing comparison of Johnson's version of Carteret's speech with that recorded by Archbishop Secker as well as that which appeared in the *London Magazine,* see B. B. Hoover, *Samuel Johnson's Parliamentary Reporting,* Berkeley and Los Angeles, 1953, p. 64.

[20] *The Works of Samuel Johnson, LL.D.,* Vol. VI, pp. 137-8.

[21] D. J. Greene, ' "Logical Structure" in Eighteenth-Century Poetry', *Philological Quarterly,* Vol. XXXI, 1952, p. 332.

chief'.[22] Certainly Johnson places side by side, as though inviting the reader to see a directly causal relationship between them, the reprehensible measures of the government and the moral and even physical degeneracy of the nation. In this way he gives a more consistently political slant to his moral satire than did Juvenal.

One interesting example of this occurs towards the end of the poem. In the corresponding passage of Johnson's original, the Roman poet, complaining of the present number of criminals in the state, exclaims:

> What furnaces, what anvils, are not groaning with the forging of chains? That is how our iron is mostly used; and you may well fear that ere long none will be left for plough-shares, none for hoes and mattocks.

And Juvenal continues: 'Happy, you would say, were the forbears of our great-grandfathers, happy the days of old which under Kings and Tribunes beheld Rome satisfied with a single gaol'.[23] This last part of Juvenal's verse-paragraph Johnson translates as follows:

> A single jail, in ALFRED's golden reign,
> Could half the nation's criminals contain.

And this reference to a glorious past is given further point by the political allusions of the preceding lines:

> Scarce can our fields, such crowds at Tyburn die,
> With hemp the gallows and the fleet supply.
> Propose your schemes, ye Senatorian band,
> Whose Ways and Means support the sinking land;
> Lest ropes be wanting in the tempting spring,
> To rig another convoy for the k - - g.

These lines, following on the 'fiery fop', 'frolick drunkard', and 'midnight murd'rer' passages, show how Johnson frequently links social and political immorality within the city. Whereas Juvenal had feared that all the iron needed for agriculture would be unproductively used as fetters for criminals, Johnson's allusion to 'rope' wittily juxtaposes an overcrowded gallows at Tyburn and George II's visits to Hanover on behalf of his very un-English interests and German mistress.

Not only is the King, as MacDonald Emslie has said, 'deserting the floundering nation, just in time, by ship',[24] but 'sinking' in this

22 'A Discourse concerning Satire' (prefixed to the volume containing Dryden's own translations of Juvenal), in G. Watson (ed.), *John Dryden: Of Dramatic Poesy and Other Critical Essays*, Everyman's Library, Vol. II, London, 1962, pp. 145-6.

23 *Juvenal and Persius*, pp. 55, 57.

24 M. Emslie, 'Johnson's Satires and "The Proper Wit of Poetry"', *Cambridge Journal*, Vol. VII, 1953-4, p. 351.

Plate IXa   The Palladian bridge at Wilton, by Roger Morris and the
Earl of Pembroke, 1737. National Buildings Record photograph.

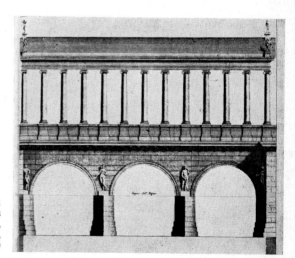

Plate IXb   Elevation of a
bridge, from Giacomo Leoni's
edition of L. B. Alberti,
Ten Books on Architecture,
1726, Plate 50

Plate Xa   Monument to James Craggs by Giovanni Battista Guelfi after a design by James Gibbs, 1727. Westminster Abbey, Warburg Institute photograph.

Plate Xb   Portrait of David Garrick by Thomas Gainsborough, 1769. Formerly in the possession of the Corporation of Stratford-on-Avon, since destroyed.

passage also carries those associations of 'decline', 'decrease', and 'decay' which Johnson attributes to the word in his *Dictionary*. The moral degeneracy of the nation is thus seen to be implicitly the result of its corrupt administration and court.

Later verse-paragraphs can be linked in this way because the connexion between a degenerate court and a degenerate populace has been prepared for throughout the poem. Thales awaits transport to the country at its threshold, Greenwich, a spot which, as the birthplace of Elizabeth, reminds both him and his companion of a former race of monarchs, the defeat of the Armada, and a very different foreign policy towards Spain,

> Ere masquerades debauch'd, excise oppress'd,
> Or English honour grew a standing jest.

The former conqueror has been enslaved by the conquered, and Thales laments:

> Ah! what avails it, that, from slav'ry far,
> I drew the breath of life in English air;
> Was early taught a Briton's right to prize,
> And lisp the tale of HENRY's victories;
> If the gull'd conqueror receives the chain,
> And flattery subdues when arms are vain?

In a previous passage Thales, going even further back in time, invites 'Illustrious EDWARD'—Edward III, the victor at Crecy as Henry had been at Agincourt—to survey once again this former land of saints and heroes. The 'rustick grandeur', the 'surly grace', is no longer to be seen. Not merely enslaved but even emasculated by its traditional enemies, the nation presents a sorry contrast to its former greatness:

> Behold the warrior dwindled to a beau;
> Sense, freedom, piety, refin'd away,
> Of France the mimick, and of Spain the prey.

Although Juvenal also complains of the degeneracy of the present by comparison with the past, Johnson develops this theme with a more obvious sense of history. Edward III has no historical counterpart in Juvenal's third satire. Moreover, in Johnson's *London* the contrast between country and city becomes, so to speak, an extended metaphor containing his essentially political theme. In the first ten lines of the poem he opposes to London those strongholds of the ancient Briton—Wales, Scotland, and Ireland. To Thales, a living example of the true Briton, the present corrupt capital seems an alien city, and he therefore resolves to fix his home 'on Cambria's solitary shore'. His journey to Wales is prompted not by a desire for rural retirement so much as by a willingness to associate himself with the spirit of his country's ancient inhabitants. Like the monarchs of a former age, and unlike the present administration, Thales gloried in the name of Briton.

In this respect we note a difference between Thales and Juvenal's poetical 'friend'. Admittedly Umbricius is also conscious of the dignity of the simple, agricultural life of the ancient Roman stock, as well as of the present degenerate state of life in the capital. He finds it insulting to be forced at every turn to give place to ingratiating foreigners; and because of his scruples he is unable either to accept contracts for degrading occupations or to share the bosom secrets of despicable men in high places. Yet he is, in a sense, merely cutting his losses by proposing to retire to the country, for every day finds his stock of capital depleted in a city which offers no reward for his honest labours. Johnson's Thales, on the other hand, though he hints at the lack of personal return in the corrupt city, inveighs more sternly against its vices. His tone has nothing of the jaunty astringency of his Roman counterpart's. Nor, to recall Johnson's later *Marmor Norfolciense,* has Thales become a patriot because of his disappointment at court. Drawing on a sense of his country's past during even the monstrously corrupt present, he can give overwhelming reasons for seeking a home in the country. He is

> Resolved at length, from vice and LONDON far,
> To breathe in distant fields a purer air.

Morally purer, that is. Juvenal, however, either treats the prospect of retirement ironically—as when he says that 'it is something, in whatever spot, however remote, to have become the possessor of a single lizard' [*unius lacertae*][25]—or seems more prepared to indulge this notion, as in the conclusion of his poem. There Umbricius expresses his willingness to leave his retreat whenever his friend should wish to read him satires at his own place in the country. These lines suggest little more than a literary companionship between like-minded friends living in country retirement. But Thales's final words ring with a more active spirit of opposition:

> Then shall thy friend, nor thou refuse his aid,
> Still foe to vice, forsake his Cambrian shade;
> In virtue's cause once more exert his rage,
> Thy satire point, and animate thy page.

Thales is, then, Johnson's portrait of a true modern Briton who, refusing to sell his birthright or succumb to political oppression, has, unlike the present court and administration, the good of the nation at heart. In this sense Pope was to use the word in his satire,

25 *Juvenal and Persius*, p. 49.

One Thousand Seven Hundred and Thirty Eight: Dialogue II,
published two months after Johnson's *London*:

> Here, Last of *Britons*! let your Names be read;
> Are none, none living? let me praise the Dead. (ll. 250-1)

Several years earlier, in a letter to William Pulteney, a leading
opponent of Walpole, Swift had, with characteristic brevity, bequeathed to his friend 'an epitaph for forty years hence, in two
words, *Ultimus Britannorum*' [the last of the Britons].[26]

Johnson's description of the country also carries overtones of that
romantic past celebrated by earlier chroniclers and poets. With
Thales's resolve to 'Give to St. David one true Briton more', it is
interesting to compare a passage from Drayton's *Poly-Olbion,* a
poem of which, as W. B. C. Watkins has noted, Johnson was
'extremely fond'.[27] In the fifth Song Drayton describes as follows
'holy *Davids* seat':

> Of all the holy men whose fame so fresh remaines,
> To whom the *Britans* built so many sumptuous Fanes,
> This Saint before the rest their Patron still they hold:
> Whose birth, their ancient Bards to *Cambria* long foretold;
> And seated heere a See, his Bishoprick of yore,
> Upon the farthest point of this unfruitful shore;
> Selected by himselfe, that farre from all resort
> With contemplation seem'd most fitly to comport;
> That, voyd of all delight, cold, barren, bleake, and dry,
> No pleasure might allure, nor steale the wandring eye.
> (ll. 333-42)

Those who have suggested that Thales should be identified with
Richard Savage, who left London for Swansea in July 1739, fourteen
months after *London* was published, seem to have forgotten in
what sense Thales was described as a 'hermit'![28] At St David's Thales
would find the perfect hermit's retreat. There his 'safety', like that
of the ancient Briton who 'in poverty defy'd his foes', would be
assured, whether his enemy were the foreign invader or, as the poem

[26] *The Correspondence of Jonathan Swift,* ed. H. Williams, Oxford, Vol. IV,
1963-5, p. 303.

[27] W. B. C. Watkins, *Johnson and English Poetry before 1660,* Princeton,
1936, p. 7.

[28] F. V. Bernard, reopening this question, has suggested resemblances between
Savage and Thales: 'Savage was single, profligate . . . line 4 refers to him
[i.e. Thales] as a "hermit"; line 20 mentions his "dissipated wealth"' (*Notes and
Queries,* Vol. CCIII, 1958, p. 398). Johnson's *Dictionary,* however, defines a
'hermit' as someone who is 'single' in a very special sense: '1. A solitary; an
anchoret; one who retires from society to contemplation and devotion. 2. A
beadsman; one bound to pray for another'. The further suggestion that Thales's
'dissipated wealth' refers to Savage's profligacy does violence to the context in
which these words appear. Thales's wealth has been 'dissipated' by 'malice,
rapine, accident' (l. 13).

more expressly implies, those forces of moral corruption which, so rife in court and city, made any other form of invasion needless.

Indeed, Thales's sense of foreign oppression is so acute that he even contemplates emigration—supposing, that is, he could find some 'secret island' or 'peaceful desart yet unclaim'd by SPAIN'. But England's foreign policy of course makes this impossible. He therefore proposes that his companion should, like himself, find refuge in some corner of their own neglected country:

> Could'st thou resign the park and play content,
> For the fair banks of Severn or of Trent;
> There might'st thou find some elegant retreat,
> Some hireling senator's deserted seat;
> And stretch thy prospects o'er the smiling land,
> For less than rent the dungeons of the Strand.

In this passage Johnson depicts the modern Briton's equivalent of Horace's Sabine farm. Its mood has much in common with Horace's in his most stoical moments, for the poet is celebrating neither pastoral ease for its own sake nor uncommitted retirement. The country not only offers a refuge from vice but imposes a duty. Since the whole land is in need of rejuvenation, the hireling senator must be replaced by such men as are prepared to provide anew the backbone and moral fibre of the nation. Thales therefore goes on to suggest the contribution which the eighteenth-century patriot can make by substituting a virtuous simplicity for corrupting luxury, sturdy independence for sycophantic dependence, and restored vitality and beauty for moral ugliness and decay:

> There prune thy walks, support thy drooping flow'rs,
> Direct thy rivulets, and twine thy bow'rs;
> And, while thy grounds a cheap repast afford,
> Despise the dainties of a venal lord:
> There ev'ry bush with nature's musick rings,
> There ev'ry breeze bears health upon its wings;
> On all thy hours security shall smile,
> And bless thine evening walk and morning toil.

Certain references in this *beatus ille* passage are interesting in the light of that country-city contrast through which Johnson gives expression to his political theme. The 'hireling senator' or 'venal lord' may be taken to represent one of Walpole's toadies who had sold his ancient birthright for a seat in a government bent on ruining the nation. Significant, too, I believe, are Johnson's references to the Severn and the Trent. Since London, situated on the Thames, had been lost to virtue and liberty, the poet is forced to celebrate instead the second and third rivers of the kingdom. The Severn especially was an appropriate dwelling-place for the modern Briton to choose. According to a tradition accepted by both Milton in *Comus* and Drayton in his *Poly-Olbion,* Sabrina, the goddess of the Severn, was a descendant of the Trojan founder of Britain. The modern Briton who inhabited her banks would therefore have been acknowledging his descent from his spiritual forbears. The allusion of the Trent is, perhaps, more personal. Miss Lascelles has noted that Johnson's birth-place, Lichfield, was a country town 'built round a confluence of springs and streams feeding the Trent'.[29] On these grounds alone the young provincial to whom Walpole's policy was so repugnant might have associated the natural seat of the true modern Briton with his own corner of England.

By now it will be clear how I read Johnson's contrast between the country and the city. Yet the extent of *London*'s political theme can only be fully recognised once it is established that Orgilio, the most prominent satirical portrait in the poem, was intended to represent Walpole himself.

Orgilio is mentioned twice in *London,* and in each instance this name must obviously refer to the same figure. The first mention is in line 84, 'Who shares Orgilio's crimes, his fortune shares', where Orgilio is a substitution for Juvenal's Verres. In the second passage, beginning at line 194, Orgilio stands for Juvenal's Persicus or the master of the 'great house of Asturicus' [*magna Asturici . . . domus*]. Each of these substitutions will be considered in turn and the appropriateness of their application to Walpole suggested.

During Walpole's administration the most influential opposition paper was the *Craftsman.* In its pages, as Dr J. H. Plumb has remarked, 'Walpole and his ministry were subjected to an endless stream of vilification and criticism which made not only England but Europe roar with delight'.[30] The dedication ('To the People of England') prefixed to the first volume of the collected edition (1731-7) frankly acknowledged Walpole in his public capacity as Prime Minister to be this paper's target. And to this first volume was also prefixed a motto from Cicero's famous indictment of Verres, the implication obviously being that what could be said of the wicked governor Verres could equally be said of Walpole as a second Verres. Nor was this all. In 1737 the eighth volume appeared, containing one paper (No. 259) which undertook to spell out in plain English, for the benefit of female readers, the meaning of the earlier motto from Cicero. Here Verres is obviously meant to stand for Walpole. He is represented as a man 'already condemn'd by the *general Voice of the People*', as 'a *Plunderer of the Treasury*' and 'an *Invader of the antient Rights of the City*' (p. 25). Indeed, he is

29 'Johnson and Juvenal', p. 44.
30 J. H. Plumb, *Sir Robert Walpole: The King's Minister,* Boston, 1961, p. 141.

said to have 'busied himself very diligently, as if he had been born and bred nearer to our Latitude and Times, in plundering and harassing the poor People, over whom he presided' (p. 24). No contemporary would have failed to see that a likeness to Walpole was intended in this portrait, even though the author prudently made the satire more oblique by comparing his ostensible subject with the *'whoreson round Man'* and knight, Sir John Falstaff. Sir John and Sir Robert, we are asked to conclude, were alike in both their physical dimensions and moral character, for Sir John was similarly deemed to be a *'Robber of the Exchequer'* who publicly invited 'his *Prince* to take Share of the Plunder' in the same way that Verres himself 'always distributed a Share of the Booty among his *chief Officers* and *Projectors of his Jobs*' (p. 26). In Johnson's later words: 'Who shares Orgilio's crimes, his fortune shares'. This practice of reading Walpole for Verres thus makes it more than probable that Orgilio as a translation of Verres represented none other than the hated Walpole.

Clearly readers of poetry were practised in making such substitutions since Pope, in his *One Thousand Seven Hundred and Thirty Eight,* which was published within days of Johnson's *London,* also strongly hinted at the identification of Walpole with Verres. Lines 51-2 of the first edition read:

> *Agysthus, Verres,* hurt not honest FLEURY,
> But well may put some Statesmen in a fury.

Moreover, in revised editions of his companion piece of the same year Pope again invited his readers to link the names of Walpole and Verres:

> But let me add, Sir ROBERT's mighty dull . . .
> But pray, when others praise him, do I blame?
> Call *Verres, Wolsey,* any odious name? (ll. 133, 136-7)

Although the first edition had read 'Clodius' for 'Verres', the revision is an improvement. For Publius Clodius, the unscrupulous and profligate tribune, Pope substituted that enemy of the people and national interest who could easily be identified, along with Wolsey and Walpole, as a type of the wicked statesman.

Before discussing Orgilio as a translation of Persicus, we may note that it was the contemporary practice to regard Walpole as a type of Wolsey,[31] and that this fact is probably not without its relevance

---

[31] For extensive documentation that Walpole was currently satirised as a second Wolsey see C. B. Ricks, 'Wolsey in *The Vanity of Human Wishes'*, *Modern Language Notes,* Vol. LXXIII, 1958, pp. 563-8, though I disagree with Ricks's suggestion that 'there may be an altogether delicate allusion' to Walpole in Johnson's portrait of Wolsey.

for Johnson's portrait of Orgilio. The name itself is suggestively symbolical and may have served to recall the example of Wolsey. In his *Dictionary* Johnson defined 'orgillous' as 'proud; haughty', though he surprisingly failed to record the more usual form, 'orgulous'. Now Wolsey had become the accepted prototype of the proud or orgulous statesman. *The Vanity of Human Wishes* refers to his 'full-blown dignity' and 'pride of aweful state'; while in the first article preferred by Parliament against Wolsey in 1529, and recorded in Lord Herbert of Cherbury's *Life and Reigne of King Henry the Eighth*, 1649, objection is made to Wolsey's 'high, orgullous, and insatiable mind' (p. 266). Might not Johnson have therefore expected his readers to interpret Orgilio as a satire on a second Wolsey as well as on a second Verres? At any rate, the *Craftsman* No. 8 had already compared Walpole and Wolsey in terms of their *superbia* or pride. The gist of its motto, from Seneca's *De Tranquillitate Animi*, is as follows:

> Those . . . whom an unkind lot has placed in a critical position, will be safer by reducing their pride in the things that are in themselves proud (*superbiam detrahendo rebus per se superbis*) and [by] lowering their fortune . . . to the common level.[32]

The details of Wolsey given in this paper are clearly reminiscent of Walpole also. Wolsey, though 'of a *low Education*', rapidly made a fortune of which his use was 'extravagant and ostentatious to the highest Degree': 'He built *Palaces*; and his Train out-shone his *Master's* so much, that when he retir'd into the Country, on a Party of Pleasure, the Court became desart' (*Craftsman*, Vol. I, p. 46). Similarly Walpole, through his triumphant manipulation of power and finance, obliterated all vestiges of his provincial past. He built at lavish expense the magnificent Houghton Hall in his native Norfolk, to which, as Dr Plumb remarks, 'his colleagues—dukes, earls, barons—rode post haste . . . at his call'. His levees, held three times a week, were thronged with noble supplicants, and by 1733 he controlled under his own hands all diplomacy, finance, and patronage. We are told that ambassadors and consuls also knew their duty, and gratified with expensive gifts Walpole's passion for paintings and sculpture.[33]

If, as I believe, Orgilio as a translation of both Verres and Persicus is an oblique reference to Walpole, we should note the significance of certain similarities between the above account of Walpole and Johnson's extended description of Orgilio. On such a reading Orgilio's 'palace' may be interpreted as an allusion to

---

[32] *Seneca, Moral Essays*, trans. J. W. Basore, Loeb Classical Library, rev. ed., Vol. II, London, 1951, p. 253.
[33] Plumb, *Sir Robert Walpole*, pp. 249, 98, 266, 85-6.

Walpole's palatial residence, the destruction of which is necessarily represented as hypothetical because no 'just bolts' from heaven destroyed Houghton Hall. Yet the imagining of such an event as a parallel to the Latin original at least allows the poet appropriately to suggest the 'sudden wealth' which produced Orgilio's 'golden pile'. Moreover, the 'gaudy vassals' who 'crowd with sudden wealth the rising dome' can readily be interpreted as an allusion to Walpole's placemen:

> With well-feign'd gratitude the pension'd band
> Refund the plunder of the beggar'd land.

The 'beggar'd land' may be taken to stand for England itself, of which the wealth seemed to the political satirist to flow into Walpole's own pockets.

The parallel passage in Juvenal is also relevant for the interpretation of Orgilio as an oblique satire on Walpole. In it the poet attacks that social evil of imperial Rome whereby rich and heirless old men and women were shamelessly courted by fortune-hunters [*captatores*] who hoped for a large legacy in return for their persistent favours and attendance. Thus Persicus, 'the most sumptuous of childless men' [*orborum lautissimus*], when his house is destroyed by fire, has it rebuilt with even greater splendour from the costly gifts contributed by legacy-hunters. Of course the Roman poet is here indulging in rhetorical exaggeration: as we learn from Juvenal's other satires, such parasites usually bought their obsequious gifts in the meat-market! Johnson, however, utilises this episode of his original by giving it a decidedly political context. The 'pension'd band' has already received its political rewards. Thus the destruction of Orgilio's 'palace' elicits a tribute from 'the laureate tribe in servile verse'. We learn, too, from E. L. McAdam's recent editing of the poem, that in Johnson's manuscript this couplet had read:

> With servile grief dependent nobles sigh
> And swell with tears the prostituted eye.[34]

Such nobles could scarcely have been 'dependent' on anyone except Walpole himself. Prudence, then, might well have dictated that this couplet should not appear in the published version of the poem. Yet there also the political overtones are obvious enough in the lines which follow, for the 'gaudy vassals'

> The price of boroughs and of souls restore,
> And raise his treasures higher than before.

Although Johnson gives us various portraits, especially in the *Rambler,* of the captator-like tactics of distant relatives hot on the

---

[34] *Samuel Johnson: Poems,* p. 57n.

scent of a fortune, the social evil which prompted Juvenal's scorn had no exact counterpart in contemporary London. According to a 'MS note in Dr Johnson's hand-writing',[35] the London bookseller Charles Hitch had 'justly remarked' the Orgilio portrait 'to be no picture of modern manners, though it might be true at Rome'. Arguably Johnson never intended Orgilio to be read without any political overtones as a simple substitution for Persicus. Nevertheless, it seems certain that he wanted his readers to remember also the Latin example. In his letter to Cave prior to the poem's publication Johnson insisted that the corresponding passages from Juvenal should 'be subjoined at the bottom of the Page, part of the beauty of the performance (if any beauty be allow'd it) consisting in adapting Juvenals Sentiments to modern facts and Persons'. Later, in his Life of Pope, Johnson, commenting on Pope's imitations of Horace, shows that he clearly expected the alert reader of such an imitation to have a 'knowledge of the original'; though he there freely admits the difficulties which an Augustan translator faced, acknowledging that the resulting 'work will be generally uncouth and party-coloured; neither original nor translated, neither ancient, nor modern'.[36] The young Johnson, however, brilliantly solved this difficulty by accommodating the example of Persicus to his own distinctive theme. When the Roman satirist attacked the *captator-orbus* relationship, part of his scorn was clearly directed against that childless society which, by disregarding marriage, bred such an insidious form of corruption. Similarly the implication is that Walpole, by fostering dependence, was perverting, in favour of a host of sycophants, those honours which should rightly have been the prerogative of merit. Johnson's famous line on 'poverty' is therefore to be read as something more than the despairing cry of a young provincial struggling to establish himself in the capital. Thales exclaims:

> Quick let us rise, the happy seats explore,
> And bear oppression's insolence no more.
> This mournful truth is ev'ry where confess'd,
> SLOW RISES WORTH, BY POVERTY DEPRESS'D:
> But here more slow, where all are slaves to gold,
> Where looks are merchandise, and smiles are sold;
> Where won by bribes, by flatteries implor'd,
> The groom retails the favours of his lord.

These are ills which the poet implicitly lays at Walpole's door, the example of Orgilio-Walpole inviting a connection between the

[35] *Poems*, p. 5.
[36] Samuel Johnson, *The Lives of the Most Eminent English Poets*, corrected ed., Vol. IV, London, 1783, pp. 203-4.

social evils of the day and the contemporary political scene. Apart
from a possible reference to George II and another to either 'Orator'
Henley, a propagandist hired by Walpole, or to Lord Hervey,
Queen Caroline's confidant and Walpole's most trusted agent in
the palace, Orgilio is the first person satirised in the poem. And
apart from the contemptuous reference to the King in line 247 he
is also the last. Together with the poem's other anti-Walpole allusions, these references to Orgilio make Walpole's presence felt as a
pernicious influence throughout much of the poem. In the poet's
view, he was clearly to be held responsible for all those ills that
plagued the nation.

Contemporary readers would, moreover, have recognised that in
associating a general moral turpitude with political corruption
Johnson was exploiting a familiar *topos*. For example, Pope's
version of Donne's fourth Satire contains an interesting example of
this. The courtier pours his gossip into the unwilling poet's ear,
whose reaction is then as follows:

> Nor more Amazement seiz'd on *Circe*'s Guests,
> To see themselves fall endlong into Beasts,
> Than mine, to find a Subject staid and wise,
> Already half turn'd Traytor by surprize.
> I felt th' Infection slide from him to me. (ll. 166-70)

Swift, too, in the letter to Pulteney cited earlier,[37] had outlined the
effects of such a creeping form of moral disease and corruption:

> It is altogether impossible for any nation to preserve its liberty
> long under a tenth part of the present luxury, infidelity, and a
> million of corruptions . . . Such hath ever been human nature,
> that a single man, without any superior advantages either of
> body or mind, but usually the direct contrary, is able to attack
> twenty millions, and drag them voluntary at his chariot-wheels.
> But no more of this. I am as sick of the world as I am of age
> and disease.

A clearer statement of the same sentiment had previously occurred
in *Craftsman,* No. 413:

> If a *Minister* should be exalted here, with a Disposition to mind
> nothing but the Increase of his private Fortune, and conse-
> quently aim at nothing so much as to continue Himself in his
> Employment, tho' the Means were ever so flagitious . . . our
> Ruin would follow as certainly from Him, as it could from any
> other. If He singly set about this Work, by playing our own
> Corruption upon us, by reducing all the Corporations into a
> venal Habit, by bestowing only upon such as were qualified to

37 See note 26.

elect Members of Parliament the inferior Employments, and afterwards by confining the larger and more lucrative to the Parliament, thus chosen, and to such of its Members, as would accept them upon the base Tenure of doing all his Drudgery; if This should ever happen, the Increase of our Corruption must easily be foreseen. (Vol. XII, p. 230)

Indeed, the author goes on to envisage the loss not only of morals but of liberty itself, in a passage which could well stand as the motto of Johnson's poem.

The above reading of *London* enables us to view in a new light its structure and theme. Once we recognise those associations of ideas shaping Johnson's organisation of particular passages, we may well be inclined to disagree with one recent critic who dismisses the poem's 'plan' as 'jejune',[38] or with the Yale editor of Johnson's poems when he argues that 'the topical elements of *The Vanity of Human Wishes* are . . . structurally more essential' than those of *London*.[39] In *London* the corruption of the whole city is imaginatively linked with the current political scene: its 'vice' is ultimately of political origin since 'the dregs of each corrupted state' become, in effect, 'the cheated nation's happy fav'rites'. The juxtaposition of ideas in lines like

> Ere masquerades debauch'd, excise oppress'd,

or

> Behold the warrior dwindled to a beau

suggest that social and political vice are inseparable. Moreover, whenever the country is mentioned, juxtaposition again becomes a significant feature of the poem's structure. The praise of 'illustrious EDWARD' and Britain's former 'rustick grandeur' follows immediately on the poet's contemptuous reference to 'a French metropolis'. A clearer example of the importance of this contrapuntal arrangement of material for Johnson's satiric theme occurs in the second half of the poem where the *beatus ille* passage follows on the portrait of Orgilio and precedes the 'fiery fop' and 'midnight murd'rer' paragraphs. Here the mutually exclusive alternatives facing the still virtuous citizen are significantly juxtaposed. Thales, seeking to preserve intact his moral character and his liberty, dissociates himself from the corrupt city, exhorting the poet to do likewise. The country, as the antithesis of all that Orgilio-Walpole stands for, has become the logical home of this 'true' though 'harrass'd' Briton. The sympathetic contemporary reader, like Walpole's opponent,

---

[38] Greene, ' "Logical Structure" in Eighteenth-Century Poetry', p. 331.
[39] *Samuel Johnson: Poems,* p. xviii.

George Lyttelton, who carried a copy of the poem in high glee to Pope, would surely have recognised the political overtones of this country-city contrast. Indeed he might well have been impressed by the originality which the unknown poet showed in transforming his Latin model and giving imaginative coherence to his theme.

Nor do I feel less confident in remarking on this originality when reminded of Boswell's later, and in some ways rather enigmatic, comments on the poem. Instead I am tempted to borrow the useful distinction once made by David Nichol Smith and suggest that not even all eighteenth-century readers were necessarily Johnsonians.

The Apocalypse of Christopher Smart

(A preliminary sketch)

A. D. Hope

The critical history of Christopher Smart's *Jubilate Agno* or *Rejoice in the Lamb* resembles that of his most famous poem, *A Song to David*. To the later eighteenth century *A Song to David* seemed an insane poem, demonstrating that though its author had been discharged from the asylum, he was as mad as ever. To the nineteenth century it seemed a glorious extravaganza displaying a wild and unusual imagination, but not insane. Only in the last forty or fifty years has it become apparent that it is in addition a highly organised poem, extremely complex in its design and as intellectual as it is ecstatic. Admittedly it conceals a system of ideas which no one has quite succeeded in making explicit and a mysterious symbolism of numbers and correspondences which still eludes complete explication. But it is neither an insane poem in itself nor does it suggest an insane mind. *Jubilate Agno,* on the other hand, may be both a poem written by a deranged man and itself an insane poem. It was probably begun in the early part of 1759 when Smart was living in lodgings near St James's Park after he had been discharged from St Luke's Hospital for the Insane uncured and with no prospect of cure—in fact he probably went from St Luke's to a private madhouse. Before the end of the year he was probably back in confinement at Turlington's Asylum in Chelsea where he remained till his release in January 1763. Dates, and probably datable remarks, in the text of the poem show it to have been written over this period. If Dr Johnson, Mrs Piozzi, and other friends of Smart were right in thinking that he was not seriously deranged, neither they nor his enemies, nor specialists like Dr Battie, the superintendent of St Luke's, were ever in any doubt that he was mad to *some* extent.[1] The first reactions to the poem were probably that it was clear evidence of Smart's insanity, since The Reverend Thomas Cawar-

---

[1] Devlin, *Poor Kit Smart,* London, 1961, Chs. 6-10.

dine and William Hayley, friends of Cowper, seem to have been
interested in it as an illustration of poetic mania when Cowper
became insane in 1763 shortly after Smart's release from his final
period of confinement. Thereafter the manuscript, or the fragments
we have, remained in the possession of the Cawardine family, and
the poem was only discovered and published by William Force
Stead in 1939.[2] Stead was able to show that many of the ideas, and
the association of ideas which at first glance look like the ravings of
a lunatic, are in fact often lucid enough reminiscences and associations based on Smart's immense and curious readings in the natural
sciences, the occult and mystical writers, especially the Cambridge
Platonists, in books of travel, Biblical criticism, and so on. But
Stead's introduction and notes show that he did not credit Smart
with more than an extraordinary memory. The poem as a whole he
treated as naïve, incoherent, and the work of an author not in
control of his associations. W. H. Bond's edition, published in
1954 under the title of *Jubilate Agno*,[3] showed, I think convincingly,
that the text published by Stead was not complete, but a
series of fragments of a mutilated original of which some two-thirds
is now missing, and in which each verse beginning with *Let* was
meant to be followed or matched by an antiphonal verse beginning
with *For*. He was able to restore the original order in the surviving
fragments and it immediately became apparent that the work is
less incoherent and more rationally planned than had been suspec-
ted. Bond has pointed out that the peculiar verse form is almost
certainly Smart's attempt to adapt to English verse some of the
principles of Hebrew poetry as expounded by Bishop Lowth in his
De sacra poesi Hebraeorum published in 1753. He has pointed out
its resemblance to some of the Psalms and to parts of the Anglican
Liturgy, has noted the fact that Smart's *Psalms* were designed to
replace the Prayer Book version, and suggests that 'the *Jubilate*
was initially conceived as the opening move in this campaign of
reform'[4] of the Anglican order of service. This is getting warm. But
Bond I think has missed the fact that *Jubilate Agno* contains in
itself the explanation of a plan of reform, if it can be called that, so
revolutionary, that it amounts to an apocalyptic vision. Smart's
references to his theory of the universe are by no means systematic,
as is natural in a hymn of praise, but they are sufficient to show
that the poem itself is based, not as Stead and Bond seem to think,
on chance reminiscences from Smart's extensive reading and on a

2 *Rejoice in the Lamb: A Song from Bedlam,* ed. W. F. Stead, London, 1939.
3 References to the text throughout are to *Jubilate Agno,* ed. W. H. Bond,
London, 1954, by fragment and line.
4 Ibid., p. 20.

random collection of rather cranky theories about numbers, letters, names, animals, angels, the composition of matter, contemporary politics, mystical and symbolical history, and so on; but on a single fairly coherent theory of the universe which must have been elaborated before his confinement and which he probably continued to hold after his cure, for it appears to some extent in *A Song to David* and in the *Hymns* and *Psalms*.

But before going on to outline Smart's theory of the universe I should like to say a little more about the plan and method of the poem itself.

Basically it is planned on the lines of the *Benedicite Omnia Opera,* which begins:

> O all ye works of the Lord, bless ye the Lord
> praise him and magnify him for ever.

And then it proceeds to invoke all creatures in their classes and calls on them to praise the Lord. Finally there are the specific names.

> O Ananias, Azarias and Misael
> bless ye the Lord, praise him and magnify him
> for ever.

These three characters reappear in Smart's poem in consecutive verses, showing that he had the *Benedicite* in mind. What Smart apparently decided to do was to extend the notion of the *Benedicite* and the *Te Deum* in such a way that not only the main classes of non-human created things but each sub-species should be named with its appropriate qualities and should be invited to praise God in conjunction with a human being in each case. As the poem stands it begins with this program.

> Rejoice in God, O ye Tongues; give the glory
> to the Lord, and the Lamb.
> Nations, and Languages, and every Creature, in
> which is the breath of Life.
> Let man and beast appear before him, and
> magnify his name together. (Fragment A, ll. 1-3)

The list begins appropriately enough, with Noah and all his company, and runs through the patriarchs, each praising with one of the beasts which may be naturally associated with him, Abraham with the ram, Balaam with the ass, Ishmael with a tiger, and so on. Old Testament names keep Smart going for a fair time; then he moves into the New Testament. We do not know how the series went in the middle of the poem for here only the *For* verses have survived, but when we come to a series of *Let* verses again Smart is using Hebrew names, sometimes of places and sometimes of persons, taken mostly from the Books of Ezra and Nehemiah. The beasts in the earlier part were taken first from all orders of creatures, and these were followed by lists of birds and fishes. Now Smart gives lists of plants. After another gap in the manuscript, we find lists of Englishmen, now asked to praise God in company with various precious stones, then with plants and an occasional bird or beast.

The reason why Smart includes precious stones among his creatures and why the list of human names in the pairs is confined to Biblical characters and Englishmen will become apparent later. It is not as mad or as arbitrary as it looks and neither is the scheme of this immense *Te Deum* of all the living creatures by species and of men by individual names. Smart calls it his Magnificat.

Smart apparently took the antiphonal form of the *Let* and *For* verses from the Psalms and the Book of Job where such verses occur sporadically. He may well have taken verses such as 34 and 35 of Psalm 69 for his model.

> Let the heaven and earth praise Him, the seas,
>   and everything that moveth therein;
> For God will save Zion, and will build
>   the cities of Judah; that they may dwell
>   there and have it in possession.

The connexion between *Let* and *For* verses here is not at all clear. Smart sometimes connects the *Let* with the *For* verse, but often there is little or no connexion, and he may in fact be following the Bible in this. The *Let* series is more often continuous with itself and the *For* series with itself. But both have odd and often inexplicably abrupt changes of subject, or intrusions of what were obviously some of Smart's fixed ideas. As the poem goes on it appears to lose order and control in details though it retains the general plan of an enormous hymn of praise based on the last three of the Psalms of David, in which Smart himself appears as the singer of a new song unto the Lord, a sort of super-psalm with himself in the character of the new David, celebrant of the new Israel at the coming of the millenium. The poem itself is incoherent enough, especially in its fragmentary form. Though it depends on a system of ideas, it does not expound these ideas systematically. Indeed it is not concerned to expound, but to praise the Lord. It is the hymn of creation, not its conspectus. This in part accounts for previous failures to recognise the evidence of a system of the universe on which it is based. In fact the outlines of this system only begin to appear when the poem is taken to pieces and all the references to one aspect of the system, now scattered through the structure, are brought together in one place. All I can say at this stage of my investigation is that these outlines appear very probable and that there are very many details which I have not yet succeeded in fitting into place. Indeed a complete demonstration may not prove possible since so much of the poem is missing. It is, of course, not impossible that some day the missing portions will be recovered.

Perhaps another reason that the existence of a system has not been noticed, or, if noticed, not pursued, is the assumption that the ideas in the poem, like the poem itself, are the product of Smart's period of insanity. In fact they probably go back to Smart's residence in Cambridge as a student and later as a fellow of Pembroke Hall. The evidence for this is in the surviving catalogues and the registers of borrowing by the fellows from the Pembroke library, between 1739 when Smart matriculated and 1749 when he left Cambridge. It is clear from these records that the fellows borrowed much the same range of books and that they lent them to one another and to members of other colleges. Ten names, including Smart's, constantly occur in this way and it is safe to conclude that the books they borrowed and lent and reborrowed were connected with common interests and discussions. Smart, when he wrote the *Jubilate*, apparently felt he was very fortunate to have been of this company. Cambridge is the right and brightest of the two universities and Pembroke Hall was founded more in the Lord than any college in Cambridge (B2, ll. 617-18). One group of books borrowed and shared in this way is concerned with the popular topic of Covenant Theology and theories concerning the millennium. Among the titles are such works as Sir Isaac Newton's *Observations upon the Prophecies of Daniel and the Apocalypse of St John*[5] and his *The Chronology of Ancient Kingdoms Amended*,[6] Stillingfleet's *Origines Sacrae*,[7] Richard Kidder's *A Demonstration of the Messias*,[8] and the library contained a number of similar works including William Whiston's *The Accomplishment of Scripture Prophecies*.[9] It is probable that it was here that Smart formed the outline of his own millennial theory. The friends also borrowed works which were concerned with current theories of cosmology. Burnet's *Sacred Theory of the Earth*[10] was a favourite and there were Derham's

[5] London, 1733.
[6] London, 1728.
[7] Edward Stillingfleet, *Origines Sacrae, or a Rational Account of the Christian Faith as to the Truth and Divine Authority of the Scriptures*, etc., London, 1662.
[8] *A Demonstration of the Messias, in which the Truth of the Christian Religion is defended, especially against the Jews*, London, 1700.
[9] From the Boyle Lectures, 1708.
[10] Thomas Burnet (*Telluris Theoria Sacra*); *The Sacred Theory of the Earth: Containing an Account of the Original of the Earth, And of all the GENERAL CHANGES which it hath already undergone, or is to undergo till the CONSUMMATION of all Things*, London, 1681-9.

Physico-Theology and *Astro-Theology*,[11] Henry Pemberton's *A View of Sir Isaac Newton's Philosophy*,[12] Newton's *Principia*,[13] and J. Keill's *An Examination of Dr Burnet's Theory of the Earth, together with some remarks on Mr Whiston's Theory of the Earth*.[14] So they probably read William Whiston's *A New Theory of the Earth*[15] and Richard Burthogge's *Of the Soul of the World and of Particular Souls*,[16] which is connected with Keill's work. Smart's own remarkable cosmology draws, as is his habit, on all these and many other sources, but appears to have more affinity with Keill and Burthogge than any others. These now forgotten attempts to establish a spiritual and animistic cosmology as a rival to the materialist one are the very basis of Smart's own system. It is important to remember that such theories, however wild they may look today, were held by learned and rational men and that Smart's was probably elaborated in discussion with serious scholars at a time when he held the post of praelector in philosophy. In fact almost all aspects of his system can be traced to the same period including his special theory of David, the psalmist. Delaney's *An Historical Account of the Life and Reign of David King of Israel*[17] was one of the books this group of university scholars borrowed and lent to one another. It is known to be one of the sources of Smart's references to David in *Jubilate Agno* and *A Song to David*.

It is impossible to give all the evidence in a short paper of this kind but in very brief outline Smart's system seems to be as follows:

The universe as created by God is both a spiritual and corporeal hierarchy of beings. The sun and the moon and the other heavenly bodies are also spirits: the sun, says Smart, is an improving angel (B2, ll. 315-16; B1, l. 102). Flowers have their angels (B2, l. 499), precious stones are able to praise God. Earth itself has an intelligence and a voice and a propensity to speak in all her parts (B1, l. 234). All fire is a form of spirit. Air, which has an important part

11 William Derham, *Physico-Theology: or a Demonstration of the Being and Attributes of God from His Works of Creation*, London, 1713; *Astro-Theology: Or a Demonstration of the* BEING *and* ATTRIBUTES *of God from a* SURVEY *of the* HEAVENS, London, 1715.
12 London, 1728.
13 Sir Isaac Newton, *Philosophiae Naturalis Principia Mathematica*, London, 1687.
14 Oxford, 1698.
15 *A New Theory of the Earth, From its Original, to the Consummation of all things, where in the Creation of the World in Six Days, the Universal Deluge, and the General Conflagration as Laid down in the Holy Scriptures are shown to be perfectly agreeable to Reason and Philosophy*, London, 1696.
16 *Of the Soul of the World and of Particular Souls, in a Letter to Mr. Lock*, London, 1699.
17 (Patrick Delaney), *An Historical Account of the Life and Reign of David, King of Israel, in Four Books . . . by the Author of Revelations examined with Candour*, London, 1740-2.

in Smart's system, is a very benign spirit, which can be contaminated by curses and purified by prayer (B1, ll. 263, 221), and one could go on quoting instances of this animist view of the whole creation in which every atom has life (B1, l. 160). Moreover God is immanent in his creation: tides are the life of God in the ocean (B1, l. 157). All motion is, in fact, life, and the centripetal and centrifugal forces are God sustaining and directing (B1, ll. 161-3). The attraction of the loadstone is the life of God in it (B1, l. 167). There is evidence that in part this spiritual physics and cosmology may owe something to the eighteenth-century scientist Derham's *Astro-Theology* and *Physico-Theology*,[18] but it collects its material from many different sources. For example, Smart, who had presumably read Newton's *Opticks* while an undergraduate,[19] attacks Newton's theory of colours (B2, ll. 650 ff.).

> For Newton's notion of colours is αλογος unphilosophical
> For colours are spiritual.

This idea, it has been suggested,[20] comes from Berkeley's 'First Dialogue between Hylas and Philonous', where it is argued that to say 'the red and blue which we see are not real colours, but certain unknown notions and figures which no man ever did see, are truly so' is false. Berkeley proves that colours are spiritual and attacks Newton's theory of white light. But the borrowings from the Pembroke library show that optics, and Newton's theory of optics in particular, must have been matters of interest while Smart was in residence, and he may have picked up many of his scientific and philosophical notions from discussion and argument among the dons rather than from systematic reading. For example, another book in the Pembroke library, borrowed on a number of occasions and probably discussed during Smart's residence, was Keill's *An Examination of Dr Burnet's Theory of Earth, together with some remarks on Mr Whiston's Theory of the Earth.*[21] Keill's account of Richard Burthogge's theory of the soul of the world has close resemblance to some of Smart's ideas: of Burthogge, Keill says:

> But a new philosopher has much outdone any I have yet mentioned in a book lately Printed concerning Reason.[22] Here he assures us that there is but one universal Soul in the World, which is omnipresent and acts upon all particular organised Bodies. . . .[23]

[18] *Jubilate*, p. 67, n. 4; Stead, *Rejoice in the Lamb*, p. 205, Sect. IX, n. to l. 13.
[19] Library register of Pembroke College, 1743.
[20] D. J. Greene, 'Smart, Berkeley, the Scientists and the Poets. A Note on Eighteenth Century Anti-Newtonianism', *Journal of the History of Ideas*, Vol. XIV, No. 3, June 1953.
[21] Oxford, 1698.
[22] Burthogge, *An Essay upon Reason and the Nature of Spirits*, London, 1694.
[23] Keill, *An Examination*, p. 6.

Burthogge felt that Keill had not quite understood him and in 1699 he took the trouble to set him right in a work entitled *Of the Soul of the World and of Particular Souls*; he explains his particular notion,

> . . . which in short is this; that the Mosaical Spirit (called *Gen.* 1.V.2 the Spirit of God) being a Spirit of Life, and present everywhere, in all the Parts of the Universe, is the Original of all the Energy, Motion and Action therein, especially that which is Animal. And that particular *Souls* (for such I acknowledg there be) are Portions of that Spirit acting on the several particular Bodies in which they are according to the Capacities, Dispositions and Qualities of those Bodies . . . To make it imaginable, let us suppose a vast Organ, consisting of innumerable Pipes of different Sizes and Fabrick, and this Organ to be filled with Wind blown into it, and the Wind to be received and some portion of it by each particular Pipe: Imagine also innumerable Fingers playing upon those several Pipes . . . The World is such an Organ (an orderly aggregate;) and the several Sorts of Bodies that compose it are as the several Pipes of that Organ—and as *those* inspired with Wind, being played upon, do sound different Notes or Tunes; so *these* animated with their respective Portions of the Mosaical *Spirit,* being impressed and acted upon by Objects, do perform their several vital functions . . . .[24]

Smart probably read Keill's discussion of Locke's *Essay,* and he may or may not have gone on to read Burthogge's reply; many points of his system are close to points made by Burthogge—the spontaneous generation of life, the rejection of *Vis Inertiae,* the analogy and correspondence of the creatures who form part of the universal creature, the equation of mind with light, and so on. Yet it is impossible to say that Smart borrowed his system from Burthogge's two books. If one compares Burthogge's image of the world as an Organ with the *For* verses in Fragment B1 (ll. 223-55), there seems to be some correspondence, especially in statements such as the following:

> For EARTH which is an intelligence hath a voice
> and a propensity to speak in all her parts. (B1, l. 234)

> For the VOICE is from the body and the spirit—
> and is a body and a spirit. (B1, l. 239)

> For the TRUMPET of God is a blessed intelligence
> & so are all the instruments in HEAVEN.

> For GOD the father Almighty plays upon the HARP
> of stupendous magnitude and melody.

24 Burthogge, *Of the Soul of the World,* p. 6.

> For innumerable Angels fly out at every touch and
> his tune is a work of creation. (B1, ll. 245-7)

Yet the very considerable differences are such as would be explained
by Smart's having picked up the general idea from listening to discussion of Burthogge's theory rather than from perusing and medi-
tating on the passage itself. This applies to almost every attempt to
pin down Smart's debt to any single source. His method was
thoroughly eclectic and he left nothing he borrowed unchanged.

When we come to consider the relation of this vital organic and
intelligent world to its creator it is evident that it is activated by
forces unknown to modern physics, but familiar enough to earlier
speculation. It is a system dominated by the idea that 'nothing is
so real as that which is spiritual' (B1, l. 258). The creation is
arranged in a great hierarchy of creatures seen in their spiritual
aspects which form a Jacob's ladder up to God through Paradise
(B2, l. 392) and all things are moving towards God. Fountains and
springs, for example, are the life of the waters working up to God
(B1, l. 204). Like Blake, Smart seems to have held some theory of
double vision: there is ordinary sensory vision and there is 'seeing
in the spirit' (B1, l. 230). An idea is the mental vision of an object
and prayers are visible to those who possess the double vision
(B1, l. 240). In this system, air and light have special importance.
Air is that which conveys praise (the importance of praise will
become clear in a moment). In its character as a spirit it propagates
sound in all directions and spreads praise everywhere, which, in
fact, may account for Smart's continuous and loud praying in public.
Light, Smart associates with divine conception (B1, l. 284; B2, l. 325),
and hence he holds that its propagation is instantaneous to all
parts of this non-Newtonian universe in which everything is both
body and spirit. Cold and darkness are not only therefore the work
of the devil but the conditions under which he works (B2, l. 296).
Fire and electricity, associated as forms of light, are also given a
special importance in Smart's system. In case all this sounds like
made-up nonsense or lunatic system-making it is worth while to
repeat that Smart seems to have got most of his details from his
wide reading in contemporary scientific experiments and theories,
and that views similar to his were the subject of serious scientific
and philosophic discussion at the time. Keill, a mathematician, and
Burthogge, a doctor, are not in the main stream of the scientific
tradition but they were serious scholars. Burthogge in particular
seems to have anticipated some of Kant's theories. The celebrated
William Whiston, from whom Smart seems to have taken some of his
views on matters like the determination of longitude, eclipses, and
the waters under and above the earth, was not only a leading

scientific figure in Cambridge and successor to Newton in the Lucasian Professorship a generation before Smart's residence there, but his *New Theory of the Earth,* a rival to Burnet's *Sacred Theory of the Earth,* displays just that union of scientific speculation with Covenant Theology which is characteristic of Smart. It is interesting to note that Whiston in 1746, the year in which Smart was re-elected to his praelectorship in philosophy at Pembroke, declared in a lecture given at Tunbridge Wells that the millenium would take place in 1766.[25] Smart predicted it in 1760.

But there is a more important aspect of Smart's system of the universe. To those granted double or spiritual vision, so that all creatures are perceived in both their aspects, it appears that there is a series of mysterious correspondences between creatures, and here we come to the significance of Smart's pairing them in his great Magnificat. What this connexion is is suggested in Fragment B1, l. 43.

> Let Jubal rejoice with Caecilia, the woman and the
> slow-worm praise the name of the Lord.
> For I pray the Lord Jesus to translate my MAGNIFICAT
> into verse and represent it.

Caecilia is the name of the lizard who is to rejoice with Jubal the inventor of music. But Caecilia is of course also the patron saint of music. This verse and some others which appear at first sight to be mere puns and verbal associations are to be connected with the sections of the work where Smart gives special significance to people who have the names of animals, like Pigg, Cock, Grub, Lamb etc. (B1, l. 114):

> Let Tirzah rejoice with Tylus which is the Cheeslip and food
> for the chicken.
> For I have a providential acquaintance with men who
> bear the names of animals.
> Let Hoglah rejoice with Leontophonos who will kill the
> lion, if he is eaten.
> For I bless God to Mr Lion Mr Cock Mr Cat Mr Talbot
> Mr Hart Mrs Fysh Mr Grub, and Miss Lamb. (B1, ll. 113-14)

Just what this bond between man and creature was, is not clear, but when Smart assembles them by pairs:

> Let man and beast appear before him and
> magnify his name together (A, l. 3),

these pairs are meant to be mystically and physically appropriate and significant. Arthur Sherbo has recently challenged Stead's view that Smart had read extensively in the works of the Cambridge

25 *Dictionary of National Biography.*

Platonists, the Kabbala, Cornelius Agrippa, and so on.[26] But it is clear that he had some acquaintance with some of these writers and Jacob Boehme's *De Signatura Rerum,* 1621, was one of the books borrowed in the Pembroke library in Smart's day and may well have contributed particular details to the general theory of the interconnexion of creatures which he seems to have taken from Burthogge, who asserts:

> There is a sensible *Analogy* and Correspondence in Fabric and Composition, not only between the several *Species* of *Animals* (which is very manifest in *Comparative Anatomy*); but also, in a good degree, between *Plants* and *Animals,* and *Minerals* and *Plants.*[27]

In the form in which it appears in the *Jubilate Agno* the connexion is partly a system of names and secret signatures that God has put on all things. 'All good words are from God' (B1, l. 85). The languages of men are given by God, especially Greek, Latin, Hebrew, and English, and everything in them has a divinely intended significance and power. Thus the series of verses on the significance of the Hebrew letter Lamed as it appears in the texture of plants and animals: where this shape is found in leaf or flower it is God's signature and signifies El, the Hebrew name of God. The editors think Smart was confused here as El is the name of the *English* letter corresponding to Hebrew Lamed and in English El does not mean God. But Smart, as we shall see, was reasoning correctly in terms of his elaborate system.

The series on the mystical significance of the bull, who is an animal and also 'the word of Almighty God' (B2, l. 676), further indicates this mysterious series of verbal, physical, and spiritual correspondences. How strange and complex it is may be illustrated by B2, ll. 402-3:

> For all the stars have satellites, which are
> terms under their respective words.
> For tiger is a word and his satellites are Griffin,
> Storgis, Cat and others.

The reference to all the stars having satellites may come from Derham's *Astro-Theology,* but may also owe something to Huygens's *Cosmotheoros. Hugenii Opuscula* was one of Smart's borrowings at Pembroke.[28] But the extension of the theory which makes the satellites 'words' and the tiger equivalent to a star with its satellites

---

26 'Christopher Smart's Knowledge of Occult Literature', *Journal of the History of Ideas,* Vol. XVIII, No. 2, April 1957.
27 Burthogge, *An Essay upon Reason,* p. 247.
28 Christiaan Huygens, *Cosmotheoros,* 1698.

which are also 'words', shows how Smart elaborates on the original borrowings in ideas.

The function of this universe of creatures is praise and adoration. God is primarily the great artist and creator and is conceived as the Musician of the Universe. In one of his Seatonian prize poems Smart addresses God as the Poet of the Universe. He makes the same point in *Jubilate Agno* in the passage already quoted:

> For GOD the father Almighty plays upon the HARP of
> stupendous magnitude and melody.
> For innumerable Angels fly out at every touch and his
> tune is a work of creation. (B1, ll. 246-7)

The whole creation is engaged in an antiphonal song of praise in answer to this divine creative music and in this way the fallen creation is gradually purified and restored. This is why David the psalmist is called 'The beginning of victory to the Lord'. The end of the world or the second coming of Christ will occur when all men join in this praise (B2, l. 344).

The most remarkable aspect of Smart's system is its mystical history. At the fall of man, man and the earth suffered together; the earth lost its fertility. God through his chosen people and chosen prophets begins the work of regeneration, which has a number of stages. The first appears to be from Adam to Abraham, the second from Abraham to David, the third from David to the Babylonian exile, the fourth from the Babylonian captivity to Christ, the fifth from Christ to the year 1760, which is the 'millenium of the millenium foretold by the prophets' and the year in which Smart is composing the *Jubilate*. The key points in this process are Abraham, David, Christ. Between David and Christ there is a further degeneration of man and nature. Man becomes smaller and loses the glorious horn he once wore in his forehead. Finally at the coming of Christ the Jews cease to be the chosen people of God, as Smart explains in the twelfth of his Parables of our Lord. Their place is to be taken by the English, who are to lead the nations in the regeneration of the world by praise and by the practice of agriculture. In one section of the *Jubilate* Smart explains that 'the ENGLISH are the seed of Abraham and work up to him by Joab, David, and Naphtali' (B2, l. 433). Moreover the Romans and the English are one people (B2, l. 434). The Welsh are the children of Mephibosheth and Ziba 'with a mixture of David in the Jones's' (B2, l. 435). These derivations of all the modern races from the tribes of Israel and peoples of the Old Testament are not, of course, Smart's invention. It was a common enough type of theory and an ancient one, which in one form or another, as Stead remarks, persists in England from the time of Bede till the middle of the nineteenth century. In fact it still persists in theories like those of the British Israelites though it no longer is taken seriously by educated people. In Smart's system the merit of being the chosen people did not pass at once to the English but to the Chinese.

> For I pray God bless the Chinese which are of
> ABRAHAM and the Gospel grew with them at the
> first. (B1, l. 77)

Now, however, the English are the chosen race and the successors to the Kingdom; the Church of England, one of the Seven Churches of Revelations, is now the chief church and the candlestick of the Lord (B1, l. 125). The English language replaces Hebrew as the new sacred tongue and language of God and is to be the language of the West (B1, l. 127). The English will undergo a great spiritual revival. The spirit of God will descend on them, they will recover man's original stature and be the first of nations to recover the glorious horn on the forehead (C, ll. 128-30). England is to be the head of Europe in the spirit. Earth will recover through the industry of man (C, ll. 155-60). Christ will become King of England (C, ll. 85-7).

Smart's part in this millenial scheme is indicated throughout the *Jubilate Agno*. Not only are the English of the seed of Abraham in a general sense but Smart is of the seed of Abraham in the specific sense (B1, l. 73). He appears to claim to be of the seed of David (B1, l. 86). The very seed of Jesus is in his body (B1, l. 144). Although he is afflicted and despised he is destined to be a prince in the New Canaan, in which he is to own estates. He is also of the seed of St George who is the same as Agricola (both names meaning a farmer) (B1, ll. 54 and note, 137, 231). It is to be noted that part of Smart's mystical biology includes the idea that the soul is divisible and a portion of the spirit may be cut off from one and attached to another. As every atom is a spirit as well as a body we could conclude from this point that one can be of the seed of David without actual physical descent. Whatever Smart's conception here, however, it is plain that he sees himself as the psalmist, the new David of the new order. God has chosen him for the illumination of the people (B1, l. 27). He has divine inspiration through his chastity:

> For CHASTITY is the key of knowledge as in Esdras,
> Sr Isaac Newton & now, God be praised, in me.

> For Newton nevertheless is more of error than of
> the truth, but I am of the WORD of GOD. (B1, ll. 194-5)

This probably refers to Newton's millenial theories more than to his physics. Smart is the bearer of the Lord's cross and his builder

281

and mason, in both senses of the terms (B1, ll. 94, 109). He is the Renewer of Adoration among Englishmen (B2, l. 332). He is the Lord's News-Writer—the scribe-evangelist (B2, l. 327). He has the gift of prophecy (C, ll. 57-8) which he exercises to the end of this section. Above all he is the composer of hymns of praise (D, l. 199) and of new psalms on which he invokes God's blessing (D, ll. 208, 210, 217, 220). He asks God to magnify the idea of Smart singing hymns on this day (5 Nov. 1762, N.S.) in the eyes of the whole University of Cambridge (D, l. 148); and so on. The peculiar importance of David in this historical process is stressed in the reference to him in the *Jubilate* (A, l. 41).

> Let David bless with the Bear—The beginning of victory to the Lord—to the Lord the perfection of excellence—Hallelujah from the heart of God, and from the hand of the artist inimitable, and from the echo of the heavenly harp in sweetness magnifical and mighty.

This by God's grace was to be Smart's importance in the new order.

One may naturally ask why Smart did not make open reference to his system elsewhere in his works, especially after he wrote *Jubilate Agno.* There are several possible reasons. His praying aloud in public seems to have been one of the reasons for his being confined, and his release in 1763 was not because he was considered to have recovered but mainly because the efforts of energetic friends and a parliamentary inquiry into private madhouses aided his escape. Once out, Smart had every reason to avoid actions which might return him to an asylum. He seems to have been alarmed as well as angry at the remarks of the *Monthly Review,* which followed his retort to the reviewer of his *A Song to David,* and both reviews clearly hint at his insanity.[29] No doubt he had constantly in his mind the warning which Imagination gives to Reason in the fable he published the same year, 1763:

> You dwell alone, and are too grave;
> You make yourself too much a slave;
> Your shrewd deductions run a length,
> 'Till all your Spirits waste their strength:
> Your fav'rite logic is full close;
> Your morals are too much a dose;
> You fly your studies 'till you risk
> Your senses—you should be more brisk—
> The Doctors soon will find a flaw
> And lock you up in chains and straw.[30]

At any rate all the testimony of his behaviour after his release from

29 Devlin, *Poor Kit Smart,* pp. 152-5.
30 'Reason and Imagination: A Fable', in *Poems by Mr. Smart,* London, 1763.

THE APOCALYPSE OF CHRISTOPHER SMART

the asylum is to the effect that he withdrew very much into himself and behaved with great circumspection. He had strong reasons for this. But stronger, I think, must have been the fact that the great day of the millenium actually arrived and passed and left him still a prisoner. The last section of the poem has a flatness and a mechanical quality about it which may be due, as some have thought, to the fact that the author was growing saner, but may equally be due to the apathy following a great disappointment. This apathy towards the world around him certainly marked his later years.

All this is speculative, of course, but if it can be sustained, it throws light on a good many things that are dark. It explains the purpose, nature, and form of the *Jubilate Agno,* as the great Magnificat from God's chosen successor to Orpheus and David, produced to greet the beginning of the millenium. We see why English and Biblical characters are called on to praise with their pairs in the spiritual creation. We see the peculiar importance of King David to Smart and the peculiar importance attached to his own version of the Psalms; and why in spite of his admiration and reverence for the psalmist he takes such liberties with the text while faithfully writing a stanza for every verse in the Bible. For Smart's psalms are more than free paraphrases. He rewrites the Old Testament Psalms in the sense and spirit of the New. These are the new model Christian psalms, in the exact mould of the old. There were precedents for this in the eighteenth century, but there is an added significance in Smart's hymnal and psalms if we see him writing as the new David for the Church of England which is to be the new temple of the millenial Jerusalem to be built in England's green and pleasant land.

Above all if Smart can be shown to have such a systematic theory of the universe, it would throw a great deal of light on the poem we chiefly remember him for, the great *A Song to David.* It is obviously an elaborately systematic poem but no account of it I have read is quite satisfactory. What tends to be missed is that it is a great metaphysical and in a sense an eschatological poem built round the conception of the universe created by a musician-artist-Creator. A world which is restored and redeemed in two steps, first by the law of Moses embodied in Smart's exercise on the decalogue (stanzas 40-8), then by divine sacrifice and grace in Christ. But the essential step between these is that of the poet-musician—King David. The exercise on the seasons has as its main theme the natural function of the whole creation—adoration. The creatures do it naturally. But just as the old law of Moses is completed and subsumed in the New Testament of Christ the Redeemer, so *natural* adoration is completed and transcended by divine poetry. David represents the messianic and redemptive function of music and poetry and is therefore properly his ancestor in the flesh.

This magnificent poem, I would suggest, is not properly understood unless we see it in the setting of Smart's system and its relation to himself as a successor of David. Then it becomes not only a song to David but a celebration of a metaphysical theory about poetry.

Smart's system may be as crazy as Smart himself seems to have been at times. But this central idea as to the nature and function of poetry can be taken quite seriously, and this is what interests me more than any speculations as to whether Smart's system can be reconstructed or not. I have very little faith, as a professional critic of literature, in most of the descriptions or definitions of poetry on which the various schools depend. 'The imitation of nature', 'the overflow of powerful emotions', a 'criticism of life'—well, yes and no: none of them seems to me a satisfactory basis of criticism. As a poet, I find them exasperating. I know of no definition of the nature and function of poetry that satisfies me better than that which is the theme of *A Song to David*: the view of poetry as celebration, the celebration of the world by the creation of something that adds to and completes the order of nature. *A Song to David* has the added beauty, for me, of being itself a celebration of what to me is the real nature of the poet's art.

The Classical Learning of Samuel Johnson

M. N. Austin

The subject I propose to consider in this paper is but a facet of the massive and miscellaneous erudition of one who in the famous phrase was 'a robust genius, born to grapple with whole libraries'. Nevertheless it constitutes an intelligible field of study and offers a significant view of Johnson's unique intellectual and moral genius. For Johnson's specifically classical learning—his mastery of Latin and his knowledge of Greek—is integral to his personality and to what he called his 'literature and his wit'. Although he was interested in and had some acquaintance with other tongues and literatures, in particular French, Italian, and Dutch, there can be no question that the classical languages, especially Latin, in which he excelled, were almost as important to him as his native English. It is easy to see that the pride which he takes in his own language derives from his sense that it may stand on its own merits with the ancient classics.

In the Preface to the *Dictionary* he writes:

> I have devoted the labour of years to the honour of my country
> . . . The chief glory of every people arises from its authors.
> Whether I shall add anything by my own writings to the
> reputation of English literature must be left to time . . . I shall
> not think my employment useless or ignoble, if by my assist-
> ance foreign nations and distant ages, gain access to the propa-
> gators of knowledge and understand the teachers of truth.[1]

Elsewhere he declares that 'modern writers are the moons of literature; they shine with reflected light, with light borrowed from the
ancients. Greece appears to me to be the fountain of knowledge;
Rome of Elegance'.[2]

[1] *Johnson's Dictionary: A Modern Selection,* ed. E. L. McAdam jun. and
G. Milne, London, 1963, p. 27.
[2] *Boswell's Life of Johnson* (hereafter cited as *Life*), ed. G. B. Hill, rev. and
enlarged L. F. Powell, Oxford, 1934, Vol. III, p. 333.

I propose to deal first with Johnson's own 'classical' education at school and university, secondly with his Latin learning, thirdly with his knowledge of Greek, and lastly with some of his comments on his favourite authors and opinions on classical studies. Each of these aspects would require more space for its adequate treatment than can be here allowed, and the subject as a whole, in its many bearings, demands a comprehensive and detailed study. The evidence is scattered everywhere throughout Boswell's *Life* and Johnson's own writings. Much of it is incidental and minutely particular—a quotation in a conversation or a motto at the head of an essay—but when taken in its gross and scope it tells us more than is actually said. There are, to be sure, the purple passages when the theme is treated deliberately by Boswell or when Johnson himself expands on a classical topic and is prodigal of his rich stores. Perhaps the best known of the former is the episode involving the Greenwich Waterman, and of the latter the numbers of the *Rambler* dealing with the pastoral and the *Eclogues* of Virgil. However, over and above these and other illustrations of Johnson actively using and enjoying his classical learning there is the more important evidence stamped on or assimilated into his own original works. This is not always easy to discern, and even when it is palpable and confessed, as in the two great poems, it is difficult to disengage and discuss. Since this has been done, or rather attempted, by scholars with the necessary competence, I shall excuse myself from attempting to expound and assess the influence of the classical tradition on his poetry, prose style, and criticism, and confine myself to a more purely circumstantial and factual exposition. If this is the less rigorous and critical approach to the subject I have hopes that it will be the more entertaining, because it will enable me, for the most part, to let Johnson speak for himself. He loved to 'fold his legs and have out his say'. I shall try to follow Boswell's example and, inevitably, I must draw largely on his aid.

Johnson was taught Latin at school from about the age of seven. It does not appear that he was *taught* anything else. He certainly learned Latin and much else besides, for he emerged in his maturity as one of the 'great modern masters of the Latin tongue' and as a veritable polymath, one who, in the words of Adam Smith, 'knew more books than any man alive'.[3] His education was based on the antique humanistic tradition and for the most part it was ignorantly and brutally applied. Motivation was secured by means of the rod. Johnson, though critical of its misapplication, never questioned its value both in general and in his own case.

[3] Ibid., Vol. I, p. 71.

Mr. Langton one day asked him [says Boswell] how he had acquired so accurate a knowledge of Latin, in which, I believe, he was exceeded by no man of his time; he said, 'My master whipt me very well. Without that, Sir, I should have done nothing'.[4]

Although constitutionally indolent he could at times be stirred to exertion and to astonishing accomplishment. He liked to excel and was proud of his distinction even at school. This was considerable, for the record, though incomplete, shows clearly his exceptional powers of mind, his wide reading, and his skill in translation and verse-composition. His memory was phenomenal and quite early he was marked as a scholar.

In 1734 Johnson began to keep some autobiographical notes in Latin. They are headed '*Annales*'. The third entry records for 1 November 1728, '*S.J. Oxonium se contulit*'.

It was at Oxford that he first showed the learned world striking evidence of his proficiency or rather his brilliance in Latin. The record here is mainly anecdotal, though there are some documents of considerable interest. Boswell assiduously collected such reminiscences as Johnson gave him and sounded the oral tradition as preserved by those of Johnson's seniors and contemporaries who survived into the time of his public fame. Johnson told him:

I had looked into a great many books, which were not commonly known at the Universities, where they seldom read any books but what are put into their hands by their tutors; so that when I came to Oxford, Dr. Adams, now master of Pembroke College, told me, I was the best qualified for the University that he had ever known come there.[5]

Then there is the celebrated incident on the first evening when his father introduced him to his tutor.

His father [says Boswell] seemed very full of the merits of his son, and told the company he was a good scholar, and a poet, and wrote Latin verses. His figure and manner appeared strange to them; but he behaved modestly, and sat silent, till upon something which occurred in the course of conversation, he suddenly struck in and quoted Macrobius; and thus he gave the first impression of that more extensive reading in which he had indulged himself.[6]

It is not possible to discover precisely what Johnson's formal course of study consisted in or what he actually read, apart from Boswell's statement that 'Horace's Odes were the compositions in

4 Ibid., Vol. I, pp. 45-6.
5 Ibid., Vol. I, p. 57.
6 Ibid., Vol. I, p. 59.

which he took most delight, and it was long before he liked his Epistles and Satires'.[7] There are notes setting out plans of methodical reading, computations of the number of lines at a given rate per day that could be read in a week, a month, or a year. Such programs are not uncommon pious exercises performed by students, but they are not conclusive evidence of reading actually done. Neither, in general, are the books in their possession. We have by chance a list of the books in the quite considerable personal library which Johnson brought with him to Oxford. It comprised 115 volumes.

One might linger over this fascinating catalogue together with that other invaluable document, the sale catalogue of the books from his personal library at the time of his death. The Latin authors represented in his undergraduate collection are: Virgil, Horace, Ovid, Lucretius, Cicero, Quintilian, Livy, Tacitus, Suetonius, Seneca, Lucan, and Catullus. However, what is particularly striking is the presence among these classics of numerous later writers of Latin: the two Scaligers, Vida, the *Colloquies* of Erasmus, More's *Utopia,* Buchanan, the Scottish humanist for whose Latin poetry he had the highest admiration, John le Clerc, Claudius Quillet, and John Barclay. There were also some of the Latin works of Milton.

It is perhaps worth mentioning at this point, though it anticipates an event later than the Oxford period, that Johnson's first serious proposals for a literary or scholarly work were for printing by subscription the Latin poems of Politian.

But to return to Oxford and his studies there. Apart from occasional verses at which he showed great virtuosity, he wrote, at the suggestion of his tutor, a Latin translation of Pope's *Messiah.* He completed the 119 lines in a few hours. It was greatly admired and a copy reached Pope himself, who commented favourably upon it. Another copy reached Johnson's father, who had the verses printed. Johnson himself was furious when he heard, and said violently that 'if it had not been his father he would have cut his throat'. At any rate it was the first of his compositions to be published for it was included in a *Miscellany of Poems,* edited by a young Fellow of Pembroke in 1731.

Johnson has a couple of entries in his Latin diary in October 1729. The first is very characteristic: 'I bid farewell to sloth, being resolved henceforth not to listen to her syren strains'. Here it is in Latin: *'Desidiae vale dixi syrenis istius Cantibus surdam posthac aurem obversurus'.* There is an echo here from Horace, but the Horace of the *Satires* (II.3.14): *'Vitanda est improba Siren/Desidia'.*

In December he left Oxford. *S.J. Oxonio rediit.* He had hoped to

7 Ibid., Vol. I, p. 70.

Plate XIc Mezzotint by James McArdell after Sir Joshua Reynolds's portrait of Horace Walpole, 1755-6.

Plate XIb The Stone Hall at Houghton, Norfolk, by William Kent, completed 1731. *Country Life* photograph.

Plate XIa Nymph in the grotto at Stourhead, copied from the 'Sleeping Ariadne' in the Vatican. From Oswald Siren, *China and the Gardens of Europe in the Eighteenth Century*, New York, 1950.

Plate XII   Sampson Gideon, later Earl Eardley of Spalding, with
his tutor, by Pompeo Batoni, Rome, 1767. The National Gallery
of Victoria, Melbourne.

return for he left his books behind. He ultimately recalled them when he was about to open a school after his marriage and doubtless felt the need of them. What he did in the years immediately after leaving Oxford is not known in any detail. The little Latin jottings continue for the next few years, recording his readings or plans of reading.

The other diary entries from a later period of his life are for the most part in English with an occasional Latin phrase or single entry. For instance we find this rather extreme example of his intellectual curiosity expressed in the decent reticence of the universal language of science. 'I shaved the hairy part of my arms and little above the wrist to see how long it would take for the hairs to grow again'. About two years later he records in Latin the inception but not the result of a further experiment along these lines, but extending it to the hairs of his chest.

Finally, there is the journal he kept through five months in the last year of his life till within a few weeks of his death. It is called *Aegri Ephemeris* [A sick man's journal]. Apart from the prayers interspersed it is entirely in Latin. He had told Mrs Thrale that 'Dr. Lawrence had said that medical treatises should be always in Latin'. This Dr Lawrence had attended Johnson during a serious illness two years before in 1782. Johnson wrote a series of letters to him in Latin reporting his symptoms and condition. One of the letters is made up of a set of jesting verses—'*Nugae anapaesticae in lecto lusae*' [Anapaestic trifles composed in bed]. It has a sub-title. '*Medico Aeger S.*' [Sick Sam to his doctor].

I have strayed from Johnson's Latin studies to some of the uses to which he put his skill. His reading in mature life is too vast to document here and is likely to have been far more extensive than the actual record proves. I have deferred to the last part of this paper some consideration of his favourite Latin and Greek authors. I would like to complete this account of his use of Latin with references to some of his occasional compositions and conversational Latin. I can but allude to the remarkable series of letters to George Strahan on the learning of Latin.

With the Latin letters on his physical condition written late in life to Dr Lawrence we may associate one which he wrote after leaving Oxford at a time when his congenital melancholia was afflicting him to an almost unendurable degree, a time when he even 'strongly entertained thoughts of suicide'. He consulted a Dr Swinfen of Birmingham on his condition and wrote in Latin a complete statement of his symptoms and fears of insanity. The doctor was so impressed with its 'extraordinary acuteness, research and eloquence' that he showed it to several people, with the result that Johnson never really forgave his breach of confidence.

There are also the two polished formal letters which he wrote to the Vice-Chancellor of the University of Oxford acknowledging the honorary degrees conferred on him, the famous epitaph for Goldsmith and, of course, the Latin poems and verses that make up the bulk of his poetical works. I shall have occasion to glance at his Latin verse later.

Besides reading and writing Latin Johnson spoke Latin, as occasion required, with wonderful fluency and elegance. His friend Baretti said: 'Though he is a great critic in French, and knows almost as much Italian as I do, he cannot speak either language, but he talks Latin with all Cicero's fury'. Boswell writes:

> While Johnson was in France, he was generally very resolute in speaking Latin. It was a maxim with him that a man should not let himself down, by speaking a language which he speaks imperfectly. . . In a Latin conversation with the Père Boscovitch, at the house of Mrs. Cholmondeley, I heard him maintain the superiority of Sir Isaac Newton over all foreign philosophers, with a dignity and eloquence that surprized that learned foreigner.[8]

And again:

> When Sir Joshua Reynolds, at one of the dinners of the Royal Academy, presented him to a Frenchman of great distinction, he would not deign to speak French, but talked Latin, though his Excellency did not understand it, owing perhaps, [suggests Boswell] to Johnson's English pronunciation.[9]

On this is a very relevant passage in the Life of Milton:

> About this time Elwood the quaker, being recommended to him as one who would read Latin to him, for the advantage of his conversation; attended him every afternoon, except on Sundays. Milton, who, in his letter to Hartlib, had declared, that 'to read Latin with an English mouth is as ill a hearing as Law French', required that Elwood should learn and practise the Italian pronunciation, which, he said was necessary, if he would talk with foreigners. This seems to have been a task troublesome without use. There is little reason for preferring the Italian pronunciation to our own, except that it is more general; and to teach it to an Englishman is only to make him a foreigner at home. He who travels, if he speaks Latin, may so soon learn the sounds which every native gives it, that he need make no provision before his journey; and if strangers visit us,

8 Ibid., Vol. II, pp. 404, 125.
9 Ibid., Vol. II, p. 404.

it is their business to practise such conformity to our modes as they expect from us in their own countries.[10]

As a final tit-bit here is a sample. 'When in Paris, Johnson thus characterised Voltaire to Freron, the Journalist: *"Vir est accerrimi ingenii et paucarum literarum"*' [A man of very acute intellect and little literature].[11]

Perhaps the best appreciation of Johnson's Latin learning is that of De Quincey, who, while admitting that Johnson did not understand Latin 'with the elaborate and circumstantial accuracy required for the editing critically of a Latin classic', describes his Latin attainments as follows:

> But if he had less than *that,* he had also more: he *possessed* that language in a way that no extent of mere critical knowledge could confer. He wrote it genially, not as one translating into it painfully from English, but as one using it for his original organ of thinking. And in Latin verse he expressed himself at times with the energy and freedom of a Roman.[12]

To this we must add the sensitive and perceptive comment of David Nichol Smith, so characteristic both of the passion and reserve of his *anima naturaliter Johnsoniana.* 'There were thoughts and feelings which asked for utterance in verse and for which it was the only language.'

> In order to get this picture at its truest, we have to read his Latin verse as well as his English. Latin was a living language to Johnson and it was the language which he preferred for the expression of certain moods and feelings. His very last poem, written on his death bed, was in Latin.

He also instances the lines he wrote expressing his feelings on the completion of the *Dictionary* as he mused on the drudgery it cost him, and his recollections late in life of his happy childhood in Lichfield: 'as he viewed it through the mists of memory, again Latin is necessarily his language. Poems about himself and his feelings he did not write in English'.

Let us now consider Johnson's Greek. In his age Latin was virtually indispensable and inescapable but Greek was, as it has been at most times since the revival of learning, something of a luxury. Johnson's famous remark is well known. 'Greek is like lace; every man gets as much as he can.' How much then did he get?

Boswell devotes a passage of special pleading to the subject.

[10] *Lives of the Poets,* Worlds Classics, Vol. I, Oxford, 1946, p. 95.
[11] *Life,* Vol. II, p. 406.
[12] Quoted in *Life,* Vol. I, p. 272n.

A very erroneous notion [he says] has circulated as to Johnson's deficiency in the knowledge of the Greek language, partly owing to the modesty with which, from knowing how much there was to be learnt he used to mention his own comparative acquisitions. When Mr. Cumberland talked to him of the Greek fragments which are so well illustrated in *The Observer,* and of the Greek dramatists in general, he candidly acknowledged his insufficiency in that particular branch of Greek literature. Yet it may be said, that though not a great, he was a good Greek scholar. Dr. Charles Burney, the younger, who is universally acknowledged by the best judges to be one of the few men of this age who are very eminent for their skill in that noble language, has assured me, that Johnson could give a Greek word for almost every English one; and that although not sufficiently conversant in the niceties of the language, he upon some occasions discovered, even in these, a considerable degree of critical acumen. Mr. Dalzel, Professor of Greek at Edinburgh, whose skill in it is unquestionable, mentioned to me in very liberal terms, the impression which was made upon him by Johnson, in a conversation which they had in London concerning that language. As Johnson, therefore, was undoubtedly one of the first Latin scholars in modern times, let us not deny to his fame some additional splendour from Greek.[13]

We have no record of when he began to learn Greek, but we may suppose that it was at the point where he introduces it into his plan of studies for a grammar school just after the pupils have been well drilled in Latin. 'Practise in the Latin rules till they are perfect in them; afterwards in Mr. Leed's Greek Grammar . . . afterwards they proceed to Virgil etc. . . . and to learn Greek'.[14] In a summary to the document he says:

> I believe it will be most for your advantage to apply yourself wholly to the languages [note the plural], till you go to the University. The Greek authors I think it best for you to read are these: Cebes [that is the pinax or tablet of Cebes] Aelian, Lucian by Leeds [i.e. edited by Mr. Leeds of the Greek Grammar], Xenophon [Attik]; Homer [Ionik]; Theocritus [Dorick]; Euripides [Attik and Dorick].[15]

As Johnson was no innovator in educational practice we may assume that his own studies began in this way.

He was certainly reading Homer while still at school. At the time when he made his first translations from Virgil and Horace he also put into English verse—heroic couplets—part of the dialogue between Hector and Andromache from *Iliad,* Book VI, in which he

13 *Life,* Vol. IV, pp. 384-5.
14 Ibid., Vol. I, p. 100.
15 Ibid.

showed his independence of the popular version of Pope. His cousin, Nathaniel Ford, the witty and worldly Parson Ford, as well as introducing him to Martial (a taste which later shocked more staid observers) may also have directed his attention to Anacreon, a bibulous and erotic lyricist, for whom the moralist always retained an affection. He told Mrs Thrale that the verses in Anacreon's *Dove* were the first Greek verses to make a deep and lasting impression on him and that he had planned a translation at sixteen, though the lines were not completed until he was sixty-eight.

During the two-year period between school and university when he was helping in the bookshop he did a lot of reading. The books he read then, he told Boswell, were not works of mere amusement, 'not voyages and travels, but all literature, Sir, all ancient writers, all manly; though but little Greek, only some of Anacreon and Hesiod'. However, of his studies at Oxford he told his biographer that 'what he read *solidly* at Oxford was Greek, not the Greecian historians, but Homer, Euripides and now and then a little epigram'. The last item would mean epigrams from the Greek Anthology. He had a great fondness for this type of literature. He composed both Latin and Greek epigrams at different times, and in the last year of his life we read that 'During his sleepless nights he amused himself by translating into Latin verse, from the Greek many of the epigrams in the *Anthologia*'.

The Greek component of his Oxford library was not extensive, but the items are interesting. Besides a Grammar and a Greek New Testament he had his two-volume Sophocles, Homer's *Iliad*, Theocritus, Dionysius of Halicarnassus, Longinus, and Anacreon. If we compare with this modest list the sale catalogue of the books in his library at the time of his death, it is clear that his interest in Greek continued and expanded throughout his life. The catalogue lists only some seven hundred and fifty of the five thousand odd volumes in the full collection. Apart from lexica and grammatical works there are over fifty volumes of Greek texts, some authors being represented by several different editions. It is a scholar's collection. Nearly all the great poets and prose writers are there. It cannot be doubted that Johnson had at least read in them, in his own way of reading, as well as in many other Greek books that he chanced upon during his long life. Wherever he goes he is nosing about for books in other people's houses. Everyone of these writers and many another is cited or spoken of in his *Life, Diaries, Letters,* or *Works.* The allusions are manifold and ubiquitous, although there are not many references to his actual reading of particular Greek books, except the Greek New Testament which he read and reread as assiduously and as systematically as his nature allowed. Boswell found him with his great folio edition open and 'beheld him with a reverential awe, and would not intrude upon his time'. Perhaps Boswell was thinking of the occasion when Johnson knocked down with just such a mighty folio a man who had had the temerity to insult him.

There are a couple of notes in his private diary written in his middle sixties which illustrate his determination to keep up his Greek.

> Advent Sunday. I considered that this day, being the beginning of the ecclesiastical year, was a proper time for a new course of life. I began to read the Greek Testament regularly at 160 verses every Sunday. This day I began the Acts.

Two years later he appended this to a prayer he had composed—'purposed to apply vigorously to study, particularly of the Greek and Italian tongues'.

Quite early in their acquaintance Johnson advised Boswell 'when settled in any place abroad to study with eagerness after knowledge, and to apply to Greek an hour every day'. Sixteen years later we find that Boswell had not in fact acted in accordance with this advice.

> Having regretted to him [he says] that I had learnt little Greek, as is too generally the case in Scotland; that I had for a long time hardly applied at all to the study of that noble language, and that I was desirous of being told by him what method to follow; he recommended to me as easy helps, Sylvanus's 'First Book of the Iliad'; Dawson's 'Lexicon to the Greek New Testament'; and 'Hesiod' with *Pasoris Lexicon* at the end of it.[16]

Johnson was not a Greek scholar, but an amateur. The great age of Greek scholarship was beginning in the last quarter of the century, led by the genius of Porson, and represented among Johnson's friends by Burney and Dr Parr, who composed the epitaph on Johnson's memorial. Thomas Gray, as a scholar poet, was probably a better Grecian. When his friend Langton spoke of his learning by heart the epistle of St Basil, 'Sir,' said Johnson, 'I never made such an effort to attain Greek'. Perhaps one of his best remarks was when, hearing a lady commended for her learning, he said: 'A man is in general better pleased when he has a good dinner upon his table than when his wife talks Greek'.

Johnson had an astonishing range of familiarity with Greek writings, but he does not display exact and comprehensive knowledge of the Greek dramatists, historians, and philosophers. However, one Greek poet profoundly appealed to him—Homer. I shall

16 Ibid., p. 1036.

now say something about this and move on to a consideration of the three Latin poets he seems to have known best and loved most.

Homer, he venerated, as 'the prince of poets'. He considered the advice given to Diomed by his father, when he sent him to the Trojan War, was the noblest exhortation that could be instanced in any heathen writer and comprised in a single line:

αἰὲν ἀριστεύειν καὶ ὑπείροχον ἔμμεναι ἄλλων
[Be ever best, and o'ertop other men].

To a dozen or more of his *Ramblers* he prefixes an Homeric motto or treats in the text some passage or point of critical interest. In No. 92 he calls Homer 'the father of all poetical beauty' in introducing, with quotations in the original followed by Pope's translations, an examination of the claim put forward by Dionysius of Halicarnassus that Homer 'of all the poets exhibited the greatest variety of sound' and mastery of sound echoing sense. He considered the *Iliad* the greatest work of entertainment in the world and thus praises the opening lines of the *Iliad* and *Odyssey*. 'If the exordial verses of Homer be compared with the rest of the poem, they will not appear remarkable for plainness or simplicity, but rather eminently adorned and illuminated.' He then quotes ten lines from the *Odyssey* and adds:

> The first verses of the Iliad are in like manner particularly splendid and the proposition of the Eneid closes with a dignity and magnificence not often to be found even in the poetry of Virgil.

He praises the wonderful multiplicity of Homer's sentiments and descriptions. In the Preface to his edition of Shakespeare he says: 'Perhaps it would not be easy to find any author except Homer who invented so much as Shakespeare'; and again:

> The poems of Homer we yet know not to transcend the common limits of human intelligence, but by remarking that nation after nation, and century after century, has been able to do little more than transpose his incidents, new name his characters, and paraphrase his sentiments.[17]

'He and my lord spoke highly of Homer', writes Boswell, recording a conversation in Scotland between Johnson and Lord Monboddo. Johnson cites with approbation the scenes depicted on the shield of Achilles in *Iliad*, Book XVIII, and goes on, 'there are in Homer such characters of heroes, and combinations of qualities of

---

17 'Preface to Edition of Shakespeare', in *Shakespeare Criticism: A Selection, 1623-1840*, ed. David Nichol Smith, Oxford, 1946, p. 107.

heroes, that the united powers of mankind ever since have not produced any but what are to be found there'. And they go on to discuss the characters.

Later he enters into a discussion of what soon was to emerge as the Homeric problem with a Mr McQueen, who alleged that Homer was made up of detached fragments. Dr Johnson denied this, observing that it had been one work originally, and that you could not put a book of the *Iliad* out of its place; and he believed the same might be said of the *Odyssey*.

It should be mentioned that Johnson once confessed that he had not read the *Odyssey* right through in Greek.

On another occasion he was in conversation with General Paoli.

> The General said he did not imagine Homer's poetry was so ancient as is supposed, because he ascribes to a Greek colony circumstances of refinement not found in Greece itself at a later period, when Thucydides wrote. JOHNSON. 'I recollect but one passage quoted by Thucydides from Homer, which is not to be found in our copies of Homer's works; I am for the antiquity of Homer, and think that a Grecian colony by being nearer Persia might be more refined than the mother country.[18]

I am afraid I must merely allude here to Johnson's famous eulogy of Pope's Homer in his Life of the poet. It is too long to quote, but it is one of the finest and most discriminating things he wrote. Nothing better shows his mastery of relevant knowledge and his large generosity of mind. Anyone who knows Bentley's aphorism: 'A pretty poem, but we must not call it Homer', should read what Johnson has to say about the *English Iliad*.

We may turn now from Johnson's appreciation of Homer to his remarks on Virgil by way of some comparisons that he made between the Greek and Roman epics. In *Rambler* No. 121 on imitation in literature he writes:

> The warmest admirers of the great Mantuan poet extol him for little more than the skill with which he has by making his hero both a traveller and a warrior, united the beauties of the *Iliad* and the *Odyssey* in one composition; yet his judgement was perhaps sometimes overborn by his avarice of the Homeric treasures; and for fear of suffering a sparkling ornament to be lost, he inserted it where it cannot shine with its original splendour.

And he instances Virgil's adaptation of Ajax's silent repulse of the advances made by Odysseus in the underworld, which he considers appropriate to the character of the blunt, uneloquent warrior, to

[18] *Life*, Vol. III, pp. 330-1.

the meeting in the shades of Aeneas and Dido, who turns away in mute disdain from her perfidious lover. While it is possible to disagree with Johnson's opinion here, it is scarcely possible not to admire the force and precision with which he makes his point. The whole passage is worth reading. He concludes, 'If Virgil could be thus seduced by imitation there will be little hope that common wits could escape'.

At another time he said that the dispute as to the comparative excellence of Homer or Virgil was inaccurate.

> We must consider (said he) whether Homer was not the greatest poet, though Virgil may have produced the finest poem. Virgil was indebted to Homer for the whole invention of the structure of an epick poem, and for many of his beauties.[19]

In a footnote to this passage Boswell says:

> I am informed by Mr. Langton, that a great many years ago he was present when this question was agitated between Dr. Johnson and Mr. Burke; and, to use Johnson's phrase, they 'talked their best'; Johnson for Homer, Burke for Virgil. It may well be supposed to have been one of the ablest and most brilliant contests that ever was exhibited.

In the Life of Dryden Johnson discusses some of the problems of translation and makes these further remarks on the Homer-Virgil comparison:

> The discriminative excellence of Homer is elevation and comprehension of thought, and that of Virgil is grace and splendour of diction. The beauties of Homer are therefore difficult to be lost, and those of the Virgil difficult to be retained. The massy trunk of sentiment is safe by its solidity, but the blossoms of elocution easily drop away.[20]

To this we may add these further remarks, from the Life of Pope, on translating Homer;

> Minute enquiries into the force of words are less necessary in translating Homer than other poets because his positions are general, and his representations natural, with very little dependence on local or temporary customs . . . among the readers of Homer the number is very small of those who find in the Greek more than in the Latin, except the musick of the numbers.[21]

Despite his admiration for Pope's translation of the *Iliad* he makes an admission: that it wants 'Homer's awful simplicity, his artless grandeur, his unaffected majesty . . . cannot totally be denied'.

[19] Ibid., Vol. III, pp. 193-4.
[20] *Lives of the Poets*, Vol. I, p. 330.
[21] Ibid., Vol. II, pp. 252-3.

Of Johnson's intimate familiarity with Virgil there can be no doubt. In his seventy-fourth year he said:

> I have this year read all Virgil through. I read a book of the Aeneid every night, so it was done in twelve nights, and I had great delight in it. The Georgicks did not give me so much pleasure, except the fourth book. The Eclogues I have almost by heart. I do not think the story of the Aeneid interesting. I like the story of the Odyssey much better; and this not on account of the wonderful things it contains; for there are wonderful things enough in the Aeneid;—the ships of the Trojans turned to sea-nymphs,—the tree at Polydorus's tomb dropping blood. The story of the Odyssey is interesting, as a great part of it is domestick.[22]

In *Adventurer* No. 92 he makes a magisterial review of the ten *Eclogues*. It is headed by a motto from the *Epistles* of Horace (II.2.110). *Cum tabulis animum censoris sumet honesti.* This he translates:

> Bold be the critic, zealous to his trust,
> Like the firm judge inexorably just.

And then he begins:

> Sir, in the papers of criticism which you have given to the public, I have remarked a spirit of candour and love of truth, equally remote from bigotry and captiousness; a just distribution of praise amongst the ancients and the moderns; a sober deference to reputation long established, without a blind adoration of antiquity; and a willingness to favour later performances, without a light or puerile fondness for novelty.
> I shall therefore venture, to lay before you, such observations as have risen to my mind in the consideration of Virgil's pastorals, without any enquiry how far my sentiments deviate from established rules or common opinions.

With this essay should be read, of course, the two famous, or perhaps we should say notorious, *Ramblers,* Nos. 36 and 37, on the pastoral. If in reading these essays we feel that both scholarship and criticism have progressed and sensibility has undergone changes in two hundred years we can still find much to admire and enjoy in the courage, manliness, and wit with which Johnson gives expression to opinions and judgments that are completely his own. He singles out the first and tenth Eclogues for special commendation. He makes some excellent observations on Theocritus. The following long single sentence is a good example at once of his learning, judgment, and style.

[22] *Life,* Vol. IV, pp. 218-19.

Yet, though I would willingly pay to Theocritus the honour which is always due to an original author, I am far from intending to depreciate Virgil; of whom Horace justly declares, that the rural muses have appropriated to him their elegance and sweetness, and who, as he copied Theocritus in his design has resembled him likewise in his success; for, if we except Calphurnius, an obscure author of the lower ages, I know not that a single pastoral was written after him by any poet, till the revival of literature.

If this shows Johnson's characteristic stride—the steady dignified gait of the *megalopsychos,* here is an example of his power to modulate his sentence into another mode as his subject may require. Still talking of the dogmatic theory of the pastoral, he says:

In consequence of these original errors, a thousand precepts have been given, which have only contributed to perplex and confound. Some have thought it necessary that the imaginary manners of the golden age should be universally preserved, and have therefore believed, that nothing more could be admitted in pastoral, than lilies and roses, and rocks and streams, among which are heard the gentle whispers of chaste fondness, or the soft complaints of amorous impatience.

And here we have a categorical judgment: 'All the modern languages cannot furnish so melodious a line as: *"Formosam resonare doces Amarillida silvas"* ' [Thou dost teach the woods to re-echo the name of lovely Amarillis].

Johnson loved Horace—at school, where he translated *Integer vitae* and *Nec semper imbres,* at Oxford, as we have seen, and all his life. The evidence is abundant: the echoes and quotations in his letters, the mottoes prefixed to his essays, the incidental allusions throughout his works, the translations (the last, significantly, was *Diffugere nives,* written within five weeks of his death) and his own Latin poems in Horatian metres. In Boswell's *Life* there are about seventy allusions to or quotations from Horace. A large proportion come from the *Ars Poetica,* a classic text in the armory of Johnsonian criticism, but *Satires* and *Epistles* are represented as well as the *Odes.*

He devotes a number of the *Idler* to a consideration of some difficult allusive passage in the *Odes.* Whether one agrees or not with the solutions of the cruces which he puts forward there is no question as to the ease and assurance with which he handles his author. It appears, from sundry slips, that he usually quoted from memory in these periodical essays, which he often wrote in odd places and at the very deadline with the printer's boy at the door. His attitude can be gauged from a remark in *Idler* No. 9—itself a delightfully ironic Horatian essay 'In praise of Idleness'. Johnson is quoting an imaginary correspondent:

> You may publish, burn, or destroy this just as you are in the humour; it is ten to one but I forget that I wrote it before it reaches you. I believe you may find a motto for it in Horace, *but I cannot reach him without getting out of my chair*; that is sufficient reason for not fixing any.

Johnson did not need to get out of his chair; he had it all in his head, or as Boswell puts it, 'his memory being stored with innumerable passages of the classicks'. He recalls in his *Journal of a Tour in the Western Highlands* Johnson standing in the bow window at Slains Castle which fronted the sea and repeating *Iam satis terris* (*Odes* I.2), and, a little later, after a rough crossing from the mainland to one of the western islands, Johnson declares:

> This is now the Atlantick. If I should tell you at a tea-table in London that I have crossed the Atlantick in an open boat, how they'd shudder, and what a fool they'd think me to expose myself to such dangers.

Then he repeated Horace's Ode:

> *Otium divos rogat in patenti*
> *Prensus Aegaeo . . .*

and on for forty lines—

> For calm he prays when overwhelmed by storm out
> in the open sea. . . .[23]

At another time Boswell tells us of his repeating many of the *Odes* while driving in a post-chaise and that he particularly remembered *Eheu fugaces*. With this should be placed a snatch of conversation from the *Journal of a Tour*. 'We talked of memory and its various modes. *Johnson.* "Memory will play strange tricks. One sometimes loses a single word. I once lost *fugaces* in the Ode *Posthume, Posthume*".'

Percy Hazen Houston makes an excellent comment on the first of these two passages I have just given:

> When a post chaise is mentioned in connection with Johnson we at once think of the remark of the sage that the thing he preferred doing above any other was driving with a pretty woman in a post chaise—surely as Horatian a sentiment as any other.[24]

[23] James Boswell, *Journal of a Tour in the Western Highlands*, ed. R. W. Chapman, Oxford, 1934, p. 265; cf. *Life*, p. 845.
[24] P. H. Houston, *Dr Johnson: A Study in Eighteenth Century Humanism*, Cambridge, Mass., 1923, p. 28.

Johnson did, indeed, always consider himself a ladies' man and was, in fact, a great favourite with women—*puellis* semper *idoneus*.

However, it is as well to look into the passage to which Houston refers and observe the qualifications and provisos of our moralist as gallant.

> If [said he] I had no duties and no reference to futurity I would spend my life driving briskly in a post chaise with a pretty woman; but she should be one who could understand me, and would add something to the conversation.

In these and other ways Johnson was more particular than either Horace, or, as we now know, Boswell himself was.

One of Johnson's lady friends was 'the learned Elizabeth Carter' whose translation of Epictetus has been the standard one for two centuries and in a revised form has just been republished. Johnson asserted that her Greek was better than Porson's; and he tried to persuade her to undertake the translation of Boethius. He wrote a Greek and two Latin epigrams to her. Another friend was Molly Aston.

> Molly [he said] was a beauty and a scholar, and a wit and a whig; and she talked all in praise of liberty; and so I made this epigram upon her—she was the loveliest creature I ever saw.

Here is the epigram:

> *Liber ut esse velim, suasisti, pulchra Maria*
> *Ut maneam liber, pulchra Maria, vale.*
> [To make me love freedom you argue so well
> That to keep this dear freedom, fair Molly, farewell.]

Mrs Thrale, who was, after his beloved and much lamented wife 'Tetty', the most important woman in his life, did even better. She got an Ode in Horatian Sapphics written in the island of Skye while Johnson was touring the Hebrides. He asks himself what his 'sweet Thralia' [*Thralia dulcis*] may be doing:

> *Seu viri curas pia nupta mulcet*
> *Seu fovet mater subolem benigna,*
> *Sive cum libris novitate pascit*
> *   sedula mentem.*
> [Now a good helpmeet mitigates her man's cares
> Now a kind mother little ones indulges
> Now to grow wiser every latest volume
>   busily reading.]

At about the same time he composed an Ode to Skye in Alcaics. So that Horace was very much in his thoughts. However, we should not forget that Horace was the classical poet most congenial to educated Englishmen of the eighteenth century. After Richard Bentley's 'sensational edition' of 1711—two years later than Johnson's birth—the continuous flood of editions, translations, and imitations testifies to the avidity of the reading public. Though Johnson shared this enthusiasm his own appreciation of Horace was deeply personal. The pagan poet with his clear-eyed outlook on life, his humour, his tolerance of human frailty, his serene self-knowledge, good sense, independence, and artistic integrity had much to offer the robust yet sensitive Christian moralist, and helped him both to enjoy life and to endure it.

We now turn finally to Juvenal, the Latin poet we most readily associate with Johnson, because of his imitations in *London* and the *Vanity of Human Wishes* of the third and tenth Satire respectively. When Boswell once regretted to him that he had not given us more of Juvenal's *Satires,* he said he probably should give more, for he had them all in his head. Some of them, however, he observed were 'too gross for imitation'. He did not give more, but there is plenty of evidence that he did have them in his head.

In his Life of Dryden he defines Juvenal's greatness in a sentence: 'The peculiarity of Juvenal is a mixture of gaiety and stateliness, of pointed sentences and declamatory grandeur'. And elsewhere he speaks of his 'massiveness and vigour'.

Johnson loved to declaim Juvenal's verses whenever a chance offered. On one occasion there was a discussion on the reputation of David Garrick, the actor.

> JOHNSON. 'No, Sir, I should not be surprised though Garrick chained the ocean, and lashed the winds.' BOSWELL [rashly]. 'Should it not be, Sir, lashed the ocean and chained the winds?' JOHNSON. 'No, Sir; recollect the original:
> *In Corum atque Eurum solitus saevire flagellis*
> *Barbarus, Aeolio nunquam hoc in carcere passos,*
> *Ipsum compedibus qui vinxerat Ennosigaeum.'*

Translated by Dryden the passage runs:

> But how did he return, this haughty brave,
> Who whipt the winds and made the sea his slave.
> (Tho' Neptune took unkindly to be bound;
> And Eurus never such hard usage found
> In his Aeolian prisons underground.)[25]

In Scotland Boswell tried to defend some 'foolish play' by repeating a few lines. *Johnson.* 'That will not do, Sir. Nothing is good but what is consistent with truth or probability, which this is not.

[25] *Life,* Vol. II, p. 227.

Juvenal indeed gives us a noble picture of inflexible virtue'—and he quotes half a dozen lines beginning:

> Esto bonus miles, tutor bonus, arbiter idem
> Integer . . .

'which', says Boswell, 'he repeated with great force and dignity'.[26] There are references, too, to Juvenal in the letters, but I shall mention only one. He writes to a friend: 'The Dr. fell to repeating Juvenal's tenth satire, but I let him see that the province was mine'. Despite this experience, this same Dr Brocklesby, who was with Johnson on his death-bed a couple of years later, when they were talking on the subject of prayer, again repeated from Juvenal: 'Orandum est, ut sit mens sana in corpore sano', and so on to the end of the tenth Satire, but in running it quickly over he happened in one line to pronounce supremum for extremum; at which Johnson's critical ear instantly took offence, and, discoursing vehemently on the unmetrical effect of such a lapse, he showed himself as full as ever of the spirit of the grammarian.

I shall excuse myself from offering any detailed comments on the two great 'imitations'. They are well known and have received the highest critical attention as well as discussion of some sort in any study of Johnson's or Juvenal's poetry. I have no gleanings to make in fields reaped and harrowed by the late T. S. Eliot, Joseph Krutch, F. R. Leavis, Mary Lascelles and John Hardy. I would only say that it is possible to read and enjoy the two English poems without a knowledge of Latin or of the poems of which they are avowedly imitations. Yet by printing beneath *London* the Latin text of Juvenal and the line references beneath *The Vanity of Human Wishes* the author obviously invited readers who could and would, to consider his poems in relationship to their models as being 'a kind of middle composition between translation and original design'.

To write such poems and to enjoy them is, according to Joseph Krutch,

> to be guilty of a kind of puerility possible to intelligent men only in an age when reverence for the classics had been carried to a point where it went beyond legitimate admiration for the virtues of the ancients and included an exaggerated interest in the ancient for its own sake.[27]

One can imagine now the sound of a tremendous volley from the Elysian fields across seven-fold Styx, an unambiguous, categorical, magisterial: 'No Sir. The mental disease of the present generation is impatience of study, contempt of the great masters of ancient

[26] *Journal of a Tour in the Western Highlands*, p. 404.
[27] J. W. Krutch, *Samuel Johnson*, New York, 1963, p. 61.

wisdom, and a disposition to rely wholly upon unassisted genius and natural sagacity'.

Yet we must not let him represent himself as a mere *laudator temporis acti*:

> I am always angry [he says] when I hear ancient times praised at the expence of modern times. There is now a great deal more learning in the world than there was formerly; for it is universally diffused. You have, perhaps, no man who knows as much Greek and Latin as Bentley; no man who knows as much mathematicks as Newton; but you have many more men who know Greek and Latin, and who know mathematicks.[28]

'Of the ancients', he writes in *Idler* No. 66, 'enough remains to excite our emulation and direct our endeavour'; and he is aware of 'the general conspiracy of human nature against contemporary merit'.

It is time to draw this study to a close, although it is not easy to find or to make an end. I shall do so by describing his memorial in St Paul's Cathedral and by means of a little fantasy inspired by a volume of essays in his honour brought out on the two hundred and fiftieth anniversary of his birth.

Johnson was interested in epitaphs. He wrote an essay on the subject, and one of his best sayings is: 'The writer of an epitaph should not be considered as saying nothing but what is strictly true . . . In lapidary inscriptions a man is not upon oath'. But in this as in other matters he held strong clear views. Once, on seeing a sepulchral inscription in English, he declared that it should have been in Latin, as everything intended to be universal and permanent should be. He himself composed a notable one for his friend Oliver Goldsmith, who was buried in Westminster Abbey. It contains the famous sentence:

> *Qui nullum fere scribendi genus*
> *Non tetigit,*
> *Nullum quod tetigit non ornavit.*

Johnson submitted this epitaph to 'the Club' and told his friends that he would alter it in any manner they pleased as to the sense of it, but he would never consent to disgrace the walls of Westminster Abbey with an English inscription. He, too, is buried in the Abbey; and it is pleasant to recall the story which he told of how once when they passed the Poets' Corner in the Abbey he had said to Goldsmith, quoting Ovid:

> *Forsitan et nostrum nomen miscebitur istis*
> [It may be that our names too will mingle with these].

[28] *Life*, Vol. IV, p. 217.

'When we got to the Temple Bar', says Johnson, 'he stopped me, pointed to the heads upon it, and slyly whispered to me: *"Forsitan et nostrum nomen miscebitur istis".'*

Johnson's memorial is in St Paul's. It appears that in the planning stage the propriety of an English or Latin inscription was canvassed among his friends. Malone, calling on a Mr Flood, maintained in conversation that the epitaph by whomsoever it should be written, ought to be in Latin. Mr Flood thought differently and sent next day in a postscript to a note on another matter, the following lines:

> No need of Latin or of Greek to grace
> Our Johnson's memory or inscribe his grave,
> His native language claims the mournful space,
> To pay the immortality he gave.

Johnson's prejudice was respected and the inscription is in Latin —brief, pointed, adequate—the work of Dr Parr, a scholar whose learned conversation he used to enjoy, but who confessed his feelings of confusion and dismay at the thought of trying to express

> the variety and splendour of Johnson's attainments, the peculiarities of his character, his private virtues and his literary publications . . . in this confined and difficult species of composition.

The monument itself consists of a colossal figure of Johnson, draped incongruously in a Roman toga, leaning against a column. On a scroll, which he holds, are the following Greek words, a modification of the quotation with which Johnson concluded the last of his *Ramblers*:

> ἐν μακάρεσσι πόνων ἀντάξιος εἴη ἀμοιβὴ
> [May he receive among the blessed fit requital for his troubles].

What, we may ask, would be a fit requital for his troubles, now that he is among the blessed?

I offer a thought. He is among the happy dead, where, as Virgil tells us, the good and worthy continue to enjoy the pleasures and pursuits which were theirs in life.

> *quae gratia . . . fuit vivis . . . quae cura*
> *eadem sequitur tellure repostos*
> [What pleasures and interests they had in life follow
> them too, now they are beneath the earth].[29]

I omit the chariot and horses mentioned by Virgil, but, of course, we might identify them for our purpose, with a post-chaise if there were any sign of the pretty woman. However, we shall play safe and

[29] Virgil, *Aeneid*, Bk VI, ll. 653-5.

let our hero enjoy the other pleasures he loved—the talk of men and books.

It is his two hundred and fiftieth birthday and he duly receives a volume: *New Light on Dr. Johnson: Essays on the Occasion of his 250th Birthday,* edited by F. W. Hilles. It bears the imprint: 'New Haven. Yale University'. Doubtless he would say: 'This is indeed taking prodigious pains about a man'. But it would surely please him that he should be read and honoured for so long and in America. We might hope that when he had perused it, he would say: 'I have got lights on the subject today, which I had not before'.

But before leaving this light fancy let us imagine that when his eye caught the title of the first essay—'The Young Waterman'—he had one of those rare blanks of memory and turned to the ever ready Boswell for enlightenment. 'Surely, Sir, you recollect. It was not long after our first acquaintance. I have the passage from the *Life* by heart:

> On Saturday, July 30, Dr. Johnson and I took a sculler at the Temple-stairs, and set out for Greenwich. I asked him if he really thought a knowledge of the Greek and Latin languages an essential requisite to a good education. JOHNSON. "Most certainly, Sir; for those who know them have a very great advantage over those who do not. Nay, Sir, it is wonderful what a difference learning makes upon people even in the common intercourse of life, which does not appear to be much connected with it." "And yet, (said I) people go through the world very well, and carry on the business of life to good advantage, without learning." JOHNSON. "Why, Sir, that may be true in cases where learning cannot be of any use; for instance this boy rows us as well without learning, as if he could sing the song of Orpheus to the Argonauts, who were the first sailors." He then called to the boy, "What would you give my lad, to know about the Argonauts?" "Sir, (said the boy,) I would give what I have." Johnson was much pleased with his answer, and we gave him a double fare. Dr. Johnson then turning to me, "Sir, (said he) a desire of knowledge is the natural feeling of mankind; and every human being, whose mind is not debauched, will be willing to give all that he has to get knowledge".[30]

The scholars of Yale and his own Oxford, (*in primis* the late David Nichol Smith) edit his works like those of the ancient classics so that foreign nations and distant ages may by their assistance meet, enjoy, and reverence a great propagator of knowledge and teacher of truth.

[30] *Life,* Vol. I, pp. 457-8.

BIBLIOGRAPHY OF WORKS BY AND ABOUT DAVID NICHOL SMITH

compiled with the assistance of the User Services Section of the National Library of Australia

WORKS BY D. N. S.

1898

Boileau-Despréaux, Nicholas, *L'Art poétique*. Ed. with introduction and notes by D.N.S., C.U.P., Cambridge (Pitt Press Series). Reissued 1902, 1907, 1931.

Brunetière, Ferdinand, *Brunetière's Essays in French Literature*. A selection, trans. D.N.S., Fisher Unwin, London.

1899

Macaulay, Thomas Babington, *The Lay of Virginia*. Introduction and notes by D.N.S., Blackie, London (Blackie's English Classics).

Shakespeare, William, *King Henry the Eighth*. Ed. D.N.S., Blackie, London (The Warwick Shakespeare).

1900

Dryden, John, *Dryden's Essay of Dramatic Poesy*. Ed. with introduction and notes by D.N.S., Blackie, London (Blackie's English Classics).

Macaulay, Thomas Babington, *Life of Johnson*. Ed. with introduction and notes by D.N.S., Blackwood, Edinburgh (Blackwood's English Classics).

1901

Hazlitt, William, *Essays on Poetry*. Ed. D.N.S., Blackwood, Edinburgh (Blackwood's English Classics).

1902

Shakespeare, William, *King Lear*. Ed. D.N.S., Blackie, London (The Warwick Shakespeare).

1903

Blackie's Standard Shilling Dictionary. Blackie, London.

Eighteenth Century Essays on Shakespeare. Ed. D.N.S., MacLehose and Sons, Glasgow. 2nd ed., Clarendon Press, Oxford, 1963.

'William Hazlitt'. In *Chambers's Cyclopaedia of English Literature,* new ed. by D. Patrick, Vol. III, Chambers, London, pp. 79-85.

1905

'Criticism'. In *The Harmsworth Encyclopaedia*, Vol. III, Amalgamated Press, London, pp. 1713-17.

'Quarrel of Ancients and Moderns'. In *The Harmsworth Encyclopaedia*, Vol. VII, Amalgamated Press, London, pp. 5005-7.

1909

The Functions of Criticism. A lecture delivered before the University on 22 February, Clarendon Press, Oxford.

1910

Jeffrey, Francis, *Jeffrey's Literary Criticism*. Ed. with introduction by D.N.S., Henry Frowde, London (Oxford Library of Prose and Poetry). Reissued Humphrey Milford, London, 1928 (The Oxford Miscellany).

Macaulay, Thomas Babington, *Essay on Johnson*. With introduction by D.N.S., Clarendon Press, Oxford (Oxford Plain Texts).

1911

'Ancients and Moderns'. In *Nelson's Encyclopaedia*, Vol. I, Nelson, London, pp. 409-11.

'Criticism'. In *Nelson's Encyclopaedia*, Vol. VII, Nelson, London, pp. 349-57.

1913

'Johnson and Boswell'. In *The Cambridge History of English Literature*, ed. A. W. Ward and A. R. Waller, Vol. X, C.U.P., Cambridge, pp. 157-94.

1914

Burnet, Thomas, *The Letters of Thomas Burnet to George Duckett, 1712-1722*. Ed. D.N.S., printed at the University Press by Horace Hart, Oxford (for presentation to the members of the Roxburghe Club).

1915

Courtney, William Prideaux, *A Bibliography of Samuel Johnson*. Revised and seen through the press by D.N.S., Clarendon Press, Oxford (Oxford Historical and Literary Studies: Vol. IV). Reissued 1925.

1916

'Authors and Patrons'. In *Shakespeare's England: An Account of the Life and Manners of his Age*, ed. Sir Sidney Lee and C. T. Onions, Vol. II, Clarendon Press, Oxford, pp. 182-211. Reprinted 1916, 1926, 1932, 1950.

Shakespeare Criticism: A Selection. With introduction by D.N.S., O.U.P., London (World's Classics No. 212). Reprinted 1923, 1926, 1930, 1934, 1936, 1939, 1942, 1944. *Shakespeare Criticism: A Selection, 1623-1840*. O.U.P., London, 1946. (World's Classics No. 212). Reprinted 1949, 1953, 1954, 1958, 1961, 1963, 1964.

1918

Characters from the Histories and Memoirs of the Seventeenth Century. With an essay on the character and historical notes by D.N.S., Clarendon Press, Oxford. Reprinted 1920, 1929, 1936, 1953, 1963.

James Colin MacLehose, 2nd Lieut., Rifle Brigade, 1897-1917. Glasgow University Press, Glasgow (printed for private circulation).

1920

Swift, Jonathan, *A Tale of a Tub, to which is added The Battle of the Books and the Mechanical Operation of the Spirit*. Together with the History of Martin, Wotton's Observations upon the Tale of a Tub, Curll's Complete Key etc. Ed. with introduction and notes, historical and explanatory, by A. C. Guthkelch and D.N.S., Clarendon Press, Oxford. 2nd ed., 1958. Reprinted 1965.

1921

Wordsworth, William, *Poetry & Prose*. With essays by Coleridge, Hazlitt, De Quincy. With introduction by D.N.S., and notes, Clarendon Press, Oxford (Clarendon Series of English Literature). Reprinted 1956.

1925

Dryden, John, *Poetry and Prose*. With essays by Congreve, Johnson, Scott, and others. With introduction and notes by D.N.S., Clarendon Press, Oxford (Clarendon Series of English Literature).

1926

Oxford Book of Eighteenth Century Verse. Chosen by D.N.S., Clarendon Press, Oxford. Reissued 1951.

Raleigh, Sir Walter Alexander, *Letters (1879-1922)*. Ed. Lady Raleigh, with preface by D.N.S., Methuen, London (2 vols.). New and rev. ed. 1928.

Raleigh, Sir Walter Alexander, *A Selection from the letters of Sir Walter Raleigh, 1880-1922*. Ed. Lady Raleigh. With preface (abridged) by D.N.S. Methuen, London, 1928.

'The British Grenadiers'. An Account of the Origin of the Song, with a facsimile of the issue of 1780, *Household Brigade Magazine*, Summer, 1926, pp. 202-5.

Wise, Thomas James, *The Ashley Library, a catalogue of printed books, manuscripts and autograph letters*. Collected by T. J. Wise. Vol. VIII, with introduction by D.N.S., London (printed for private circulation).

1927

'Life of William Aldis Wright (1831-1914)'. In *Dictionary of National Biography 1912-1921*, ed. W. H. C. Davis and J. R. H. Weaver, O.U.P., London, pp. 595-7.

1928

'Johnson's Revision of his Publications, especially *The Rambler, Rasselas,* and *The Idler*'. In *Johnson & Boswell Revised by Themselves and Others*, three essays by D.N.S., R. W. Chapman, and L. F. Powell, Clarendon Press, Oxford, pp. 5-18.

Shakespeare in the Eighteenth Century. Three lectures delivered in Birkbeck College, London, in November 1927, Clarendon Press, Oxford. Reissue announced 1967.

1929

'Johnson's Irene'. In *Essays and Studies by Members of the English Association*, Vol. XIV, Oxford, pp. 35-53. Reprinted Dawson, London, 1966.

Samuel Johnson's Irene. Clarendon Press, Oxford (reprinted in part from *Essays and Studies by Members of the English Association*, Vol. XIV).

Warton's History of English Poetry. British Academy, Warton Lecture on English Poetry, 1929, Milford, London.

'Warton's History of English Poetry'. In *Proceedings of the British Academy*, London, Vol. XV, pp. 73-99.

1930

Jonathan Swift. A lecture delivered in Abercromby House in the University of Liverpool, 23 May, Tinling, Liverpool.

1931

'The Degree of Doctor of Philosophy (Ph.D., or D. Phil.)'. A paper read on 8 July, University Press, Oxford.

'The Standard and the Conditions of Candidature for Ph.D. in relation to other post-graduate qualifications'. In *Report of Proceedings of the Fourth Congress of the Universities of the Empire, 1931*, Bell, London, pp. 83-8 (for the Universities Bureau of the British Empire, London).

1932

Percy, Thomas, *Ancient Songs Chiefly on Moorish Subjects*. Trans. from the Spanish by T. Percy, with preface by D.N.S., O.U.P., London.

1933

'The Newspaper'. In *Johnson's England: An Account of the Life and Manners of his Age,* ed. A. S. Turberville, Vol. II, Clarendon Press, Oxford, pp. 331-67.

1934

Essays and Studies by Members of the English Association. Vol. XIX, collected by D.N.S., Clarendon Press, Oxford.
'The Contributors to *The Rambler* and *The Idler'*, *Bodleian Quarterly Record,* Vol. VII, No. 84, pp. 508-9.

1935

'Jonathan Swift: Some Observations'. A paper read before the Royal Society of Literature, 13 March. In *Essays by Divers Hands: being the transactions of the Royal Society of Literature of the United Kingdom,* London, New (3rd) Series, Vol. XIV, ed. the Earl of Lytton, pp. 29-48.
Swift, Jonathan, *The Letters of Jonathan Swift to Charles Ford.* Ed. D.N.S., Clarendon Press, Oxford.

1937

'Life of Sir Walter Raleigh (1861-1922)'. In *Dictionary of National Biography 1922-1930,* ed. J. R. H. Weaver, O.U.P., London, pp. 701-4.
Some Observations on Eighteenth Century Poetry. The Alexander Lectures in English at the University of Toronto, 1937, O.U.P., London. 2nd ed., University of Toronto Press, Toronto, 1960. Reprinted 1964. Paperback edition, 1965 (Canadian University Paperbooks).

1938

Chapman, George, *An Humorous Day's Mirth, 1599.* Prepared with assistance from D.N.S., printed for the Malone Society by John Johnson at the O.U.P., London (Malone Society Reprints).
'Robert Burns'. A lecture delivered at the Sorbonne, 19 January, *France-Grande Bretagne; bulletin des relations franco-britanniques,* No. 173, février, pp. 29-40.

1939

'Edmond Malone'. A lecture delivered before the University of London, 10 May 1938, and subsequently revised, *Huntington Library Quarterly,* Vol. III, October, pp. 23-36.

1940

Byron, George Gordon Noel, *Poetry & Prose.* With essays by Scott, Hazlitt, Macaulay, etc., with an introduction by Sir Arthur Quiller-Couch and notes by D.N.S., Clarendon Press, Oxford (Clarendon Series of English Literature).
'James Boswell (1740-1795)'. In *Cambridge Bibliography of English Literature,* ed. F. W. Bateson, C.U.P., Cambridge, Vol. II, pp. 650-4.
'Samuel Johnson (1709-1784)'. In *Cambridge Bibliography of English Literature,* ed. F. W. Bateson, C.U.P., Cambridge, Vol. II, pp. 613-28.
Viga-Glúms Saga. Ed. G. Turville-Petre, O.U.P., London (Oxford English Monographs, Vol. I, general editors: D.N.S., J. R. R. Tolkien, C. S. Lewis).

1941

Johnson, Samuel, *The Poems of Samuel Johnson*. Ed. D.N.S., and E. L. McAdam, Clarendon Press, Oxford. Reprinted 1951.

'The Early Version of Shenstone's Pastoral Ballad', *Review of English Studies*, Vol. XVII, January, pp. 47-54.

1943

'Hazlitt's Depth of Taste'. An overseas broadcast especially for Indian students, 15 January 1943, *The Listener*, Vol. XXIX, 28 January, pp. 118-19.

'Samuel Johnson's Poems'. An address to the Johnson Club, 11 December 1941, *Review of English Studies*, Vol. XIX, January, pp. 44-50.

'Thomas Warton's Miscellany: The Union'. A paper read to the Oxford Bibliographical Society, 5 December 1942. *Review of English Studies*, Vol. XIX, July, pp. 263-75.

1944

Percy, Thomas, *The Percy Letters*. General editors: D.N.S. and Cleanth Brooks, Louisiana State University Press, Baton Rouge, 1944-58 (5 vols.). Reprinted Yale University Press, New Haven, 1960-1 (6 vols.).

1946

The Saintsbury Centenary Oration. Delivered by D.N.S. at the 27th meeting of the Saintsbury Club, 23 October 1945, privately printed at the Curwen Press for the Saintsbury Club, London.

1947

Arden of Feversham, 1592. A facsimile reprint of White's London edition of 18 December 1592, prepared by H. Macdonald with assistance from D.N.S., printed for the Malone Society at the O.U.P., Oxford (Malone Society Reprints).

1948

Lyly, John, *Mother Bombie, 1594*. Prepared by K. M. Lea with assistance from D.N.S., with facsimiles, printed for the Malone Society by Charles Batey at the O.U.P., Oxford (Malone Society Reprints).

1949

Kyd, Thomas, *The Spanish Tragedy (1592)*. Reprint of the original version, prepared by W. W. Greg and D.N.S., with reproductions of title pages of early editions, printed for the Malone Society by Charles Batey at the O.U.P., Oxford (Malone Society Reprints).

1950

'A Centenary Tribute'. In Saintsbury, George, *A Last Vintage: Essays and Papers*, ed. J. W. Oliver, A. M. Clark, and A. Muir, personal portraits by D.N.S., D. M. Stuart, and H. Waddell, Methuen, London, pp. 11-17.

John Dryden. The Clark Lectures on English Literature, 1948-9, C.U.P., Cambridge. Reprinted Archon Books, Hamden, Connecticut, 1966.

Johnsonians and Boswellians. The Presidential Address, 1949, Lomax's Successors, Lichfield (Johnson Society Address No. 29).

'The Poetry of Sir Walter Scott'. The Sir Walter Scott Lectures for 1950, *University of Edinburgh Journal*, Vol. XV, pp. 63-80.

1952

'A Boswell Fragment'. A previously unpublished extract from an address, 'Samuel Johnson & the New Boswell Papers', delivered in 1951 at the University of Melbourne by D.N.S., *Meanjin* No. 50, Spring, pp. 292-3.

1957

'A Note on MUM, an Eighteenth-Century Political Ballad', *Transactions of the Edinburgh Bibliographical Society,* Vol. III, Pt 4, pp. 249-52 (printed for the Society by R. & R. Clark).

1958

'Armstrong College Fifty Years Ago', *Durham University Journal,* Vol. L, No. 2, N.S. Vol. XIX, No. 2, March, pp. 49-57.

'The Constance Meade Collection and the University Press Museum', *Bodleian Library Record,* Vol. VI, February, pp. 427-33.

1959

'Johnson's Poems'. In *New Light on Dr. Johnson: Essays on the Occasion of his 250th Birthday,* ed. F. W. Hilles, Yale University Press, New Haven, pp. 9-17.

'Thomson and Burns'. In Clifford, James L., *Eighteenth-Century English Literature: Modern Essays in Criticism,* O.U.P., New York, pp. 180-93.

MANUSCRIPTS OF D. N. S.

held in the National Library of Australia

MS 1521   Nichol Smith—Hugh Macdonald correspondence.

1521/1-47   43 letters, David Nichol Smith to Hugh Macdonald, 10 June 1932-4 January 1955.

1521/54-176   87 letters, Hugh Macdonald to David Nichol Smith, 7 June 1932-10 November 1944.

The letters discuss mainly college and literary matters. For instance, there is a short series of letters from D.N.S. containing comments on Dryden, relating to Macdonald's preparation of *John Dryden; a bibliography of early editions and of Drydeniana* published in 1939.

MS 1771   Nichol Smith, David.
                2 letters written to Professor Herbert Davis from Adelaide, 1951. Also papers relating to D.N.S. collected by H. J. Davis, including a xerox copy of D.N.S.'s inaugural lecture, 1909; and excerpts from letters referring to him, including one comment by D.N.S. himself, and memories of him by his youngest daughter, Mrs Anne Phipps.

Tape record-   A recording of D.N.S. speaking on Robert Burns and reading
ing 14   3 pieces of verse by Burns. Transcript, 2 pp.

WORKS ABOUT D. N. S.

Essays on the Eighteenth Century. Presented to D.N.S. in honour of his seventieth birthday, Clarendon Press, Oxford, 1945.

'David Nichol Smith 1875-1962: Obituary', by James Sutherland. In *Proceedings of the British Academy,* London, Vol. XLVIII (1962), pp. 449-59 (portrait).

'Prof. David Nichol Smith', *The Times,* London, 19 January 1962, p. 14d (obituary).

'Nichol Smith, Prof. David'. In *Merton College Register 1900-1964,* Blackwell, Oxford, pp. 141-2.

Australia, National Library, *The David Nichol Smith Memorial Seminar in Eighteenth Century Studies*. National Library of Australia, Canberra, 1966 (18 pp., facsimiles and portrait).

Short title catalogue of books printed in the British Isles, the British Colonies and the United States of America and of English books printed elsewhere, 1701-1800, held in the libraries of the Australian Capital Territory. Ed. William J. Cameron and Diana J. Carroll, National Library of Australia, Canberra, 1966 (2 vols.). (Published as a contribution to the David Nichol Smith Memorial Seminar in Eighteenth-Century Studies, Canberra, 15-19 August 1966).

Subscribers

Richard Abel & Co., Inc.
Barr Smith Library, University of
  Adelaide
W.E.A. Bookroom, University of
  Adelaide
Marcia Allentuck
Penelope Allum
Angus & Robertson, Ltd
F. G. Atkinson
M. N. Austin
Australian National University
  Library

R. J. Barnes
R. J. Bird
B. H. Blackwell, Ltd
V. H. Blain
Edward A. Bloom
Bodleian Library
G. C. Bolton
The Library, University of Bombay
O. M. Brack
A. T. Brissenden
J. T. Burke

W. J. Cameron
Mrs John Cannon
L. N. Cantrell
Diana J. Carroll
John Cashmere
F. W. Cheshire Pty Ltd
Ralph Cohen
John Colman
John Colmer
The Library, University of Colorado
Columbia University Libraries
Jane D. Crisp

James Dally, Antiquarian Booksellers
L. J. Davies
Herbert Davis
Dennis Davison
Direct Book Service
Mrs A. M. Dobson

Public Library, Dunedin
Diana Dyason

I. Ehrenpreis
J. O. Ekpenyong
The Library, University of Essex

Mrs J. F. Ferry
Franklin L. Ford
R. G. Fraser

Thelma Gelfond
Aubrey H. L. Gibson
Anne Godfrey-Smith
Joel J. Gold
I. A. Gordon
Helen Gray
Dorothy Green

J. P. Hardy
Harvard College Library
W. Heffer & Sons Ltd
Jill Hocking
A. D. Hope
C. J. Horne
Mrs P. B. Horner
Sir Leonard Huxley

The Library, University of Iowa

M. K. Joseph

Bruce Kent
Gwin J. Kolb
Paul J. Korshin
Leonie Kramer

J. T. Laird
J. A. La Nauze
The Library, Latrobe University
Leicester University Bookshop
Nola M. Leov
Jay A. Levine
G. L. Little
H. H. R. Love

Dougald MacMillan
Bruce McPherson
The Library, Macquarie University
W. M. Maidment
Department of English, University of
  Malaya
The Library, University of Manchester
Baillieu Library, University of
  Melbourne
W. Milgate
J. D. S. Moore
C. Morrow
D. C. Muecke
Englisches Seminar, Münster

Bonar Law-Bennett Library,
  University of New Brunswick
The Library, University of New
  England
The Library, University of Newcastle
The Library, University of
  Newcastle-upon-Tyne
The Library, University of New
  South Wales
Public Library of New South Wales
The National Librarian, Wellington,
  New Zealand
The Library, University of
  Nottingham

C. J. H. O'Brien
Pamela Oettlé
J. P. O'Gorman
The Library, University of Oregon
The Library, University of Otago

I. J. Page
P. E. Parsons
A. C. Partridge
Mrs af Petersens
Henry Pettit
Mrs A. L. Phipps

Arthur Pollard
C. J. L. Price
Irwin Primer
The Library, Princeton University

George Rudé
G. H. Russell

The Library, University of Sheffield
Educational Book Centre, Ltd,
  Singapore
The Library, University of
  Southampton
O. H. K. Spate
T. D. Sprod
Albrecht B. Strauss
The Library, University of Sussex
Rosemary H. Sweetapple
Fisher Library, University of Sydney
The Library, University of Sydney

State Library of Tasmania
Joyce Thomson
J. H. Tisch
Michael J. Tolley

State Library of Victoria

The Library, University of Warwick
Ian P. Watt
N. S. Wayer
The Alexander Turnbull Library,
  Wellington
Library Board of Western Australia
The Library, University of Western
  Australia
Jean P. Whyte
Richard M. Wilding
R. M. Wiles
N. E. Williams
Roy S. Wolper
David Woolley

Index

Abington, Francis, 116, 117
Adam, James, 239
Adam, Robert, 239, 244
Adams, Elizabeth, 63
Adams, J., 20
Addison, Joseph, 215, 235n.; and the fable, 193; and Latin verse, 71; and the Rule of Taste, 240; and Swift, 198; as dramatist, 73, 110, 112n.; moral purity, 76; and *Spectator*, 84, 211-12
Addison, Robert, 38, 39
Adelaide, University of, xvii; Library, 37, 45, 47, 48
Aelian, 292
Aesop, 195, 196, 200, 202, 203, 204
Agreeable Miscellany, 63
Aiken, Miss, *see* Barbauld, Anna Laetitia
Akenside, Mark, 121, 181
Alberta, University of, Library, 45
Alembert, Jean le Ronde de, 24, 155n.
Alexander Lectures, Toronto, ix, 7, 8, 14
Alexander Turnbull Library, Wellington, 35, 46
Allport, W. H., 142, 146
Altick, Richard, 50
Ammianus Marcellinus, 68n.
Anacreon, 293
Anderson, Robert, 127n.
Andrew Brice's Old Exeter Journal, 56
Anglomania, 207, 208
Annual Register, 147-8
Apelles, 238
Apollo Belvedere, 245
Arden of Feversham, 3
Aristotle, 160
Armstrong College, Newcastle upon Tyne, xvii
Art Bulletin, 239
Art collectors, 235-6
Ascham, Roger, 231, 232n.
Ashburner, Thomas, 63
Astley, Thomas, 58, 59
Aston, Molly, 301

Atkinson, D. T., 135n.
Atkinson, Richard, 38, 39
Atterbury, Francis, 68
Auckland libraries, 45, (Public Library) 47, (University Library) 47, 48
Augustan mode, 171-90 *passim,* 191-2
Augustan tradition, 67-88
Augustus Caesar, 69, 70, 72, 73, 74, 75, 77
Ault, Norman, 246n.
Austen, Jane, 86, 96
Australian National Library, *see* National Library of Australia

Bacon, Francis, 234
Bagehot, Walter, 125
Bailey, Nathan, 90n.
Baird, T., 138n.
Balderston, Katharine C., 116n.
Baldwin, Richard, 58
Barbauld, Anna Laetitia (Miss Aiken), 96n., 111
Barclay, John, 288
Baretti, Giuseppe, 290
Baron, Hans, 73n.
Barrett, Charlotte, 109n.
Bartolo, Taddeo di, 233
Barton, George, 52
Barwick, G. F., 59n.
Basle, 209
Basore, J. W., 263n.
Bateson, F. W., 80, 81
Bath, 84, 243
Batoni, Pompeo, 247
Battie, William, 269
Beale, William, 39
Beccaria, Cesare Bonesana, Marchese di, 23, 27
Becker, Carl, 18
Bellamy, George Anne, 117n.
Benedicite Omnia Opera, 271
Benkowitz, C. F., 220
Bentham, Jeremy, 19, 22, 165-6, 167, 168, 169
Bentley, Richard, 296, 302, 304
Berge, E. G. von, 210

317

Chatman, S., 171n.
Chester Courant, 63
Chester Miscellany, 63
Christchurch, N.Z., libraries, 45
Christchurch College, New Zealand, 39
Christian humanism, 25
Churchill, Awnsham and John, 58
Churchill, Charles, 130-1
Chyrtaeus, Nathan, 234
Cicero, M. T., 139n., 261, 288
Circulating libraries, 52-3
Clarendon, Edward Hyde, First Earl of, 79-80
Clark, G. N., 81n.
Clark, William, 135
Clay, John, 55
Clerc, John le, 288
Clifford collection, *see* National Library of Australia, Clifford collection
Clifford family, of Ugbrooke, 34
Clive, Kitty, 116, 117
Cobban, A., 18
Cobham family, 248-9
Cohen, R., 89n.
Coleridge, S. T., 40
Collection of Voyages and Travels, 58
Collins, A. S., 49
Collins, Benjamin, 56n.
Colosseum, 243
Colvin, S., 236, 237
Comte, Auguste, 28
Condillac, Etienne B. de, 23, 157
Condorcet, M. J. A. N. Caritat, Marquis de, 22, 28
Congreve, William, 110, 113-14
Connoisseur, 245
Cook, John, 58n.
Cook, Thomas, 232
Corn Laws, abolition of, 80
Corneille, Pierre, 110
Cosmological theories, 273-5, 277, 278-9
Cotton, Sir John Hynde, 10
Counsell, George, 135
Courthope, W. J., 4
Courtney, W., 5
Covenant Theology, 273
Cowper, William, 86, 122-3, 232
Crabbe, George, 86
Craftsman, 49, 261, 263, 266-7
Crane, R. S., 60
Cranfield, G. A., 60n., 61n., 63n.
Croker, J. W., 109n.
Cumberland Pacquet, 62

Currie, H. M., 252
Curtis, L. P., 134n.
Cust, L., 236, 237

Daily Courant, 60
Dalhousie University Library, 45, 48
Dallaway, J., 241n.
Dalzel, Andrew, 292
Daniells, R., 217n.
Dante Alighieri, 73, 224
Davies, Thomas, 116, 117
Davis, Herbert, 74
De Beer collection, *see* Otago University Library, De Beer collection
Defoe, Daniel, 51, 68
Delaney, Patrick, 274
Denham, Sir John, 82
De Quincey, Thomas, 291
Derathé, Robert, 23n.
Derham, William, 273-4, 275, 279
Descartes, René, 22, 25, 139
Deventer, Hendrik van, 135, 143, 147-8
Devis, Anthony, 240
Devlin, Christopher, 269n., 282n.
Diderot, Denis, 19, 23, 25, 155n., 156n.
Dionysius of Halicarnassus, 75, 293, 295
Dixson Library, N.S.W., 32, 45, 47
Dobrée, Bonamy, 130
Doncaster Flying Post, 61
Donne, John, 266
Doran, A., 135n., 136n., 149n.
Downer, A. S., 111n.
Drayton, Michael, 259, 261
Dryden, John, 1, 3, 4, 31, 76, 302; and the Augustan mode, 172-5, 187-8; and Charles II, 67-70; and classicism, 237-8; and satire, 255-6; as dramatist, 110-13; as fabulist, 193, 196
Duckett, George, 5
Dunedin libraries, 45
Dyer, John, 119, 124, 128-31, 177-8

Eachard, Laurence, 75
Edwards, T. R., 190n.
Eighteenth Century Essays on Shakespeare, 2, 3, 8
Einsiedeln Itinerary, 232-3
Eliot, T. S., 251, 303
Ellwood, Thomas, 290
Elwood, the quaker, *see* Ellwood, Thomas
Empsom, William, 96
Emslie, MacDonald, 256

319

South Australia, Public Library, 45, 47

Spatial process in Augustan poetry, 172-6, 185, 191

Spectator, 84

Spencer, H. R., 135n.

Spingarn, J., 4

Staiger, E., 222n.

Stamm, R., 217n.

Stead, William Force, 270, 275, 278, 280

Steegmann, J., 239

Steevens, G., 112n.

Stephen, Leslie, 22

Sterne, Jaques, 134

Sterne, Laurence, 83, 133-54

Stillingfleet, Edward, 273

Stirling, James H., 18

Stoicism, 25

Stone, Walter, 36, 39

Storz, G., 225n.

Stosch, Philip von, 236

Stowe, 248-9

Straumann, H., 215n.

Strich, Fritz, 205

Stubbs, George, 147

Sublime, the, 227-9

Sudheimer, H., 226n.

Suetonius, 288

Summerson, Sir John, 242, 244

Sussex Weekly Advertiser, or Lewes Journal, 53

Sutherland, James, 2, 11, 61, 69, 123

Swift, Jonathan, 72; and the Augustan tradition, 73-4, 77, 78, 87, 173-6; and D.N.S., 5, 9-13, 83; and William Pulteney, 259, 266; as fable poet, 193-204; National Library of Australia collection, 33, 37, 43

Swinfen, Samuel, 289-90

Switzer, Stephen, 240n.

Sydney, Philosophical Society Library, 39

Sydney, University of, Library, *see* Fisher Library, University of Sydney

Tacitus, 288

Tarleton, Richard, 115

Tasmania, University of, Library, 48

Tasmanian libraries, 45

Taste, 231-50

Tatler, 53, 54

Temple, Sir William, 195

Terence, 110, 112

Thackeray, W. M., 87

Theobald, Lewis, 13, 112

Theocritus, 292, 293, 298-9

Thicknesse, Philip, 145

Thomasius, Christian, 21

Thomson, James, 68, 121-2; and the Augustan mode, 179-82, 185-9, 191

Thoyras, Paul de Rapin de, 57

Thrale, Mrs Hester, *see* Piozzi, Hester Lynch (Mrs Thrale)

Thucydides, 296

Tickell, Thomas, 71, 119

Times, The, xvii, 8

Tindal, Nicholas, 57

Tinker, Chauncey Brewster, 14

Tisch, J. H., 217n.

Todd, W. B., 59n.

Tofts, Mary, 139n.

Topham, Francis, 145

Topping, Thomas, 39

Toronto, Public Library, 47

Toronto, University of, Library, 33, 35, 43, 45, 46, 48

Travels of the late Charles Thompson, Esq., 57

Trickett, Rachel, 172-3

Trinity College, Cambridge, 10

Tristram Shandy, 133, 136, 137-43, 145-6, 150-3

Turgot, A. R. J., Baron de l'Aulne, 23, 28

Turnbull Library, New Zealand, *see* Alexander Turnbull Library, Wellington

Turner, Florence Maris, 53

Turner, Thomas, 53

Tyburn, 256

Ullathorne, William B., 41

Universal Spectator, 51

Upwell, Norfolk, 38

Utilitarianism, 165-9

Uz, Johann Peter, 208

Vanbrugh, Sir John, 110, 113, 196

Van Dyck, Sir Anthony, 238

Vanity of Human Wishes, The, 15

Varma, D. P., 52

Vico, Giovanni Battista, 19

Victoria, State Library of, 37, 45, 46

Victoria University of Wellington, Library, 33, 48

Vida, Marco G., 237-8, 288

Vignon, Pierre Alexandre, 243

Virgil, 85, 122, 217, 286, 288, 295, 296-9, 305

327

Wholly set up and printed by Edwards & Shaw Pty Ltd, Sydney.
Set by Harley & Jones Pty Ltd in Linotype Baskerville 10 on 11 point, with Monotype Baskerville headings. Printed on Periotone DM 68 paper, and bound by Stanley Owen & Sons Pty Ltd.
Designed by Edwards & Shaw, Sydney.

ARNULFO L. OLIVEIRA MEMORIAL LIBRARY
1825 MAY STREET
BROWNSVILLE, TEXAS 78520